Hospitality

AN INTRODUCTION

Fourteenth Edition

Robert A. Brymer
Florida State University

Misty M. Johanson
DePaul University

Kendall Hunt
publishing company

Book Team

Chairman and Chief Executive Officer   Mark C. Falb
President and Chief Operating Officer   Chad M. Chandlee
Vice President, Higher Education   David L. Tart
Senior Managing Editor Ray Wood
Assistant Editor Bob Largent
Editorial Manager   Georgia Botsford
Senior Developmental Editor   Lynne Rogers
Vice President, Operations   Timothy J. Beitzel
Assistant Vice President, Production Services   Christine E. O'Brien
Senior Production Editor   Beth Trowbridge
Permissions Editor   Carla Kipper
Cover Designer   Suzanne Millius

Kendall Hunt
publishing company

www.kendallhunt.com
Send all inquiries to:
4050 Westmark Drive
Dubuque, IA 52004-1840

To God and all the blessings He's given me. To Renee and Ryan Melin, their awesome son Parker Ryan Melin (my grandson) and the incredible gift they've all been to my life.

Robert A. Brymer

May you know one day the goodness and mercy you have brought to my life.

Misty M. Johanson

BRIEF CONTENTS

CONTENTS

We believe that it is important to give students a well-rounded background in hospitality to pique their curiosity. But from there, it is equally important to identify as many career paths as possible, so that students can identify areas about which they want to learn. Many students come from other disciplines and say, "Oh, if I had known all these choices, I would have switched majors." It is up to us, to show them how vast the industry is, and how many choices and options they can have. We believe this book provides this focus.

There are many introduction to hospitality textbooks available. However, while this book explores many of the general topics common to traditional business and hospitality topics in the first three sections, this book is unique in that it also explores many different career paths. We wanted to discuss the common areas so that students could understand the context in which the industry is housed. However, the topics that make hospitality distinctive lie in the wide variety of options available in each grouping.

Hospitality: An Introduction is systematically organized for the introductory student. The book begins with a broad overview exploring how and why the industry developed into the different components and how the past trends may shape the future of our industry. It is important to understand the realities and opportunities that students may not be aware of in hospitality so we wrote chapter four. The second section, *Hospitality Companies,* gradually narrows the focus to include an introduction to different forms of organizations and management that are available. These three topics discuss the different business structures that are available in hospitality. While other industries also use these formats, hospitality abounds with them and has honed them to a fine science. From there, we wanted to get students involved in the industry and offered chapter eight to learn what associations and rating programs everyone should be aware of and to inspire them to join so that they can begin their valuable networking and learn the applications of the theory from our classes. These first two sections give students the overall knowledge they need to learn more about this exciting industry and understand the general scope.

The third section, *Hospitality Operations,* explores six of the general areas of business: operations management, marketing, managing revenue & expenses, human resources, law & ethics and physical plant management. Except for physical plant, these topics can be found in a business curriculum. However in this book, we explore the subjects that are similar yet different in the service industry. In the final section, *Hospitality Career Menu,* we review many specific industry segments and career options available to prospective managers. The goal is to provide a survey approach to hospitality, while offering the information needed to help students proceed into more advanced courses and readings.

As you can see, this book has a vast amount of knowledge for students that both excites them and allows them to go deeper into the subjects that most interest them. Because we have a chapter on each topic, it allows students to have enough basic knowledge to know whether the world of hospitality is for them and most importantly, where they might fit in.

ACKNOWLEDGMENTS

The fourteenth edition of this book is a collection of readings written by numerous authors representing colleges and universities across the United States. These authors have written papers specifically for this book, and without their generous contributions the publication of this edition would not have been possible. They have truly created an outstanding edition, and we are very grateful for the special role each and every author played.

Donna Albano, The Richard Stockton College of New Jersey
Bradley Beran, Waukesha County Technical College
Daniel Bernstein, Seton Hill University
Sherie Buezina, Florida Gulf Coast University
Ronald J. Cereola, James Madison University
Michael D. Collins, Coastal Carolina University
Wanda M. Costen, University of Tennessee
John C. Crotts, College of Charleston
Molly J. Dahm, Lamar University
L. Taylor Damonte, Coastal Carolina University
Christopher DeSessa, Johnson & Wales University
Robin B. DiPietro, University of South Carolina
Brad Engeldinger, Sierra College
Donald G. Farr, Florida State University
Reginald Foucal-Szocki, James Madison University
Christian Hardigree, University of Nevada, Las Vegas
Bradford T. Hudson, Boston University
Joe C. Hutchinson, University of Central Florida
Keith Mandabach, New Mexico State University
Karl J. Mayer, University of Nevada, Las Vegas
S. Denise McCurry, Gordon and Rees
Robert A. McMullin, East Stroudsburg University
Richard J. Mills, Jr., Robert Morris University
Gail J. Myers, Suite Harmony Corporation
Ken W. Myers, University of Minnesota, Crookston
Radesh Palakurthi, Drexel University
David Rivera, Jr., East Carolina University
Chris Roberts, DePaul University
Denis P. Rudd, Robert Morris University
Chay Runnels, Stephen F. Austin University
Michael S. Scales, The Richard Stockton College of New Jersey
Joseph Scarcelli, Niagara University
Neha M. Shah, Pittsboro-Siler City Convention & Visitors Bureau
Linda J. Shea, University of Massachusetts, Amherst
John Stefanelli, University of Nevada, Las Vegas
Marcia Taylor, Florida Gulf Coast University
Patrick Tierney, San Francisco State University
Kirsten Tripodi, Fairleigh Dickinson University
Jan van Harssel, Niagara University
Mel Weber, East Carolina University
Michele Wehrle, Community College of Allegheny County

Robert A. Brymer

Robert A. Brymer, CHA, is the Cecil B. Day Professor of Hotel Management, Florida State University, College of Business, Dedman School of Hospitality. He is nationally recognized in hotel management and education in the following ways.

- Ranked 34th in hospitality research influence and 20th in hospitality research productivity worldwide
- Certified Trainer in Stephen Covey's *7 Habits of Highly Effective People*
- Recognized in Harvard University's *Profiles in Business & Management: An International Directory of Scholars and Their Research*
- Appointed to the *White House Conference on Travel and Tourism*
- Stevenson Fletcher CHRIE Achievement Award
- Van Nostrand Reinhold CHRIE Research Award
- Elected a Fellow in the American Institute of Stress
- Florida State University Teaching Award
- Certified Hotel Administrator by the American Hotel & Lodging Association

Dr. Brymer has over 30 years of management, consulting, and education experience in the hotel industry. He has held management and supervisory positions with Hyatt Hotels, Westin Hotels, and Hospitality Management Corporation. In 2000, while on sabbatical from Florida State University, he worked for several months in daily operations at The Ritz-Carlton Hotel, in Sydney, Australia. His management seminars have been presented for more than 7000 managers in the hotel industry, including Four Seasons, Walt Disney World, Ritz-Carlton, Marriott, Hyatt, Hilton, Westin, Inter-Continental, and many five-star independent hotels and resorts.

Dr. Brymer earned his doctorate in Psychology from The University of Denver, where he specialized in executive and management psychology. He has an M.B.A. in Hotel, Restaurant, and Institutional Management from Michigan State University and a B.S.B.A. in Hotel and Restaurant Management from The University of Denver. He is one of the hotel industry's leading authorities in managerial and organizational psychology, and has conducted research in the areas of executive personality, leadership behavior, ethics, service excellence, and managerial stress.

Misty M. Johanson

Dr. Johanson attended Michigan State University for her BA, MS and PhD degrees in Hospitality Business and Tourism. She comes to DePaul University's School of Hospitality Leadership in Chicago as an Associate Professor, after seven years as a tenured faculty member with the University of Hawaii-Manoa, and four years as faculty at George State University. Her industry experience includes managing and training in resort hotels and restaurants in the U.S., Hawaii, Caribbean and throughout Asia. She has contributed to the industry as a consultant to several international hospitality organizations including: Starwood, Marriott, Hilton, Disney, the RARE Hospitality Group and NAMA.

Dr. Johanson has actively served as a member of ICHRIE—The International Council for Hotel, Restaurant and Institutional Education, for over 12 years. She currently stands as Director of Education for one of its U.S. Federations and serves as the association's Executive

Editor for the top ranking *Journal of Hospitality and Tourism Education.* Dr. Johanson has produced over 50-refereed scholarly publications and has been recognized and awarded internationally for her research in the field. Further, she has served in an administrative capacity to cohesively lead efforts in redesigning undergraduate and graduate program studies in hospitality education.

Hospitality Industry

Welcome to Hospitality

Robert A. Brymer, Florida State University
Misty M. Johanson, DePaul University

LEARNING OBJECTIVES
- An overview of the industry
- An overview of this book so that you will know what to expect

CHAPTER OUTLINE
The Service-Hospitality Connection
Key Content
Hospitality
    Lodging
    Food Service
Summary

KEY TERMS
Ambience or servicescape
Moment of truth
Service
Service experience
Service product

Welcome to the EXCITING world of HOSPITALITY! This book introduces you to one of the fastest-growing industries globally. It comes to you at a time when the wonderful world of hospitality has never been more dynamic! On a broad scale, hospitality enterprises are part of the service industry and possess unique characteristics that differentiate them from manufacturing firms. Most important for you to understand is that the hospitality product is intangible. This means that, unlike a pair of jeans that you can take back and exchange, a service once offered or experienced cannot be taken back. Once a guest meets and interacts with the employee—which is known as the moment of truth—the service experience is created, for better or worse. Overall, hospitality encompasses those service organizations that offer food, drink, lodging, and entertainment. In the modern industry, you will find that many of these fields are interrelated. You may not realize, for instance, that sculptors are needed in food organizations to create ice and edible displays for banquets and restaurants. Interior designers are needed to help create the exotic fantasy of a casino's pirate world or a themed Chinese restaurant. Meeting and event planners can organize weddings at Disneyland or a meeting of the local bar association or perhaps even a convention of 10 thousand attendees. Hospitality enterprises need quality employees and leaders with many different types of skills, from artists to public relations to accountants. It needs special individuals who like people and truly want to help make the guests' experience the best possible. The authors in this book will introduce you to an industry that is a "people" business. Chapter after chapter will reaffirm that, in the world of hospitality, taking good care of the guest is the single most critical element for success.

The Service–Hospitality Connection

For a better understanding of where the industry fits in the economy, please refer to Figure 1.1. Starting at the top of that chart—The Economy—you will see

3

FIGURE   1.1   **The Service-Hospitality Connection**

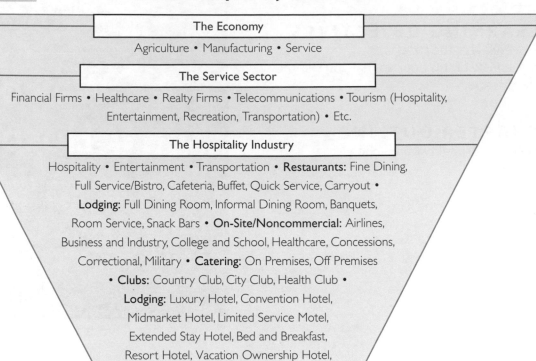

that the economy is made up of agriculture, manufacturing, and service. They are three separate parts of the economy, yet each plays a role in the service part of the economy. In the past, agriculture and manufacturing contributed the most to the economy. Agriculture focuses on growing the food that is necessary for survival. Once that production process is stable and people have enough to eat, the economy moves on to manufacturing. Manufacturing helps build products that make life easier. We can evaluate these products with our five senses like touch or smell. As other countries have developed cheaper labor, American manufacturing has changed. Now the service sector is the most dominant contributor.

This shift of dominance from agriculture and manufacturing to service has required people to acquire different skills. In an agricultural economy, people were engaged in growing crops and getting them prepared for consumer consumption. Service played a very small role because most of the focus was on climates and crops. In a manufacturing economy, people were occupied with the process of creating a product and what machinery can be used to speed up the process. Service played a more important role because more people were involved in the process. In today's service economy, there is no tangible product—the product is mostly service—and the quality of that product rests in the mind of the guest.

In a hotel, the room is the tangible product. However, in picking the hotel, the guest spends more money for the ambience and the service. By the same token, people go to a restaurant to eat, but the way they are treated is just as important. Think about your best experience in a restaurant. You enjoyed the food, of course. However, what if the server was rude? What would happen to your feeling about the restaurant experience? Herein lies the difficult and exciting part of this industry: forecasting the guests' service expectations. The skills necessary to survive in an agricultural economy and manufacturing economy are physical and mental. In the service economy, they are more interpersonal and intellectual. For many people, this is quite a change and a difficult transition. Figure 1.1 illustrates the relationship between the economy, service, and the hospitality industry.

Key Content

Hospitality: An Introduction is systematically organized for the introductory student. The book begins with a broad overview exploring how and why the industry developed into the different components and what the current trends are that are shaping the future of the industry. Further, it is important to understand the realities and career opportunities that you may not be aware of in hospitality; therefore, we present you with Chapter 4. This first section gives you the overall knowledge you need to learn more about this exciting industry, where it's been, where it's going, and how you can fit in!

The second section, *Hospitality Companies,* gradually narrows the focus to include an introduction to different forms of industry expansion, organizations, and management that are current in the industry. Next, *Hospitality Operations,* explores six of the general areas of business key to success in the industry. In the final section, *Hospitality Career Menu,* we review many specific fields in the industry and career options available to prospective managers. Please see Figure 1.2 for a graphic view of how the book is organized. The goal is to provide a survey approach to hospitality, while offering the information needed to help students proceed into more advanced courses and readings.

Hospitality

The hospitality industry includes many different segments, as can be seen in Figures 1.1 and 1.2, including recreation, entertainment, travel, food service, lodging, and many others. We will devote a little more time in this chapter to lodging and food service, the two single largest sectors. Although they are the largest, they are closely related and work hand in hand with many other vital segments of this vast industry.

Lodging

If you were to ask 10 people to give you an example of the lodging industry, you might get answers like: a resort in the Bahamas or Hawaii; a small inn in Vermont; a bed and breakfast in Cape May, New Jersey; a small exclusive converted castle in France; a roadside motel in Akron, Ohio; a 1,200-room luxury hotel in New York; a 100-room budget motel in Fresno, California; an all-suite hotel in Memphis; a mega hotel in Las Vegas; and an apartment hotel in London. All these answers, although different in some ways, represent examples of the lodging

FIGURE **1.2** **Organization of the Book**

Hospitality Industry
Welcome to Hospitality • Hospitality History • Current Trends and Future Issues • Career Expectations and Realities

Hospitality Companies
Independent and Entrepreneurial Operations • Chain Operations and Franchising • Contract Management • Hospitality Trade Associations and Rating Services

Hospitality Operations
Operations Management • Marketing • Managing Revenue and Expenses • Human Resource Management • Law and Ethics • Physical Plant Management

Hospitality Career Menu
Lodging: Lodging Segments • Hotel Operations • **Food and Beverage:** Food Service Segments • Restaurant Operations • Bar and Beverage Operations • Culinary Arts • Food, Wine, and Distribution Services • Facility Layout and Design Consulting • Real Estate in Hospitality • **Tourism:** Golf Management • Sports and Entertainment Centers • Attractions Management • Travel Management Companies and Tour Operators • Meetings and Events Management • Private Club Operations • Casinos • Cruise Ships • **Special Career Paths:** Senior Services Management • Education Careers in Hospitality • Management Consulting

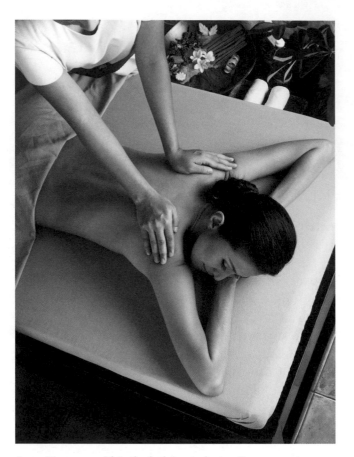

Amenities vary within the lodging industry. Some resorts include a spa. © 2011 by Hywit Dimyad. Used under license of Shutterstock, Inc.

industry. The common bond is that they all have sleeping rooms.

However, the amenities and quality of service will vary from concept to concept. A Motel 6 will give you a clean room with bed and bath, while a Marriott might provide you with additional amenities like a fitness center and a swimming pool. A resort will allow you to walk around the grounds and play golf or go to the spa and have a clean room with bed and bath. Some will have extensive food service with two or three restaurants with different cuisines and 24-hour room service. Some will have one restaurant that serves breakfast, lunch, and dinner. An apartment or residential hotel may provide the guests with a fully equipped kitchen. A bed and breakfast will serve only breakfast. Some will have no food service except for a vending machine with snacks and soft drinks. The profitability percentage of a sold guest room is usually higher than selling a meal. Therefore, many owners make the decision not to have food service in their properties because of the profitability picture and the difficulty of operating a food service

facility. In some cases, lodging owners want to provide food service for their guests and will lease the food service facility.

Some lodging facilities will have five employees to service each room, while others will have two or more employees per room. The Peninsula Hotel in Hong Kong changes your linens and towels several times a day to provide the ultimate in service, while other hotels will ask you to throw the towels on the floor only when you want them changed to protect the environment. If you think about how much water and soap it takes to wash all those sheets and towels, you can see that even using towels one more day before washing them can make a big difference in water usage. In places that regularly have droughts, like California, this is an important factor. It is amazing that there are over 50,000 lodging operations in the United States. What incredible opportunity.

The lodging industry is very broad and varied, with each segment requiring a different skill set. Can you imagine the amount of experience you would need to run one of those mega properties in Las Vegas with 4,000 to 5,000 rooms? You would actually be running a medium-sized corporation. You would need to have experience in all facets of hotel operations, excellent interpersonal and leadership skills, extensive food and beverage experience to run 12 to 24 different venues, plus excellent knowledge of the gaming industry. Obviously, to run a 100-room or less property without food and beverage would require much less experience than the Vegas property. Some managers of these properties have less than 5 years of experience in the lodging business.

The basic strategy in the lodging business is to sell rooms; that is pretty obvious. The challenge for marketing is to bring people in to buy rooms. Once the guest is at the property, a challenge might be to sell them the kind of room they desire at a price that represents value to the guest. Like quality, the guest, not the management of the property, determines value. A guest room is a perishable product. If it is not sold on any one night, that revenue is lost, so the challenge is to know how to sell that room based on the guests' expectation and their perception of value.

Food Service

This part of the hospitality industry is growing at a dramatic rate. The reason for this growth is that consumers are changing their eating habits. In the 1950s, the woman stayed at home and cooked for her husband and two children. The measure of her success as a wife and mother was her cooking abilities and how much time she labored in the kitchen. Going out to eat was only for special occasions. Now, there are varieties of households, ranging from singles to one-parent families to couples with no kids to the two-parent family. To meet their economic needs, the adults in the family are working longer hours. Therefore, there is less time to spend buying groceries and preparing meals. As a result, more people are consuming meals away from their homes or are bringing prepared food home to eat. The increase in second-income families and the inadequate time to prepare meals is a significant factor in this trend.

However, this industry is far more than just food and service. For example, how many different reasons can you think of for going out to eat? Hunger, of course. However, what else? How about getting together with friends to socialize or impressing a special someone, or creating a romantic mood. Because there are so many different reasons for eating out, it makes sense that restaurants come in all types of price ranges and service qualities to meet the needs of their guests. For example, quick-service restaurants cater to our frantic on-the-go lifestyle. Family restaurants attempt to keep kids occupied with activities like placemats that they can draw on while they wait for their food. At the upper end of the spectrum are restaurants that serve great food and deliver exceptional service. In each of these different venues, understanding the guests' needs and providing the kind of food and good service they want is important.

However, there is another aspect of any service environment: ambiance or servicescape. Ambiance is made up of the décor, the sound level, the lighting, the furniture, and the symphony of dining sounds created by both the diners themselves—their conversation and laughter—and the clanking of dishes and silverware. What type of ambiance do you like when going out to eat? When Windows on the World reopened in 1996, the president of Windows, Joe Baum, announced at the employee orientation, "We are not in the restaurant business; we are in the entertainment business because we are creating a unique experience." He took the notion of a dining experience to the next level. Windows on the World went on to become the highest-volume restaurant in the United States. Unfortunately, that ended on September 11, 2001, when the industry and the world lost many good people.

When you go to a restaurant, the service is as important as the meal. © 2011 by bluefox. Used under license of Shutterstock, Inc.

The restaurant segment of the food service industry can be a trip around the world. In any major city, you can experience food from almost any country in the world. New taste sensations are created as chefs blend different cuisines to produce what is called "fusion" cuisine. For example, the blending of the flavors from Chinese and French cuisine produces a new, unique taste. Creative themes and décor can enhance the eating experience by transporting the guest to any country in the world or make them feel like they are in the eighteenth or the twenty-third century. The diversity of the restaurant segment is immense. As a customer, you can spend 5 dollars for dinner or you can spend 100 dollars for dinner. You can select from an assortment of 5 beverages or a selection of 1,000 varieties of wine. You can also experience an operation that is owned by an individual who has one restaurant and works at it all the time or a restaurant that is one of a thousand restaurants owned by a corporation, where the owners are never around. For the employee, both entrepreneurial properties and franchises have advantages and disadvantages.

In addition, the food service industry is made up of more than just restaurants. The noncommercial food service industry feeds students—elementary, secondary, and college—as well as patients and corporate employees. The challenge is to offer food they will eat and that is nutritious. In some college dining programs, a cafeteria is set aside just for vegetarians.

That goes a long way to meet and exceed the expectations of the customer. There will be many students who will choose that university because they have a vegetarian cafeteria. Hospital food service is challenging in that meals must be suitable for all kinds of diets that are required by patients. Many institutional dining facilities (hospitals, schools, companies) have gone to branding. Branding is taking a known brand like McDonald's and opening that facility in a hospital or a school. This trend brings to the operation the name recognition and appeal that goes with it, as well as the standards of operation for that brand.

An often-overlooked segment of the food service industry is the private club segment. Private clubs are owned and run by its members. Therefore, the focus is on satisfying the needs of a small group of people. You know these people because they come in regularly, and they expect that you will know their names and their preferences for drinks and food. These operations can provide an exciting, interesting place to work, especially if the club has a large food service facility that serves à la carte and has catering for special events. In addition to the food service operation, a manager could end up managing the challenges of other activities like a golf course or tennis courts.

Probably the largest segment of this industry is the quick-service or fast-food restaurants. As we mentioned earlier, quick service meets our needs for food when we are on the run. As you know, you can eat in or drive through, which affords a variety of eating options like eating at your desk or in the car on the way to classes. Quick-service restaurants are continually trying to reinvent themselves, but the eating public continues to go for that hamburger, fried chicken, and pizza.

Another subdivision of the food service business is found in special events and catering. Special events include food service at outdoor concerts, golf tournaments, tennis tournaments, and huge events like the Olympics. These events are intense and many times

more difficult to operate because the dining tents and kitchens are normally temporary. During the Winter 2002 Olympics, the food service people were providing 100,000 meals per day. The dining tent in the Olympic Village housed 1,300 seats, a huge kitchen, and a full-service McDonald's. Working in stadiums and arenas is a unique challenge because they contain almost every segment of the food service industry: concession stands, private clubs, luxury skyboxes, à la carte restaurants, and catering for special events. As a free bonus, you get the excitement of watching a major sporting event. As you can see, food service has a broad variety of venues that will be explored in this book. Knowing about all these different types will allow you to decide whether this is the career path for you.

Summary

The bottom line in the hospitality business is managing the *moments of truth*. A moment of truth is any time the guest comes in contact with anything that represents the operation. The perception of that contact could be positive or negative. Those contacts could be the condition of the parking lot, the friendliness of the voice on the phone when the reservation was made, the cleanliness of the entranceway, the greeting by the front desk person or a hostess, the speediness of the elevator, and so on. In a one-night stay or the time it takes to enjoy a meal, the guest could experience 100 moments of truth. The greatest challenge in the industry is to manage those moments of truth so that they are positive for the guest who then wants to return and tell their friends how wonderful their encounter was. These happy memories create the desire in our guests and everyone who hears their stories to come and experience the adventure. Hospitality and service are interwoven in this exciting worldwide industry. Enjoy your exploration into the industry, companies, operations, and careers. It is *our* pleasure to welcome you!

RESOURCES

Internet Sites

Career Builder: hospitality.careerbuilder.com/
Hospitality Net: www.hospitalitynet.org
HCareers: www.hcareers.com/
Hospitality Online: www.hospitalityonline.com

Review Questions

1. Why is the hospitality industry referred to as a "people" business?

2. What are the three separate parts of the economy described by the author? Define each.

3. Describe the major shift in the economy concerning manufacturing industries and service industries.

4. What is the product in a service economy?

5. Who judges the quality level of service?

6. What are the skills necessary to survive in the service economy?

7. Describe the various segments of the hospitality industry.

8. Describe the current trends in the food service industry. How and why are they changing?

9. List three to five factors that influence decisions concerning a meal away from home.

10. What is fusion cuisine?

11. What is a challenge of the noncommercial food industry?

12. Describe the different attributes of the private club segment of the hospitality industry.

13. What are the common menu choices of fast-food restaurants?

14. What types of venues are likely to cater to or hold special events?

15. What makes working in stadiums and arenas a unique challenge?

16. Give six examples of different types of lodging.

17. What is the range of employees per guest room ratio? How does that vary within the lodging industry?

18. What are the different types of food services you will find in many hotels?

19. What type of lodging management skills would be needed to run a mega-property in Las Vegas?

20. What is meant by the concept that a guest room is perishable?

21. List five examples of "moments of truth" in a hospitality setting.

22. What is one of the greatest challenges related to managing moments of truth?

CHAPTER 2

Hospitality History

Bradford T. Hudson, Boston University

LEARNING OBJECTIVES

- To acquire introductory knowledge about the history of hospitality as a business.
- To understand the ancient origins of the modern hospitality industry.
- To understand the role of economic, technological, and social context in the evolution of the hospitality industry in the past.
- To understand how the organization and structure of the hospitality industry have changed over time.
- To understand the concepts of brand heritage and heritage tourism in the modern hospitality industry.

CHAPTER OUTLINE

The Ancient and Medieval World
The Nineteenth Century
The Modern Era
Recent Developments
    Restaurants
    Cruise and Air Lines
    Theme Parks
Perspective
Summary

KEY TERMS

Auguste Escoffier
Bakken
Brand heritage
Carnival Cruise Line
Cesar Ritz
Chain
Code of Hammurabi
Conrad Hilton
Cunard Line
Darden Restaurants
Delmonico's
Disneyland
Ellsworth Statler
Ernest Henderson
Franchising
Fred Harvey

Grand tour
Heritage tourism
Hilton Hotels
Holiday Inn
Hospitia
J. Willard Marriott
Kemmons Wilson
Knott's Berry Farm
Management contract
Marriott Hotels
McDonald's
P&O Line
Parker House Hotel
Portfolio
Property
Ray Kroc

Ritz-Carlton Hotels
Samuel Cunard
Savoy Hotel
Segment
Sheraton Hotels
Silk Road
Starwood Hotels
Statler Hotels
Ted Arison
Theme park
Tivoli Gardens
Union Oyster House
Waldorf-Astoria Hotel
Walt Disney
White Castle

The Ancient and Medieval World

The history of the hospitality industry begins in the early days of human civilization. Throughout the ancient world, the business of hospitality followed the concentration of populations into towns, the development of road systems and transoceanic travel, the growth of interregional trade, and the adoption of exchangeable currency.

Among the evidence of early hospitality that exists today is a stela (or stone marker) displayed at the Louvre Museum in Paris, which contains laws established around 1750 BC by Hammurabi, the ruler of Babylonia. The **Code of Hammurabi** includes regulations for innkeepers and tavern keepers on issues related to pricing and licensing.[1]

During the classical period, the Roman Empire had a burgeoning hospitality sector. The Romans built an extensive network of roads throughout the Mediterranean region, which required the establishment of lodging venues for travelers. Modern tourists can visit the ruins of several *hospitia* (or guest places) in the town of Pompeii, near the modern city of Naples in Italy, which was buried by a volcanic eruption in 79 AD.[2]

The **Silk Road** encompassed a variety of ancient routes between Europe and points in Asia. Merchants and traders used this system to transport goods, including silk, spices, and gemstones. *Caravanserai* (or caravan houses) subsequently appeared throughout the region. Modern travelers can visit several such sites in Turkey, including the Sultan Han near Aksaray, which dates to 1229 AD.[3]

In Japan, a system of rest houses for travelers was first established during the Nara period circa 750 AD.[4] These evolved into inns during the later medieval period, many of which survive to the present era. Modern travelers can stay at the Houshi Ryokan in Ishikawa, which traces its origins to 718 AD.

The Nineteenth Century

Although many global civilizations have influenced the traditions and practices of hospitality, the modern business of hospitality developed predominantly in Europe and America during the nineteenth century. This period is characterized by a significant acceleration in the pace of technological and economic development, especially in manufacturing and transportation powered by steam. The Industrial Revolution created vast new wealth among investors and business owners, resulting in the development of a new managerial class to operate their huge companies, this contributed to the widespread emergence of an economic middle class.[5] These factors, in turn, resulted in a dramatic increase in leisure and business travel.

Inns and taverns were common in Europe and America prior to 1800, but they were relatively small and simple operations. During the nineteenth century, a new style of hotel appeared with luxurious amenities and opulent décor reminiscent of royal residences.[6] These palace hotels were built to accommodate wealthy industrialists and European nobility, who were taking extended international vacations. The route from Britain to Italy was known as the **Grand Tour**, a term that eventually became associated with visits by Americans to a variety of European destinations.

Famous city hotels of this period included the Hotel des Bergues in Geneva (1834), the Grand Hôtel de Louvre in Paris (1855), and the Hotel Imperial in Vienna (1873). This era also included the first resort hotels, which were built in locations that would offer either health benefits (such as near mineral spas) or cooler temperatures (such as near mountains or oceans). These included the Hotel Minerva in Baden-Baden (1872), the Hotel Victoria-Jungfrau in Interlaken (1865), and the Hôtel de Paris in Monte Carlo (1864).

The most famous hotel of the late nineteenth century was the **Savoy Hotel** in London (1889), which still operates today. The Savoy was one of the first major buildings powered entirely by electricity and one of the first hotels to offer private *en suite* bathrooms. Shortly after its construction, the owner hired Swiss hotelier **César Ritz** as Managing Director and French cook **Auguste Escoffier** as *Chef de Cuisine* (chief of the kitchen).[7] The pair would subsequently become the most famous hospitality professionals in history. Ritz eventually built his own luxury hotel empire, which has evolved into the modern **Ritz-Carlton** brand.

In the United States, the first lodging property that we would recognize as a modern hotel was the Tremont House in Boston (1829). It included innovative features such as private guest rooms and indoor plumbing, albeit with shared bathrooms.[8] Other famous early hotels included the Astor House in New York (1836) and the **Parker House** in Boston (1855).

Palace hotels also appeared in the United States during the second half of the nineteenth century. Famous city hotels included the **Waldorf-Astoria Hotel** in New York (1893–1897), the Palmer House in Chicago (1875), the Brown Palace Hotel in Denver (1892), and the Palace Hotel in San Francisco (1875). Celebrated resort hotels included the Hotel Ponce de Leon in Saint Augustine (1888), the Grand Hotel on Mackinac Island in Michigan (1887), and the Hotel del Coronado in San Diego (1888).

The Modern Era

The palace hotels of the nineteenth century defined standards that remain in effect today within luxury hotels. However, the vast majority of modern hotels are based on concepts introduced and perfected more recently in the United States.

The most famous American hotelier of the first half of the twentieth century was Ellsworth Statler.[9] After an early career as a hotel employee and restaurant entrepreneur, he built the Statler Hotel in Buffalo (1908). The hotel was so popular that he quickly expanded his business, eventually operating hotels in several major cities.

Statler Hotels featured comfortable accommodations and a full range of services previously offered only in luxury hotels, but they were moderately priced and targeted toward the economic middle class. Statler was also famous for his innovations in amenities and technology. His hotels were among the first to offer bathrooms in every guest room, telephones in every guest room, and free morning newspapers for everyone.

The seeming contradiction between high quality and moderate price was made possible by an innovative approach to building and managing hotels. Statler properties were unusually large and therefore offered economies of scale, meaning that fixed costs could be distributed across a large number of customers. They were also differentiated by the efficient design of operating systems and architectural elements, such as centralized plumbing risers.

Statler created the modern hotel for business travelers, but he was soon followed by other pioneers using the same formula. **Conrad Hilton** bought his first hotel in 1919 and built a national **chain** (or company with multiple locations) during the next two decades. **Hilton Hotels** eventually acquired the Statler chain in 1954, making the combined company the largest hotel operator in the world at the time.[10] Hilton also eventually acquired several historic properties, including the Waldorf-Astoria Hotel in New York and the Palmer House in Chicago.

Ernest Henderson started **Sheraton Hotels** near Boston in 1937. His company grew quickly, and 10 years later Sheraton was the first hotel company to be listed on the New York Stock Exchange.[11] Sheraton also eventually acquired several historic properties, including the Palace Hotel in San Francisco and the Hotel Imperial in Vienna.

J. Willard Marriott started his career as a restaurant entrepreneur in Washington, DC, during the late 1920s. He opened his first hotel in 1957 and eventually decided to focus exclusively on lodging. **Marriott Hotels** bought Ritz-Carlton Hotels in 1995, thereby acquiring an historical legacy that can be traced back to César Ritz.[12]

At the same time that chains for business travelers were being built, other pioneers were reinventing the economy hotel. Inexpensive lodging was common throughout the United States, but quality levels were inconsistent and often poor. As highway construction and maintenance improved, and as people began to travel more by automobile, the urban locations of the existing hotels also became problematic. **Kemmons Wilson** envisioned a chain of inexpensive roadside hotels oriented toward families traveling by automobile with a limited budget.[13] He founded **Holiday Inn** in 1952, and within two decades it was the largest hotel chain in the United States.

Recent Developments

The basic elements of the modern hotel were firmly established by the middle of the twentieth century, especially from the viewpoint of the guest. However, several important developments have occurred in recent years related to the structure and operations of the industry.

First, ownership of individual properties has shifted away from hotel companies. A century ago, the real estate (building and land) associated with most hotels was owned by the company that operated the hotel. However, over the past three decades, ownership and management functions have been separated for financial reasons. Most hotels are now owned by independent investors. The hotel companies still control their brand names, but they merely operate hotels on behalf of owners, based on **management contracts**.

Second, the hotel industry has been divided into parts. A century ago, there was no standardized system for understanding what to expect at a specific hotel **property** (or individual location). Now the industry is organized according to price and quality levels known as **segments**, which progress upward from the economy segment to the luxury segment.

Third, the industry has become consolidated through acquisition. A generation ago, almost every hotel brand was owned and operated separately. However, over the past three decades, the major hotel companies have assembled **portfolios** (or collections) of hotel brands. These have been created to fulfill the growth ambitions of parent companies, to diversify investment and risk, and in response to the increasing segmentation of the industry. Hilton was the first to acquire a major competitor (the now defunct Statler brand) and has subsequently acquired or created nine other brands, including Waldorf-Astoria, Doubletree, Embassy Suites, and Hampton. A real estate investment group named **Starwood Hotels** purchased Sheraton Hotels and then acquired or created eight other brands, including St. Regis, Westin, and W Hotels. Marriott Hotels has acquired or created more than 10 different hotel brands, including Ritz-Carlton, Renaissance, Courtyard, and Residence Inn.

Restaurants

The hotel and restaurant industries were connected throughout much of history, as meals were typically provided by inns or taverns that also offered lodging upstairs. This tradition continues to the present day, as a portion of revenues in full-service hotels continues to derive from restaurants on premise or from banquet operations.

The dining industry grows every year as people spend less time cooking and more time eating out. © 2011 by Andresr. Used under license of Shutterstock, Inc.

Independent restaurants (separate from hotels) emerged in Europe and America during the eighteenth and nineteenth centuries.[14] The social and economic factors that contributed to the rise of the hotel industry also helped create the burgeoning restaurant business. The first American establishments that we would recognize as modern restaurants were the **Union Oyster House** in Boston (1826) and **Delmonico's** in New York (1837), both of which are still operating.

The earliest chain restaurant operator was probably **Fred Harvey**, who opened a restaurant in the railroad station at Topeka, Kansas, in 1876. The company succeeded based on his formula for excellent food, good service, and reasonable prices. By the turn of the century, the Fred Harvey Company operated an extensive network of restaurants and hotels along the route of the Atchison, Topeka and Santa Fe Railway Company.[15]

The most important early pioneer in the quick service segment is **White Castle**, which opened its first hamburger restaurant in Wichita, Kansas, in 1921. White Castle established a system involving counter service, mass production of a limited menu, strict sanitation procedures, and a chain of identical units.[16]

The White Castle formula was adopted by the McDonald brothers, who opened the first **McDonald's** restaurant in California two decades later (1948). Shortly thereafter, an enterprising milkshake machine salesman named **Ray Kroc** convinced the McDonalds to sell the franchise rights to their concept. Kroc subsequently created the largest restaurant brand in the world.[17]

Several important developments have occurred in recent years related to the structure and operations of the restaurant industry. First, **franchising** has become a widespread method of growing restaurant brands. This is a technique in which an independent entrepreneur pays for the rights to use the brand, recipes, and operating system of a leading restaurant company. Second, the restaurant industry has been organized into **segments** based on price and quality, which progress upward from the quick-service (or fast-food) segment to the fine dining segment. Third, the industry has become consolidated through acquisition. For example, **Darden Restaurants** owns several major brands, including Capital Grille, Red Lobster, and Olive Garden. Fourth, the chain restaurant paradigm has matured to encompass concepts in every segment, including fine dining restaurants operated by celebrity chefs such as Wolfgang Puck.

Cruise and Air Lines

Ships have been an established mode of transportation for thousands of years, but a new style of passenger ship was introduced during the nineteenth century. Steamships were larger and faster than their predecessors. They also had features and interior decor that resembled luxury hotels, intended to cater to wealthy industrialists and their families, who were traveling from America to Europe (and within Europe) on the Grand Tour.

The **Cunard Line** was founded in 1839 by **Samuel Cunard** to operate transatlantic vessels between Britain and the United States. By the early twentieth century, it had become one of the most prestigious shipping companies in the world. A leading competitor was the White Star Line, which owned the ill-fated ship *Titanic*. The two companies eventually merged (1934), and shortly thereafter Cunard built the famous ships *Queen Mary* and *Queen Elizabeth*.[18]

The original purpose of ocean liners was to transport people and cargo from point to point, in a manner similar to modern airlines. The Peninsular and Oriental Steam Navigation Company (or **P&O**) advertised a new type of service in 1843, offering voyages with a series of stops in the Mediterranean for tourists interested in visiting historical sites.[19] This was the start of leisure cruising.

A century later in 1958, the jet engine was introduced to commercial passenger aircraft, making intercontinental air travel fast and safe. Ships could no longer compete, and the oceanic passenger industry effectively disappeared within a decade. Many of the ships were scrapped, but some were adapted for leisure cruising. However, the passenger profile remained essentially the same, predominated by older and wealthier customers.

In 1972, **Ted Arison** purchased a former ocean liner from the Canadian Pacific Line and offered cruises from Miami to the Caribbean. Arison believed that a market existed for moderately priced voyages aimed at a younger audience, with extensive onboard activities and without the formality of the transatlantic ocean liners. He called his company **Carnival Cruise Line**, renamed his first ship *Mardi Gras,* and adopted the slogan "The Fun Ships." This was the start of the modern cruise industry.[20] Within two decades, Carnival had become the largest cruise line in the world and had acquired the historic Cunard and P&O brands.

Theme Parks

The Industrial Revolution not only generated phenomenal wealth for capitalist barons, but it also created a new economic middle class with increasing amounts of disposable income and leisure time. Entrepreneurs naturally created new products and services to meet the growing demand for entertainment.

Dyrehavsbakken or **Bakken** is an amusement park in Copenhagen, Denmark, that traces its origins to the sixteenth century. The park was opened to the public on a seasonal basis for festivals in 1756. By the late nineteenth century, Bakken had evolved into a permanent venue, offering rides and other amenities found in modern amusement parks.[21] Meanwhile across town, the famous **Tivoli Gardens** opened in 1843. Both are still operating.

Theme parks emerged as a special type of amusement park, in which every aspect of the park had a story or design with a shared theme. The first operations that we would recognize as modern theme parks were Sea Lion Park (1895) and Steeplechase Park (1897) at Coney Island in New York, the former with an ocean theme and the latter with a horseracing theme.[22]

Another pioneer in the theme park industry was **Knott's Berry Farm**, which started as a farm stand and restaurant in Buena Park, California (1928). A few years later, to give restaurant customers something to do while waiting for a table, the Knott family built a western "ghost town" attraction, which has evolved into a full-scale theme park.[23]

Perhaps the most important moment in the history of theme parks occurred when **Disneyland** opened in Anaheim, California (1955). **Walt Disney** was originally a commercial artist, who founded a cartoon movie production company in Hollywood in 1923. Three decades later, he was a major producer of both live action and animated films. Disney envisioned an amusement park that would allow guests to immerse themselves in the imaginary worlds depicted in Disney cartoons and movies, where both adults and children could enjoy the entertainment together. The company subsequently opened Walt Disney World in Orlando, Florida (1971). The latter has grown into a vast entertainment complex encompassing four subsidiary theme parks and numerous hospitality operations, constituting the largest single-site employer of any type in the United States.[24]

Perspective

You may be wondering, if we are preparing hospitality students for the future, why are we focusing here on the past? Although seemingly arcane, business history is actually quite relevant to contemporary issues in hospitality management. Faculty members at Harvard Business School have argued persuasively that the historical approach can be applied to modern business education in important ways.[25] The historical perspective contributes to an appreciation of the economic, technological, and social factors that influence business. An understanding of the evolution of industries and the history of specific firms also contributes to our analysis of the strategic dynamics of modern companies. Those who understand the history of our industry will be better prepared to anticipate its future, especially in identifying the next generation of opportunities that may emerge.

History is also embedded within the identities of older companies, products, and places. **Brand heritage** is an emerging topic within the marketing discipline, which suggests that the consumer appeal of products and services offered by older companies may be enhanced by the historical characters of their brands.[26] Many of the hospitality companies and properties discussed in this chapter continue to operate today, and their historical status is one reason that customers choose such offerings over competitors. Historic Hotels of America is an organization devoted exclusively to marketing for older hotels. It represents more than 200 famous hotels throughout the United States, which are currently managed by a variety of hotel companies.

Heritage tourism is a related topic that considers travel to historic cities, ancient ruins, museums, and other locations that consider our past.[27] This explains the interest in sites from classical antiquity for travelers on the Grand Tour of Europe during the nineteenth century. It also explains the attraction of historical sites throughout the United States today, such as Colonial Williamsburg in Virginia.

Summary

The hospitality business has its origins in the ancient past. Over the centuries, the standards and practices of hospitality have evolved as civilization has progressed. The industry has developed in response to changes in social structure and cultural norms, travel and migration behavior, industrial and economic systems, and technology. Two patterns are particularly clear. First, the hospitality industry has been influenced by transportation technology and infrastructure such as roads, railroads, steamships, automobiles, and aircraft. Second, the hospitality industry has been influenced by the vast increase in the scale and distribution of wealth resulting from the Industrial Revolution.

RESOURCES

Internet Sites

Many of the companies, hotels and restaurants described in this chapter still exist. You can find their Web sites by using any popular search engine, such as Google. Some of these Web sites have subsidiary pages that describe the history of the company or property. These are often located in sections such as "About Us" or "Company Information." The pages usually have titles such as "Our History" or "Company Heritage." To find these sections and pages, review the links at the bottom of the main page or use the "Site Map" feature.

Historic Hotels of America (*www.historichotels.org*) is a marketing organization that represents more than 200 historic hotels, which are currently managed by a variety of hotel companies. This is a good place to start if you are seeking information about specific properties.

ENDNOTES

1. King, L. W. (1898). *The Letters and Inscriptions of Hammurabi [etc.].* London: Luzac; Kent, C. F. (1903). The Recently Discovered Civil Code of Hammurabi. Biblical World, 21 (3), pp. 175–190.

2. O'Gorman, K. D., Baxter, I., and Scott, B. (2007). Exploring Pompeii: Discovering Hospitality through Research Synergy. *Tourism and Hospitality Research,* 7 (2), pp. 89–99.

3. Yavuz, A. T. (1997). The Concepts That Shape Anatolian Seljuq Caravanserais. In G. Necipoglu (ed.), *Muqarnas XIV: An Annual on the Visual Culture of the Islamic World,* pp. 80–95. Leiden: Brill.

4. Japan Ryokan Association. (2010). *Origins and History of the Japanese Ryokan.* Tokyo: Japan Ryokan Association.

5. Chandler, A. D., Jr. (1977). *The Visible Hand: The Managerial Revolution in American Business.* Cambridge: Belknap.

6. Denby, E. (1998). *Grand Hotels.* London: Reaktion; Donzel, C., Gregory, A., and Walter, M. (1989). *Grand American Hotels.* New York: Vendome; Sandoval-Strausz, A. K. (2007). *Hotel: An American History.* New Haven: Yale University.

7. Jackson, S. (1964). *The Savoy: The Romance of a Great Hotel.* New York: E. P. Dutton; Ritz, M. L. (1938). *César Ritz: Host to the World.* Philadelphia: J. P. Lippincott.

8. Lee, H. (1965). Boston's Greatest Hotel. *Old-Time New England,* 55 (200), pp. 97–106.

9. Turkel, S. (2005). Ellsworth Milton Statler: Hotel Man of the Half Century. *Lodging Hospitality,* 61 (5), pp. 64–68.

10. Hilton, C. (1957). *Be My Guest.* Englewood Cliffs, NJ: Prentice Hall; Hilton Buys Chain of Statler Hotels. (1954). *New York Times,* August 4, p. 1.

11. Stock Exchange Notes. (1946). *New York Times,* May 21, p. 36.

12. O'Brien, R. (1977). *Marriott: The J. Willard Marriott Story.* Salt Lake City, UT: Deseret; Marriott to Acquire a Ritz-Carlton Stake. (1995). *New York Times,* March 7, p. D4.

13. Brewster, M. (2004). Kemmons Wilson: America's Innkeeper. *Business Week,* October 11.

14. Spang, R. (1999). *The Invention of the Restaurant.* Cambridge: Harvard University.

15. Fried, S. (2010). *Appetite for America: How Visionary Businessman Fred Harvey Built a Railroad Hospitality Empire that Civilized the Wild West.* New York: Bantam.

16. Hogan, D. G. (1997). *Selling 'em by the Sack: White Castle and the Creation of American Food.* New York: New York University.

17. Love, J. (1986). *McDonald's: Behind the Arches.* New York: Bantam.

18. Hyde, F. E. (1975). *Cunard and the North Atlantic, 1840–1973: A History of Shipping and Financial Management.* Atlantic Highlands, NJ: Humanities Press.

19. P&O Cruises. (2010). History. (www.pocruises.com.au)

20. Garin, K. A. (2005). *Devils on the Deep Blue Sea: The Dreams, Schemes and Showdowns That Built America's Cruise-Ship Empires.* New York: Viking.

21. A/S Dyrehavsbakken. (2010). The History of Bakken. (www.bakken.dk)

22. Sterngrass, J. (2001). *First Resorts: Pursuing Pleasure at Saratoga Springs, Newport & Coney Island.* Baltimore: Johns Hopkins University.

23. Knott's Berry Farm. (2010). Historical Background. (www.knotts.com)

24. Smith, D. (1996). *Disney A to Z: The Official Encyclopedia.* New York: Hyperion; Walt Disney Company. (2010). Corporate History and Walt Disney World Facts. (www.corporate.disney.go)

25. Kantrow, A. M. (1986). Why History Matters to Managers. *Harvard Business Review,* 64 (1), pp. 81–88.

26. Hudson, B. T. (2011). Brand Heritage and the Renaissance of Cunard. *European Journal of Marketing,* forthcoming; Urde, M., Greyser, S. A. and Balmer, J. M. T. (2007). Corporate Brands with a Heritage. *Journal of Brand Management,* 15 (1), pp. 4–19.

27. Dallen, T. J. and Boyd, S. W. (2003). *Heritage Tourism.* London: Prentice Hall.

Review Questions

1. How old is the hospitality business?

2. Identify a specific example of the hospitality business prior to the year 1700.

3. Identify a famous hotel that was built during the period 1800–1899.

4. Identify one pioneering company in each of the following parts of the hospitality industry: hotel, restaurant, cruise line, theme park. Briefly describe the history of each of these companies, and identify the individuals who founded these companies.

5. How did economic, technological, and social context influence the evolution of the hospitality industry in the past? Explain and provide a specific example.

6. How have the organization and structure of the hotel industry changed over time? Explain and provide a specific example.

7. What is brand heritage? What is heritage tourism? How do these concepts relate to each other? Define and explain.

Current Trends and Future Issues

Brad L. Engeldinger, Sierra College

LEARNING OBJECTIVES

- Identify current trends that are influencing the hospitality industry.
- Examine future challenges that hospitality professionals may encounter.
- Comprehend the changing role of technology within the industry.
- Examine the prominent role of social media and its impacts.
- Explore the importance of sustainability and green hospitality.
- Recognize ethical challenges and moral decision-making practices.

CHAPTER OUTLINE

KEY TERMS

Ad targeting
Consumer Behavior
E-Commerce
E-Hospitality
Globalization
Green Hospitality
Segmentation
Shared Technological Services
Social Media
Social Networking
Sustainability

2011: A Year of Transformation

The hospitality industry must transform itself to keep up with demands set on the relationship between guest and services, which are becoming more complex with customer knowledge and increasing expectations, causing preferences to change. Changes in the past decade are creating a new environment in which hospitality services need to do more with less to secure growth and competitive differentiation in today's economy to ultimately meet the challenges of the next decade. The modern customer has become more dynamic than ever by developing expectations built around personal needs refined from performing significant amounts of research prior to travel. Further, globalization is creating growth markets, influencing the hospitality map, and is a recent development that will need to be capitalized on. Professionals must be able to effectively adapt to these changes by closely monitoring consumer behavior to maintain effectiveness in guest services as new segments of customers from differing parts of the world with significant financial clout and unique discrepancies of needs will expand the volume of the global marketplace.

What will the future bring? Though no one can predict the future, we can hypothesize outcomes based on past and present behaviors. Now ask yourself, what current trends, ideas, and actions will likely shape the outlook of the world in which we live? If the terms *technology* and *social media, sustainability,* and *ethical decision making,* come to mind, then you have already begun to recognize the important key issues in the progression of modern society. It will be critical for you to become familiar with such current issues and to develop an understanding of what skills professionals will need to cultivate to manage the challenges that lie ahead.

Technology and Social Networking

E-Hospitality

E-commerce is a form of Web retailing that features the buying and selling of goods and services on the Internet, consisting of direct retail shopping (with a global reach and a 24-hour availability) and has become a multi-billion-dollar industry for world business. Multiple distribution channels are used through Web sites, third-party Web sites (such as social media network advertisements), and telephone reservation systems. There are several key aspects of e-commerce, which include the following:

- Virtual storefronts on Web sites with online catalogs
- Gathering and usage of demographic data
- Business-to-business exchange of data, buying, and selling
- The use of e-mail, instant messaging, and social networking
- Security of business transactions

E-commerce has influenced the hospitality industry to create and develop its own form of electronic commerce. E-hospitality is an innovative service known as "total solutions" where distributing, servicing, and supporting hospitality products to all sizes of organizations in the industry to offer more amenities and support services to potential guests. Hotels, for example, are now using this resource to improve availability to accommodate the needs of guests around the clock. To be skilled in ever-changing commerce technology, formal on-the-job training must transpire. There are now video blogs with brief interviews with industry experts, which discuss important topics such as online marketing, e-commerce, and sales and marketing learning materials. Some of the most prominent benefits are reduced labor costs, increases in productivity, revenue, consumer service convenience, and a competitive advantage in the market.

Social Networking

Today, social networking is a $1.8 billion industry. Web sites are now being created where students and professionals in the hospitality industry can do it all—participate in forum discussions, read/write blogs, search for/post jobs, promote events, chat, and facilitate business connections. Today, hospitality professionals can share insider information with up-and-coming students to discuss topics of interest in forums, groups, by means of private messages, or in a chat room, which may lead to new friendships, career exploration, and professional development.

Now that online social networks have become an established method of communication for many consumers, online communication is now more likely to transpire through social media than via e-mail. Social media is a marketing technique that has gained momentum over the past several years with promising projections for future success. Though Web sites such as Facebook, Twitter, YouTube, and Flickr are

the most prominent, there are currently 246 social media sites/networks up and running. It will be critical for companies not to put all their stock into a single resource but rather to diversify their connections with multiple networking outlets, as consumers from a broad range of demographics are now regular users of various social media sites.

Social marketing allows companies the freedom to do creative things online that cannot be done on a Web site at a relatively inexpensive cost. Companies now improve their online presence by:

- Ensuring Web site content and media is up-to-date and optimized
- Developing and implementing a social media plan
- Tracking consumer behavior on the Web
- Responding quickly to the evolving needs of guests who are traveling less frequently
- Using YouTube for virtual tours of facilities, services, and amenities at casinos, resorts, golf courses, and hotels
- Featuring hotel special events and promotions on Facebook

Though this is an effective marketing technique, companies must not wait for these trends to shape their businesses, but rather maintain control and use them to their advantage.

Ad Targeting

Ad targeting is a craze that has changed online advertising more in the last two years than in the previous decade, benefiting businesses and consumers alike. Through sophisticated audience-targeting ad technology, consumers form travel-related site content, and it categorizes each individual into a group based on her/his online behavior. With this approach, for example, a hotel can buy an audience rather than space on a travel-related sight by extending behavior including lifestyle, news, entertainment, and general interest sights. Segmentation is based on behavior, allowing companies to reach travelers who are most likely to book reservations.

Text Message Marketing

Text messaging has become a prevalent development in contemporary communication, which is written information in text format sent from one party to another by way of cellular phone exchange. This is a fast, convenient, effective technique to relay messages and is growing in popularity with the opportunity to expand.

- 86% of the population ages 13 and up have cell phones.
- 95% of cell phones have text message capability.
- Over 90% of texts are opened and read versus only 40% of e-mails.
- There were over 1 trillion texts sent by mobile phone users in 2009.

Businesses are beginning to text coupons, new product information, company updates, sales, and Web links in a manner that is inexpensive, convenient, and transformative.

Shared Technological Services

A model is being developed to dramatically alter the cost performance landscape for the hotel industry through the sharing of many technological services such as guest room device management, concierge, point of sales, housekeeping, facilities management, and human resources and is now being used by multiple hotel companies. These services offer efficiencies and execution practices that will improve standards of delivery, quality, and performance for hospitality technology functionality for years to come.

Sustainability and Green Hospitality

Sustainability—or the capacity to maintain, support, or endure—is an ecological term that describes how biological systems remain productive through diversity over an extended period of time. The challenge to sustain is to necessitate the present without compromising the ability of future generations to meet their own needs, while balancing environmental, social, and economic demands.

The drive of human manifestation has taken a toll on Earth's ecosystem, which is altered by population and impact per person determined by the ways in which resources are used (consumption). The depleting of natural resources and pollution have been top environmental concerns over the past several decades. There are moral, ethical, social, and political factors for taking action to improve conditions. To become sustainable, we must be able to efficiently manage the environmental, social, and economical aspects of the world in which we live.

In the second half of the twentieth century, the world population doubled, food production tripled, energy use quadrupled, and overall economic activity quintupled. Historically, there has been a significant correlation between economic growth and environmental degradation: As technology advances, the environment declines. Unless resource use is monitored, modern global civilization will collapse through overexploitation of its resource base. Sustainability efforts help to reduce the amount of resources such as water, energy, and materials that are needed for production, consumption, and disposal, through economic management, product design and the implementation of new technology.

Future business leaders must be able to balance ecologic, economic, and social concerns, which is most commonly known as the triple bottom line. Uneconomical growth is growth that depletes the ecosystem resulting in a declined quality of life. Conservation techniques such as waste reduction and energy efficacy reduce costs, liability insurance, environmental penalties, and disposable costs, and many lead to an increase in market share from an improved public image. Several key principles have been developed to guide sustainability efforts, including

- Intergenerational equity by providing future generations the same environment potential as the present
- Decoupling economic growth from environmental degradation—less resource intensive and to reduce pollution
- Integration of environmental, social, and economic sectors with developing sustain policies
- Ensuring environmental adaptability and resilience—enhancing the adaptive capability of the environmental system
- Preventing irreversible damage
- Accepting global responsibilities
- Education and grassroots involvement

Over the past several years, there has been increasing pressure on the hospitality industry to implement "green" initiatives in response to demands from the government, environmental groups, and the general public. This is commonly referred to as green hospitality. The goal of green hospitality is to improve the ability of business while increasing its positive impact on the environment. The challenges faced by the hospitality industry to sustain are the costs of increased pressure on the natural, social, and environmental resources generated by increased number of tourists in concentrated tourism destinations. Moreover, climate change threatens many of the prized tourism destinations such as beaches, islands, and coral reefs.

Expanded tourism destination development has spread travelers across the globe at the expense of natural and social environmental assets. Tourism has a major impact on local communities in tourist destinations. On the one hand, it can be a significant source of income and employment for local people; on the other, it can pose a threat to an area's social fabric and its natural and cultural heritage, on which it ultimately depends. These destinations can be conserved if responsible planning and careful management of facilities and resources transpires. The challenge and goal for the future is to incorporate win–win solutions with travelers and tourist destinations, which will require dynamic thinking and creative solutions. The hospitality industry has developed the following goals to promote sustainability:

1. Design equipment that uses fewer resources.
2. Use sustainable food and beverage options.
3. Decrease environmental impacts while increasing profitability.
4. Integrate sustainability management systems while staying ahead of the competition.
5. Increasing the reputation of an operation to attract investment by incorporating responsible marketing and corporate social responsibility policies.

More specifically, many hotels are now developing resourceful methods to promote sustainability by implementing

- Low-flow showerheads
- Faucet aerators
- Low-flow lawn sprinkler systems
- Compact fluorescent lighting
- Energy-efficient central heating and air-conditioning units
- Bulk soap and shampoo dispensers in showers
- Recycled paper tissues
- Unbleached stationary
- In-room recycling deposit
- Organic cotton linens
- Air and water filtrations systems
- Environmentally safe cleaning products

A recent study has shown that 70% of tourists are willing to pay an extra 9% to 10% in premiums when it comes to environmentally friendly lodgings.

An innovative approach practiced by the Fontainebleau Hilton Resort and Towers in Miami Beach, Florida, is to reuse laundry detergent barrels as garbage bins. "Greening" hotel towels and linens is a resourceful conservation method now practiced where guests and housekeeping agree to leave the same towels and linens for use in rooms for multiple days, reducing water and detergent expenses; this is most commonly referred to as the linen and towel program. These techniques have been used in hotels such as The Hampton Inn, Embassy Suites, Best Western, and Comfort Inns across the nation.

Ethics in Hospitality

Ethical behavior has been and always will be a challenge for corporate executives, managers, employees, and guests alike. Hospitality, travel, and tourism is the fastest-growing industry in the world, governed by powerful corporate and political influences. As discussed in this chapter, many companies are using technology to improve productivity and reduce labor costs. However, if labor costs are being reduced as a result of technology, then that means employees are losing hours, income, and jobs.

As businesses and services expand, revenue increases, which requires meticulously detailed financial management and allocation of funds. One could ask if it is ethical to pay hospitality employees minimum wage with no health insurance, medical benefits, retirement, vacation, or sick days when they have families to support. Other hospitality employees may have jobs where tips are associated as supplemental income. However, corporate mandates instruct them to share their tips with other non-tip-generating employees and allows the company to reduce labor costs by lowering hourly employees' pay at the expense of the staff. Where do we draw the line between profit and employee relations?

A corporate executive may implement a rule at the expense of management and hourly employees to increase revenue for company shareholders; a risk management analysis may elect to not fix a problem that will likely cause personal injury to save money; restaurant managers may offer preferential shifts to servers in exchange for personal favors; a cruise line director may deflect blame on an employee instead of taking personal accountability for a mistake; a guest may exaggerate an dissatisfactory experience to get monetarily compensated. The majority of theft in the workplace is committed by employees. Will a blackjack dealer pocket a one hundred dollar casino chip or bartender embezzle a bottle of vodka, will a hotel maid steal guests' personal belongings while cleaning a room, or will a theme park employee scalp employee entry passes for cash? These are all dishonest actions that may compromise the integrity of the service industry. It will be critical for hospitality professionals of the future to demonstrate ethical behavior over myriad situations and circumstances to minimize corruption and maintain legitimacy within the industry.

Summary

The hospitality industry is changing at a rapid rate due to technological advancements that will require future professionals to be skilled in technology while conserving natural resources to sustain our environment. Leisure professionals will need to exceed guest expectations from a growing clientele and accommodate their ever-changing needs to stay relevant. Future leaders must be able to analyze and identify current trends to understand future consumer behavior by conducting research while maintaining ethical behavior to uphold integrity within the industry.

RESOURCES

Internet Sites

Amadeus Technology Institute: http://www.amadeus.com

Digital Visitor Social Media Solutions: http://www.digitalvisitor.co.uk

Ecole Hoteliere de Lausanne Institute of Technology and Entrepreneurship: http://www.ehlite.com

Globally Green Hospitality Consortium: http://www.globallygreenhospitality.com

Hotel Technology Next Generation: http://www.htng.org

Hospitality Trends: http://www.htrends.com

Inn Hospitality: http://www.InnHospitality.com

Travel Mole: http://www.TravelMole.com

VFM Leonardo (online visual content management and distribution for the hotel industry): http://www.vfmleonardo.com

References

Burns, J. (2010). *Act Now to Secure Your Future, Hotels Told in New Industry Report.* Retrieved June 17, 2010, from http://www.htrends.com/trends-detail-sid-46419-t-Act_Now_to_Secure_Your_Future_Hotels_Told_in_New_Industry_Report

Chen, J., Sloan, P., and Legrand, W. (2009). *Sustainability in the Hospitality Industry.* Maryland Heights, MO: Elsevier Inc.

Ciccotelli, C. (2010). *Independent Hotels and Resorts Attract Guests, Increase Revenue Using Social Media and E-marketing to Promote Direct Website Bookings, Loyalty.* Retrieved June 17, 2010, from http://www.htrends.com/trends-detail-sid-4434-t-Independent_Hotels_and_Resorts_Attract_Guests_Increase_Revenue_Using_Social_Media_and_E-marketing_to_Promote_Direct_Website_Bookings_Loyalty

Continued Growth of Social Media Presents Marketers with New Opportunities and Challenges. (2010). Retrieved June 17, 2010, from http://www.technewsresource.com/report-2646351-opportunities_in_social_media_profiting_from_digital_conversation.html

Deyo, C. (2010). *Viewpoint: Hotels, Guests Shift to Behavioral EAdvertising.* Retrieved June 17, 2010, from http://www.htrends.com/trends/-details-sid-46535-t-Viewpoint_Hotels_Guests_Shift_to_Behavioral_Eadvertising

eHospitality Solutions Incorporated. (2010). Retrieved July 4, 2010, from http://www.ehospitalitysystems.com/about.html

Get the Bang for your Buck with Text Message Marketing. (2009). Retrieved June 10, 2010, from http://www.htrends.com/trends-detail-sid-46422-t-Get_the_Bang_for_Your_Buck_With_Text_Message_Marketing

Hatch, D. (2008). *Hotel Industry Must Further Embrace Social Networking.* Retrieved June 17, 2010, from http://www.travelmole.com/stories/1127113.php

Holleran, J. (2005). *Hospitality Sustainability Moving the Agenda Forward? Or Not?* Retrieved June 10, 2010, from http://www.hospitalitynet.org/news/4022182.search?query+sustainability+hospitality+industry

Hospitality: Future Trends. (2007). Retrieved June 10, 2010, from http://ww2.prospects.ac.uk/cms/ShowPage/Home_page/Explore_job_sectors/Hospitality/future/trends

Johnson, J. (2007). *Social Networking for the Hospitality Industry.* Retrieved June 17, 2010, from http://www.thetalentjungle.com/hospitality_blog/tiem/385

Larson, B. (2010). *New Research Shows Hotels are Ready for Shared Technology Services.* Retrieved June 17, 2010, from http://www.htng.org

Nikolis, N. (2009). *Hospitality Industry—Hotels Businesses Current and Future Trends.* Retrieved June 10, 2010, from http://www.ezinearticles.com?Hospitality-Industry—Hotels-Business-Current-and-Future-Trends

Social Networking and the Travel Industry. (2010). Retrieved June 17, 2010, from http://www.hotelmarketing.com/index.php./content/article/070207_Social_Networking_and_the_Travel_Industry

Tourism and Local Agenda 21, The Role of Local Authorities in Sustainable Tourism. UNEP and I-C-L-E-I, 2003, p. 7.

van Ketel, M. and Nelson, T. D. (2009). *E-commerce.* Retrieved July 4, 2010, from http://www.searchcio.techtarget.com/sdefinition/0,,sid182_gci212029,00.html

Vieth, J. (2010). *VIDEO: Improving your Presence Online.* Retrieved June 17, 2010, from http://vfmleonardo.com

Wilke, A. W. (2008). *Green Hospitality.* E: The Environmental Magazine, Mineola, NY: Earth Action Network, Inc.

Review Questions

1. Discuss several ways in which technology will influence the future of the hospitality industry.

2. Describe several ways in which social networking can improve the hospitality industry.

3. List four ways in which hospitality companies can improve their online presence through social media.

4. Define e-hospitality.

5. Explain how text messaging can be an effective marketing tool in the hospitality industry.

6. Why is sustainability a future concern?

7. List several ways in which hospitality services can improve sustainability.

8. Discuss some of the challenges hospitality professionals will face to maintain sustainability.

9. List and describe five creative/innovative sustainability solutions within the hospitality industry.

10. Why is the demonstration of ethical behavior critical to future success in the hospitality industry?

11. What are the greatest challenges hospitality employees will face in the future regarding ethics in the workplace?

Career Expectations and Realities

Michele L. Wehrle, Community College of Allegheny County

 LEARNING OBJECTIVES

- Explore positive and negative aspects of a hospitality career.
- Understand skills and traits needed to become successful in the hospitality industry.
- Develop an understanding of the size and scope of hospitality careers.
- Develop resume-building skills and interview strategies.

 **CHAPTER OUTLINE**

KEY TERMS

Career fair
Employment brand
Game show
Internship
Interview
Interviewee
Interviewer
Labor-intensive business
Myth
Organization's culture
Relocation
Resume
Student organizations

Choosing a career can be similar to being a game show contestant or part of a reality television series. Decisions about your future no doubt will involve competition against other players or job seekers while striving alone for a good outcome or high score. Will you win the "prize" for making the best career choice? Using popular reality television and game show formats, this chapter explores the size and scope of career opportunities within the hospitality industry. As a contestant (student), you need to answer questions to determine your career path.

Do you want to get paid to help people have fun? Do warm sunny beaches, majestic mountain views, or visiting faraway places spark your interest? How about being around delicious food in exotic restaurant locations, working on a cruise ship, coordinating events for country clubs, or owning your own food service or lodging establishment?

Workers in the hospitality industry deal with people who are looking for a relaxing vacation or mini vacation—even if it's only going out to dinner at a local restaurant! The hospitality industry offers its employees a choice of working in the kind of climate they like best.

The Myths and the Realities

◆ *Are You Smarter Than a Fifth Grader* about the hospitality industry?

What do you know about the hospitality industry? Where do you see yourself in the future? Will you love your career and look forward to going to work each day? Will you like the people you work with? You may have preconceived notions about a career in the hospitality industry. *Do you know the difference between a myth and a reality about this industry, or do you need to copy a fifth grader's answers?*

MYTH: There is a shortage of job opportunities within the hospitality industry.

REALITY: There is a shortage of qualified hospitality employees. There are many career choices and opportunities. The hospitality industry is the largest, fastest-growing industry in the world. Globally, hospitality makes up 11% of the gross domestic product, 200 million jobs, 8% of total employment, and 5.5 million new jobs annually until 2010 (www. nra.org).

MYTH: Anyone can become a successful hospitality manager.

REALITY: The myth is that all you have to do to become a hospitality manager is sit behind a desk and give orders. A career in hospitality management is not suitable for every individual. The industry is people and service oriented. A career in this field is rewarding for those seeking responsibility, opportunity for advancement, salary growth, and personal satisfaction. As a hospitality manager, you need to always try to meet and exceed your potential, treat others as you would want to be treated, work hard, learn from your mistakes, listen to your employees, and love your job. A college education and industry experiences are requirements for a successful hospitality career.

MYTH: I will spend most of my time sitting at my desk.

REALITY: A good manager is constantly on the floor working alongside his/her employees and understanding what is going on during the day and night. Solving problems is a critical skill that takes wisdom, creativity, and information. The hospitality industry is too fast paced to sit at a desk. Every day brings a new set of guests and a new set of challenges. It takes a special person to rise to the challenge.

MYTH: There is limited career advancement.

REALITY: The potential for advancement is excellent for the capable individual who is willing to work hard. There is a critical need for people with general management skills to supervise all aspects of a hospitality property. The growth of the field has translated into exceptional opportunities for graduates. The hospitality field employment outlook is excellent for people from every race and ethnic background.

MYTH: Starting salaries are low.

REALITY: Starting salaries are competitive. Unlike many industries, hospitality has more flexible working hours and pay scales. You can work and get paid by the hour. There are even some supervisory roles with this capacity. Hotels work 24/7, so you can work on many different schedules so it does not interfere with your classes. And, after a few promotions, the compensation package is tremendous.

MYTH: Graduating with a degree in hospitality is all I need to be successful.

REALITY: A degree by itself is not enough! A college education combined with relevant work experience is! Many programs include work experiences as part of the curriculum. As you learn more about the industry through hands-on knowledge, you appreciate and learn more in your classes because you understand why this material is important.

MYTH: A job in the hospitality industry is boring

REALITY: Hospitality employees have fun! Working alongside people you like, talking to new people all the time, and doing something you love. How can that be boring?

The Career: The Good and the Bad

◆ *Jeopardy*

The hospitality industry has a long history of providing meaningful employment in a variety of career fields. According to the International Council of Hotel, Restaurant, and Institutional Educators (ICHRIE), the hospitality industry is comprised of four major career fields: food, lodging, tourism, and recreation. These areas include many diverse and exciting career opportunities. Examples of career opportunities include but are not limited to club management, food service, health care, parks, lodging, resorts, casinos, catering companies, conference centers, attractions management, marinas, prisons, colleges/universities, and school food service. Just quickly glance at the table of contents for this book to start your possibilities, and these are only the beginning.

The hospitality industry offers many advantages to employees, but just like any other industry, you face challenges. *Analyzing the categories of a hospitality career allows you to increase your knowledge of the industry's good and bad points, thus reducing mistakes that could cost you time and money. After reviewing the answers, you may be motivated to seek additional information and ask additional questions.*

The Good

Let's explore the "good points" of a career in the field.

1. Extensive list of career options
2. Creative opportunities
3. Varied work environment
4. Career growth
5. Social networking

Extensive List of Career Options

The hospitality industry offers an abundance of management opportunities. In lodging, you may choose a 500-room property or a 10-room bed and breakfast, an international franchise company or a local boutique hotel, a grand hotel or a campground. On the other hand, food service opportunities can include fine dining or a cafeteria, a privately owned catering company, a nightclub or an assisted-living facility. When people want to be entertained or just recreate, hospitality includes final destination theme parks or city amusement parks, a metropolitan convention center, casinos, or museums. And always there is the shopping that everyone does. Hospitality career possibilities are endless. So, what do you want be when you grow up?

Creative Opportunities

Are you inventive? Do you have vision? Hospitality managers may design new products or remodel food service and lodging facilities. Managers may be asked to develop training programs or implement new marketing strategies. Even on a day-to-day basis, you need creativity to productively handle problem guests or motivate employees to do their best.

No other industry can offer you the chance to work almost anywhere, with interesting work and people contact. © 2011 by Phil Date. Used under license of Shutterstock, Inc.

Varied Work Environment

If you desire a 9-to-5, 5-day-a-week career—please find the nearest exit, proceed straight to registration, and change your major! Hospitality careers are fast paced, and each day begins a new work environment. Power outages, severe weather, equipment failures, a busload of guests, and staff shortages are some of the challenges that provide variety and excitement. Hospitality positions are not desk jobs. Quality customer service and meeting/exceeding guest satisfaction cannot be obtained from merely hiding in your office. Hospitality employees should consider the entire facility as their "office" and seek the opportunity to interact with guests on a daily basis.

Career Growth

The hospitality industry is widely based. You can work almost anywhere in any setting, from a small country town to a metropolitan city, from a warm sunny beach to a deep powder ski resort, from a small bed and breakfast to a casino resort, from a small town in Kansas to a foreign country. Across the nation and around the world, career opportunities abound for people of all ages, education levels, and backgrounds. No other industry can offer you the chance of working almost anywhere you choose, with interesting work, a chance for advancement, people contact, and stability of employment.

Social Networking

Surveys and statistics cannot tell you all you want to know about a career. You need to spend time with people who perform the job you want. How do you network? You want to expand your base of contacts by attending career fairs and by joining alumni associations, student organizations, and professional organizations. Meeting people is a major advantage of your career. You will have the opportunity to meet people from all over the world and all walks of life, including celebrities, political figures, wealthy clientele, top executives, professional athletes, and local community members. As in all businesses, the more people you know, the easier it is to find your dream job.

The Bad

All careers have advantages and challenges. The challenges or potential "bad points" of a career in hospitality include labor-intensive business, hours of work, and relocation. You may find the challenges to be to your advantage.

Labor-Intensive Business

Like all work environments, there is a downside that has to be put into perspective. So just how bad is it? There are three areas to be aware of in hospitality. First, the work can be very hands on at times involving physical labor. This isn't all bad because, as a manager, it gives you better empathy and appreciation for the hard work of your employees. It is a way to keep you close to the customer, which is critical to understanding your business. If however, there is never any quiet time to plan and manage, this can be a major issue. In a labor-intensive business, you can plan on being a "working" manager in this field, at least in your formative years, if not always.

Hours of Work

The hospitality industry is open 365 days a year, 7 days a week, 24 hours a day. Most managers work 10- to 12-hour days and 60+ hours a week, weekends, and holidays. This is an industry where most people spend long hours on their feet and spend each day making complete strangers feel welcome and happy. These long hours can limit the time you have available for family, friends, and your social life. A common cliché is "employees in the hospitality industry work while others play." However, you can get your household chores done faster because you have off when everyone else is working. So the lines are shorter. In addition, you can recreate or go on vacation during low season when the rates are better and it is not so crowded.

Relocation

Relocation can be defined as the act of moving from one place to another for employment advancement. You may have to consider relocating several times because hospitality organizations have facilities in a variety of geographic locations. Larger chains may offer better opportunities than small, but relocation every several years is often necessary. A willingness to relocate often is essential for advancement. The decision is difficult: remain in your current area? Return home? Relocate? However, many people find relocation exciting and a benefit of a hospitality career. Also, if you want to travel and see new countries and cultures or just go back home after your training, large hotel and restaurant chains have sites worldwide. You can transfer or even be part of an exciting start-up team.

The Skills and Qualities Needed for Success

◆ *American Idol*

A desire to serve others is a strong characteristic of successful people. Wanting to give our guests a quality experience is an important trait. It comes down to something as simple as wanting to help. Whether it is giving them directions to an area attraction or clearing and cleaning a table so they can be seated in a restaurant, this type of activity must be a source of satisfaction for you. Liking to be with others and a desire to interact with them is something that is intrinsic to most positions in this business. Being friendly, sincere, and patient and a good listener are critical skill sets for anyone contemplating success in this field. Now, these skills take time and practice to develop, and there will be days when they will be tested to the limit. However, *there are essential skills and qualities you will need to perform to the best your ability in front of the judges (employers) and the audience (guests).*

Skills and Qualities

1. Conceptual skills (planning, problem solving, and decision making)
2. Communication skills (verbal and nonverbal)
3. Flexibility and diversity
4. Leadership skills and qualities (supervising, team building, organization)
5. Personality skills (outgoing, ethical, sense of humor, energetic, like to work with people, don't like to sit behind a desk, creative, problem solver, service oriented, ambitious)

The Money

◆ *Deal or No Deal*

If you possess these skills and qualities, your earning potential can be limitless. *Don't be insulted by the banker's low offer; eliminate the low offers and strive to find the "lucky game case."* According to the National Restaurant Association (NRA), the table on the following page details potential earnings based on job positions within the hospitality industry.

Additionally, the American Hotel & Lodging Educational Institute (AH&LA) publishes information annually documenting compensation and benefits for the hospitality industry. The median salary compensation for management positions in the industry includes Sales & Marketing Director—$80,400, Controller—$73,800,

Enjoying interaction with people is essential to most positions in this business. © 2011 by Stephen Coburn. Used under license of Shutterstock, Inc.

Senior Sales Manager—$56,000, Personnel/HR Director—$61,600, and Sales Manager—$38,500. In addition to base salary, many jobs have a commission, shared gratuity, or bonus plan that pays up to 40% of salary as incentive compensation. Hospitality is an industry where pay for performance and career opportunities are especially strong. *Should you accept a position with a lower salary than you expected? The decision is up to you: Deal or No Deal?*

The Career Pursuit

◆ *The Amazing Race*

There are several key questions that you will need to address for yourself. First, what segment of the industry is right for you, and second, who are the better employers in each sector? You may not be able to find answers to these questions until you have experienced a variety of employment settings. Start becoming a student of the industry now. Read various trade publications. Track different company performances and history during your time in school. Attend open houses and talks given by hospitality employers. Attend annual career conferences. Be sure to talk to employer representatives, even if you are not looking for work at that time. It is a good skill to practice so you are comfortable with that format when it really counts. Definitely take advantage of the resources your school offers, whether they are your advisor or the career services office. *A career in hospitality may take you on an adventure around the world leading you on a successful journey of personal and professional satisfaction.*

TABLE 4.1	Earning Potential in the Hospitality Industry		
CAREER	**AVERAGE ANNUAL EARNING POWER**	**REQUIRED EDUCATION**	**FOLLOW-UP CONTACT WEBSITE**
President/Chief Executive Officer	$50,000–$350,000+	Bachelor's/Master's Degree	www.nraef.org/hba/ hba_career_ladder.asp
Owner	$35,000–$200,000+	Bachelor's/Master's Degree	www.nraef.org/hba/ hba_career_ladder.asp
Chief Financial Officer	$45,000–$200,000+	Bachelor's/Master's Degree	www.nraef.org/hba/ hba_career_ladder.asp
General Manager/Chief Operating Officer	$42,000–$200,000+	Bachelor's/Master's Degree	www.nraef.org/hba/ hba_career_ladder.asp
Director of Operations	$40,000–$150,000+	Bachelor's/Master's Degree	www.nraef.org/hba/ hba_career_ladder.asp
Regional Manager	$40,000–$100,000+	Bachelor's Degree, Associate Degree, or On-the-job training	www.nraef.org/hba/ hba_career_ladder.asp
Food and Beverage Director	$35,000–$85,000+	Bachelor's Degree, Associate Degree, or On-the-job training	www.nraef.org/hba/ hba_career_ladder.asp
Director of Purchasing	$35,000–$100,000+	Bachelor's Degree, Associate Degree, or On-the-job training	www.nraef.org/hba/ hba_career_ladder.asp
Director of Training	$35,000–$100,000+	Bachelor's Degree, Associate Degree, or On-the-job training	www.nraef.org/hba/ hba_career_ladder.asp
Unit Manager	$30,000–$70,000+	Bachelor's Degree, Associate Degree, or On-the-job training	www.nraef.org/hba/ hba_career_ladder.asp
Chef	$27,000–$60,000+	Associate Degree/On-the-job training	www.nraef.org/hba/ hba_career_ladder.asp
Catering Manager	$30,000–$50,000+	Associate Degree/On-the-job training	www.nraef.org/hba/ hba_career_ladder.asp
Kitchen Manager	$25,000–$45,000+	Associate Degree/On-the-job training	www.nraef.org/hba/ hba_career_ladder.asp
Banquet Manager	$26,000–$45,000+	Associate Degree/On-the-job training	www.nraef.org/hba/ hba_career_ladder.asp
Waiters and Waitresses	$6.50–$20.00+ per hour including tips	On-the-job training	www.nraef.org/hba/hba_career_ladder.asp
Cook	$6.30–$12.43+ per hour	On-the-job training	www.nraef.org/hba/hba_career_ladder.asp

Data from the National Restaurant Association, 2002.

The Internship

◆ *The Apprentice*

To gain experience, most colleges/universities require internships or work experiences as part of a hospitality student's major program of study. The first rule of thumb in this area is that some internships are good and some are bad, but you will always learn something from them. Obtain them through your career services office, your department, or on your own. Remember, attending a school with a hospitality program gives you kind of a built-in employment brand for this industry. With the Internet, your potential is limitless when it comes to obtaining an internship.

However, students need to avoid the trap of thinking their internship will be ideal and answer all of their questions. It won't be perfect; after all, it does take place in the real world. It may also create more questions for you than it answers. But you will learn from it, and it will go on your resume. It can be a base on which you can develop future job opportunities. You will observe various management styles in action, some that you will want to adopt, and many you will want to avoid. It may even bring a job offer for after school. This way you and the employer will be in a better position to make an informed decision about your suitability for the job and your fit within their organization's culture. *In reality, an internship is becoming an apprentice. You should strive to conquer your assignments, perform at your highest potential, and avoid being "fired." Before you begin the search process for an internship, a well-written resume is critical.*

Get "Real"—Take Control—Be Successful

♦ *Survivor*

Be the last one standing!! Outwit, outplay, and outlast your competition! How will you become the sole survivor? A well-written resume, cover letter, interview strategies, and a thank-you letter may grant you immunity.

The Resume

♦ *1 vs. 100*

A resume is a written document that lists a person's personal and professional qualifications for a position. The purpose of a resume is to provide information to people about who you are and what skills you have. Because every individual is unique in their own way, there is room for individuality and creativity when writing a resume. In reality, it is your "personal advertisement."

Writing a resume during your first year of college helps you to answer questions about yourself. Documenting your career objective, your past and present education, and past and present work experiences enables you to see what you have accomplished and where you are going. It should be well organized, concise, and written in a focused manner. A well-written resume also aids you in obtaining scholarships, internships, and professional job positions. *Your resume may be 1 out of 100 resumes received for a single open position. Make sure all the information on your resume is accurate, as one mistake may cause you to lose it*

all. There are certain headings and information that should be included in your resume:

1. Current contact information
2. Career objective
3. Education
4. Internship
5. Work experience(s)
6. Special skills and abilities
7. Awards and recognitions
8. References (People who are willing to speak with a potential employer about your personal and professional experiences. Make sure you ask them before putting their names as a reference. Make sure they will give you a positive recommendation. This includes faculty. Giving you a positive reference is not your right, but the reference's honest opinion of you.)

The Cover Letter

♦ *America's Got Talent*

Included with your resume should be a cover letter. This letter introduces you to your potential employer. The content should include highlights of your personal and professional experiences (*talents*) and a request for an interview. Many potential employers will only review your resume if your cover letter sparks their interest. *You do not want to get a big red "X" and be eliminated from the search. So, think carefully about what you are going to offer as your best skills, and please check spelling.*

The Interview

♦ *Fear Factor*

The goal of your resume and cover letter is to get you an interview with an employer of your choosing. An interview is defined as a formal meeting between two or more individuals. Interview etiquette includes dressing in a professional manner, introducing yourself, offering a firm handshake, maintaining eye contact, responding to questions, never saying anything negative, asking questions, smiling, and being enthusiastic. Enthusiasm is the single most important quality. Remember the saying, "You only get one chance to make a first impression."

During an interview, the interviewer(s) asks the interviewee questions to determine their ability to meet the expectations of a position. Your answers say

Resume

Joe S.Student

Permanent Address	**Campus Address**
17 Apple Court	23 New Street
Pittsburgh, PA 15102	State College, PA 18423
(412) 555-1212	(814) 555-1212
jstudent@psu.edu	

OBJECTIVE   To obtain a managerial-level internship within the hospitality industry.

EDUCATION   PENNSYLVANIA STATE UNIVERSITY   State College, PA
Bachelor of Science in Hospitality Management   May 20xx
Overall GPA 3.1/4.0
Course emphasis in Lodging Management
Minor: Mass Communication

COMMUNITY COLLEGE OF ALLEGHENY COUNTY   Pittsburgh, PA
Associate of Science   June 20xx
Hotel-Restaurant Management
Earned 75% of college expenses through work experience.

HONORS   Pennsylvania State University Dean's List (three semesters)

EXPERIENCE   **PITTSBURGH AIRPORT MARRIOTT**   Pittsburgh, PA
Front Desk Agent   April 20xx–Sept. 20xx
- Balanced check-in and check-out of multiple guests while responding to inquiries and needs of others. Achieved high customer satisfaction comments.
- Worked with various hotel departments to make decisions and solve problems.

KENNYWOOD AMUSEMENT PARK   West Mifflin, PA
Event Coordinator/Trainer   June 20xx–May 20xx
- Part-time and seasonal employment providing customer service for various areas of tourist-oriented theme park.
- Served as relief shift leader for up to 20 employees.
- Trained new employees in guest relations and standard operating procedures for attractions.
- Received certificate of appreciation for one year of perfect attendance.
- Promoted within three months of hire.

PAYLESS SHOESOURCE   Pittsburgh, PA
Sales Associate   May 20xx–August 20xx
- Summer employment involving retail sales of shoes on a commission basis.
- Awarded bonus for highest monthly volume sales for August.
- Recommended merchandise recovery system reducing loss by $5,000 savings in the first quarter.

ACTIVITIES   PSU Hospitality Association
Rho Alpha Tau Sorority, President and Vice President Community Volunteer, Meals on Wheels Weekend Youth Director

SKILLS   Computer: Proficient in Microsoft Office (Word, Excel, Access, PowerPoint)
                   Working knowledge of HTML and Java
Language: Fluent in Spanish

Cover Letter

Joe S. Student

17 Apple Court
Pittsburgh, PA 15102
412-555-1212

Ms. Lee Thomas
Hilton Hotel Corporation
Runway Road
Pittsburgh, PA 15102

Dear Ms. Thomas,

My unique mix of previous work experience and my status as a Pennsylvania State University hospitality student in my junior year studying hotel and restaurant management make me an ideal candidate for a summer internship with Hilton Hotel Corporation.

My experiences in sales and customer relationship management, combined with my courses in hospitality, have convinced me that hospitality marketing is a career option I would like to explore.

More important, an internship with Hilton Hotel Corporation would be mutually beneficial. Your company has an excellent reputation for customer satisfaction, and I know that the combination of my experience, education, and motivation to excel will make me an asset to your marketing department.

I am sure that it would be worthwhile for us to meet. I will contact you within a week to arrange a meeting. Should you have any questions before that time, you may reach me via phone (412-555-1212) or via e-mail (jstudent@psu.edu). Thank you for your time and consideration.

Sincerely,

Joe S. Student

a lot about who you are. The International Council of Hotel Restaurant Institutional Educators (ICHRIE) offers the 10 most common interview questions and suggestions how to answer the questions on their Web site. Questions include

- What are your weaknesses?
- Why should we hire you?
- Why do you want to work here?
- What are your goals?
- Why did you leave (are you leaving) your job?
- When were you most satisfied in your job?
- What can you do for us that other candidates can't?
- What are three positive things your last boss would say about you?
- What salary are you seeking?
- If you were an animal, which one would you be and why?

Today in many interviews, the employer wants to understand how you will perform on the job under certain circumstances. To get at this, they will present you with a series of lifelike events that happen daily on the job and ask how you would respond to them. In some cases, you may have had actual experience in dealing with similar situations earlier in your work life and will be comfortable answering such inquiries. Other questions may represent your first exposure to a certain situation. "I don't know" is not an option. The key is to remain calm and think through how you would answer the question.

Remember, an interview is a two-way street. The goal of both interviewer(s) and interviewee is to get enough information about each other to make an informed decision. Making a quality decision about going to work or not for a particular employer is just as important for you as it is for the employer

Thank-You Letter

Joe S.Student

17 Apple Court
Pittsburgh, PA 15102
412-555-1212

Ms. Lee Thomas
Hilton Hotel Corporation
Runway Road
Pittsburgh, PA 15102

Dear Ms. Thomas,

Thank you for taking the time to discuss the internship opportunities at Hilton Hotel Corporation with me. After meeting with you and observing the company's operations, I am further convinced that my background and skills coincide well with your needs.

I really appreciate that you took so much time to acquaint me with the company. It is no wonder that Hilton Hotel Corporation retains its employees for so long. I feel I could learn a great deal from you and would certainly enjoy working with you.

In addition to my qualifications and experience, I will bring excellent work habits and judgment to this position. With the countless demands on your time, I am sure that you require people who can be trusted to carry out their responsibilities with minimal supervision.

I look forward, Ms. Thomas, to hearing from you concerning your hiring decision. Again, thank you for your time and consideration.

Sincerely,

Joe S. Student

---

about whether they are going to hire you. You should develop a list of questions that you want answered prior to the interview. At some point toward the end of the interview, you may be asked if you have any questions for the employer. There is nothing wrong with pulling your list out at this point and reviewing it to see if there are any unanswered questions. There are different schools of thought about asking about salary in the initial interview. This shows the employer you are prepared and an active participant. Ideally, you should have some idea of the salary range for the position after the first interview. *During an interview, you will be challenged mentally and sometimes even physically. You must overcome your fears and not be* *afraid to answer questions and prove yourself to better and quicker than everyone else.* Send a thank-you note to the interviewer. This is rarely done and can leave a lasting impression.

The Thank-You Letter

◆ *Identity*

After completing an interview, it is important for you to write a thank-you letter to the interviewer(s). This personalized, handwritten letter should be written and mailed the same day as your interview. *A well-written thank-you letter can make you stand out from the other contestants, thus revealing your true identity.*

Summary

◆ *Dancing with the Stars*

You are about to embark on a journey that can lead to a long-term successful career in a dynamic and thriving industry. The hospitality industry is a very unique industry, and it demands certain skills and qualities like strong interpersonal skills, attention to details, and the desire to be a problem solver. The industry has different hours than most, but it has many rewards to offer someone who is willing to work hard and "earn their stripes."

Your number one priority over the coming years is to be a student, a good student. This is both from an academic skills standpoint and from the standpoint of understanding this industry. Build your resume now while in school. Develop a variety of experiences that will help you land a great starting position when you finish your schooling. Definitely pursue one or two internship experiences to add to your portfolio. Utilize all the services of your school's career office and your department to assist you in the interviewing and the job acceptance process as you finish your studies. Be prepared to take the good work and study habits you developed during school with you into the hospitality industry so that you are ready to advance your career. Keep in mind that learning is not just in school, but for the rest of your career. *Aim high, pay attention to details, perform the steps correctly, don't miss a beat, and you too can be dancing with stars.*

RESOURCES

Internet Sites

Council of Hotel, Restaurant, and Institutional Educators: www.chrie.org

American Hotel & Lodging Association: www.ahla.org

Hospitality Career Net: www.hospitalitycareernet.com

Hospitality Jobs Online: www.hospitalityonline.com

Hospitality Net: www.hospitalitynet.org

Hospitality Careers: www.hcareers.om

National Restaurant Association: www.restaurant.org

National Restaurant Association Education Foundation: www.nraef.org

Review Questions

1. Discuss several advantages and disadvantages of working in the hospitality industry.

2. List skills and qualities necessary to become a successful manager.

3. What are some common interview questions, and how would you answer?

4. What are three questions you could ask a potential employer while being interviewed?

5. How would you go about securing an internship?

6. How can you research salary ranges of hospitality management positions?

7. What is the purpose of your resume?

8. Develop a resume, cover letter, and thank-you letter for a position offered in your local newspaper.

Hospitality Companies

Independent and Entrepreneurial Operations

Robin DePeitro, University of South Carolina

LEARNING OBJECTIVES

- Describe the techniques for assessing and developing opportunities for independent operators and entrepreneurs in the hospitality industry.
- Understand the importance of the independent operator in the service industry.
- Describe the scope of the nature of the job of an independent operator.
- Explain entrepreneurship and its roles and contributions to the economic life of the hospitality industry.
- Describe entrepreneurial skills that will contribute to the hospitality entrepreneur's success.

CHAPTER OUTLINE

Independent Operations
    Opportunities for Independent Operators and Entrepreneurs in the Industry
    Advantages/Disadvantages for Independent Operations
    Independent Operations and Entrepreneurship
    Single-Unit Management
Explanation of Entrepreneurship
    Entrepreneurship and the Contribution to Hospitality
    Entrepreneurial Skills
    Types of Legal Structure for Small Business Operations
Summary
Case Study

KEY TERMS AND CONCEPTS

Angel Investor
Effectiveness
Efficiency
Entrepreneur
Independent Business Owner
Independent Operations
Leadership

Management
Multi Unit/Chain Operations
Return on Investment
Single Unit Operation
Sustainable Competitive Advantage

After reading Part 1 of this text, *Hospitality Industry,* it is clear to see that there are many different segments and many distinct organizations that are part of the hospitality industry, and they all strive to grow in sales and profits. Many individuals enjoy the thought of operating their own business and the challenge of trying to create a business that has a competitive advantage over others. The hospitality industry, with its varied types and sizes of organizations, is a great industry to get into if you strive to own your own business, as there are low barriers to entry and diverse skills and interests represented.

An independent operator is someone who owns a business and operates that business on a smaller scale than a large chain or corporate business does. They are people who enjoy working on their own to build something from the ground up and like the thrill of developing a business to be something to be proud of. In the hospitality industry, these independent operators typically own restaurants, bed and breakfasts, independent hotels, or other service-providing businesses. An independent operator is a huge driver of the economy in the United States and other countries. These people are risk takers and help to put money into the economy through the development of businesses that provide products and services to people who are looking for them. These small businesses also provide jobs that fuel the economy and help to spark economic growth.

This chapter will review the independent operator and their role in the hospitality industry. It will also discuss the characteristics of entrepreneurs and the role that they play in the economy in general and the hospitality industry specifically. This information will be used to set the framework for Chapter 6, "Chain Operations." Chapters 5 and 6 will discuss the differences between independent and entrepreneurial operations and chain operations and the responsibilities and skills that an independent business owner and/or manager and a multiunit or chain owner or manager will need to do their jobs effectively.

Independent Operations

Opportunities for Independent Operators and Entrepreneurs in the Industry

Owning your own business has been considered an American Dream for many decades, and the hospitality industry gives people the opportunity to do that with the low barriers to entry and many opportunities that are available. Low barriers to entry occur because there are lower costs to starting up many hospitality businesses than starting up a manufacturing business or other types of businesses. There are also not as many restrictions when it comes to opening a small business such as a restaurant, bed and breakfast, or many of the other types of hospitality businesses that can be independently owned and operated.

There are many opportunities for hard-working, innovative people to start a new company or to open their own small business in the hospitality industry in such segments as bed and breakfast inns and restaurants. There are more than 30,000 bed and breakfasts in North America, and the majority of these are independently owned operations (McMullin, 2004). The National Restaurant Association reports that in the United States, almost half of all eating and drinking establishments are owned by one person (sole proprietorships) or owned by partnerships (owned by two or more people). These facts show that there are many opportunities for smaller, independent operations in the hospitality industry.

To put the number of independent business owners in perspective, the U.S. Small Business Administration is a hub of information on small businesses and provides resources for anyone interested in opening their own small business. There has continued to be a large increase in the number of people opening and owning small businesses. In 1970, the U.S. Small Business Administration reported that there were approximately 200,000 new companies started, and in more recent years the number has increased to 3.5 million new start-up businesses. To further show the importance of small business ownership in the economy, in 2007, it was reported by the U.S. Census Bureau (2010a) that 78.8% of businesses are small enough to have no paid employees. It was also reported that minorities own 86.7% of small businesses that don't employ any paid employees (U.S. Census Bureau, 2010b). These facts show that there are a lot of opportunities for independent business owners to start their own business, and minority business owners play a large role in the U.S. economy with regard to small business ownership. Small businesses create excellent opportunities for minorities and women. There are a lot of opportunities for many types of people to create small businesses and be successful in a variety of settings. In 2007, women owned 191,919 accommodation and food service businesses (U.S. Census Bureau, 2010c), once again showing the importance of minority and women small business ownership.

Advantages/Disadvantages for Independent Operations

Independent operations are those operations that have one unit up to a few units that have distinct characteristics from other units. These types of operations typically have different looks and feels from other units. For example, think of all the hamburger restaurants that you have eaten at or driven by. They probably have certain characteristics that are similar and then some characteristics that are different. Some of these restaurants are called chain restaurants and all look alike, and some are independent operations that have a look and a feel of their own.

Independent operations can have many advantages over a chain operation. Because there are a small number of units, they are easy to implement changes to. Also, they tend to have smaller corporate headquarters, and therefore there is typically less red tape and corporate policies and procedures to slow down any changes desired in the operation of the business. For the most part, independent operations can take place in a small storefront to set up an ice cream shop or a vending cart to sell hot dogs, or in a home such as a bed and breakfast operation. Other advantages to the independent operation are that the owner/operator of an independent business can make the policies and procedures that the business will be operating by, and these can be changed very quickly and without much effort in comparison to a large chain or corporate operation.

Some of the disadvantages of an independent operation are that they do not have the backing of a corporate headquarters in either financial or operational ways. A chain operation has a corporate headquarters that can help to provide advice and support to an individual unit and the management staff. There are also economies of scale that large companies have that small businesses do not. For example, financial institutions and vendors may give chain operations a better deal because they will purchase food in larger quantities and may be more apt to borrow larger quantities of money as they expand operations, whereas an independent operation may expand more slowly and will only need supplies and purchases for the single unit. Another disadvantage of an independent operation is that they have not usually proven themselves to the public, so advertising

and marketing becomes more critical to get the name out to the public and to get people to try the business. As guests try out new operations, they have to prove to be of good quality and consistent to drive repeat business and potentially brand loyalty. Because of the lack of multiple units of independent operations, the lack of brand knowledge may dissuade new customers from trying something new when they are not familiar with the business.

Independent Operations and Entrepreneurship

Independent operations are those businesses that are owned and usually operated by one or two people. These businesses can operate from as few as no paid employees to many paid employees, depending on how big the business and operations are. Many small businesses are started with a single owner, someone who is driven to create a business that is unique and is willing to work hard to ensure that the business survives. They put their financial, emotional, and sweat equity into the business to make it successful. An independent operation is one that is a single unit, and the goal of the owner is typically for revenue growth, but not necessarily unit growth. The definition of an independent operator is someone who operates a business on their own without any large corporation and infrastructure behind them.

The definition of an entrepreneur is someone who is willing to take the risk to start a business, manages a business, and assumes the risk and rewards of a

A successful entrepreneurship needs to have a well-defined oppourturity, adequate resources, and a cohesive team. © 2011 by Konstantin Chagin. Used under license of Shutterstock, Inc.

business. They also would like to grow the business in revenue as well as in the number of units. An entrepreneur may grow the business through opening more units on their own, or through selling franchises or through selling the entire concept to a corporation to develop and grow the business. The entrepreneur is typically someone who is not afraid of risk taking and often has creative and innovative ideas of their own that they wish to grow and develop. Many people use the terms *independent operator* and *entrepreneur* interchangeably, but from the preceding definitions, the difference is primarily in the purposes of developing the business as well as in the risk-taking characteristics.

An angel investor is someone who is interested in investing in a new business or business concept, and they can help the independent operator or entrepreneur to get enough capital to start the business. An angel investor is often someone of substantial wealth that wants to give capital in exchange for ownership equity in the company. There can also be angel investor groups that can pool their money to help to fund one or more projects and business ideas.

It is important when putting together your ideas for a new business that you create a carefully laid out business plan. This business plan should help you to determine what people need to be gathered around you to ensure that you have the proper expertise to open and operate a new business venture. You need to assemble a team that has diverse skills and backgrounds to ensure that all needs for the business will be able to be met. Investors will be looking at your business plan, and the team that you have gathered around you to be able to determine if the business will be successful or not. When an investor looks to put money into a new business, they look to see if there are people capable of growing a business and developing future growth plans to ensure that they will recoup their initial investment.

A successful business plan will lay out the foundation for the where, when, how, and why of a new company. It is important to be able to show that there is a need for a new product or service, and the business plan should show how your company will fill a need in the marketplace and will have a competitive advantage over other companies in filling that need.

As an independent operator, it is important that you show through the business plan how you plan to derive a successful return on investment for any investors in the business. In the hospitality industry, there are many fixed expenses such as land and building, as well as variable expenses such as food costs and labor costs, that need to be accounted for. A complete understanding of forecasted revenues and expenses, as well as critical financial documents such as income statement, balance sheet, and payroll forms are important for a business owner to have to obtain funding for the new venture.

Single-Unit Management

Single-unit management refers to managing one unit. That unit can be part of any industry in the economic sector of the world. Whatever the business, a single-unit manager has only the responsibility of the single unit as their primary focus. When someone is an independent operator, they typically own and manage that independent business. This makes the management function smaller in scope than the multiunit operator, but not necessarily easier to perform. An independent operator has the typical task of managing a single unit along with the ownership responsibilities of the business, such as financing, providing for taxation of the business, ensuring legal representation, and the burden of ownership that can mean protecting yourself from lawsuits, following government regulations, and potential risks and rewards of business ownership.

A single-unit manager has the responsibility of ensuring that the unit is set up and opened for business on a daily or consistent basis. They are traditionally responsible for staffing the unit with reliable, talented people that can ensure that guest service is taken care of. The staffing of the unit is very important to the success of the business. Most of the competitive advantages that an organization can have are short lived and can often be reproduced by other companies in the same industry. A competitive advantage is something that your organization has that other organizations do not have. An example of this may be a new technology that you introduce into the marketplace that other organizations have not mastered yet; for example, the iPod was first introduced by the Apple Corporation. Other companies soon followed with Mp3 players that used the same technology, so the competitive advantage was very short lived. Even McDonald's only had a patent on the components of the Big Mac for so long, and then the competition could create similar hamburgers.

People in a service business are often one of the sustainable competitive advantages that an organization can have. The people provide the key component in a service business, the service. Therefore hiring the right people and retaining them become essential components of the business. The responsibility of the single-unit manager to staff that single unit can be critical to the short-term and long-term success of an organization.

The single-unit manager or independent operator is often the "go-to" person in operational, marketing, and financial issues and concerns that have to do with the single unit. They are the person that is in the front line on a consistent basis and tends to have a strong operational focus in the business. They are able, for the most part, to take care of the business operationally from any facet. The single-unit manager or independent operator has various broad areas of responsibility, including: operations, finance, accounting, marketing, human resources, and all the areas that this entails.

In a study done by Reynolds (2000), it was found that the top five characteristics required of a single-unit restaurant manager were organizational skills; interpersonal skills; restaurant experience, knowledge, and skills; honesty, integrity, and strong ethics; and leadership skills. This research was done through interviews with industry leaders in top chain restaurants, and the skills were found to be similar to key success factors required of managers in a variety of other business organizations. These key characteristics have been found in other studies as well (Boulgarides & Rowe, 1983; Kakabadse & Margerison, 1988; Van Der Merwe, 1978) and would be similar characteristics that independent operators would need to have as well.

Through this research, it can be seen that a strong operational background, human resource skills, and honesty and ethical traits help managers to be successful in their jobs. A successful manager needs to be organized to help to organize their organization to achieve their goals.

Explanation of Entrepreneurship

Entrepreneurship and the Contribution to Hospitality

Entrepreneurs are innovative risk takers that enjoy starting and growing businesses. They are often involved in creating new business ventures and then growing them to be chain locations in multiple destinations or multiple units. Many of the chains of today in the hospitality and tourism industries were started by entrepreneurs of the past. For example, Ray Kroc bought the rights to McDonald's from the McDonald brothers in California because he saw the potential of the fast-food hamburger restaurant industry. Harlan Sanders started Kentucky Fried Chicken, as he had a vision for how to make quality chicken in a fast-paced environment with friendly people and clean surroundings. An A&W Root Beer restaurant with nine stools gave a young J. Willard Marriott a vision for how great service could be. This beginning started the chain of Marriott hotels and ventures through Marriott's entrepreneurial vision and created an organization that is stronger today than ever.

There is a lot of overlap between an entrepreneur and an independent operator, as both take risks and are willing to put forth hard work and effort in starting a business and building that business up in terms of sales and/or number of units. Often entrepreneurs are creative and try to find new and interesting ways of doing things, and they are stronger risk takers. There are also people called "serial entrepreneurs," who are great at starting up concepts, growing them, and then moving on to another concept. Entrepreneurs are often developing businesses and growing them for the thrill of the victory of doing it. The following discussion looks at the skills that many entrepreneurs have and what makes them successful.

Entrepreneurial Skills

The skills that are necessary to be an entrepreneur vary based on the type of business that you want to open, but many of the skills overlap. It is important that an entrepreneur possess leadership skills, managerial skills, and the ability to be creative and work under some stressful and unknown situations. There is always a certain level of risk when starting your own business, and entrepreneurs are willing to take risks to reap the potential future rewards.

Entrepreneurs are willing to take action, to pursue opportunities that are often left alone by other people, and they typically see risks as challenges. They exhibit behaviors that are often seen as dynamic, risky, outgoing, and creative and innovative. The entrepreneur usually has a lot of capital invested in terms of time and money and is willing to risk that to be successful in their current venture. Entrepreneurs see it as a challenge to invest a lot and to see if they can get the return on their investment that they would like.

To gain a competitive advantage over other businesses that are similar, an entrepreneur needs to be innovative with products and services provided to

An entrepreneur usually works alone and is helpful in business.
© 2011 by Goodluz. Used under license of Shutterstock, Inc.

people. Often the products are similar to others in the field, so trying to gain a competitive advantage in the level and type of service provided will help in the hospitality and service industries.

Another characteristic of an entrepreneur is that they often work alone, and this is helpful in business, but can also be a challenge. By working alone, they can often avoid confrontation on issues or differences in beliefs on policies and procedures that other people may have. Entrepreneurs may also need to hire other people to supplement their skill set and expertise, depending on what talents they have and what talents they need to make the business successful.

Entrepreneurs have an intense level of commitment and perseverance, which is critical in any situations where you have to fight adversity. When you develop your own business, you have to make sure that you have the capability to fight off other competition and to beat the doubts that may get to you. It is important to keep on pushing through any problems that you may have.

Before you decide to start your own business, you should ask yourself some very important questions that will help to evaluate whether you are ready to open your own business or not.

1. How do you feel about people and are you willing to serve them?
   - Taking care of guests is the reason that you go into business, and so before you start your own business you have to be ready to work with people and through people to get things done.
2. Do you have the energy to start your own business?
   - It takes a lot of energy and hours to start up a business—are you prepared to work hard to create a business that you can be proud of?
3. How persistent and flexible are you?
   - You have to be ready to work through problems and be creative with solutions that make the most sense for you and your guests.
4. What is your hands-on quotient, and are you ready to provide unwavering service?
   - When you start a business, you need to be hands on and do what it takes to create a name for yourself and your business. Being available and working on the front line will allow you to do that.
5. How do you feel about business and the ability to get things done through other people?
   - You have to be able to delegate and get things done through other people to maintain a work–life balance.
6. How well do you handle conflict?
   - Part of owning and operating a business is being able to handle conflicts that come up through day-to-day operations—conflicts with vendors, guests, employees, etc. Being able to effectively handle those conflicts is going to be important in the overall operation of the business.
7. How is your sense of humor?
   - Keeping a positive attitude and sense of humor will help you achieve your goals and will help you deal with any situations that may come along.

Types of Legal Structure for Small Business Operations

Before you decide to open your own business, you need to determine what type of legal structure is best suited for your organization. The three primary types of options for how organizations can be set up for ownership are sole proprietorship, limited liability corporation (LLC), and S corporation. The type of organizational setup should be based on the type and size of organization that you will own and the amount of liability that you want to have if something goes wrong.

A sole proprietorship is very easy to form, and there are no costs to start this up. You as the owner of the business make the decisions, and therefore the management of the business entity is up to you. There are no operational formalities, and all expenses and revenues are tied directly to you. The primary concern with this is that all liability is tied to you as well, so your personal assets are exposed.

A limited liability corporation (LLC) limits the amount of exposure that the owner has to have on their personal assets. The liability is limited to the assets of the corporation. There are a few more things that need to be done when creating an LLC, and they involve costs and ease of formation. There are some fees because you have to register with the secretary of state, and if you hire an attorney, you have to pay for them as well. You also have to create a document stating how the company will be set up and how the organization will be structured. You can make the structure as simple or complicated as you would like, but all financial information has to be kept separate from your personal financial information.

An S corporation is similar in setup to an LLC, but it is more formal and therefore there are more documents to complete. You have to have a board of directors, and there is not as much flexibility with the operations. There must be shareholder meetings, notice requirements, and annual filings and fees. There are more administrative issues and higher costs to operate. You are taxed like a corporation, and your personal assets are protected.

Summary

In this chapter, you learned in great detail about the independent operator and their important role in the hospitality industry. The chapter wrapped up with a discussion of the characteristics of entrepreneurs and the role that they play in the economy in general and the hospitality industry specifically. This information now can be used in order to set the framework for Chapter 6, "Chain Operations." Through Chapters 5 and 6, it will be important to see the differences between independent and entrepreneurial operations and chain operations and the responsibilities and

skills that an independent business owner and/or manager and a multiunit or chain owner or manager will need to do their jobs effectively.

Case Study

Tim Chase was a multiunit manager of a large casual dining restaurant chain called Chico's. Tim's territory included eight stores in the Atlanta area; he has held this position for approximately 1 year. Tim is one of 12 multiunit managers in the chain. He prides himself in being a fair and knowledgeable manager and has over 12 years of industry experience. His last position was with a well-known national restaurant chain named Phil's, where he held the position of general manager for 6 years. Tim enjoys his position as a multiunit manager, but is beginning to realize that he has many creative ideas that are not allowed to be done in a chain or corporate setting. He feels like he is being kept from creating menu items and working creatively with customers and employees on solving problems on a more regular basis. This is his first job as a multiunit manager, and he occasionally feels as if there are too many rules and regulations for him to be successful.

Chico's is an established national restaurant chain, founded in the late 1980s. It is part of the Tuxedo Corporation, which has produced several other chains, all corporately owned and operated. Richard Keller, a respected entrepreneur in the restaurant industry, is the owner of the Tuxedo Corporation. Keller got his start operating fast-food hot dog restaurants in the Chicago area. Keller is known for his integrity, which permeates throughout his company.

Tim was promoted because he was an excellent supervisor and had an excellent "rapport" with the employees of the restaurant. However, since Tim's promotion, Tim has noticed that he is not quite the multiunit manager that he had hoped he would be.

Tim has decided to talk to Richard Keller about the skills and abilities that he has that have allowed him to start businesses and be successful in developing Tuxedo Corporation and Chico's. Tim feels that he may have what it takes to start his own restaurant company and wants to get Richard's input into this. Tim doesn't have a college degree, but he has taken some college courses in accounting and management. He has always been a hard worker, has had perseverance, and never had a problem with working with different kinds of people. He is good at coming up with creative ideas, he tries to surround himself with great people who complement his skills, but he does have a hard time following other people's rules if they get in the way of providing great service to guests or to employees.

Tim asked Richard to talk with him about his success, and Richard said, "Tim, I don't know what it is, but I always wanted to be my own boss. I always had a hard time when bosses of mine created rules to put roadblocks in my way so that I had a hard time changing things that didn't make sense. I like serving people, and when I work for someone else, I have to do that their way. I also am a risk taker, and I try to do things that other people would only dream about doing. I'm not afraid of investing in something that I truly believe in."

Tim responded by saying, "I admire that trait in you and I feel the same way. I feel that if you believe in something and work hard enough, it can be successful. As long as you have great people around you to complement your skill set, you can do almost anything in the service business."

Richard nodded his head and asked Tim, "Why are you so interested in what made me successful?" Tim responded with a smile and said, "I think I want to make the leap and start my own business, be an independent operator of a restaurant. I wasn't sure at first, but now I know this is what I want to do"

After having this conversation with Richard, Tim realized that he may have what it takes to start his own business and be an independent operator.

Discussion Questions for Case Study

1. What skills does Tim believe that he has that would make him a great business owner?
2. How has Richard Keller been so successful over the years?
3. What is good or bad that Tim talked to his boss, Richard Keller, about his entrepreneurial skills? Why?
4. Is it important to understand Tim's management style to answer the preceding questions? Why or why not?

RESOURCES

Internet Sites

U.S. Small Business Association: www.sba.gov
U.S. Census Bureau: www.census.gov
Entrepreneur Magazine: www.entrepreneur.com

References

Boulgarides, J. D., & Rowe, A. J. (1983). Success patterns for women managers. *Business Forum, 8*(2), 22–24.

Haim, A. W., & Olander, K. W. (1996). *The entrepreneur's complete sourcebook.* Upper Saddle River, NJ: Prentice Hall.

Kakabadse, A., & Margerison, C. (1988). Top executives: Addressing their management development needs. *Leadership & Organization Development Journal, 9*(4), 17–21.

McMullin, R. A. (2004). Independent and entrepreneurial operations. In R. A. Brymer (Ed.), *Hospitality and Tourism* (11th ed., pp. 81–85). Dubuque, IA: Kendall/Hunt Publishing Company.

Pine, B. J., & Gilmore, J. H. (2004). *The experience economy: Work is theatre & every business a stage.* Boston: Harvard Business School Press.

Reynolds, D. (2000). An exploratory investigation into behaviorally based success characteristics of foodservice managers. *Journal of Hospitality & Tourism Research, 24*(1).

Robbins, S. P., & Coulter, M. (2002). *Management* (7th ed.). Upper Saddle River, NJ: Prentice Hall, p. 6.

U.S. Census Bureau (2010a). Retrieved July 14, 2010 from http://www2.census.gov/econ/sbo/07/prelim/all_emp_pie.pdf

U.S. Census Bureau (2010b). Retrieved July 14, 2010 from http://www2.census.gov/econ/sbo/07/prelim/minority_emp_pie.pdf

U.S. Census Bureau (2010c). Retrieved July 15, 2010 from http://factfinder.census.gov/servlet/IBQTable?_bm=y&-_lowValue=&-filter=SEX;in;002&-ds_name=SB0700CSPRE01&-_highValue=&-geo_id=01000US&-_filterValue=002&-_selOp=eq&-fds_name=EC0700A1

Van der Merwe, S. (1978). What personal attributes it takes to make it in management. *Ivey Business Quarterly, 43*(4), 28–32.

Review Questions

1. Imagine being an independent owner/operator of a small grocery store in a large urban area of the country. What are the skills that you would most likely use on a regular basis, and what are the skills that you would need to be a manager of a chain grocery store unit in that same area?

2. What are the similarities and differences of the management functions of planning and organizing?

3. What is the primary management style that you use when you lead people?

4. What is the management style that your manager uses, and is it effective? Why or why not?

5. How can the model of management help with a new manager just starting off in her career in the management of a service organization?

6. What skills does it take to be an entrepreneur in the hospitality and service business? Do you have those skills?

7. Who owns the business that you work for? Is it a corporation or an independent operation? Or some other format of ownership?

Chain Operations and Franchising

Radesh Palakurthi, Drexel University

LEARNING OBJECTIVES

- Define and understand what chain operations and franchising means in the hospitality industry.
- Understand the distinction between brands and chain operations.
- Comprehend the different business forms of hospitality chain operations.
- Recognize the advantages and disadvantages of hospitality chain operations.
- Identify the largest multiunit operations in hospitality.

CHAPTER OUTLINE

Brands versus Chains
Multiunit Operations Business Models
    Simple Form
    Mixed Franchise Form
    Management/Franchise Form
    Brand Management Form
Advantages of Chain Operations
Disadvantages of Chain Operations
The Big Chains in Hospitality

KEY TERMS

Advantages of multiunit operations
Brand
Chain operations
Disadvantages of multiunit operations
Franchise
Multiunit business forms

Joan Tortza is a bright, young, enterprising undergraduate student in Hospitality Administration at a reputed national university. Ever since Joan started the program, she had harbored a passionate desire to start her own restaurant. With her excellent culinary abilities, people skills, and superior knowledge of management techniques (gained through hard work at school and internships), she was confident that she would be successful. During the end of her senior year, Joan put together a business plan for her proposed restaurant concept for the capstone class in strategic management. Joan's professor for the course was very impressed and offered an opportunity to present her plan to potential investors in the hospitality industry. Soon after graduating from school, Joan was making presentations to groups of investors that asked her poignant questions about the feasibility of her business plan.

Joan was eventually able to convince one local group of investors about the soundness of her proposed restaurant concept, and they agreed to convert one of their existing restaurants, that was not performing up to standards, into the concept proposed by Joan. After months of planning and renovation, the new restaurant opened with much fanfare. It was instantly a huge success, confirming that Joan's assessment for the need for such a restaurant concept was on the mark. In fact, the restaurant concept was so successful that the investors decided, with Joan's approval, to open a chain of additional restaurants using the same name and restaurant concept theme. Within a couple of years after graduation, Joan was overseeing four of her restaurants in the region. Needless to say, Joan was very happy with her success.

One fine day, a customer at one of her restaurants approached Joan to ask if she was interested in expanding her operations nationwide. Joan could not believe what she was hearing because the thought

had crossed her mind. However, she was restrained by her original agreement with the investment group and also their relatively limited resources to expand rapidly nationwide. Additionally, the cash flow from her four restaurants was not high enough to expand rapidly in many markets simultaneously. If she decided to use only the profits from her restaurants to expand, the expansion would be very slow, and other people with more money to invest could beat her to the market. The customer suggested that Joan consider the franchising route. In such a business model, many individuals or investors from across the country would make the capital investment to buy the land, build the restaurant, license Joan's restaurant name and logo, and agree to operate the new restaurants according to Joan's standards. In return, Joan would receive part of the new restaurants' sales as franchise fees and royalties, even though she had not made any additional investments. She could also charge them a management fee if they decided to allow Joan's employees to operate the restaurants. While Joan was thrilled with the prospect of turning her four-restaurant concept into a national chain, she was immediately concerned with all the management issues that might crop up in the process. After all, the devil is in the details, isn't it? For example, Joan wondered if such rapid expansion would enable her to maintain control over the quality of the restaurant products that she now has. How about the fact that she now will have to deal with hundreds of investors (franchisees) from across the country, all with different personalities and financial goals? Will she be able to find an adequate number of employees with the required skills to run her restaurant concept nationwide? What about legal responsibilities of her company and the franchisees? Reflecting on such issues, Joan sat down to do some careful planning to set the course for the future of her company.

The vignette offers a scenario in developing chain operations. It describes one of the ways by which a hospitality chain operation can be created and the underpinning issues involved in growing it. The vignette also describes a chain operation without unfolding the specifics. The purpose of this chapter is to throw light on hotel and restaurant

chain operations and discuss the nuances of structuring such chains.

Brands versus Chains

A chain operation can simply be defined as a business under one management or ownership. More specifically, chain-operated hotels, restaurants, and other similar businesses are owned by the same company and offer similar goods and services, but are found in different geographic locations. Although there is no magic number in commerce that converts similar operations into a chain, generally, six similar type operations could be considered to be a chain. The scope of a chain operation could be regional, national, or international. A few examples of international hospitality chain operations include McDonald's Restaurants, Burger King Restaurants, Holiday Inn Hotels, and Marriott Hotels.

Although the concept of a chain operation is easy to understand, structurally, it may become more complex with increasing size. The complexity comes from the ownership and management contracts that form the basis of the relationships between the unit operators and the corporate office. In addition, the distinction between a chain and a brand confounds the issue. A brand is a specific identity of a business that is intentionally created through a careful combination of the design of its products and services and other forms of business identity such as name, logo, slogans, and signs. The aim is to convey a personality for the business and to infuse a consistent image of what the business stands for in the minds of the guests each time they think of or hear about the brand.

Multiunit Operations Business Models

A brief description of each of the business models is described next.

Simple Form

In its simplest form, a chain can consist of a single owner/investor that has full equity stake in all the units owned by company. In such a chain, the parent company fully owns and operates all the units in its chain. All the profits obtained by running the chain belongs to the parent company. All the employees of the unit operations are the employees of the parent company. For accounting purposes, the parent company may consolidate the sales and costs of all the unit operations to determine the total profit or loss for the parent company. Any marketing campaigns conducted would be at the expense of the parent company and would be performed for the benefit of all the unit operations. Usually, this type of structure is found in local or regional chain operations, and they constitute a large percentage of the smaller chains in hospitality. Figure 6.1 illustrates the simple form of structure of chain operations in hospitality.

Mixed Franchise Form

In this type of a chain, there is a mix of ownership, with some units being owned and operated by the

FIGURE 6.1 Simple Form of Chain Operations in Hospitality

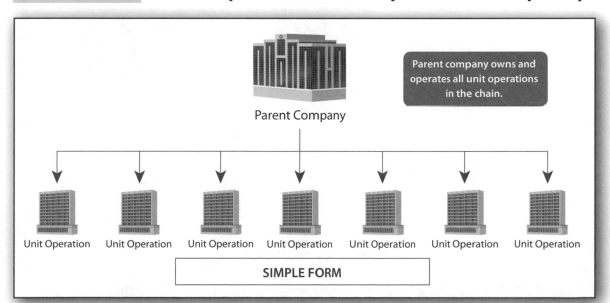

Parent company owns and operates all unit operations in the chain.

Parent Company

Unit Operation | Unit Operation | Unit Operation | Unit Operation | Unit Operation | Unit Operation | Unit Operation

SIMPLE FORM

parent company (known as the franchisor) and the rest owned and operated by many other owners/investors (known as franchisees). Depending on the size of the chain, the number of franchisees can be large. The percentage of the total units owned that are franchised also determines the number of franchisees. Many of the franchisees may own multiple units through business partnership entities of their own. It is not uncommon for some of the franchisee partnerships to own more units than the parent company. The franchisor derives their revenues through multiple revenue streams: Franchising Fees (franchise application fees and a flat fee as a percentage of gross sales); Incentive Fees (an additional fee based on the level of profitability of the unit operation); Royalty Fees (a fee for using the name, logo, and standard operating systems of the parent company); Marketing Fees (an additional fee to pay for marketing the entire chain through different campaigns); and Other Fees (for project consulting, employee training, and inventory/supplies management). It should be noted that although all such fees are reported as revenue for the franchisor, the gross sales of the non-company-owned (franchisors) units is not reported as revenue

of the parent company. Although the fees charged by the parent company can be a major part of the costs of a franchisor, the benefits derived can also be substantial. For example, the franchisor will not have to worry about the soundness or feasibility of the business concept because it is already a proven business model. In addition, the operating systems are already laid out with clear plans for design, operations, and personnel management. Even the marketing for the units is undertaken by the parent company (franchisor), although the entire chain's brand name is emphasized rather than any individual unit. Figure 6.2 illustrates the structure of a mixed franchise form in hospitality.

Management/Franchise Form

When the parent company (franchisor) also engages in offering professional management services for its non-company-owned (franchised units), the company can be said to be using the management/franchise form of chain operations. The difference is that in this form, the parent company has an additional stream of revenue called "management fees" (i.e., fees that it charges the non-company-owned units

FIGURE   6.2   Mixed Franchise Form of Hospitality Chain Operations

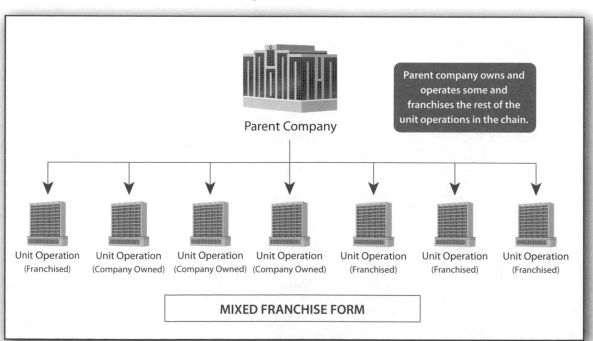

for managing their operations). The parent company also charges the costs involved in running the units directly to the units. The employees of the unit operations that are managed but not owned by the parent company (franchisor) are the employees of the parent company (franchisor). Some management/franchise parent companies also help fund the investment projects of the franchisees such as opening a new unit or renovating an existing unit. All such functions may be conducted through a separate financial subsidiary of the parent company. Any profits obtained from such funding are retained by the parent company. Many such financing operations of the franchisors are currently more profitable than the franchise operations because of the low interest rates on loans. Many regional and national chain operations use this business model. A point to note in this model is that the franchisees may be free to hire any other professional operations management company rather than the parent company. In such a case, the unit will be owned by an investor and managed by an outside company that will operate the business strictly by the standards established by the parent company. The fee structure of the outside management company may be similar to that of the parent company. However, the outside management company may be operating many other operations that belong to other chains. If fact, the outside management company may also be a partial or full business partner in some unit operations it manages. Figure 6.3 illustrates the management/ franchise form of structure in hospitality.

Brand Management Form

When a megacorporation owns multiple chain operations under the same parent umbrella structure, it prefers to refer to each of such chain operations as a brand

FIGURE **6.3** **A Management/franchise Form of Hospitality Chain Operations**

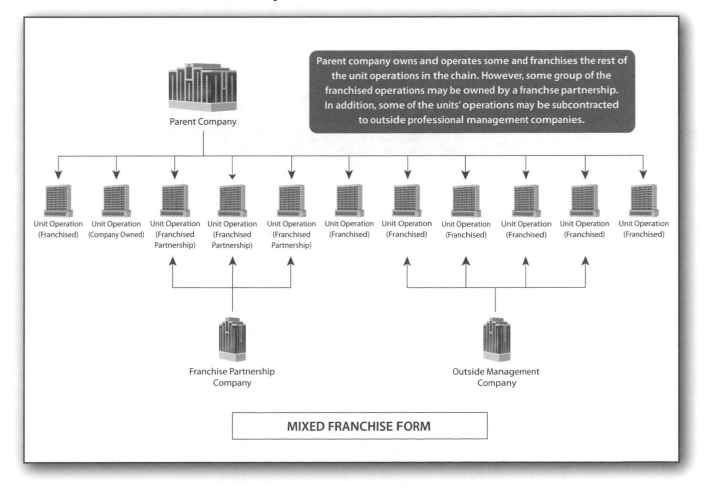

rather than a chain to emphasize the importance of the distinctive brand image of each of the brands in its portfolio (Figure 6.4). For example, as of 2010, Marriott International owns seventeen brands. Each of the brands has a distinctive position and covers specific market segments of the lodging industry.

For example, the JW Marriott Hotels & Resorts is an elegant and luxurious brand for business and leisure, whereas the Residence Inn by Marriott is designed to be a "home away from home" and caters to travelers who stay for an extended stay of five or more nights.

FIGURE 6.4 The Megacorporation Form Structure of Hospitality Operations

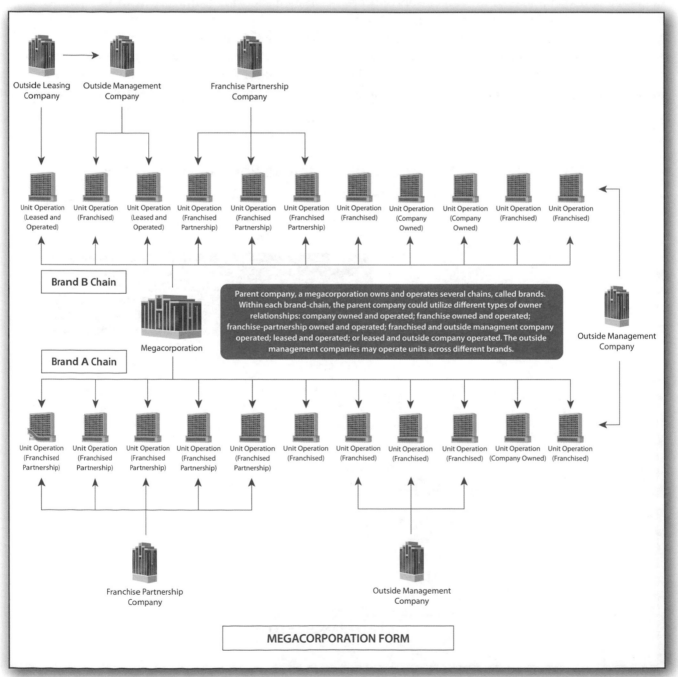

Each chain within the brand management form operates similarly to the management/franchise form in terms of the franchisor–franchisee relationships. The chain's units may be operated by the parent company directly, sole owners as franchisees, partnership-owners as franchisees, or a management company as a third-party operator for a franchisee. The large size of the megacorporation may also allow it to raise funds through the financial markets to make direct investments in real estate across the globe. In such a case, the parent corporation may buy land, build new establishments, or buy existing establishments and convert them into one of their brands. Such investments also allow the megacorporation to

offer the invested properties on a lease to third parties that may choose to operate the establishment or hire a professional management company to run it for them. The complexity of such relationships may be compounded when the megacorporation chooses to enter into a joint venture or other similar partnership with a foreign entity to enter and expand in foreign countries. Figure 6.5 shows the partial portfolio of Marriott International. It can be seen that the company owns, manages, leases, and franchises its properties, although at a different level for each brand. The company uses different brand strategies for each chain within its portfolio. For example, although almost all units in the Fairfield Inn chain

FIGURE **6.5** **Partial Portfolio of Lodging Chain Operations of Marriott International**

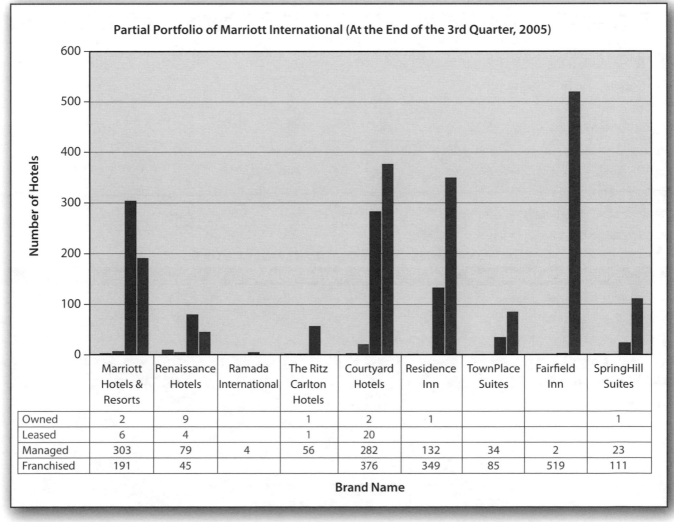

Partial Portfolio of Marriott International (At the End of the 3rd Quarter, 2005)

	Marriott Hotels & Resorts	Renaissance Hotels	Ramada International	The Ritz Carlton Hotels	Courtyard Hotels	Residence Inn	TownPlace Suites	Fairfield Inn	SpringHill Suites
Owned	2	9		1	2	1			1
Leased	6	4		1	20				
Managed	303	79	4	56	282	132	34	2	23
Franchised	191	45			376	349	85	519	111

Brand Name

Source: http://www.Marriott.com; Company Reports.

are franchised, none of the units are franchised in the Ritz Carlton Chain. Instead, all the Ritz Carlton hotels are managed through full ownership or direct management contracts. This ensures full control of the quality of this upscale brand.

Similar to Marriott Corporation, other megahotel chains also follow a strategy of their own in terms of managing and franchising their properties. Table 6.1 shows the top 10 hotel franchisees and managers of hotel properties in the world. In the table it can be seen that all the major chains prefer to extensively franchise their hotels and manage them to a letter extent. Some of the chains such as Cendant and Choice Hotels franchise all the hotels in their chain.

On the other hand, the Tharandson Enterprise prefers to manage all the hotels in the company.

Advantages of Chain Operations

Hospitality chains operations have many advantages that can broadly be classified into the following categories:

- **Market Reach:** How many times have we wished that one of our local favorite restaurants also traveled with us so we never have to miss the food we love? That is precisely the need that chain operations aim to fulfill by

TABLE   6.1   Top 10 Franchises and Managers of Hotel Chains

COMPANIES THAT FRANCHISE THE MOST HOTELS		
COMPANY	TOTAL FRANCHISED	TOTAL HOTELS
Cendant Corp.	6,396	6,396
Choice Hotels International	4,977	4,977
InterContinental Hotels Group	2,971	3,540
Hilton Hotels Corp.	1,900	2,259
Marriott International	1,658	2,632
Accor	949	3,973
Carlson Hospitality Worldwide	864	890
Global Hyatt Corp.	505	818
Starwood Hotels & Resorts	310	733
Worldwide Louvre Hotels (Societe du Louvre)	307	887
COMPANIES THAT MANAGE THE MOST HOTELS		
COMPANY	HOTELS MANAGED	TOTAL HOTELS
Marriott International	889	2,632
Extended Stay Hotels	654	654
Accor	535	3,973
InterContinental Hotels Group	403	3,540
Tharaldson Enterprises	360	360
Global Hyatt Corp.	316	818
Interstate Hotels & Resorts	306	306
Starwood Hotels & Resorts	283	733
Hilton Hotels Corp.	206	2,259
Worldwide Louvre Hotels (Societe du Louvre)	227	887

Source: Hotel Giants' Survey, 2005.

replicating a successful product in as many geographic regions as they can. In this way, chain operations have an advantage over single independent restaurants because they "reach" out to many markets with the same concept. Reaching new markets means increased sales and thereby increased profits (hopefully!).

- **Economies of Scale:** Economies of scale refers to the cost advantages that a company can derive because of its large size. Because chain operations have multiple units, all products and supplies they buy are also multiples of the requirements of a single independent unit. Therefore, a chain operation will be able to negotiate better rates for its products and supplies from vendors compared to a single-owner unit. In addition, chain operations will also be able to derive cost savings through synergy. For example, a single-unit operation may have to have a different functional department (marketing & sales, finance, human resources, etc.) for running the operation, whereas in a chain the same single functional department may manage many units in the chain. In other words, the chain operation could have the same departments (and staff) help run many units in the chain (say regionally). Therefore, the chain operation is able to spread the costs of such functional departments across many units compared to a single-unit operation and thereby reduce the overall unit cost of such functions for all units in its chain. Such synergies can only be derived in a chain operation.

- **Streamlined Operations:** Chain operations often standardize the products and services offered to streamline their operations. The standardization also extends to operating procedures resulting in commonly understood requirements for managing all resources (people, finances, and equipment). Such standardization makes it easy for consolidation and reporting of performance across the chain. It also makes it easy to compare unit performance across the chain and assign accountability to individuals.

- **Enhanced Marketing Power:** The marketing power of chain operations comes from increased visibility gained through greater

A global business environment is creating opportunity for rapid international expansion. © 2011 by Chubykin Arkady. Used under license of Shutterstock, Inc.

market reach. The greater visibility allows the chain to use mass media such as TV, radio, and newspapers for marketing purposes. It also allows the chain to embark on multiple marketing campaigns at the same time in different geographic regions. An added benefit of such campaigns is that successful campaigns in one geographic region can be repeated in other regions, ensuring a more effective use of marketing dollars.

- **Value-Added Service Options:** Chain operations are often able to provide additional services both to the customers and the unit chain operations. Such services range from providing a reservations service to full-fledged consulting for running the operations. For the customers, the chain may provide a loyalty program to make sure they spend most of their product-related expenses with the chain. They may also have a full-fledged customer relationship management (CRM) program that keeps track of the customers' expenses and their likes and dislikes. For the unit chain operations, the parent company may offer preopening services, architectural and construction consulting services, employee training and certification services, operations and revenue management services, information technology consulting services, owners and franchisee services, and guest satisfaction survey services.

- **Access to Finances:** The larger size of the chain operations may mean the company may have multiple options for raising money for growth. The cheapest way is to fund growth may be through operational cash flows, which will be higher in chain operations compared to a single and independent operation. However, the chain may be able to borrow money from banks, savings & loans, and other financial institutions such as insurance companies and other financial institutions. The chain may also be able to borrow money by issuing bonds on the stock market. All such funds raised can be used to fund operations, make capital investments for growth, or in turn be lent to the unit operations for a fee and a reasonable interest rate. Such increased assess to finances means that a chain may be able to grow more rapidly than a nonchain operation.
- **Professional Management:** Because of the enhanced legal requirements and the complexity of operations in a chain, many such companies are realizing that it is prudent to hire professionals such as students graduating from hospitality management programs. With professionalism and specialization comes a better understanding of a company's operating needs. In that regard, chain operations are becoming incubators of good management practices in hospitality.

Chain development strategy is prudent in global business today.
© 2011 by Lilya. Used under license of Shutterstock, Inc.

Disadvantages of Chain Operations

Depending on the perspective of the owner (or the parent company/franchisor) and the operator (or the franchises/management company), some of the advantages listed earlier can also be seen as drawbacks for managing hospitality chain operations. The disadvantages can broadly be listed under three categories as discussed next.

- **Operational Constraints:** Although the parent company may want standardized operations throughout the chain to control costs and efficiency, it may put a lot of restrictions on the franchisees or owners that may want to vary in some small ways. For example, the ownership contracts may disallow independent marketing in the local areas by any unit operations without prior approval by the parent company. The type of marketing and the collateral used may also be restricted by the parent company. Such restrictions are only enforced to ensure a consistent image of the brand in the minds of the consumer in all geographic areas where the chain operates. In final analysis, the power of the brand comes from maintaining the image of the brand, and hence, the parent company is often very stringent with their requirements. In fact, all chain operations have some form of quality-assurance program where they perform surprise inspections of their unit operations to ensure compliance with all company rules and regulations. Units that repeatedly violate the company requirements are dropped from the chain after proper notice.
- **Financial Strain:** Another disadvantage of belonging to a chain operation may be the strain put on the financial resources of the company. Not only do unit operations have to contribute to the parent company through royalties, incentive, franchise, marketing, and other such areas, but they may also incur additional expenses if the parent company requires additional capital investments to comply with a new requirement they initiated across the chain. For example, if the parent company of a 300-hotel chain decides that the lighting in the guest bathrooms must be increased from 400 lumens to 500 lumens for better visibility and safety, each hotel may have to incur thousands of dollars in expenses to refit

each guest bathroom in the hotel they operate. If one such hotel in the chain has 250 rooms and it costs about $300 to make the lighting change in each bathroom including equipment, labor, and downtime costs, this particular hotel will have to spend $75,000 to meet the parent company's requirements. Extending the calculation, across the chain, it may cost up to $22.5 million to meet this new parent company requirement.

- **Legal Forces:** The complex structure of most chain operations, along with many types of owner–operator contracts and partnerships, often plagues it with legal woes. Invariably, a difference of opinion or perspective on the same issues may have no other recourse than the local courthouse. Consider again the example of the guest bathroom lighting enhancement requirement described earlier. This cost of improving the bathroom lighting at the unit level will have to come at the expense of the profit of the unit operations, and that is always a contentious issue between the parent company and the unit managers. The parent company may have a more holistic view of the costs associated because they believe that such an investment may pay off through lower guest accidents in the bathroom that may in turn reduce insurance costs and legal expenses. If the unit managers can be convinced of the justification of the costs, then the cost of making the lighting changes in the bathroom will be seen as an investment rather than an unjustified cost rained on them by the parent company. However, if the costs are seen as unjustified, the unit operations may first try to wield control by collective representation through unions or partnerships. If that fails, the parent company may have to deal with the issue in a court of law.

The Big Chains in Hospitality

The increasing globalization of the hospitality industry is rapidly being reflected in the geographic profiles of large hospitality corporations, especially in the hotel industry. It is now commonplace for major hospitality corporations to consider the entire global market as their potential domain. Table 6.2 lists the number of countries each of the major hotel corporations operated in 2010. The top five companies operated in more than half the nations in the world.

TABLE 6.2   15 Hotel Corporations Operating in Most Countries: 2010

COMPANY NAME	NUMBER OF COUNTRIES
InterContinental Hotels Group	100
Starwood Hotels & Resorts	100
Accor	90
Best Western International	82
Hilton Group plc	81
Carlson Hospitality Worldwide	77
Marriott International	66
Le Meridien Hotels & Resorts	56
Golden Tulip Hospitality/THL	47
Wyndham Hotel Group/ Cendant Corp.	44
Global Hyatt Corp.	43
Choice Hotels International	42
Rezidor SAS Hospitality	41
Club Mediterranee	40
TUI AG/TUI Hotels & Resorts	28

Source: Corporate Web sites and Annual Reports.

In addition to the countries in which the hotel companies operate, the country in which the companies are based is also truly global in scope. Table 6.3 lists the top 15 hotel chains in the world in terms of number of rooms. In the table, for example, the world's largest hotel company, InterContinental Hotels Group, is based in United Kingdom, and Accor, the fourth largest, is based in France. Although many of the other larger chains are based in the United States, the ownership profile is changing rapidly with cross-national mergers and acquisitions such as the Hilton brand, which is now partly based in Herts, England, and in Beverly Hills, California, under two different ownership companies.

Unlike the hotel industry, the food service chains are currently dominated by American quick-service restaurants. Table 6.4 lists the top 12 food service chains in the world. The top eight chains have substantial international operations, with most of their growth actually coming from the overseas markets. It is interesting to note that although McDonald's Restaurants is still ranked first in terms of sales, the Subway Restaurants chain is the largest in terms of the number of units. It can also be seen that the more traditional quick-service concepts such as Burger King and Wendy's are either in mature or decline stage; newer restaurant concepts such as Starbucks and Sonic Drive-In are rapidly growing. Not unlike the hotel industry, the food service industry also has a penchant for franchising with some of the chains such as Subway and Dunkin' Donuts franchising almost all their restaurants.

TABLE	6.3	Top 15 Hotel Chains in Terms of Number of Room (2003–10)				
RANK 2010	RANK 2003	COMPANY HEADQUARTERS	ROOMS 2010	ROOMS 2003	HOTELS 2010	HOTELS 2003
1	1	InterContinental Hotels Group Windsor, Berkshire, England	650,402	536,318	4,421	3,520
2	3	Marriott International Washington, D.C., USA	607,252	490,564	3,489	2,718
3	2	Wyndham Hotel Group/Cendant Corp. Parsippany, N.J., USA	593,000	518,747	7,090	6,402
4	4	Accor Paris, France	506,234	453,403	4,101	3,894
5	5	Choice Hotels International Silver Spring, Md., USA	485,245	388,618	6,045	4,810
6	6	Hilton Hotels Corp. Beverly Hills, Calif., USA	438,408	348,483	3,504	2,173
7	7	Best Western International Phoenix, Ariz., USA	308,237	310,245	4,013	4,110
8	8	Starwood Hotels & Resorts Worldwide White Plains, N.Y., USA	292,242	229,247	983	738
9	9	Carlson Hospitality Worldwide Minneapolis, Minn., USA	196,143	147,624	1,080	881
10	10	Hilton Group plc Watford, Herts, England	176,257	98,689	514	392
11	11	Global Hyatt Corp. Chicago, Ill., USA	122,317	89,602	424	208

Source: Corporate Web sites.

TABLE	6.4	Top Food Service Chains in the World in 2009		

2009 RANK	CHAIN	SEGMENT	2009 SYSTEMWIDE SALES ($MIL)	TOTAL UNITS
1	McDonald's	Burger	$54,928	32,478
2	Subway	Sandwich	$14,256	33,188
3	Wendy's/Arby's Group	Burger/Sandwiches	$12,412	10,563
4	Yum Brands (KFC, Taco Bell, Pizza Hut, Long John Silver's, A&W, and All-American Foods Restaurants Brand	Burger/Sandwiches	$11,204	37,345
5	Starbucks	Snack	$9,775	16,706
6	Burger King	Burger	$8,956	12,134
7	Dunkin' Donuts	Snack	$6,380	8,8,35
7	Domino's Pizza	Pizza/Pasta	$5,587	8,952
9	Sonic Drive-In	Burger	$3,770	3,511

Source: Company Annual Reports and Web sites.

In an increasingly competitive world, chain development strategy offers an opportunity for hospitality companies to take control of costs and harness their strengths. With the short time it now takes for the diffusion of innovation and migration of ideas across the world because of rapidly evolving telecommunication facilities, the world is swiftly shrinking and creating immense business opportunities for growth globally. As people around the world share the same information and ideas, they may also develop the same preferences for hospitality products and services. In such an environment, growing through the application of chain development strategy is prudent for business. Needless to say, the concept of hospitality chain operations will only get stronger in the future.

RESOURCES

Internet Sites

IHG Corporate Information: http://www.ihgplc.com/
Marriott Corporate Information: http://www.marriott.com/corporateinfo/glance.mi
Wyndham Hotels Group: http://www.wyndhamworldwide.com/about/at_a_glance.cfm
Accor Corporate Information: http://www.accor.com/en/group/accor-company-profile.html
Choice Hotels Corporate Information: http://investor.choicehotels.com/phoenix.zhtml?c=99348&p=irol-aboutchoice
Hilton Hotels Corporation Information: http://www.hilton.com/en/hi/brand/about.jhtml
Best Western Corporate Information: http://www.bestwestern.com/aboutus/index.asp
Starwood Hotels Corporate Information: http://www.starwoodhotels.com/corporate/company_info.html
Carlson Hospitality Corporate Information: http://www.carlson.com/our-company/
Hilton Group PLC Corporate Information: http://www.hiltonworldwide.com/aboutus/index.htm
Hyatt Global Corporate Information: http://investors.hyatt.com/phoenix.zhtml?c=228969&p=irol-irhome
McDonald's Corporate Information: http://www.mcdonalds.com/us/en/our_story/our_history.html
Subway Corporate Information: http://subway.com/StudentGuide/

Wendy's Corporate Information: http://ir.wendysarbys.com/phoenix.zhtml?c=67548&p=irol-IRHome

Yum Brands Corporate Information: http://yum.com/company/ourbrands.asp

Starbucks Corporate Information: http://www.starbucks.com/about-us/company-information

Burger Kings Corporate Information: http://investor.bk.com/phoenix.zhtml?c=87140&p=irol-IRHome

Dunkin Donuts Corporate Information: https://www.dunkindonuts.com/aboutus/company/

Dominos Corporate Information: http://www.dominosbiz.com/Biz-Public-EN/Site+Content/Secondary/About+Dominos/Fun+Facts/

Sonic Corporate Information: http://www.sonicdrivein.com/business/profile/index.jsp

Review Questions

CHAPTER 6

1. Define what is brand is describe how it is related to multichain operations. Explain with an example.

2. What are the key elements of a multiunit chain operation in hospitality?

3. How is brand management related to franchising? Explain with an example.

4. Describe the four business forms that exist in hospitality chain or multiunit operations.

5. What are some of the key advantages and disadvantages of hospitality chain or multiunit operations?

6. Identify five major hotel and restaurant chain operations in hospitality. Pick one chain from each segment and research the different brands they operate. Describe how are the brands different from each other.

Contract Management

Wanda M. Costen, University of Tennessee

LEARNING OBJECTIVES

- Understand the roles of owner and contractor.
- Know the components of a management contract.
- Understand the key criteria for selecting a hotel management contractor.
- Be able to explain the roles of host, client, contractor, and self-operated.
- Be able to describe the different segments of the on-site food service industry.
- Know the key players in the on-site food service industry.
- Understand the career opportunities available in contract services management.

CHAPTER OUTLINE

KEY TERMS

Base fees
Board plan
Branding
Client
Contract services management
Host
Incentive fees

On-site food service management
Operator
Operator loan and equity contributions
Operator system reimbursable expenses
Owner
Self-operators
Term

Have you ever thought about owning a lodging business but weren't sure you knew enough to make a profit? You may not realize it, but when you stay at a hotel or motel, sometimes the company that runs or operates the hotel is not the same company that owns the property. Similarly, when you eat in your university's dining facilities, there is often a separate organization providing the food service. After all, you wouldn't expect the university administrators to know all the details of how to feed all those students. The organization that manages lodging or food service operations for owners are called *operators*.

Over the years, real estate has been an attractive and lucrative investment. Many investment companies choose to purchase real estate and subsequently build a lodging property on the land. These investment companies typically do not have the expertise necessary to operate a hotel or motel, but they believe that lodging would be a sound investment strategy. Therefore, they hire another organization to run the property. Likewise, most managers of businesses, universities, and hospitals know their own industries, but they have no desire to gain the knowledge and expertise necessary to feed employees or students. Because this is a secondary concern, they may not want to hire a department just to feed everyone. Therefore, they do not operate their own cafeterias. They, too, hire outside organizations to run their food service operations. The agreement between the owners and the operators is called a contract, and thus this segment of the hospitality industry is referred to as *contract services management*.

There are two types of operators: chain operators and independent contractors. Chain operators, as the name implies, are affiliated with major hotel chains like Marriott, Starwood, and Hilton. In recent years, there have been many mergers of these chains creating megabrands. As a result of acquisitions, this group of major chains is becoming smaller each year. For example in July 2007, Blackstone Group purchased Hilton Hotels Corporation for $26 billion! Blackstone operates under the name brands of Wyndham, Extended Stay America, La Quinta, and Boca Resorts. They purchased Starwood that contains the following brands: Sheraton, Westin, W, Four Points, and St. Regis. All these chain operators have name brand recognition, a history of successful performance, and efficient operating systems.

Independent contractors are not affiliated with any specific brand. They purchase brands and locations based on their assessment for compatibility with their objectives. For example, The Hotel Group manages 25 properties under brands like Double Tree, Sheraton, Crowne Plaza, Microtel, Best Western, Embassy Suites, and even Courtyard by Marriott.[1] Another independent contractor, Hostmark Hospitality Group, has managed over 250 hotel properties in 40 states, the Caribbean, Canada, and the Middle East since its founding in 1965. Currently it manages hotel properties under the names of Hilton, Radisson, Sheraton, and Embassy Suites.[2]

Hotel Contract Management

The concept of separating the ownership and operation of a lodging property fueled much of the capital needed to fund the expansive growth of the lodging industry in the 1970s and 1980s. Investors were able to purchase land all over the country without having to be concerned with the challenges of running a lodging property. They simply bought great locations for hospitality ventures, and then turned them over to contract managers to ensure profitability. By the same token, successful management companies were able to grow their brand names and expand into new markets without huge capital expenditures. It was a win–win situation for both parties.

The Contract Parties

Ultimately, there are three parties involved in hotel management contracts: operators, lenders, and owners. Each party has its own objectives or incentives for entering into the contract. Operators desire an increase in both market presence and market share, maintaining control over the day-to-day management decisions, and long-term stability.[3] However, their knowledge about the industry and operations is no longer a monopoly as lenders and owners stay in the business longer and learn from their ventures.

The most significant change in the contract negotiating process over the past few years has been the more active involvement of lenders and an increase in the power of the owners. Lenders are typically concerned with generating an adequate rate of return and protecting the investment. However, in recent years, as their knowledge about the process and success factors increases, lenders have become more involved in the negotiation of these contracts.

Owners are primarily interested in generating cash flow and ensuring that their capital investment appreciates or grows in value. As a result, owners have developed more knowledge about hotel operations as they acquire more properties and experience. In addition, there is an increase in the number of hotel operators (i.e., competition), which has shifted the bargaining power to the owners.

The Contract

Management contracts are comprised of several key provisions, which explain the contract. One key provision is operator loan and equity contributions. As a result of the increase in competition among operators, many are now choosing to make loan or equity contributions. In the past, operators were solely responsible for managing the hotel property, but today operators are willing to contribute funding, which demonstrates the operator's commitment to the success of the property.

All contracts include an initial term or length of the contract and guidelines for renewing the contract. The length of the initial term for chain operators is approximately 8 to 10 years, with one or two 3- to 5-year renewals. Independent contractor initial terms are typically 1 to 3 years, with one or two 2-year renewals. Owners desire shorter terms because they believe this will entice the operator to perform well for the contract to be renewed. Operators obviously prefer a longer contract term because they want stability. Operators also argue that shorter termed contracts force them to focus on short-term goals instead of long-term strategy.[4]

Management fees, which have decreased in recent years, are paid to the operators. In general, basic management fees have been on the decline, and incentive fees have become more challenging for operators to achieve. These trends are a result of the increase in owner negotiating power and operator competition. Basic management fees for chain operators of full-service hotels average 2.25% of gross revenues without an operator equity contribution and 2.5% of gross revenues with an operator equity contribution. Independent contractors receive base fees of 1.5% and 2.5%, respectively.[5]

Incentive fees are now based on cash flow after debt service or return on equity. Cash flow after debt service is the amount of cash that flows through the company after paying for its debts. Return on equity is the amount of profit a company makes with the money shareholders have invested. In the past,

operator incentives were determined by gross operating profit, or the amount of revenue generated after the costs associated with the goods and services sold are removed. This shift indicates that owners expect operators to contribute to the bottom-line profit of the venture, not just the revenue.

Another important area that must be addressed in the contract is operator system reimbursable expenses. The owner pays the operator for centralized services provided by the operator. For example, operators provide their own PMS systems, marketing, and advertising programs; centralized reservations systems; accounting and management information systems; purchasing services; as well as risk management and insurance. Owners pay these fees because these systems are provided by the operator's corporation, and the property benefits from them. For chain operators, these expenses range from 2% to 4% of gross revenues, whereas independent contractor expenses range from 0% to 1% of gross revenues.[6] Independent contractor fees are significant lower because they do not have an affiliation with a major hotel chain.

As with individual employee performance, operating companies must be held accountable for achieving certain outcomes. These performance standards are included in the contract. Typically, these performance provisions should be evaluated each year. Often the measures include year-to-year growth, based on an initial 3- to 5-year gross operating profit projection. When the hotel first opens, an operator may have 1 or 2 years grace period before the performance criteria are fine-tuned. If the operator assumes control of an existing property, the operator usually has a 6-month grace period. When operators fall short of their projections due to changes in the economy or market, owners make allowances for lower-than-expected performance. If the operator simply does not meet the performance criteria, they are usually required to pay the owner the difference. In addition, owners often include options for terminating a contract based on continued poor performance.

The specific conditions under which a contract may be terminated by either party is a crucial component of every contract. Once again, there is a huge benefit to being a chain operator. In general, owners cannot terminate a contract with a chain operator at any time. However, after some period of time in the contract, owners may terminate the operator. Owners must pay operators a termination fee, which ranges from 2 to 4 times the management fee for chain operators, and 0.5 to 2 times the management fee for independent contractors.[7]

The final component of the contract is the degree of input the owner has in decision making related to running the hotel. Owners are beginning to negotiate the right to have input on the annual budget and hiring the executive staff. In general, the executive staff (general manager, controller, directors of marketing, human resources, rooms, food and beverage, housekeeping, and engineering) are employees of the operating company. The hourly workers are employed by the owners.

It is important to note that as with all contracts, each provision or component is negotiated. A management contract is a written agreement between two organizations that outlines each party's responsibilities and consequences for not fulfilling its obligations. As mentioned earlier, today owners have gained a slight advantage in negotiating, but major chain operators are still able to influence the provisions that matter most to them.

Choosing a Hotel Management Company

Given the large number of hotel operators today, it is important for owners to develop criteria for selecting a management company. Research shows that there are five key areas that should be examined and evaluated when choosing a company to operate a hotel. First, if the owner has other hotel properties, one should look at the operating performance of the current contracted companies. If the owner has no previous experience with other operators, he/she should rely on feedback from clients with existing management contracts with potential operators. Next, the owner should try to determine how accessible the operating company's senior management is. How willing is the operator's senior management to meet with the owner and work through issues or discuss opportunities for growth? The owner should also try to get a feel for the overall integrity of the operating company. What is the operator's reputation in the industry? Does the operating company's organizational culture and values align with those of the owner's company? Finally, the owner should measure the marketing strength and penetration of the operator.[8]

Hotel owners and operators must work together to create a successful hotel that delivers or exceeds the level of customer service expected by its guests. The process of negotiating a management contract is one of give and take. Each party has its own goals, but must be flexible to create a mutually beneficial contract. Today, owners have more bargaining power than operators, which is forcing the operators to invest in the property and to meet increasingly challenging performance expectations. In addition, this shift has resulted in lower base and incentive fees for operators and more flexible terms for owners.

Contract Food Service Management

The evolution of the term used to describe food service management contracts also explains the transition of this segment of the hospitality industry. Contract food service management was initially called institutional food service because most contracts were with hospitals, industrial plants, and correctional facilities. The focus was on producing mass quantities of food that could be delivered quickly. Not surprisingly, quality was not a high priority. Today this segment of the food service industry is known as on-site food service management or managed services. The quality of food and service provided in business organizations, hospitals, schools, colleges and universities, and recreational facilities today often rivals that of top restaurants. The difference is that the food service is provided on-site (i.e., at the hospital, business organization, or recreational facility). Furthermore, today's providers of on-site food service now manage other services (copy centers, on-site child care, company stores) as well. This segment totals approximately $230 billion of the $800 billion global food service industry.[9]

The Players

To grasp the difference between on-site food service management and restaurants, one must first understand the terminology and the roles of the players. First, the *contractor* is the organization that provides the food service. The *host* is the organization that hires the contractor. The *client* is the person within the host organization that serves as the host organization's representative and is responsible for monitoring the contractor's performance. In a general sense, the term *client* is also used to refer to the entire host organization.

Some host organizations decide to operate their own food service instead of hiring an outside contractor. These organizations are *self-operated*. In these situations, the food service operation is a division of the host organization, and all the managers and employees in the food service operation work for the host company. Many school districts operate their own food service organizations, but there is a trend toward outsourcing, that is, hiring an outside firm to handle all the food operations. It is often difficult for organizations to operate two separate organizations profitably. Until 2001, the largest and most successful self-operated on-site food service organization was Motorola. Its Hospitality Group generated revenues in excess of $55 million in 2001.[10] However, the pressure to reduce costs, while maintaining quality and generating revenues became too challenging, and Motorola hired Compass Group North America to run its food service in September 2001.

On-Site Food Service Management Companies

The largest on-site food service management company is Sodexho Alliance. Sodexho is based in France and is expected to generate $19 billion in revenue.[11] Sodexho operates in 80 countries and employs approximately 332,000 people.[12]

The next largest on-site food service management company is also a global company, Compass Group. This organization is based in Britain and is expected to generate revenue in excess of $10 billion in 2007.[13] Compass operates in 70 countries with over 400,000 employees.[14] Each of its businesses operates as a separate entity under the following brands: Surest, Bon Appétit, Restaurant Associates, Me direst, Morrison, Scrotal, Chart wells, Secularist, Levy Restaurants, ESS, and Canteen.[15]

The third largest on-site food service management company is ARAMARK Services, Inc., which is the only major player based in the United States. In 2006, ARAMARK generated $11.6 billion in revenue.[16] It operates in 18 countries and employs 240,000 people.[17] As the numbers indicate, these companies manage the overwhelming majority of contracts in the on-site food service segment of the hospitality industry.

On-Site Food Service Segments

The on-site food service industry is divided into market segments based on where the food service is provided. The first market segment is business and industry.

Approximately 85% to 90% of this segment is operated by on-site managed services organizations.[18] In this market segment, on-site food service contractors operate dining facilities in corporate offices. These facilities include multiple food stations, often with different ethnic cuisines. Today the trend is toward exhibition cooking and meal replacement. Many on-site food service contractors prepare take-home meals for their customers. Customers can now eliminate a stop on the way home, and this increases the revenue of the operation. The focus is on providing what the customers want and exceeding their expectations, while remaining profitable. Not surprisingly, these are the same goals of a free-standing restaurant.

The education segment of the industry comprises K–12 schools, as well as colleges and universities. Approximately 60% to 65% of college and university food service is operated by managed services companies, while only 15% to 20% of K–12 food service is contracted out.[19] With the reductions in federal funding, the focus in K–12 schools is on reducing costs and increasing participation. Managed services providers are also offering on-site child care (before and after-school programs). Moreover, occasionally the food service operator extends its services to adult daycare centers, preschools, and private schools that are nearby. Centralized production kitchens often allow the on-site food service contractor to serve these other organizations with little increase in costs.[20]

Food service operations on college and university campuses have two types of operations. One is the *board plan,* and the other is termed *retail.* The board plan allows students to prepurchase a set number of meals throughout the semester. These

Approximately 60% to 65% of college and university food service is managed by service companies. © 2011 by Don Tran. Used under license of Shutterstock, Inc.

all-you-can-eat meals are typically offered in the campus dining halls. Retail operations resemble shopping mall food courts. Students transfer money to a debit card, which is used to purchase items in the food courts and kiosks around campus. Managed services providers use branding (which will be discussed later) to increase participation.

Health care is probably the most challenging segment of the on-site food service industry because it includes patient feeding in addition to operating on-site dining facilities. Not only are there nutrition and dietary concerns in this segment, but also patient treatment has shifted from inpatient to outpatient services and shorter hospital stays. This shift has resulted in lower food service revenue projections. Managed services companies have opted to offer additional services like housekeeping and facilities maintenance to offset these reductions. This shift might also explain why only 40% to 45% of this segment is managed by on-site food service companies.[21]

Recreation and leisure is the fastest-growing segment of this industry, with 35% to 40% of the business being operated by managed services companies. This segment includes ballparks, stadiums, arenas, and national and state parks. Today's sports fan can find a wide variety of menu options ranging from clam chowder and garlic fries at AT&T Park in San Francisco to a Dodger Dog at Dodger Stadium in Los Angeles. In addition, many of the top stadiums and arenas today have deluxe skyboxes, where gourmet meal packages are offered.[22]

Corrections or prison feeding is the final segment in this industry. Not surprisingly, only 10% to 15% of this industry is managed by on-site food service contractors.[23] Security is only one of the challenges in this segment. Prison food service production facilities were not built to accommodate the recent increase in the prison population, which presents many challenges for food service operators. In addition, similar to K–12 schools and hospitals, the correctional nutrition requirements pose unique challenges in designing menus. Moreover, the workers in these facilities are inmates, which can present management challenges.

Branding

On-site food service management companies have realized the importance of branding for increasing revenues. In each segment, the dining facilities include national, regional, and corporate brands.

Branding has shifted the ambiance of on-site dining from a cafeteria to a "market-style eatery."[24] National brands include fast-food eateries like KFC and Pizza Hut, as well as Starbucks. Regional brands allow the management companies to bring in foods that are unique to the local area. Finally, each of the major on-site food service companies has developed their own in-house brands. For example, you might find a Coyote Jack's Grill next to a Burger King kiosk in a Compass account, or a Miso Noodle Bar next to a Quizno sub outlet in an ARAMARK account.

Career Opportunities

Like the restaurant industry in general, there are vast career opportunities in on-site food service management. In operations, a recent college graduate can expect to spend 2 to 3 months in a comprehensive training program, followed by an assignment as an assistant food service manager at a particular location. Within 3 to 5 years, an assistant manager can move up to a food service director position (depending on the complexity of the operation). Most food service operators aspire to reach a district manager position. This position oversees on-site food service operations within a specific geographic region and reports to a regional vice president. One of the primary benefits of a career in this segment is the hours. Typically, food service managers work during the hours of operation for their location. Thus, if a business and industry account operates Monday to Friday, 7:00 A.M. to 6:00 P.M., the management team typically provides breakfast and lunch, and does not have to work late nights and weekends. This structure allows those with a passion for the food service business to have a quality of life also.

Summary

Contract services management allows the ownership and operation of a hospitality venue to be separated. The owner and operator enter into a binding legal contract, which outlines the nature of the relationship and each party's responsibilities. Although hotel management contractors are facing increasing competition, which is affecting their bargaining power, on-site food service organizations are gathering up more of the market. This segment of the hospitality industry offers unique, challenging, and exciting career options, which provide options for hospitality majors

RESOURCES
Internet Sites
Society for Food Service Management: www.sfm-online.org

    This site contains information about the on-site food service management segment of the hospitality industry.

American Hotel and Lodging Association: www.ahla.com

    It is the premier Web site for the lodging industry. This site contains information on professional certifications, career opportunities, conferences, and more.

National Restaurant Association: www.restaurant.org

    It is the premier Web site for the food service industry. This site contains information about professional certifications, career opportunities, current news, and more.

www.hotelresource.com

    This Web site provides a vast amount of resources and information about hotel management companies.

ARAMARK Corporation: www.aramark.com

Compass Group: www.compass-group.com

Sodexho Alliance: www.sodexho.com

ENDNOTES
1. The Hotel Group Website. (2007). http://www.thehotelgroup.com/about_history.asp
2. Hostmark Hospitality Group. (2007). http://www.hostmark.com
3. Eyster, J. (1993, February). The revolution in domestic hotel management contracts. *The Cornell HRA Quarterly,* 16–26.
4. Eyster, J. (1997, June). Hotel management contracts in the U.S. *The Cornell HRA Quarterly,* 21–33.
5. Ibid.
6. Ibid.
7. Ibid.
8. Rainsford, P. (1994, April). Selecting and monitoring hotel-management companies. *The Cornell HRA Quarterly,* 30–35.
9. Reynolds, D. (2003). *On-site foodservice management: A best practices approach.* Hoboken, NJ: Wiley.
10. Ibid.
11. Sodexho Alliance. (2007). *Sodexho profile* at http://www.sodexho.com/group_en/the-group/profile/profile.asp
12. Ibid.
13. Compass Group. (2007). Interim Report at http://static.digitallook.com/digitalcorporate/cms/25/assets/COMPASS_INTERIM_2007.pdf
14. Compass Group. (2007). *About Us* at http://www.compass-group.com/aboutus/
15. Compass Group. (2007). *Markets* at http://www.compass-group.com/aboutus/markets.htm
16. ARAMARK Services, Inc. (2007). *Company Snapshot* at http://www.aramark.com/ContentTemplate.aspx?PostingID=369& ChannelID=203
17. ARAMARK Services, Inc. (2007). *About Us* at http://www.aramark.com/MainLanding.aspx?PostingID=336&ChannelID=187
18. Reynolds, D. (1999, June). Managed services companies: The new scorecard for on-site food service. *The Cornell HRA Quarterly,* 64–73.
19. Ibid.
20. Ibid.
21. Ibid.
22. Ibid.
23. Ibid.
24. Ibid.

Review Questions

1. Define contract management services.

2. What is a hotel management contract?

3. Describe three key provisions of a hotel management contract.

4. What are some of the challenges hotel management contractors face today?

5. What are the two terms used today to describe contract food service management?

6. Describe the market segments in the contract food service management industry.

7. Name the three key contract food service management companies.

8. What are some of the benefits of a career in contract food service management?

Hospitality Trade Associations and Rating Services

Chay Runnels, Stephen F. Austin University

LEARNING OBJECTIVES

- Identify and recognize leading industry associations.
- Define the terms: *Industry association, bylaws, member benefits, rating services.*
- Be able to understand the importance of industry associations.
- Understand the rating systems in the United States.

CHAPTER OUTLINE

KEY TERMS

Bylaws
Hotel ratings system
Industry association
Member benefits

Mission statement
Networking
Restaurant ratings system

What Is an Industry Association?

Industry associations are professional organizations that assist members by providing opportunities for networking, education and training, recognition, and support within a given industry. Some associations are formed for the purpose of promoting a particular industry to the public. For example, originally the Automobile Association of America (AAA) was primarily dedicated to assisting members with their driving plans for vacations. The automobile was the up and coming transportation mode during the 1950s because it was economical to take the whole family for two weeks to see America and visit the family in other states. AAA provided people with rated places to sleep and eat along with attractions that would keep the children in the back entertained when they said, "Are we there yet?"

Other associations are formed to keep members informed about legislative issues that may affect their industry or business. The American Gaming Association (AGA) filled a need to act as liaison between the federal government and the casino industry. With the bad reputation of the gaming industry in the early 1900s, the casinos needed to have a voice in Washington to protect their interests against lobbyists supported by antigambling groups. The AGA helped turn around their image and get information to the people who were voting on the issues. In addition, the National Indian Gaming Association (NIGA) protected the Native American casinos from legislation that would chip away their rights as sovereign nations.

The hospitality industry has many associations that provide members with current information on industry trends while also keeping the general public aware of the industry through marketing and public relations efforts. The National Restaurant Association sends out periodicals each month to keep their members informed on what is happening in the industry. Then to aid their members on learning what is new in the supply side, they have an annual trade show convention in Chicago in May. This is the largest restaurant show in the country designed to allow suppliers to show off their newest product lines, to give workshops on different trends, and to allow industry people to network. The American Hotel and Lodging Association (AH&LA) is also one of the largest in hospitality because it caters to businesses that allow people a place to rest overnight. Members benefit from product and service discounts, training opportunities, in-depth research and information, and a voice in Washington. Typically in November, their trade show and convention meets at the Javits Center in New York City.

Although these two are the largest and broadest associations, there are also many smaller associations that cater to the different segments. Hospitality Sales and Marketing Association International (HSMAI) organizes marketers, while Professional Convention Management Association (PCMA) informs the convention segment of industry. National Society of Minorities in Hospitality (NSMH) segments by diversity and multiculturalism, and the International Hotel and Restaurant Association (IH&RA) combines countries into a global network. To find associations that are relevant to your interests, there is a set of books called the Encyclopedia of Associations, in your library. Every association is listed by name, address, purpose, contact information, number of members, and areas of specialization. One of the volumes is searchable by topics. So, it is easy to find an association that suits your particular needs and interests.

Associations in the hospitality field may be organized on several different levels. Associations may be created to meet the needs of individuals, businesses, and organizations in a certain geographic area. Many communities and cities have specific industry associations for lodging-, food service- and tourism-related organizations. For example, there is the New Orleans Restaurant Association, which is a branch of the National Restaurant Association. This allows members to network and organize projects that are necessary for their city. After 9-11, the New Orleans Restaurant Association began a media campaign to

set aside one night to take someone out to dinner to create awareness that restaurants were failing without customers and tourists. An industry association could be an organization formed by bed and breakfast owners in a community or region. The American Bed and Breakfast Association (ABBA) is a national organization to improve marketing efforts. However, there are also organizations like the California Association of Bed and Breakfast Inns or the Bed and Breakfast Association of Virginia. States also have hospitality and tourism associations that serve the needs of members on a state-wide level.[1] (See Industry Association Profile.)

Large national associations may include not only individual and business members, but also colleges and universities, affiliated industry partners, vendors, institutional members, and student members. These large associations, like the National Tour Association, may have thousands of members. Finally, some industry associations are international. Membership in these global associations is often made up of smaller industry associations from around the world. Many international associations also have national, statewide, or local chapters. These chapters are smaller, affiliated groups that share the same or similar purpose as the "parent" association. The International Council on Hotel, Restaurant and Institutional Education (ICHRIE) is an association of educational hospitality programs around the world. There are states that are grouped together by region in the United States forming federations, and there are international federations that are part of ICHRIE but also operate independently in their own countries. These different regional groups offer special programs to help their students develop research studies as well as networking opportunities.

Determining Member Needs

No matter what the size or scope of membership, almost all industry associations will have governing documents that will include a mission, and/or vision, bylaws, and a board of directors or advisors that oversees the organization.

Industry associations will have a mission—a statement of purpose—that should concisely describe why the association was formed and for what purpose. You should be able to look at an association's mission statement and immediately understand the purpose and scope of the organization. The **mission statement** is developed by the membership or governing board of an organization and often serves as the guide for the activities of the association. Industry associations will also have bylaws that govern the membership, board of directors or advisors, and any paid staff that the organization may employ. **Bylaws** are rules or laws that govern the association's actions and internal operations. Bylaws are typically developed internally by an association and adopted by the membership. With the membership's approval, bylaws may be amended or changed to meet the needs of an association. A **vision statement** is typically an umbrella statement about where the organization sees itself in the context of the industry as a whole. Vision statements tend to be broader in scope than mission statements and may include goals that the association hopes to achieve in the future.

Governing documents like bylaws and mission and vision statements help associations run smoothly. Many smaller industry associations have volunteer or part-time staffs. These associations rely on boards of directors or advisors to guide the organization's activities. Larger industry associations may employee both full- and part-time staff members to assist the association's board and membership in the day-to-day activities of the organization.

Why Join an Industry Association?

Everyone always says networking is important. And it is. But, what does it mean? How do you network? Some students believe that if they become president of the student chapter of the restaurant association that they don't have to do any more than have the name on their resume. However, networking is more than that. It is meeting someone for the first time, exchanging business cards, and getting to know them. Then it is time to follow up. E-mail them a week later to say what a pleasure it was to meet them and how you would like to learn more about what they do and their company. Call them and set up an appointment to talk. Afterward, send them another e-mail thanking them for taking the time to talk to you. Make sure at the next meeting, you say "hello." This is the process for getting to know someone. In this way, people learn who you are, but it is a gradual process, not a one-shot deal. Then once you become friends, you can ask for help finding a job or learning about opportunities in their company, and they will spend the time to ask around. If you are a perfect stranger, why should anyone go out of their way to help? Networking is building relationships.

Why should you join an association? Let me give you a personal example. I used to teach in a large ski school for many years. I did my job and had a lot of fun. Then, it came time for me to look for more responsibility. I didn't know anyone outside my ski school, so I bought a book of ski areas and sent out over 500 letters to people I didn't know. Well, I got back around 20 rejections and wasted a lot of time and effort, but finally managed to get a job. I thought to myself, "There must be a better way." So I joined a number of associations, then volunteered for some committees, and talked to people. People began to know who I was. Then, the next time I wanted a better position, I called five people and within two weeks, I had six interviews and one offer. What made the difference? Networking. My five friends were trusted by a lot of people, and when they vouched for me, people listened. Networking takes time and effort, but it makes life much easier when you need help. Associations provide the contacts, but you must provide the energy.

In today's economic climate, networking and putting forth extra effort may separate you from your fellow soon-to-be graduates. Employers take notice of students who volunteer in the field and go the extra mile to position themselves as "future professionals and colleagues."

Most industry associations provide excellent networking opportunities for members through educational seminars, annual meetings, conventions and conferences. Many industry associations maintain Web sites and are now providing e-mail updates in addition to printed newsletters. Becoming a member of an industry association may also give you a competitive edge in your chosen hospitality career path. Some associations extend **member benefits** to employees whose companies have institutional memberships or are affiliated with the association on some level. Member benefits may include newsletters, updates, and educational opportunities.

Although most industry associations charge annual dues, many are now offering reduced rates for student members or serve as parent organizations for student chapters. By joining a student chapter or joining an organization as a student member, you can gain valuable experience in your given field. First, you are meeting future colleagues who share your interests, and if they are working now, they are potential information sources about jobs and companies. Second, most student chapters invite guest speakers from the industry, so you have the opportunity to meet a professional who cares about helping students, otherwise they wouldn't be there. Third, become a leader. Leaders must interface with industry to get speakers and outside resources for the chapter. This is an excellent way to show your interest, demonstrate your leadership abilities, and network. Fourth, go to parent chapter meetings. Every student chapter has at least one industry liaison who is interested in helping you. Take advantage of that friendship. Have them introduce you around at the meetings. Talk to people about what they do and what kind of company they work for. This allows you the opportunity to learn the industry, meet new friends, and develop contacts. People begin to recognize you as an interested, involved person, not just a student.

When you become a member of an industry association, you are joining a network of professionals. There are many leadership opportunities in industry associations. You may be a chapter officer or hold a statewide position within a larger national association. Some associations have both state and regional annual meetings in addition to larger national meetings. These meetings are opportunities for professionals in the hospitality field to learn about industry trends and share ideas with colleagues. Also, many associations offer certifications in several areas. Although there are years of experience requirements, many associations will waive some years for someone obtaining a degree in the field. Working on a certification allows you to bond with others by studying together and to give you a competitive advantage by having a degree and a certificate from a reputable, national professional organization. The certificate gives you credibility from a practitioners' perspective, and the degree provides you with the theoretical knowledge, internship experience, and many different perspectives on handling the same problem. It is the best of both worlds.

Associations in the Food and Lodging Arena

Because the hospitality industry is so diverse, many associations have been created to meet the needs of professionals in the different arenas. We will take a look at some of the major industry associations for professionals in food and lodging. Remember that many states have their own food and lodging industry associations.

Founded in 1919, the *National Restaurant Association* represents over 60,000 members and over 300,000 restaurant establishments. The organization offers memberships to restaurants, allied industries, educators and students, international companies, and not-for-profit organizations. The National Restaurant Association promotes the restaurant industry and related career paths, promotes dining out, and is committed to food safety in the industry.

With over 65,000 members the *American Dietetic Association* (ADA) promotes healthy lifestyles grounded in good nutrition and well-being. The *American Culinary Federation* (ACF) is the nation's largest organization for professionals working in the culinary arts, including chefs, bakers, and cooks. The ACF sponsors competitions, awards, and educational events for chefs, including a comprehensive certification program for chefs. Both the ADA and ACF have student membership categories. Other important food and nutrition–related industry associations include the *American Association of Wine and Food,* the *International Food Service Executives Association* and the *Catering and Institutional Management Association.*

Professional organizations are also an important part of the lodging industry. The *American Hotel & Lodging Association* (AHLA) promotes the interests of hoteliers throughout the United States and internationally. The AHLA offers student memberships and extensive educational opportunities for members. Other lodging-related organizations include the *International Hotel Association*, the *International Executive Housekeeper's Association,* and the *Hospitality Sales and Marketing Association International.* Each of these organizations sponsors conferences, conventions, and educational opportunities for those interested in the lodging industry.

Associations in the Travel and Tourism Arena

A number of associations in the travel and tourism arena have been organized to serve the needs of tourism professionals. Many of these associations also promote the industry externally by encouraging people to travel and visit destinations. The *Tourism Industry Association of America* (TIA) works with partnering organizations to promote travel within and to the United States. Through press releases, advertisements, and other marketing efforts, TIA encourages travel throughout the country with its "See America" campaign.

The World Tourism Organization (UNWTO/ OMT) is a specialized agency of the United Nations. The organization is a leading international organization in the field of tourism. According to the mission of the UNWTO, the organization "serves as a global forum for tourism policy issues and practical source of tourism know-how."[2] The organization also encourages sustainable and regional tourism worldwide and sponsors tourism-related research internationally. Other tourism industry associations like *Destination Marketing Association International* (DMAI), formerly known as International Association of Convention and Visitor's Bureaus, and the *National Tour Association* (NTA) provide services to members in a very specific segment of the industry. These organizations promote travel and tourism awareness and also encourage travel to the United States. The *Club Managers Association of America* (CMAA), the *Meeting Professionals International* (MPI), and the *American Association of Travel Agents* also are leading tourism-related industry associations that offer networking and educational opportunities to their members. The *Travel and Tourism Research Association* works with educators, tourism marketing professionals, and other industry associations to promote research in the field, provide networking opportunities, and give career information.

As you can see, many hospitality industry associations have been organized to assist professionals in their chosen fields. Joining an industry association could

- Help you develop your professional skills
- Foster a sense of belongingness in a large and diverse industry
- Provide important networking opportunities
- Communicate information about issues, trends, and legislation affecting the industry

In addition to personal and professional development, many associations also recognize industry leaders and innovators and set standards within the hospitality profession. Some industry associations provide mentoring programs and scholarship opportunities for early and midcareer professionals. No matter what part of the industry you are interested in, there is an association for you.

Rating Systems

Just as industry associations set standards for professionals in the hospitality field, **hotel and restaurant ratings systems** also set standards with definite

The American Hotel & Lodging Association promotes the interests of hoteliers throughout the United States and internationally.
© 2011 by Chee-Onn Leong. Used under license of Shutterstock, Inc.

criteria. Although there are no government rating systems of the hotel and restaurant industry in the United States, the American Automobile Association (AAA) and Forbes Travel Guide (formerly Mobil Travel Guide) both provide independent rating services for hotels and restaurants.[3]

AAA and Forbes Travel Guide use professionally trained inspectors to evaluate and rate hotel and restaurant properties based on a system of standards and guidelines. The goal of the ratings system is to provide an indicator for excellence in hospitality. The Forbes Five-Star Award indicates that a dining or lodging experience is one of the best in the country. Properties with this award have been found to consistently provide an unparalleled level of service and quality that distinguishes them from their peers.[4]

While Forbes Travel Guide assigns stars to properties that meet certain criteria, the AAA uses a classification system that awards diamonds to qualifying properties. The Five-Diamond award is the highest award bestowed on a restaurant or hotel by AAA. The AAA inspects over 57,000 properties in the United States, Canada, Mexico and the Caribbean. Less than one-half of one percent of the evaluated properties receive the coveted five-diamond award each year. In 2006, more restaurants were added to the list than hotels, bringing the number of five-diamond ranked properties to 150. According to Michael Petrone, director, AAA Tourism Information Development and head of the AAA Diamond Ratings, this reflects trends seen in the hospitality and tourism industry. It's not surprising to Petrone that "the greatest numbers of Five Diamond restaurants are in areas of high tourism. As a nation, we are becoming more enlightened diners. Consumer demand is resulting in an emerging trend for more high quality dining experiences in our travel and vacations."[5]

Do Ratings Matter?

As the use of the Internet for trip and travel planning increases, more and more Web sites use rating systems to help consumers make decisions on where to stay and where to dine. Some travel agents continue to rely heavily on ratings, whereas others trust their own experience with properties—rated or unrated. When a hotel or restaurant loses a star or diamond or is downgraded from a higher category, it suggests that the service and product have been reduced. "When a hotel's been downgraded, we pay attention," says Walter Littlejohn, president of Teaneck, N.J.–based Great Vacations. "Then we start to look for properties in the same area that are newer or have higher ratings."[6]

How Rating Systems Work

Hotel and restaurant inspectors evaluate properties based on a set of guidelines. The AAA Diamond-Ratings System uses the following criteria for restaurants, for example:

- One-diamond restaurants must meet basic standards for management, quality, and cleanliness. These restaurants tend to have limited service menus and offer food at an economical price.
- Two-diamond restaurants have expanded menus and feature upgraded service and atmosphere. These restaurants are family friendly and may have enhanced or themed décor.
- Three-diamond restaurants employ professional chefs and offer entry-level fine dining. They exhibit a degree of refinement, and there is an emphasis on quality and service.
- Four-diamond restaurants are distinctive and are focused on fine dining. Often expensive,

these restaurants are for those seeking a high-quality experience.
- Five-diamond properties are "world class" and leaders in innovative menu selection and fine service. These properties are distinctive and feature "haute cuisine" and impeccable service.

Summary

Industry associations are professional organizations that assist members by providing opportunities for networking, education and training, and support within a given industry. Associations in the hospitality field may be organized on several different levels: community, statewide, regional, national, or international. They may include only one segment of the industry or encompass the hospitality and tourism industry as a whole. Industry associations will have governing documents that will include a mission, and/or vision, bylaws and a board of directors or advisors that oversees the organization. Hospitality and tourism industry associations are important because they provide a voice for the industry and also provide many benefits to members. Industry associations may also set standards and guidelines for the hospitality industry.

Just as industry associations set standards for professionals in the hospitality field, hotel and restaurant ratings systems also set standards with definite criteria. Although there are no government rating systems of the hotel or restaurant industry in the United States, the American Automobile Association (AAA) and Forbes Travel Guide both provide independent rating services for hotels and restaurants. Forbes Travel Guide assigns stars to properties that meet certain criteria, whereas the AAA uses a classification system that awards diamonds to qualifying properties. Both the AAA and Forbes Travel Guide use professional inspectors to determine what properties will receive star or diamond ratings. The highest awards given by both organizations are highly sought by world-class hotels and restaurants.

RESOURCES

Internet Sites

The National Restaurant Association: http://www.restaurant.org

The American Hotel & Lodging Association: http://www.ahma.org

International Executive Housekeeper's Association: http://www.ieha.org

Hospitality Sales and Marketing Association International: http://www.hsmai.org

Meeting Professionals International: http://www.mpiweb.org

American Society of Travel Agents: http://www.astanet.com

Destination Marketing Association International: http://www.iacvb.org

Tourism Industry Association of America: http://www.tia.org

Travel and Tourism Research Association: http://www.ttra.org

American Automobile Association: http://www.aaa.com

Mobil Travel Guide: http://www.mobiltravelguide.com

ENDNOTES

1. 2006 Hospitality Associations. (2005, December). *Lodging Hospitality,* 16–18.

2. Mission Statement of the United Nations World Tourism Organization. Retrieved January 18, 2008, from http://www. unwto.org/aboutwto/index.php

3. Rowe, M. (2003, December). Lost in translation. Meetingsnet.com, 34.

4. Mobil Travel Guide Announces the 2006 Mobil Five-Star and Four-Star Winners. Retrieved February 21, 2006, from http://rez.mobiltravelguide.com/mtg/template.jsp?id=20413; http://rez.mobiltravelguide.com/mtg/template.jsp?id=2041

5. Graziani, J. (2006, November). AAA names 13 new Five Diamond lodgings, restaurants for 2006. Retrieved January 15, 2006, from http://www.aaanewsroom.net/Main/Default.asp?CategoryID=8&ArticleID=407

6. Webber, S. P. (2000, February). Stargazing. *Travel Agent.* 298. Retrieved February 1, 2006, from the Business Source Premier Database.

7. Personal conversation with Scott Owings, director of Membership, Texas Travel Industry Association, February 21, 2006.

Review Questions

CHAPTER 8

1. What are some of the benefits to joining an industry association in the hospitality or tourism field?

2. How can you determine for what purpose an industry association is formed? What are some of the basic governing documents of an industry association?

3. Explain the process of rating a hotel or restaurant property. What are the oldest, most-respected rating organizations in the United States?

4. If a hotel or restaurant is downgraded in a rating system, travel agents may take notice. Do you think industry ratings matter? Why or why not?

Hospitality Operations

Operations Management

Richard Mills, Robert Morris University
Denis Rudd, Robert Morris University

LEARNING OBJECTIVES

- Identify the importance of operations management.
- Define the role of the manager in the hospitality and tourism industry.
- Discuss the consequence of the recent materialization of management as a field of work and study.
- Show how management is a set of balanced, problem-solving techniques rather than a group of inborn abilities and traits.
- View planning as an organizational process that goes on at all levels.
- Outline the general procedure of staff planning and identify and describe the major tools that are used in that process.
- Examine how service principles play a major role in operations management.

CHAPTER OUTLINE

Understanding Operations Management
    The Managers' Role
    Managing Change
    Basic Qualifications for a Successful Operations
        Manager
Levels of Management
    Top Management
    Middle Management
    Supervisory Management
Implementing Management Functions
    and Services

Planning Service
Organizing Service
Staffing Service
Controlling Service
Leading and Directing in Hospitality
    Management
    Leadership Qualities
    Organizational Success
    Why People Follow the Leader
    Enthusiasm for the Industry
    Developing Your Own Style

KEY TERMS

Conceptual skills
Control
Empowering
Ethics
Interpersonal skills
Labor intensive

Moral development theory
Organizing
Planning
Staffing
Technical skills
Vision

Understanding Operations Management

Students considering a career in hospitality must first understand the management concept. The word *management* has two meanings. First, management is a collective noun to identify those in charge of directing business affairs. Management is a group of persons or individuals who receive their authority and responsibility from ownership or a directive from organizations to oversee the entire operation. Managers use this authority, along with the resources that are supplied from the business, to produce a product or service that creates an operation. Second, management becomes a service. From the sale of products and services, the operation itself becomes an additional product that engages management compensations, employee wages, and dividends paid to owners. Therefore, operations management becomes an act, the job that management does, and the first task at hand is to define exactly what management *does*. Second is to understand how these managerial tasks are learned, applied, and implemented. This defines the different operations that encompass the hospitality industry today. To be successful in the industry, it is imperative that students have a basic understanding of what management actually *performs* and why particular managerial styles, leadership skills, and personal qualities enhance the direction and overall outcome of any operation.

The Managers' Role

There have been many definitions applied to the term management, but the one that seems to get directly to the point is: Management is the process of getting tasks accomplished through people. A manager is a person who is responsible for the work of others, deciding the tasks people should perform, and ultimately how they can accomplish these goals. Managers can accomplish their goals by acquiring skills and knowledge and passing these qualities on to employees. Manning and Curtis (2007) discusses how a manager can improve skills and assign work more effectively.

- **Consider the availability of the employee's time and whether this is the ideal person to do the job.** If the employee's schedule is heavily loaded, explain the priorities of the job. It is important not to overwork the employee because the overworked employee does not know the priority of many assignments, and the underworked employees are wasted or never developed.
- **Use work assignments as a means of developing people.** If a job does not have a deadline, an employee may be *tired* in the task.
- **Know exactly what you want to communicate before giving an order.** This eliminates confusion and encourages confidence in employees. If you are giving a speech to employees, practice it and be concise and clear. Write it down if it is complex to avoid confusion.
- **If many duties or steps are involved in an order, follow oral communication with a note, and keep a copy.** Keeping records of important conferences, orders, and rules can be helpful to keep memos to a minimum, as this practice encourages defensive behavior.
- **Ask rather than tell, but leave no doubt that you expect compliance.** This approach shows both courtesy and respect.
- **Use the correct language for the employee's training level.** Recognize that many people will not understand your words and terms as readily as you do.
- **Make assignments in a logical sequence, using clear and concise language. Break up assignments into easily achieved goals so that everyone understands the process.**
- **Be considerate but never apologetic when asking someone to do a job.**
- **Talk deliberately and authoritatively, Avoid shouting across a room or making an unnecessary show of power.**
- **Take responsibility for the orders you give.**
- **Give people the opportunity to ask questions and express opinions.**
- **Follow up to make sure assignments are being carried out properly, and modify them if the situation warrants.**

Identifying *who management is* may be easier than defining *what management does*. The average employee may not see what management *does*. Supervision, in a service business, is more complex than that in a factory, and for this reason, hospitality supervisors face a unique challenge. Manufactured products and labor are driven by volume and easily visible quality. Service employees work under different conditions. The "product" of their work is not visible or measurable with our five senses. A satisfied guest is the goal of our employees. As a result, the work situation changes from guest to guest and changes with each individual guest. Because we are working with people, mundane tasks are always adapted to suit the new personality or problem a guest has. This keeps the supervisor on their toes because reactions to situations are unpredictable.

Managing Change

Management is a relatively modern institution, and ultimately, it must view the problems of work in an expanding and increasingly wealthy society. This new way of viewing employee productivity has become one of the strongest forces in the last 100 years. Because of the rapid development of technology and the service business, our view of the role of management has changed dramatically. Management responsibilities continue to adapt to the dynamic society in which it operates, and those who aspire to a career in management must be prepared to adjust to these changes.

Management styles change with the fluctuations in society. In colonial times, management was easy: Do as I say or you are fired. Today's managers do not have the same set of goals that were evident in colonial America or the sweatshops in the Industrial Revolution. These rules would be intolerable for today's managers housed in computer-age, air-conditioned, sanitary workplaces. There is a different set of rules for managing today's workers. We've learned that employees are more productive when they are happy and motivated, so the role of management has changed to coaching and facilitating.

Basic Qualifications for a Successful Operations Manager

Technical Skills

Technical skills involve having the knowledge of, and the ability to perform, a particular job or task. One requirement of a competent operations manager is that he/she thoroughly understands the specific, technical aspects of the operation of his/her unit or department.

Manning and Curtis (2007) set forth three levels of managers: *Top managers* set forth the direction of the company by establishing the organization's goals, overall strategy, and operating policy. These individuals officially represent the organization to the external

environment. However, in terms of knowledge, their technical skills are not as important as their conceptual ones. *Middle managers* are responsible for implementing the policies and the plans developed by top management. As a result, they break down the strategies and operating policies into smaller, measurable, objectives that can be delegated to various departments. They also supervise and coordinate the activities of lower-level managers. Depending on the company's entrepreneurial spirit, middle managers can be sources of innovation when given the privilege. Again, middle managers are developing their conceptual skills while still maintaining their technical skills. *Front-line managers* spend a large proportion of their time coordinating, facilitating, and supporting the work of front-line employees. Because they are directly involved with the operation of a department, front-line managers must possess the technical skills and specific know-how of the particular systems they supervise. As part of their responsibilities, they train and direct employees on a daily basis. This includes developing standard operating procedures; using participative management principles: developing effective training, maintaining safety assurance, encouraging personnel to use efficient methods; and motivating men and women to do a better job by stimulating pride in their products and services. For example, it would be difficult for an executive chef to supervise workers in a kitchen without knowledge of culinary arts and kitchen procedures. Similarly, a front office manager in a hotel needs to know the operation of the computer system at the front desk and the procedures for registering a guest. Therefore, although people who are front-line managers need to have excellent technical skills, as one progresses up the managerial ladder, conceptual skills take primary importance.

Judgment

Judgment can be described as having "good sense." Individuals who hope to be qualified leaders must possess the ability to make sound and wise decisions. Sound thinking accompanies creative thinking, innovative brilliance, and invention. Change for the sake of change can be detrimental unless it is balanced with common sense.

Being negative is never a substitute for judgment. If an individual approaches an idea with a negative history, the idea, no matter how creative, may be perceived as one that *will not work*. Enthusiasm and a positive attitude are important talents required of a leader whose judgment and decision-making activities will be tested daily.

Conceptual Skills

The organizational manager must have the ability to conceptualize the company or department as a whole and understand how the different parts work together. This involves technical skills utilized for problem solving, decision making, planning, and organizing. Managers with conceptual skills are able to look at problems from a broad perspective and see them from different points of view. Conceptual skills are important at all levels of management, but they are essential for top managers who make decisions that can dramatically affect the future of the hotel or restaurant company.

Manning and Curtis (2007) discuss conceptual skill as having knowledge about and being able to work with concepts and ideas. As a result, this includes the ability to think abstractly, implement long-range planning, create strategic decision making, and weigh ethical considerations in employee, customer, and government relations. Examples can include a labor relations vice president evaluating a proposed labor agreement or a company president deciding whether to support a community service project

Interpersonal Skills

Interpersonal or human skills include a manager's ability to lead, motivate, and communicate with those around them. The ability to understand people and work well with them on an individual basis and also in groups is usually a developed skill because very few people are innately gifted. It requires focusing on active listening and observing body language. Some say that 70% of communication is through nonverbal behavior. For example, making eye contact with another individual or recognizing facial expression or hand movements are all useful when interacting with others. Another factor in interpersonal skills is being aware of cultural differences. With the diverse workforce of today, it is important to speak other languages as well as recognize that different ethnicities may have different reactions. For example, something as simple as eye gaze can change perceptions. Many cultures like Asians and Hispanics lower their eyes as a sign of respect to people with more status. A typical American might perceive this to be a sign of lying. Because all managers must deal directly with people, and in particular guests, interpersonal skills are essential at all levels of management.

Integrity and a Sense of Ethics

A person's level of morality is imperative and determines whether the leader is respected. An organizational manager must have a set of principles or ethics to enhance interaction with others. Ethics should govern the general behavior of managers and guide them in making business decisions. The quality of one's integrity manifests itself in many ways, but the honesty and sincerity of an effective organizational manager must be unquestionable. This quality applies to *true leaders* and should not be compromised. Operational managers are responsible for the ethical treatment of five different groups of people: customers, employees, suppliers, owners, and the community at large. Ethical behavior means fair and consistent treatment toward members of each of these groups. A personal code of ethics is imperative for a qualified organizational manager to ensure truth, a lack of bias, consistency, and respect when interacting with others. Unethical behavior of a corporation through its managers can result in negative attitudes toward the business by the public. Many times, this results in a drop in profits because the community at large doesn't trust the managers or the products they create.

Levels of Management

It is agreed that all managers carry out the same functions; these functions become less important, relative to the others, as the manager moves up or down the organizational ladder. This shifting emphasis distinguishes the different levels of management. Although the line between the levels is often blurred, management is separated into three levels: *top management, middle management,* or *supervisory management.*

Top Management

Top management includes only a limited number of senior executives within the organization. In small properties, like an individually owned and operated enterprise, the owner-manager is the sole member of top management. But in large corporations or organizations, members of top management usually have titles such as chairman of the board, chief executive officer, chief operating officer, president, or executive vice-president. Top managers determine the direction of the company by recognizing and identifying the basic mission and objectives of the company. They develop goals and established plans for the purpose of reaching the company's overall objectives or operational outcomes. Top managers possess conceptual skills and are responsible for strategic planning and decision making.

Middle Management

In middle management, the department heads, perhaps 2 to 20, are next highest in responsibility. Several titles are frequently used for middle managers in the hospitality industry: regional director, general manager, rooms division manager, and food and beverage director. Although this group is larger in number than top management, there are still fewer middle managers than supervisory managers. Middle managers have relational skills and coordinate and plan implementation.

Supervisory Management

The line supervisor, who is the first manager up the managerial ladder and the last one down, is the most difficult to identify as management. Typical titles of supervisory managers are front office manager, executive housekeeper, or restaurant manager. Supervisory managers implement the goals and plans of the organization by directing work of the line-level employees, who provide guests with products and services. They are closer to the operative employees than they are to other managers. In many instances, they have earned their promotions because of excellent operative skills. The ambiguity of who they are is reinforced by the lack of management title. This manager may be considered first-level management and demonstrate technical skills and implementation.

Different managers rely on different skills: the sales manager is expected to be more outgoing; a good server may become a host; a skillful bartender may be promoted to chief or head bartender; and a room attendant may become the floor inspector. Different managerial positions call on different elements of the personal and professional package that each individual brings to the position or job.

Implementing Management Functions and Services

Planning Service

Planning is based on the establishment of goals and objectives. Thus, management must decide how to accomplish these goals. Planning is often referred to as the primary management function, and the result of inadequate planning is chaos. Successful companies train at all management levels to ensure successful goals.

Successful service is best achieved through careful planning with a vision of the customers and the end result. The service vision is defined by the results produced for the customers. Kandampully suggests the following:

1. The core service (or services) it proposes to offer to the customer;
2. The facilitating and supporting services it proposes to offer to the customer;
3. How the basic package is to be made accessible to the customer;
4. How customer interactions are to be developed; and
5. How customers are to participate in the process. (Kandampully, 2007)

Organizing Service

Managers must determine what activities are to be done and how employees are grouped to accomplish specific tasks. Reservations, housekeeping, or maintenance are examples of how groups of individuals are organized to perform a specific task. In addition, at a higher level, many large hotel companies are divided into several divisions, according to the geographic location of their property or the product or service they provide.

Operational functions are an integral part of the organizing process. Many service organizations go to the trouble of guaranteeing its service offering. It is important to actually guarantee a service and not use the "guarantee" as a marketing tool. There are several levels of guaranteed options, and it is imperative that management enforce the guarantees. Customers expect a promise to mean something and contain real value. If management is cautious, guarantees will not reach beyond the capabilities of enforcement; they will be easy to enforce and fulfill. There are several benefits of guarantees:

1. They will encourage sales;
2. Enhance customer feedback;
3. Improve service delivery-systems;
4. Identify fail points;
5. Increase customer satisfaction;
6. Improve employee performance;
7. Develop a general service-oriented culture; and
8. Maintain competiveness in the marketplace. (Kandampully, 2007)

The staff is the front line of every hotel. © 2011 by Norman Pogson. Used under license of Shutterstock, Inc.

Staffing Service

Staffing is the process employed to service guests at a lodging, food or beverage, or tourism establishment. Managers involved with staffing have several responsibilities: They determine the number and type of employees needed; they recruit and select employees; and they develop and implement training programs. In addition, they must determine compensation and benefits received by employees.

The staff is the front line of every hotel, restaurant, or other hospitality industry. The first person the customer sees often determines the value of the establishment and what the customer expects. The attitudes, emotional behavior, and general appearance gives a real sense of the behavior of the entire organization. The staff must show the quality and integrity of the establishment; this is evident in grooming, hygiene, and overall appearance. Some managers may have difficulty critiquing employees on such a personal level, but it is important for the entire establishment to do so.

Controlling Service

Controlling is the process of comparing the performance of employees in a workforce to the objectives and goals that have been set by the company. The purpose of any control system is to ensure that the company is headed in the right direction and is capable of making corrections when necessary. There are three distinct types of control: *preliminary controls* take place before an event occurs, such as the planning of a major banquet; *concurrent controls* take place during an actual event, such as a server's responsibility;

and *postactional controls* take place after an event has taken place, as when a general manager reviews a monthly "profit and loss" statement for a hotel.

Mangers are also responsible for internal service employee controls. For example, safety is a manger's responsibility, and safety features must be built in to the control of the staff. Instructions are included in employee training sessions for the purpose of providing a healthy and safe environment for the staff. Several controls are necessary for the establishment to follow so they can acquire insurance protection. These include health and safety regulations provided by the state in which they operate. Without these health and safety enforcements, the operation will lose its license to operate in that state. One such regulation is that governing the service of alcoholic beverages and enforcing the laws established in the state of operation.

Leading and Directing in Hospitality Management

Leadership Qualities

An organizational manager must instill and influence others for the purpose of channeling their activities toward assisting the hotel or restaurant's goals. Leadership can be viewed as having two separate components or elements: success and effectiveness. A successful leader demonstrates a quality that followers want to emulate; an effective leader instills a desire to follow in the same direction. Leadership may be defined in several ways. Often these qualities consist of the leader, the group, and the situation. Leadership is a *personal* and a *human* experience, as animals and computers cannot lead. Leadership is both an *art* and a *science* and is subjective in nature. There are fundamentals of leadership that can be learned and are based on research and observation. Leadership is *active,* as leaders must do something; leadership is one element of a three-part dynamic; the leader, the group, and the situation are always in *interaction* and tension with one another.

Organizational Success

Organizational success requires a leader to have many qualities, but perhaps the most important is *vision.* Management author Peter Drucker once said, "The best way to predict the future is to create it." Drucker's difference begins with a vision for change; this creativity may be one of the most important ingredients a leader possesses. A vision alone will not ensure success; there are five necessary components for organizational success: vision, skills, incentives, resources, and an action plan. When all five are present, organizational success is achieved. If any one is removed, the end result will change.

- Vision + Skills + Incentives + Resources + Action Plan = Organizational Success
- (remove Vision) Skills + Incentives + Resources + Action Plan = Confusion
- Vision (remove Skills) + Incentives + Resources + Action Plan = Anxiety
- Vision + Skills (remove Incentives) + Resources + Action Plan = Gradual change
- Vision + Skills + Incentives (remove Resources) + Action Plan = Frustration
- Vision + Skills + Incentives + Resources (remove Action Plan) = False Starts.

The word *vision* suggests a future orientation and implies a standard of excellence or virtuous condition and has the quality of uniqueness. Vision is an ideal image of what could and should be. The leader must ask three questions to test his or her vision: (1) Is this the best direction? (2) Are these the most productive goals to reach my projected end? (3) Is this the best time? Once the decision is made, the leader must share this vision and have it supported by others who are involved in the project. A leader must (1) take responsibility for initiating change; (2) create a vision and strategy for the organization; and (3) trust and support others.

Why People Follow the Leader

People enter an organization and perform their work for various reasons. They follow the leader of the organization for the purpose of being financially and socially successful. The most basic reason that people work is to provide themselves and their independents with food, shelter, and clothing. This is often identified as a *selfish* reason for working. In contrast, there is a more positive motive for *following the leader.* This is most evident when people seek work for societal goals. Making enough money to achieve both needs and wants supports the aspirations of the worker. Personal satisfaction is therefore necessary for individuals to pursue work. Through hard work and diligence, one is rewarded with independence, encouragement, praise, and recognition.

Followers must freely accept the efforts of the leader for leadership to occur. Followers must

A successful manager is confident and enthusiastic. © *2011 by Francesco Ridolfi. Used under license of Shutterstock, Inc.*

voluntarily align their will with that of the leader. A leader must manifest good qualities without threats of discipline or punishment for followers to function within their own free will. It is only when followers make a true choice to follow the leader that true leadership occurs.

Enthusiasm for the Industry

An enthusiasm for the industry is often identified as having the business "in their blood." For the purpose of developing a desire to work in this industry, it may be necessary to have a passion for the business. Leaders are the best "cheerleaders" for their organization and their people. They display enthusiasm or passion and instill it in others. They possess poise, stability, clear vision, and articulate speech. Their enthusiasm is often described as *infectious* and motivates workers that are in their presence.

Successful managers are confident that their abilities are up to the task of their actions and are able to gain the trust and support of workers. A manager must first be enthusiastic, with a passion for the position, and second the manager should be confident. It is obvious when these qualities are displayed; self-confidence helps the manager adjust to the ever-changing direction of the industry.

Developing Your Own Style

We are impressed and often amazed with the ability of certain managers and their leadership style. All are unique, and top managers are uncommonly different; they are extraordinary people who can adjust from one role to another without losing momentum or hesitation in thought or action. The roles of managers may also reflect the styles of the managers. A leader possesses standards and values within the organizational culture. The manager is responsible for what happens in the organization in such areas as personnel choices, marketing, financial, and public affairs decisions. The manager is the chief tactician, strategist, spokesperson, negotiator, observer, and the one who ultimately represents the organization beyond whom decisions do not pass without a final determination.

RESOURCES

Internet Sites

Hospitality Operations Management—Hotel Lodging Operations HEI: www.heihotels.com/operations/leadership.cfm

Baldridge National Quality Program: http://www.quality.nist.gov/

Center for the Study of Work Teams: http://www.workteams.unt.edu/

Creative Learning: http://www.creativelearningcentre.com/default.asp

REFERENCES

Brymer, Robert A. *Hospitality & Tourism,* 11th ed. Dubuque, IA: Kendall/Hunt Publishing, 1977.

Fisher, William P., & Muller, Christopher C. *Four-Dimensional Leadership.* Upper Saddle River, NJ: Pearson/Prentice Hall, 2005.

Kandampully, J. *Service Management the New Paradigm in Hospitality.* Upper Saddle River, NJ: Pearson/Prentice Hall, 2005.

Manning, George, & Curtis, Kent. *The Art of Leadership.* New York: McGraw-Hill, 2007.

Nykiel, Ronald A. *Hospitality Management Strategies.* Upper Saddle River, NJ: Pearson/Prentice Hall, 2005.

Powers, Thomas F. *Introduction to Management in the Hospitality Industry,* 2nd ed. NewYork: John Wiley & Sons, 1979.

Powers, Tom, and Barrows, Clayton W. *Management in the Hospitality Industry,* 8th ed. Hoboken, NJ: John Wiley & Sons, 2006.

Vallen, Jerome J., & Abbey, James R. *The Art and Science of Hospitality Management.* East Lansing, MI: The Educational Institute of the American Hotel & Motel Association, 1987.

Review Questions

1. What is the author's definition of management?

2. What do managers do within operations?

3. What is the difference between management and operations?

4. How has management changed historically?

5. List the basic qualifications for a successful operations manager.

6. Define technical skills as a management function.

7. Define judgment as a management function.

8. Define conceptual skills as a management function.

9. Define interpersonal skills as a management function.

10. What five groups should managers be concerned with when ethics is applied?

11. What are the three traditional levels of management?

12. What are the primary duties of top management?

13. What are the primary duties of middle management?

14. What are the primary duties of supervisory management?

15. What are the four functions of operations management?

16. Define planning as a management function.

17. Define organizing as a management function.

18. Define staffing as a management function.

19. Define controlling as a management function.

20. List some basic leadership qualities that operations managers should be concerned with.

21. List some basic reasons why people follow. And what role does leadership play?

22. From the authors' perspective why is enthusiasm for the industry important?

23. What is meant by developing your own style?

24. What are Kohlberg's three levels of moral behavior development?

25. What are some future concerns for operations managers?

26. What five key ingredients are needed for leaders with a vision?

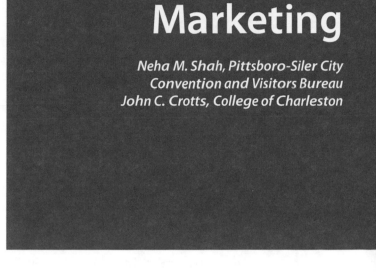
Marketing

Neha M. Shah, Pittsboro-Siler City
Convention and Visitors Bureau
John C. Crotts, College of Charleston

LEARNING OBJECTIVES

- To be able to recognize the various factors influencing supply and demand.
- To have a working knowledge of the marketing mix, traditional and the additions.
- To understand the hospitality marketing system, plus the marketing messages and means of delivery.
- To be able to recognize the lodging facility segments and organizational structure.

CHAPTER OUTLINE

Consider for a moment: The family who vacations at a resort for a week then returns home and raves about the experience to their friends; the association meeting planner who has just finished a successful convention; and the restaurant manager of a fine Italian bistro who has just opened a new account with a food wholesaler. At one time, all three of these satisfied customers were no more than a lead or prospect. In each case, someone in the marketing and sales department for the resort and/or destination marketing organization (DMO), the convention hotel, and the food wholesaler did something right in gaining these buyers' attention and winning their business.

Make no mistake, the hospitality and tourism industry is competitive, and customers have a tremendous amount of choice regarding with whom they do business. It takes more for a firm to be successful than to simply put an *open for business* sign in the window. It takes effective marketing and sales efforts to create the level of awareness, interest, desire, and ultimately action (AIDA for short) on the part of consumers to make a profitable and viable business.

The goal of all organizations is to create and retain satisfied, profitable customers. This is true whether or not the organization is a tourism destination, a national hotel property, a restaurant, or for that matter, an owner-operated hospitality or tourism enterprise. For example, a hotel (which has supply) wants to sell rooms and other services to guests (who provide demand) at rates that both satisfy the guest and produce a fair profit. Bringing supply and demand together to make a profit is essential for any organization. Doing it in such a way that creates satisfied loyal customers is the key to long-term profitability. This chapter follows a framework that presents *marketing* and *sales* as an active *relationship development process* that links hospitality *supply* and *demand* in such a way that it creates *repeat patronage* and *positive word-of-mouth* (customer referrals).

The Marketing Mix

In today's marketplace, enterprises not in step with changing consumer demands are quickly replaced by companies that understand their customers.

Consumers' needs, tastes, and preferences are constantly evolving, and it's ultimately consumers who determine which hospitality and tourism products succeed. Only those businesses and destinations that can identify consumer needs and fulfill them more effectively than others in the marketplace will flourish. Success is accomplished, in part, through a mix of marketing inducements designed by the marketing and sales department to create and keep customers.

Operators of hospitality enterprises must develop a marketing strategy that will influence consumers to buy their products and services. In a single competitive environment it is not surprising to find several unique approaches to the task. Some managers believe that the only condition needed to make a sale is to deliver a quality product or service. An example of this product-approach to marketing is the restaurant owner whose primary concern is the quality of the guest experience (e.g., food, presentation, service, and ambiance). By maintaining and improving the guest's experience in terms of the owner's own taste and preferences, the product becomes positioned in the marketplace. The approach can be successful if what the restaurant offers fits consumers' tastes. However, when customer tastes change or increased competition occurs, this approach becomes a recipe for failure.

Another owner focuses his/her marketing efforts on advertising and promoting the restaurant in the marketplace. Because the restaurant's key measure of success is return on investment, investing in advertising and promotional campaigns designed to reach and influence potential customers appears logical. Over the past decade, numerous studies have reported the sources of information consumers are using in their decision making. In virtually every case, previous experience and word of mouth (recommendations from friends and relatives) have far and away dominated the response. Travel blogs such as TripAdvisor and Raveable.com are also a source of recommendations from past guests that many travelers use. Assuming that guest satisfaction contributes to both repeat patronage and positive word of mouth, perhaps the owner should find equilibrium between promoting the restaurant and ensuring a quality guest experience to best serve the restaurant's organizational goals.

It's not that either a product or promotional approach is wrong, but that it's only partly right. It is necessary that the product or service offered be of value. Only when customers begin to recognize the value of a product or service and begin buying it will you be in business. It's also necessary that the product or service is promoted effectively. Without information, the consumer cannot act; without promotions, the marketer cannot sell. However, even a combined product and promotional approach is considered insufficient in today's competitive environment. One must recognize that a successful marketing mix, like a recipe, is a blending of several ingredients to reach and satisfy customers at a profit.

The key to understanding the concept of the marketing mix is that it's a carefully developed reasoning process that is built solely around the consumer. By reasoning from the consumers' perspective, a marketing and sales manager can prepare a recipe for success (a mix of inducements to buy) that fits the needs and preferences of the target market more so than the competition does. The elements of this mix are traditionally referred to as the 4Ps: product, place, price, and promotion.

1. Design or offer a *product* (good or service) that consumers want.
2. Offer the product in a *place* (both location and channel of distribution) that is both convenient and available to the consumer.
3. *Price* the product in terms of its value to the consumer and the price of competitors.
4. *Promote* the offering to potential customers through appropriate and cost-effective activities (advertising, sales, Internet, social media, and other forms of communication channels).

Leading hospitality and tourism enterprises have added additional "Ps" to include in the marketing mix. Some of these are

1. Focus on the satisfaction of one's *personnel,* sometimes referred to as an organization's internal customers. As J. W. Marriott once said, "You can't make happy guests with unhappy employees." Likewise, Hal Rosenbluth advocates a philosophy that the "customer comes second," suggesting that satisfied frontline travel agents ultimately translate into satisfied Rosenbluth Travel clients. Both quotes illustrate the connection between employee satisfaction, customer satisfaction, and corporate profits.
2. Provide *physical cues* that offer an inviting atmosphere to guests and an indication of

the quality and experience they can expect to receive.

3. Use *packaging* that increases customer value through the bundling of multiple products and services (e.g., getaway packages that combine lodging, food and beverage, spa packages).

4. Develop *partnerships* and strategic alliances with other firms designed to creatively find ways to produce more value by effectively working with one another (e.g., airline/lodging frequent traveler programs).

It is important to remind ourselves that the 4Ps (or expanded marketing mix variables for that matter) are by themselves insufficient to ensure a firm's long-term profitability. Profitability hinges more on the ability to *retain* customers than to create new ones. Influencing a customer to make a first-time purchase through price and promotions is an expensive process. The most important customer contacts, from a marketing success point of view, are the ones outside the realm of the 4Ps and the marketing specialists. The concept of relationship marketing, adopted by many of today's leading hospitality and tourism firms, has expanded the marketing concept to a wider context where everyone in the organization has a marketing role in fulfilling promises that have been made to the visitor or guest. As such, some employees take on full-time marketing roles (e.g., marketing and sales staff), whereas those in operations assume a part-time marketing role.

Today, social networking tools reinforce the active relationship development process, and the results can include success through positive word-of-mouth referrals. Social networking tools such as Facebook, Twitter, LinkedIn and blogs are all active and continuous efforts that build excitement and brand loyalty. The interactive communication with customers can result in restaurant patrons providing valuable information in terms of feedback on a menu item or filling the restaurant with last-minute reservations if business is slower than expected.

The key concepts that we can take away from this discussion are that marketing is (1) a carefully designed strategy composed of marketing inducements intended to create and retain profitable customers, (2) a customer relationship development process that is influenced by everyone in the organization, and (3) a process that must be actively managed, often by those assigned full-time marketing and sales responsibilities.

Social networking tools help build or break excitement and brand loyalty. © 2011 by AVAVA. Used under license of Shutterstock, Inc.

Let's now look at how these ingredients of the marketing mix are used in the hospitality and tourism industry by marketing and sales professionals.

The Hospitality Marketing System

Marketing managers have several alternative ways in which to deliver their message to consumers.

1. Their direct sales force can reach potential customers *directly* through personal interactions and increasingly through technologies, such as the Internet (via Web site, social networking).

2. Their sales force can reach potential customers *indirectly* by marketing through wholesale intermediaries (such as tour operators or independent meeting planners), who might, in turn, sell to retail travel agencies, who then sell to the final customer.

3. They can reach potential customers *impersonally* through marketing promotional tools such as advertising and public relations.

Let's more closely examine the lodging sector because arguably it has the most developed marketing system in the hospitality industry. First, we will examine the nature of *demand* because demand is the determining factor of *supply.* Second, we will examine the nature of *supply.*

Lodging Facility Market Demand and Segments

Different types of hotels are designed and created to be responsive to different travelers' preferences and needs. For example, people traveling for the purposes of pleasure and driving across the United States on the interstate system need a clean, easily accessible place to spend the night. Services such as meeting rooms are not needed; consequently, limited-service hotels are usually found along these highways. On the other hand, organizations that have groups of people who need to hold meetings need other types of properties. They, for example, may need a large downtown convention hotel that offers many meeting rooms and specialized services for group meetings.

Demand for a lodging product is commonly *segmented* according to the purpose of travel: for pleasure or for business. In addition, business or pleasure travel takes place in groups or through individual travel. This creates four segments: (a) business groups, (b) business individuals, (c) pleasure groups, and (d) pleasure individuals. As a general rule, when marketing to *groups,* a sales force is the primary source of leads. When marketing to *individuals,* advertising and other nonpersonal promotional media are used to attract the segment.

Business/Organizational Segment

This segment is composed of demand from businesses and organizations of all types. Group demand comes from corporations, associations, social groups, educational groups, government groups, religious groups, and so on. Individual demand comes from individual members of these businesses and organizations who are traveling for business purposes.

Groups

Groups attending meetings and conventions are a large source of business for the lodging industry. Group sizes may range from 10 attendees (typically the minimum party size to be considered a group) to groups of thousands. On average, groups occupy hotel rooms for an average of three nights. Groups in the business/organization segment meet for a variety of reasons, including training; management development; executive and board of director retreats; national and regional sales conferences; and international,

national, regional, and state association conventions. They select meeting sites based on the facilities' ability to satisfy the purposes of these meetings.

Individual attendees do not select the lodging facility where these meetings will be held; thus, the lodging facility's sales force must identify and work through group decision makers. These include organizational executives or intermediaries such as independent meeting planners and sometimes travel agencies.

Individuals

Individuals traveling for business purposes make up a large portion of lodging industry revenues. In addition to having the potential for frequent repeat business, they are easier to identify and reach than pleasure travelers. Thus, lodging facility sales forces are able to contact the organizations from which these travelers depart and/or the local organizations where they will visit to offer accommodations and services. Most lodging facilities have at least one salesperson specializing in obtaining this type of business. In addition, advertising may be heavily used to attract this group. In addition to the lodging facility sales staff, DMOs are often contacted by the individuals or are reached by the DMOs.

Pleasure/Recreational/Personal Segment

The pleasure/recreational/personal traveler is motivated to travel by four primary factors: physical, cultural, interpersonal, and status and prestige. They choose to reach their objectives by traveling in groups or essentially alone.

Groups

The pleasure/recreation/personal segment is motivated to take trips and does so in a group form known as a tour package. Tours became an important travel segment following World War II and have expanded rapidly since 1960. Tours are put together by knowledgeable tour wholesalers and offer the traveler the advantage of security and greater affordability. These wholesalers generally offer vacation packages to the traveling public at prices lower than individual travelers would be able to arrange by themselves. Wholesalers buy travel services such as transportation, hotel rooms, sightseeing services, airport transfers (ground transportation), and meals in large quantities at discounted prices, then package the components, add a markup, and resell this package to a group of individual travelers. All retail travel agencies offer packages for sale ranging from traditional trips through the United States and Europe to exotic packaged tours to the rain forests of the Amazon.

Individuals

Individual pleasure travelers are willing to travel alone or with close companions. They do not usually require the services of a group tour operator. They are willing to contact directly, today commonly through the Internet, or through their preferred online travel agent, the specific travel suppliers needed.

As mentioned earlier, supply in the lodging industry is determined by the nature of demand. For example, group business travelers may require a convention hotel, whereas an individual pleasure traveler may require a limited-service lodging facility. A variety of hotel segments have been created to specifically match specific customer (demand) needs. Marketing and sales organizations in each of these various types of facilities will also vary.

Organizing for Marketing and Sales

Hotel chains at the national level maintain a centralized marketing office and a national sales force. Depending on the individual hotel property size and mix of market segments that they want to attract, the marketing and sales department will vary greatly. For example, in a large property (250 or more rooms) that obtains its revenue primarily from groups (50% to 75% of its revenue), you might expect to see a well-staffed and well-developed marketing and sales department. On the other hand, a limited service property may have one or no salesperson on staff with the general manager also serving as a marketing manager with support of a regional or national marketing office.

In a convention hotel obtaining 70% of its revenue from group business, marketing serves as a support for sales, where salespeople need marketing positioning and awareness to assist them in making sales. The 30% of individual travelers coming to this hotel would primarily be attracted by marketing activities as opposed to sales activities. While modern marketing attempts to create relationships between the organization and all customers, the sales staff focuses on creating relationships on a one-to-one basis with the organizational buyer (groups).

A sales force is the most expensive marketing and sales channel and therefore should not be used indiscriminately "chasing" all potential business. Instead, marketing managers need to be more selective in their use of salespeople, utilizing them solely for those customer accounts (a) large enough to justify the salesperson's costs and (b) sufficiently complex (a large group meeting is complex) that the customer cannot be handled by lower cost alternatives.

Examples of lower cost promotional alternatives include

- **Advertising**—paid, ongoing, nonpersonal communications designed to inform the consumer of the product or service in such media as newspapers, magazines, television, internet, and direct mail.
- **Promotions**—short-term inducements such as discount coupons or drawings for free prizes designed to influence nonusers to purchase the product or service in hopes that they will make repeated purchases in the future.
- **Publicity**—unpaid communication about the firm or its products in the mass media. Favorable publicity is attained by gaining the attention of news editors of newspapers, magazines, television, and radio who are always looking for stories that provide entertainment value to

Indirect marketing teams focus efforts on companies, such as tour services, who provide end contact for companies. © 2011 by egd. Used under license of Shutterstock, Inc.

their audience. Again, social networking tools like Facebook can provide positive coverage and reach different audiences and/or create new markets.

The lesson to be learned from this discussion is that the marketing and sales manager has available a number of promotional tools. Each should be used where they can produce awareness, interest, desire, and ultimately action on the part of the target market. However, costs and return on investment will influence the promotional mix to be employed.

Summary

The marketing and sales manager is a kind of a cook who is continually experimenting with new blends and new kinds of ingredients to yield the highest return on investment from his/her inventory. The manager hopes ultimately to produce the highest amount of revenue by filling the hotel or the airline, etc., with the best mix of customers based on the customer's willingness to pay.

Hospitality and tourism marketing and sales is a rewarding and challenging field. The marketing career ladder often begins in sales, and graduates will find sales positions are more abundant than marketing positions. Often students in their part-time jobs as waitstaff, front desk attendants, or any other customer contact position find their work helps to develop sales skills that will prepare them well for a professional sales and marketing career (e.g., order taking, up selling). What is needed is training that can take them to the next level of demand creators. Even those careers that are not entirely sales positions have an indirect element of sales skills necessary for success.

Marketing and sales professionals as demand creators must master their skills in market research, segmentation, targeting, and positioning. We also know that to be successful, one must possess strong people skills. Research has shown us that what buyers want in a marketing and sales professional is someone who:

- Is polite, efficient, and respectful of the buyer's time, needs, requests, and opinions.
- Has an in-depth knowledge of his/her own products and its capabilities.

- Has an in-depth knowledge of the customer's industry.
- Represents a product or service that is consistent in quality.
- Is honest and keeps promises.

Brief Case Study: Marketing Destinations

Situation

The rural town of Circle City is in the middle of the state, in the heartland. The destination marketing organization (DMO) director, Sandy Baker, strongly believes the town is a great place to visit, with a quaint historic downtown area filled with boutiques and eateries, all family owned and operated. The town is home to a fine resort and several inns, plus a lake and some historic buildings. Sandy isn't sure why, if they have something for everyone, some travelers aren't visiting and instead going to the neighboring big cities.

Challenges

- Small town surrounded by larger towns
- One resort that offers a lot of great dining and shopping but no spa or golf course on-site
- Visitors opting for big cities instead of this town

Actions

- The DMO director talked with the local day spa to see whether they could offer treatments for a special price to the resort guests or create a package weekend getaway.
- The DMO director had the same discussions with the golf course as she did with the spa.
- The DMO promoted the town as a slower-paced escape from the hustle of city life, yet with all the conveniences and luxuries of a true vacation.
- The DMO director and resort found a local transportation company to take care of getting resort guests to and from the spa and golf course.
- The resort included information about the spa and golf getaways in the monthly e-newsletter.
- One of the resort employees started blogging about the new packages available.
- The DMO and resort jointly placed an ad in the state magazine and contracted advertising for six months, with two different ads appearing alternate months.

Results

- The blog caught the attention of another blogger because it offered last-minute and online codes for special package discounts during the week.
- The resort blogger got a request for use of his pictures by a regional magazine, and the magazine editor wrote a story about the package getaways and their value for vacationers.
- The resort decided to create a Facebook page where guests could post vacation pictures
- Guests who visited the resort posted their opinions about their visit on TripAdvisor and gave feedback about the spa and golf course.
- Some of the other local businesses contacted the DMO to see whether they could create packages, even just for sightseeing for the day and offer day trips to those staying overnight in big cities but might be interested in an outing in the countryside.

What Aspects of the Marketing Mix Were Employed in the Actions? Results?

Product (service) that consumers want—Spa and golf packages.

Place, physical cues—A country getaway, escape from the city and the transportation in town from the resort to spa and golf.

Promote—Blog, TripAdvisor.

Personnel—Blogger was staff member.

Packaging, Price—Package deal for an overnight stay plus golf round or spa treatment and transportation. Bloggers posted the special package discounts during the week.

Partnerships—Resort and DMO worked together to create and promote package. Resort worked with local spa and golf course businesses. DMO contacted by additional local businesses for packages.

RESOURCES

References

Grönroos, C. (1989). Defining marketing: A market-oriented approach. *European Journal of Marketing, 23*(1), 52–60.

McNeil, R., & Crotts, J. (2005). *Selling hospitality: A situational approach.* New York: Delmar/Thompson Learning.

Crotts, J., Mason, P., & Davis, B. (2009). Measuring guest satisfaction and competitive position: An application of stance shift analysis of blog narratives. *Journal of Travel Research, 48*(3), 139–151.

Review Questions

1. What is described by the acronym AIDA? Who or what is being targeted?

2. Discuss the concept of supply and demand. Why is this especially important in hospitality and tourism?

3. Who or what is the primary target of a marketing mix?

4. Marketing is considered a relationship development process. Why? Explain fully.

5. What impact is social networking having on marketing departments within hospitality and tourism organizations?

6. Briefly describe each of the primary lodging demand segments:

    a. Business Groups

    b. Business Individuals

    c. Pleasure Groups

    d. Pleasure Individuals

Managing Revenue and Expenses

Daniel Bernstein, Seton Hill University

LEARNING OBJECTIVES

- To learn how income is evaluated in a hotel and restaurant.
- To be able to calculate and use the ratios that are used for success in the hotel and restaurant industry.
- To learn how to maximize income through selling.
- To learn how to control costs in the hotel and restaurant industry.

CHAPTER OUTLINE

Revenue in the Hotel Industry
Revenue in the Restaurant Industry
Maximizing Revenue through Selling
Controlling Costs in the Hotel Industry
Controlling Costs in the Restaurant Industry
Summary

KEY TERMS

AP (As Purchased)	Independent	Prime cost
ADR (Average Daily Rate)	Intangibility	Top-down approach
Cost control	Labor cost	Units
Discounting	Occupancy percentage	Up selling
EP (Edible Portion)	Perishability	Volume purchasing
Energy management	Portion control	Yield management
Food cost	POS (point of sale)	

The two main ingredients in making a profit are increasing revenue and lowering costs. A company may often appear to be profitable because they have a high revenue stream. However, failure to control costs may actually cause the company to lose money and eventually go out of business. This chapter will introduce different types of revenue in the hotel and restaurant industry and introduce means of utilizing cost control. Because of the unique nature of this industry, different formulas for measuring hotel and restaurant revenue are used.

Revenue in the Hotel Industry

It is important for students to understand that in reality, most of the everyday tasks completed by managers are done for the financial well-being of the firm. Specifically, most hospitality managers increase shareholder value by decreasing expenses and increasing revenues. A manager who is not concerned with the success of the company, will not likely be employed for too long.

There are various means of measuring revenue in the hotel industry, so managers can assess how successful they are. Before one measures their success, they must have a working knowledge of expectations. While, of course, hotel managers would like to sell out every room, every night, this is not always possible. Many factors can affect hotel occupancy over which the hotel manager may have very little or no control. These factors are often external forces, such as seasonality (demand for warm weather climates in winter places) and competition (new businesses in the market). These external factors may adversely affect hotel occupancy, and therefore a manager must carefully plan to overcome these problems.

To aid in the strategic plan, three tools for measuring revenue are occupancy percentage, average daily rate, and yield management.

Occupancy percentage is a ratio relating the number of rooms sold to the number of rooms available. How does a hotel manager know if their hotel is running at an acceptable occupancy percentage? Numerous factors affect determining an acceptable occupancy percentage.

What if you work for an **independent** hotel without any franchise or chain affiliation, without any specific guidelines about expected occupancy percentages of your hotel? You could find out percentages of comparable hotels in your area. Another way of estimating your occupancy percentage would be looking at a daily audit report, which will include occupancy percentage and average daily rate. When comparing occupancy percentage from past records, it is important to know what to compare. If you want to know how well your hotel will do for December 15th this year, you may assume that you should look at December 15th of last year. But that would not be accurate. December 15th of this year and December 15th of last year were on different days of the week. Hotel occupancy percentage often fluctuates by days of the week. Often business hotels have higher occupancy percentages on weekends, whereas resort hotels tend to be the opposite. So, if you want to estimate how well your hotel will do for December 15th this year, you should compare by the days of the week. If December 15th was on a Thursday this year you would compare it to the third Thursday in December

last year. The only time you would compare the same date from year to year would be holidays such as Christmas, which is always on December 25. In this case, the day of the week is of little significance compared to the actual date.

Another calculation that the hotel manager should look at in reference to occupancy is how many guests are in each room. Some hotels charge more for two guests in a room than for a single guest in a room. The reason for this is that hotels will have additional expenses for the possible use of another bed, length of time for a housekeeper to clean a room, and additional utility expenses because of an additional guest in the room. Also some hotels offer a free continental breakfast, which is an additional expense for each guest staying at the hotel.

The second measurement of hotel revenue is **average daily rate** (ADR). The ADR is computed by dividing room revenue by the number of rooms occupied. This formula is necessary when you sell rooms for more than one rate, which is often the case with most hotels. This is how managers measure how well they are maximizing revenue through double occupancy and through the selling of more expensive rooms. If the most expensive rooms are $250 per night and the lowest priced rooms are $100 per night and if average daily rate is barely above $100 per night, room revenue is not being maximized. You may be selling mostly your least expensive rooms or not charging for double occupancy. This is lost revenue for the hotel, which will affect your hotel bottom line. A hotel can have high occupancy but a low average daily rate. Both are important in calculating how well your hotel is at selling rooms and maximizing revenue.

Room (units) for Sale

1000 (Rooms available for sale) $\times$ 365 (days per year) = (365,000 Rooms)

OCCUPANCY PERCENTAGE

Number of rooms sold / Number of rooms available for sale

675 (number of rooms sold) / 1000 (rooms available for sale) = 67.5% (occupancy %)

*Always round off to the 100th place to insure accuracy. Too much rounding off will affect the accuracy of your answer. For example, 1000 rooms at 68% occupancy (Rounded off) = 680 rooms.

Double Occupancy

Number of Guests – Number of rooms sold / Number of rooms occupied

1000 (number of guests) – 750 (number of rooms sold) / 750 (number of rooms occupied)

$$\frac{1000 - 750}{750} = 33.33\%$$

What this means is that 33.33% or (1/3) of the rooms occupied had double occupancy, and 66.66% or (2/3) of the rooms had single occupancy, 500 rooms.

500 rooms × single occupancy (1)	= 500 guests
250 rooms × double occupancy (2)	= 500 guests
750 rooms	= 1000 guests

The $100 rate is simply the average price of rooms sold that night. You want to maximize revenue by selling as many rooms as possible at as high a room rate as the market will allow.

A third measurement of hotel revenue is **yield management**. Occupancy percentage and average daily rate combined are a utilization of yield management attempts to control occupancy as a means of maximizing revenue potential. You might question, why would we want to control occupancy? The answer is that we can control occupancy by holding out for a higher room rate. For example, due to seasonality, many hotels change their room rates four times a year. Any potential guest who makes a reservation during different times of year will find that rates can sometimes vary significantly due to demand. A hotel room in a resort area is likely to be quite different in January than July due to demand. The greater the demand allows the hotel to charge higher room rates, and the lower demand means the hotel should lower their room rates accordingly to maximize revenue.

Hotels that fail to adjust rates according to changing conditions will likely lose out in maximizing revenue and therefore fail to increase income. An effective hotel manager should know how to maximize the full potential of room revenue, and yield management is an effective tool for a hotel manager in maximizing income for their hotel.

Revenue in the Restaurant Industry

Revenue concerns may be even more crucial in the restaurant industry than in the hotel industry because the restaurant business failure rate is much higher than the hotel industry. Over half of independent restaurants go out of business within the first year of operation, and 90% go out of business in the first three years. There are various means of measuring revenue in restaurants. **Prime cost** is a term restaurants use for food and beverage expenses and payroll. They are referred to as prime costs because these are

Calculating Average Daily Rate

$100,000 (room revenue) / 1000 (rooms occupied) = $100 (ADR)

*Rule of Thumb—In almost all cases, the ADR cannot be less than the minimum published room rate nor greater than the maximum published room rate.

your two largest expenses in the restaurant industry. If you cannot control your two largest expenses, smaller expenses that you controlled efficiently will not likely matter. Most restaurants fail financially because they could not control their prime costs.

Labor costs, also referred to as payroll cost, consists of salaries and wages and employee benefits. Controlling labor costs can be very challenging for the restaurant manager. Low labor costs may not be an indicator of efficient management. If you are managing labor costs by being understaffed you will not be helping your restaurant's financial well-being. Customers will complain about poor service and not return. On the other hand, being overstaffed will certainly not help you manage labor costs either. Although you may have acceptable service, you will likely have employees standing around doing very little or nothing. A good manager in the restaurant industry should be upset at seeing employees being paid to stand around and do nothing.

The best means for evaluating labor needs is to have a formula for determining how much labor you need based on the amount of customers in your restaurant. An advantage restaurant labor staffing has over hotel labor staffing is that restaurants have peak and off-peak times of operation every day. Peak hours for breakfast may be 6:00 A.M. to 9:00 A.M., peak hours for lunch may be 11:00 A.M. to 2:00 P.M., and peak hours for dinner may be 5:00 P.M. to 9:00 P.M. A restaurant manager, who knows how to effectively manage labor costs would increase staff service during those peak hours and reduce staffing during the in-between off-peak hours.

Food cost is incurred when food is consumed for any reason. Food cost includes the cost of food sold, given away, stolen, or wasted. Restaurant managers determine what food they need to purchase by buying food based on their recipes, menu, and customer demand. Recipes also ensure that menu items are consistent in taste. Restaurant managers can adjust food costs by being creative about menu items. A leftover broiled chicken from dinner can become a chicken salad lunch special tomorrow. Also restaurant managers can determine the popularity of menu items from **point of sale** (POS) equipment. This technology determines the percentage of sales of each particular menu item.

However, food can also be wasted by a failure to follow recipes or improper cooking of food. Another concern is employees who steal food and beverage from the restaurant. Restaurants that secure food well and have enough managers managing day-to-day operations can lessen food and beverage theft by employees. Another factor is employees who serve food to customers and purposely do not charge for the food. Food giveaways may be accidental from servers who undercharge or forget to collect payment from customers or they may be intentional giveaways to friends of employees.

Restaurant managers can measure how effective they are by measuring their food and beverage cost percentage. Most franchise restaurants will have established desired food and beverage cost percentages from the corporate office. Independent restaurants can obtain information about desired food and beverage costs from research provided by the NRA (National Restaurant Association) or other Internet or research sources. Previously discussed concerns such as food and beverage given away, and stolen or wasted food will make it more difficult to attain desired food cost percentage.

This formula (outlined in the box below) determined that food cost was 30% of food sales. That means that $70,000.00, or 70%, was profit out of this $100,000.00. Without the necessary labor, it will be difficult to produce revenue for the restaurant. If you do not manage food and beverage purchasing, food and beverage waste, food and beverage giveaways,

Food Cost Percentage

Cost of food sold / Food Sales = Food Cost %

$30,000.00 (cost of food sold) / $100,000.00 (Food Sales) = 30% (Food Cost)

and food and beverage theft, this will adversely affect the amount of revenue you will bring into your restaurant. Managing food cost will increase your revenue, which will increase your level of success as a restaurant manager.

Maximizing Revenue through Selling

Most hotels and restaurants in this competitive environment must determine methods for maximizing revenue and gaining a competitive edge. Among the methods utilized by hospitality managers are discounting, up-selling and the top down approach.

Discounting is a method of reducing an item from the regular price. This may lead to a very logical question, "How does one charge less and still maximize revenue?" Managers must concern themselves with the perishability factor. **Perishability** refers to the shelf life or how much time you have to sell a product until it cannot be sold anymore. A hotel room, for example, that has a rack rate of $100, nets zero dollars in revenue if it doesn't sell that night. If it is discounted and sells at $80, that is $80 in additional revenue for the hotel. A hotel manager, to be successful at selling, must envision each hotel room as a perishable product. Further, managers must set a specific amount to which they may discount an item or product and no further. For example, if a hotel room regularly sells for $100, there is a price that would be so low they would actually lose money from renting that room. The price of a hotel room is not a random number made up by the hotel manager. It is a specific number based on actual expenses, rates of competition, and a reasonable expectation of a profit. If a hotel attracts a certain clientele, severe discounting may attract a different type of clientele. Regular hotel guests may decide to stay elsewhere in the future. Yet another example, restaurants must develop methods of discounting menu items to encourage customers to purchase these items. A discounted item, which is often called a special, may appeal to some customers. Customers like to order a menu item that they think might be special and think they are getting a bargain. A discounted item does not always mean a discounted menu price, however. It could mean the menu price is the same and the restaurant manager may offer something free in addition, such as a free dessert as an incentive to the customer to order that special menu

Restaurant managers must concern themselves with discounting when considering the perishability factor of food. © 2011 by Denis Vrublevski. Used under license of Shutterstock, Inc.

item. If a restaurant has to discard a menu item due to the fact that the menu item has exceeded its shelf life, that is lost revenue for the restaurant. Discounting is used more often at lower-priced restaurants and less at fine dining restaurants.

Up-selling is often not about selling more items, it is about selling higher priced items of a particular item or logical additions to an item that the customer has already expressed an interest in purchasing. For example, "For $20 more you can be upgraded to a poolside room" or "Would you like a bottle of the wine instead of three glasses?" More profitable hotel rooms for the hotel are usually their most expensive rooms. Restaurants' most profitable menu items are often the most expensive items that have the largest profit margin. So up-selling is in the best interest of the organization. If used effectively, it should help to increase hotel's average daily rate (ADR), which will in turn maximize revenue. Yet it is also about convincing the customer that a more expensive item is in the customer's best interest. A guest is not going to pay more for something if they do not perceive any benefit in paying more.

The **top-down approach** is a method of attempting to sell the most expensive item first and then offering a less expensive item next, and so on. In the restaurant industry, the top-down approach is similar to up-selling and would consist of the restaurant server recommending more expensive menu items. They can further reinforce these recommendations by informing the customer, "This is my personal favorite" or "This is the chef's specialty." This increased check average and greater tips will likely lead to more satisfied servers. This will likely benefit the restaurant by reducing employee turnover. This in turn will maximize revenue by reducing employee recruitment costs.

Controlling Costs in the Hotel Industry

Cost control in the hotel industry is an important component in maximizing profits. Without proper cost control procedures, a hotel may appear to be successful financially in terms of room sales, but missing out on controlling expenses. Two means of controlling expenses in a hotel are in the area of energy management and labor costs. Hotels who manage energy can maximize revenue potential to a greater extent. Hotels that can control labor costs also maximize revenue potential to a greater extent.

Up-selling to a poolside room will increase ADR and maximize revenue. © 2011 by jamalludin. Used under license of Shutterstock, Inc.

Energy management is the efficient management of energy usage within your establishment. In a hotel, we would concern ourselves with heat, air conditioning, water usage, electric usage, gas usage, and sewer usage. Hotels can encourage guests and employees to become part of an energy management program at a hotel. Hotels can control heat and air conditioning by regulating minimum and maximum temperatures in individual guest rooms. Water usage can be regulated by use of low-flow toilets and showerheads, which dispense less water. Also sprinkler systems can be shut off outside when it is raining. Using energy efficient or lower wattage bulbs in guest rooms can help decrease electric usage. By regulating temperatures based on changing weather conditions, hotels can control heat usage. Being aware of changing weather conditions can help to regulate energy costs.

Labor costs in the hotel industry are different than controlling labor costs in the restaurant industry. Hotels have less peak specific periods during a day, unlike restaurants, which have meal periods. Labor costs are more likely to be controlled by seasonality over long periods of time. If a hotel is operating at 90% occupancy during the summer and 50% occupancy during the winter, staffing should be adjusted accordingly. If a hotel is staffing at the same levels regardless of occupancy, they are not effectively controlling labor costs. In a hotel that has low occupancy during a particular period, they can reduce the number of guest service agents at the front desk. Guest service agents can also handle reservations, reducing reservations staff. Housekeeping can be reduced by two methods during lower occupancy. Those methods are by fewer housekeepers working full time or more housekeepers working part time. Although high labor costs by itself may not cause a hotel to go out of business, it is one of many factors that if not controlled will reduce revenue.

Controlling Costs in the Restaurant Industry

Controlling **food costs** as discussed earlier in this chapter is essential in the success of your restaurant. One means of controlling food costs is through **volume purchasing**. Restaurants can save money per pound or unit by purchasing in bulk. The supplier is willing to reduce the price because that supplier is selling

TABLE 11.1 Key Hotel Management Positions in Managing Revenue Expenses

TITLE	DEPARTMENT	REVENUE AND COST CONTROL DESCRIPTION	ADVANCEMENT OPPORTUNITIES
Executive Housekeeper	Housekeeping	In charge of all renovation and purchasing housekeeping supplies	Supervisor of more than one operation or corporate position
Catering Manager	Food and Beverage	Purchases and supervises the receipt and storage of food and beverage for the hotel.	Director of Food and Beverage
Director of Food and Beverage	Food and Beverage	Oversees entire food and beverage operation	General Manager
Director of Sales	Sales	Sells convention facilities for meetings, banquets, and receptions. Sells rooms to volume purchasers such as corporate travel directors of large companies	Resident Manager
Resident Manager	Administration	Takes over for manager in his or her absence. Usually handles duties assigned by the manager.	General Manager
General Manager	Administration	Supervises all activities with the hotel. Responsible for the coordination of all departments	Managing Director
Food and Beverage Controller	Accounting	Controls food and costs through menu planning and pricing, purchasing decisions, storage issues	Assistant Controller
Credit Manager	Accounting	Oversees accounts receivables from time of extension of credit until cash is collected	Assistant Controller
Assistant Controller	Accounting	Functions as office manager with responsibility for preparation of financial statements	Controller
Controller	Accounting	Acts as financial advisor to management in achieving profit objectives through detailed planning controlling costs and effectively managing hotel assets and liabilities	Area or Regional

more. The supplier may have a reduced profit margin, but by selling more, that supplier may increase their profit by selling in volume. A competent restaurant manager or steward (purchasing agent), should know based on sales projections how much food needs to be purchased for the restaurant. For example, a restaurant averages sales of 100 quarter-pound hamburgers in a day. Each hamburger is 4 ounces (100 hamburgers a day times four ounces equals 400 ounces); (400 ounces divided by 1 pound (16 ounces) = 25 pounds of hamburger meat). So the restaurant manager or steward purchasing about 80 pounds of hamburger meat every three days would be a reasonable amount for the restaurant to purchase. You would not purchase hamburger meat more than three days at a time due to concerns about the spoilage of

TABLE   11.2 Key Restaurant Management Positions in Managing Revenue Expenses

TITLE	DEPARTMENT	DESCRIPTION	ADVANCEMENT OPPORTUNITY
Beverage Manager	Beverages	Orders for and stocks bar to maintain inventories of liquor and glassware	Food Production Manager
Cook or Sous Chef	Kitchen	Prepares and portions out all food served	Executive Chef
Executive Chef	Kitchen	Responsible for all quantity and quality food preparation; supervision of sous chefs and cooks and menu recipe development	Assistant Manager
Purchasing Agent	Management	Orders, receives, inspects, and stores all goods shipped by suppliers	Assistant Manager
Assistant Manager	Management	Performs specified supervisory duties under the manager's direction	Food Service Manager
Food Service Manager	Management	Responsible for profitability, efficiency, and quality of the entire food service operation	Multiunit Regional Manager
Personnel Director	Management	Responsible for hiring and training of food service personnel and benefits	Regional Personnel Manager

the meat. You should always purchase slightly more than you need. As was discussed previously in this chapter, food is sometimes improperly cooked, given away, or stolen. Purchasing too much food can lead to waste as food becomes spoiled and has to be discarded, which costs the restaurant revenue with no sales in return. Purchasing not enough food may lead the restaurant to not be able to offer particular menu items. This may lead to some displeased customers, which may lead to some of those customers not returning to your restaurant.

Two additional concerns about volume purchasing are the perishability factor and the storage factor. Although a restaurant may save money from volume purchasing, it must concern itself with the perishability factor. Saving money on purchasing volume will be diminished if the food spoils and has to be discarded. If a restaurant uses 50 pounds of tomatoes in a week, they should not purchase 100 pounds because it is cheaper by the pound. Produce and dairy products are highly perishable. Those 50 pounds of additional tomatoes would not last two weeks. So the per pound savings in purchasing 50 extra pounds of tomatoes would be negatively affected by most of those 50 pounds of additional tomatoes being discarded. A

volume purchase for dry goods, canned goods, and frozen foods makes more sense because there is little or no concern about perishability of those food items. One concern about buying more dry goods, canned goods, or frozen items is the type of restaurant. A fine dining restaurant is expected by the customer who is paying more than in non–fine dining restaurant to offer more fresh items and menu items prepared from scratch. So the perishability factor is likely to be greater concern to the fine dining establishment then a family style of fast-food restaurant. The second concern is storage; you cannot buy more food than you can reasonably store. So your volume purchasing will be limited by the size of your storage area. Larger restaurants with larger storage areas can be more profitable than smaller restaurants with smaller storage areas because they can purchase in greater volume. Larger restaurants may sell the same exact item as a smaller restaurant. They may also charge the same price for the same item, but the profit will likely be greater for the large restaurant. This greater profit margin will be due to volume purchasing.

Portion control is a very necessary component of cost control in the restaurant industry. If a restaurant does not use portion control, they will never

---

Yield Factor

1 lb. / .75 yield percentage = 1.33 lbs. (quantity)

If we know the sirloin has a yield percentage of 75%, or 25% waste, we would know based on this formula to purchase 1.33 or 1 1/3 pounds of sirloin steak AP to yield 1 pound of sirloin steak EP.

---

know exactly how much money they are making on each item. Knowing how much you need will help you to know how much profit margin you have on each menu item and also how much to purchase. Portion control is not just about profit margins; it is also about uniformity. If you don't use portion controls, individual menu items may look or taste different each time. If a customer orders the same menu item again and again, they must like that item. They like that item because it tastes good to them and because it's consistent. Without portion control, this menu item may look different or taste different one time, and the customer may never come back. Portion control is also needed in food purchasing. Referring back to our hamburger purchasing, if we measured each hamburger into a four-ounce patty, we would have the correct amount that we needed. If we did not measure those hamburgers, we may be serving inadequate small hamburgers that are less than four ounces or hamburgers that are more than four ounces, affecting our profit margin. Two means of measuring portion control are (AP) **as purchased** and (EP) **edible portion**.

This means of portion control is often used with meat. In the case of meat, such as a sirloin steak, AP would mean what the steaks weighed when purchased. This is before waste of fat and bones are removed. Also as meat is cooking, it shrinks in size. The more the meat is cooked, the more the meat shrinks. The condition of the meat after waste is removed and it is cooked is known as EP, edible portion. If a recipe calls for 1 pound of sirloin steak EP, you would need to know the yield factor before you decide how much to buy.

These methods of cost control in the restaurant industry, volume purchasing, portion control, as purchased (AP), edible portion (EP), and yield percentage are essential tools of a restaurant manager concerned with cost control. Purchasing is a not always an exact science, but with the most up-to-date sales forecasts, you should be relatively accurate, which should lead to a greater likelihood of your restaurant maximizing its revenue potential.

Summary

In this chapter, we learned about managing revenue and expenses in the hospitality industry. We learned how hotels and restaurant operations must manage revenue and expenses if they intend to be successful in the competitive hospitality industry. We also learned how we need effective managers who understand revenue and expenses to successfully run those operations. In discussing revenue in the hotel, we learned about occupancy percentages, ADR (Average Daily Rate) and yield management. In the restaurant industry, we learned about the prime costs of labor and food costs. We also discussed maximizing revenue through selling by learning such methods as discounting, up-selling, and the top-down approach. In our discussion on revenue management, we learned about energy management and labor cost. For the restaurant industry, we also learned about controlling food costs through volume purchasing and portion control. We also discussed the intangibility factor in the hotel and restaurant industry and its importance. Finally, we discussed the many rewarding and challenging opportunities in managing revenue in the hospitality and tourism industry.

RESOURCES

Internet Sites

A Directory of Knowledge Management Web Sites: www.knowledge-manager.com

American Hotel & Lodging Association (AH&LA): www.ahla.com click information center

A-Z topics/Business and Financial Management/ Running your own business: www.restaurant.org/business/topics_financial.cfm

Council of Hotel, Restaurant & Institutional Educators (CHRIE); Affiliation of hotel and restaurant educators): www.chrie.org

Financial Information Advertising: www.restaurant&results.org

Financial Management HQ—Financial Management: www.financialmanagementhq.com

Gecko Hospitality (Hospitality Financial): www.geckohospitality.web.aplus.net

Hospitality Careers: www.hcarres.net

Hospitality and Food Service Management: www.cccd.edu/hospitality/resources.htm

Hospitality Financial and Technology Professionals (HFTP): www.hftp.org

Hospitality net-in depth-decision support—Revenue Management: www.hospitalitynet.org

Hotel Resource: Hotel and Hospitality Industry Resource: www.hotelresource.com

Hotel Real Estate: www.lodgingeconometrics.com

Microsystems Inc.—Fidelio—Property Management Point of Sale: www.micros.com

Profitable Hospitality Resources and Solutions for Restaurants and Hotels: www.profitablehospitality.com/links/index.htm

Restaurant Report—Top 50 Food and Hospitality Industry Web sites: www.restaurantreport.com/top100/index.htm

References

A Guide to College Programs in Hospitality and Tourism, 3rd ed. New York: John J. Wiley & Sons, 1993, pp. 13–14.

Chatfield, R. and Dalbor, M. *Hospitality Financial Management.* Upper Saddle River, NJ: Prentice Hall, 2005, p. 10.

Dittmer, Paul R. *Principles of Food, Beverage, and Labor cost controls,* 7th ed. New York: John J. Wiley & Sons, 2003, pp. 9, 12 and 549.

Vallen, G. K. and Vallen, J. J. *Check-In Check-Out, Managing Hotel Operations.* Upper Saddle River, NJ: Prentice Hall, 2005, p. 609

Review Questions

1. An occupancy percentage measures the ratio of what two factors in determining the answer?

2. Why do hotels want to determine the difference between rooms occupied and double occupancy?

3. What is another term used in the industry for rooms?

4. How can a hotel have a high occupancy percentage and a low ADR (average daily rate)?

5. What is the "rule of thumb" in determining if your ADR calculations are accurate?

6. How can controlling room rates and restricting occupancy be effective tools in yield management?

7. Why do you think the failure rate is higher for independent restaurants than franchise restaurants?

8. Why do more restaurants fail than hotels?

9. What are the two factors that make up prime cost in the restaurant industry?

10. How has labor cost changed over the last 20 years in relation to health benefits?

11. Why should restaurant managers not staff at the same levels throughout the day?

12. Name three methods of food cost incurred in which potential revenue is lost.

13. Hotels that are considered business hotels would more likely discount their rates during what part of the week?

14. In up-selling a particular item in the hospitality industry, the seller must emphasize what characteristic in what they are selling?

15. The top-down approach attempts to sell in the hotel industry what priced rooms first?

16. Name three areas within the hotel where effective energy management principles could be utilized to reduce energy costs.

17. Name the statistics in the hotel industry that may cause labor costs to vary.

18. Why would it not be cost effective to purchase food for a restaurant from a supermarket?

19. What are the incentives for restaurants to purchase larger quantities of various food items?

20. Why is the perishability factor important in the hotel industry?

21. Why should restaurants use portion control as a means of controlling costs?

22. What are three factors that reduce the portion a particular cooked from AP (as purchased) form to EP (edible portion)?

23. Why is service an intangible?

24. Why is it important for hospitality managers to be able to visualize intangibles?

25. What are the job description responsibilities of a cook or sous chef?

Human Resource Management

Mel Weber, East Carolina University

 ## LEARNING OBJECTIVES

- To describe the functions of the human resource department.
- To recognize the role any manager plays within human resource functions.
- To describe the role legislation plays in human resource management.
- To discuss the role human resources plays in guest satisfaction in the hospitality industry.
- To develop a vocabulary of human resource terminology.

CHAPTER OUTLINE

Human Resource Department Functions
    Planning
    Staffing
    Training and Development
    Turnover and Employee Loyalty
    Evaluation
    Compensation and Benefits
    Health and Safety
    Legislation
HR Is Involved in Every Supervisory or
    Management Position
Summary

KEY TERMS

Americans with Disabilities Act of 1990
Civil Rights Act of 1964
Evaluation
Human resource management
Interviewing
Job analysis
Job descriptions
Job design
Job enlargement
Job enrichment

Job rotation
Job simplification
Job specifications
Merit pay
Progressive discipline policy
Recruiting
Selection
Team building
The training cycle
Turnover

In today's business world, people are the key. Dealing with this people challenge is the human resource (HR) department. This is the department within the organization that handles the paperwork regarding selection, termination, legal mandates, benefits, training, and compensation. In the past, this department handled these responsibilities following policies formulated by top management. Today, HR managers no longer just follow policy. They are also responsible for formulating policy and assisting with strategic planning related to department functions. Although the HR department performs these functions, there is more to human resource management than paperwork. You must understand that HR goes beyond the functions of any department and is the responsibility of all supervisors/managers and every worker within the organization. Human resource management is concerned with the management and caring of the hospitality businesses' most important asset, the people who work for the organization.

J. W. Marriott, founder of the Marriott Corporation, is noted for saying that if a company takes care of the people who work for it, then the people will take care of the company. This translates into a well-balanced 360-degree company/employee/customer relationship that can be evaluated at any of the three levels. To play a productive role in the organization, HR must be involved in activities to enhance the ability of the company to meet the needs of the guest while satisfying the needs of the worker. As in every department, customer satisfaction is the bottom line. Simply stated, *Human resource management is the process of how organizations treat their people to accomplish the goals and objectives of the firm.*

Human Resource Department Functions

Planning

As a management function, planning is one of the most important activities. This certainly is the case in the HR area. Like all strategic planning, managers must understand where they are. HR continually assesses needed skills and employees who have these abilities to maintain necessary competencies. Then, the HR department must not only attempt to predict future employment needs in terms of turnover, but they must also look at future trends to assess additional skill needs or changing emphases to prepare the staff and assist the company in growth. Finally,

the third step of any planning is to develop a stepwise progression and timetable on reaching these changing objectives.

As a result, it can be seen that this is a dimension where the HR department cannot work in a vacuum. They must work with all departments to assess employment needs. In fact, if you want to meet people from all the different departments, HR is the hub. In addition, they must be kept updated regarding industry shifts to enable them to assist the workforce in handling the ongoing changes. Moreover, they must remain competitive with wages to attract the best and the brightest to our industry.

Before an organization can determine how many people are needed to meet the demands of the business, planning functions are necessary to determine what work must be accomplished, how the work should be completed, and the skills necessary to complete the job. There are tools available to the HR professional to fulfill these tasks. The first is *job analysis*. This is the information that focuses on what work needs to be accomplished. This analysis allows us to write job descriptions and *job specifications*. Job descriptions identify the tasks, responsibilities, and duties under which jobs are performed. Keeping a diary of daily activities is one way this can be accomplished. This allows for a more realistic assessment of tasks and abilities needed. It also allows HR to see how the job responsibilities change over time. Then summaries of the tasks and duties are listed and job descriptions and specifications created. *Job specifications* are the knowledge, skills, and abilities necessary to perform the position. Job descriptions and specifications are the basis for recruitment, selection, training/development, evaluating, compensation/benefits, and health/safety issues.

The task of determining how the job should be performed is the function of *job design*. This looks at how the job is organized and how it can be planned to provide both productivity to the organization and the most job satisfaction to the employee. The most widely used techniques in job design are (1) job simplification, (2) job enlargement, (3) job enrichment, (4) job rotation, and (5) team building. *Job simplification* is the process of determining the smallest components of the job and assessing how they fit into the whole job. It can be the case where the job responsibilities keep expanding to meet the needs of the department.

Therefore, this process can help break down the job to see how a division of labor can be accomplished.

In other cases, where job sharing is an option, two people may need to examine job simplification to determine how they can subdivide the tasks. *Job enlargement* is the process of broadening the job by adding tasks. There are many reasons why adding tasks is necessary. One might be the process of changing a job from part-time to full-time status.

Job enrichment is the process of adding responsibilities to the job. To prevent the job from becoming boring, adding new responsibilities can give motivation to the employee who is looking for a challenge. It might also allow people to go back to school or travel to corporate for training. *Job rotation* is allowing the employee to work at different jobs. This technique requires employees to be cross-trained. This is good for the company because it allows additional people to be on hand in case you are short-handed in another department. However, one of the issues with rotation is having more than one boss who is responsible for your schedule. If they don't communicate your schedule to each other, you could end up with a problem of having to be in two places at the same time or having double shifts. And finally, *team building* views employees as members of work groups, rather than as individuals.[1] When there are problems that need resolving, quite often a team of experts, that is people who work in that job or department, can be called together to brainstorm possible solutions. Sometimes they can be used to create policies or go across departments to offer larger alternatives.

Staffing

Once the organization determines the number and type of employment positions available, the task of staffing for these positions begins. This includes recruiting candidates for the positions and selecting the best person for the position. This must all be achieved within the guidelines set forth in both federal and state laws. Selection is not as easy as putting an ad in the paper and choosing a new employee from the stack of applications. For example, one hotel in New Orleans put a want ad in the newspaper, and 300 people arrived at their doorstep. This is good you say? However, out of the 300, they could not find one person to hire. In some cases, applicants were on government subsidies and were required to apply for jobs as part of their duties in keeping their money coming. Others explained that after 2:00 in the afternoon or weekends or holidays, they could not work because they had to be with their children. Others could not read to fill out the application.

A key element to staffing is finding the right employee for the job. © 2011 by Leah-Anne Thompson. Used under license of Shutterstock, Inc.

The key element is finding the right employee for the job. The labor market demonstrates fluctuations dependent on the economy at any given time. When the economy is tight, there are more applications; however, when the economy is booming, it is often difficult to find qualified personnel to fill the vacancies. We employ many entry-level employees in minimum wage jobs; this makes the challenge significantly greater for finding the right employee for every position. Given these variables, the current labor market conditions, and shifting dynamics inherent in the labor force, a company today must go well beyond the traditional want ad and look for innovative ways to attract good employees. Many hospitality firms guest speak at nearby colleges and universities so that they can persuade students to apply. Some hotels have even formed alumni groups of employees to ask them how to reach students. One increasingly popular tool is the Internet, with many Web sites available for the job seeker to research companies and pursue lists of jobs available. There are also services available to showcase the talents of the job seeker to any interested employer.

Once the company receives the individual's application, the task of interviewing begins. Many interviewing styles may be used; however, the overriding concern is to ensure fairness to the applicants and achieving the best match for the job. The interviewer must be sure they do not ask any questions that could be considered illegal or discriminatory in nature. Often one of the functions of the HR department is training the managers interviewing applicants in the proper methodology to conduct the interviews. One must also try to structure the interview in such a way that you can compare the candidates' qualifications without bias. Increasingly, behavioral or situational interviewing methods are used. These methods show greater validity (via statistical accumulation) in choosing the right person for the job. Other tools being used to help in the decision-making process are checking references and administering a number of preemployment tests. Many organizations today are employing outside firms to administer appropriate personality and honesty tests to obtain unbiased information suitable to a particular job and or company. The goal of this process is to find employees that will enjoy their work and fit well into the organizational structure. Some firms have six interviews per applicant to assess the candidate's personality. After all, a favorite saying is, "If the applicant doesn't smile during the interview, what makes you think they will smile on the job?"

Training and Development

Once the organization has selected the employee, the organization must train the new employee. New employee training introduces the corporate culture. It discusses the history of the company, its mission, and its priorities. This allows new employees to begin the assimilation process of identifying how they fit into this business. It is also used to introduce new employees to one another so that there is a social bond and a common experience everyone goes through. In Japan, some companies have departments climb Mt. Fuji at night so that they can share the sunrise

New employee training introduces the corporate culture and creates a social bond between participants. © 2011 by Konstantin Chagin. Used under license of Shutterstock, Inc.

together. This forms a bond between the participants. Other companies do wilderness or survival training. The hottest event, currently, is to cook together and serve a meal.

But the HR department is not only concerned with the new employees; they must continue to develop the tenured employees. To complete these tasks, the HR department may choose to use the training cycle.

1. Conduct a needs assessment—identify problems
2. Identify training objectives—goals of the program
3. Establish training criteria—benchmarks
4. Select trainees—new or tenured
5. Pretest trainees—establish a baseline of knowledge, skills, and abilities
6. Choose training methods—on the job or off the job
7. Implement training
8. Evaluate training[2]

Evaluating training usually helps the HR department identify more needs, thus the cycle starts anew.

Turnover and Employee Loyalty

Failure to perform the recruiting, selection, and training/development processes adequately will often lead to unnecessary turnover. Turnover is the term used to describe the situation when an employee leaves and must be replaced. Turnover is an expensive occurrence, as the company must not only go through the entire recruitment and selection process once again, but it must also retrain a person for the position. Frequently, this ongoing training may produce negative effects of inefficiency until the new employee can achieve the expected level of productivity that the departed employee demonstrated.

Another expense to the organization is the time a manager needs to oversee this process. The replacement also takes a manager away from other responsibilities in situations where a manager performs all the recruiting and selection duties. Previously, turnover was an accepted occurrence in the hospitality industry because there were always new bodies to fill the shoes of the departing employee. However, this is not always the case. In hospitality, the average turnover rate is around 60% to 70%. That means that one out of every three hired actually stays for more than six months. Therefore, more companies are emphasizing the need to select new hires wisely and to put programs in place to retain the existing employees. The new slogan is a job should be fun, fair, and interesting.

Retention programs can focus around activities such as softball leagues and opportunities for socialization. Still, it is widely believed that the best methods to enhance employee retention is an atmosphere of fair treatment, one where employees enjoy working, one where they feel they make a difference, and one where they are rewarded based on their own individual needs. Contrary to popular opinion, money is not the main reason for leaving a job, but it is the main excuse. Because employee satisfaction is an ongoing process, managers continually will need to monitor the climate as new generations come into the labor market. The tangible and intangible assets of the job are becoming increasingly important to successful retention programs coupled with creative packaging that either entices and/or satisfies the employee.

Evaluation

Employee evaluations take place after an employee has been selected, trained, and on the job for a period of time. Evaluations have many organizational purposes. They can be used to determine if the employee requires more training, is in the best job for them, is ready for a promotion, and is entitled to incentive pay or any situation based on job performance. The best reason to evaluate an employee's performance is for official feedback. However, the employee should be receiving feedback concerning their performance on a regular basis. A significant reason for dissatisfaction with the job results from an employee not being aware of how they are doing on the job, and this feedback must be completed in a timely fashion. This is just like a student's desire to know where they stand regarding a grade in any given class. Evaluations play a significant motivational effect on employees by encouraging the employee to improve on their performance based on the outcomes of the evaluation. The HR department's role in this process is one of providing the form, filing the evaluations for future reference, as well as training managers how best to complete the process. Evaluations are usually completed and administered by the employees' supervisor.

Employee evaluations also are used as backup documentation necessary if an employee is terminated based on performance. Although there are provisions for "employment at will" that allow an employer to terminate employment at the employer's discretion, most employers prefer to have a policy

in place where an employee's performance is scrutinized, warnings are given, and an opportunity for retraining is provided before that termination takes place. This is also known as a ***progressive discipline policy***, where employees receive increasingly more stringent discipline for infractions. In this scenario, the evaluations serve as documentation if the former employee brings discrimination charges forward.

In many organizations, employee evaluations are the link between performance and pay raises. This makes it critical that the evaluations are performed in an impartial manner to ensure consistency regarding compensation across all areas of the organization. Merit pay is the approach of identifying employees who are performing at or above expected levels and providing them with increased wages. You must make every effort to evaluate the employee on the promised anniversary date, as it is one of the most contentious complaints employees levy against their supervisors. Failing to evaluate and process the appropriate paperwork is essential to maintaining a professional posture and image.

Compensation and Benefits

Employees receive compensation for the work that they do in three ways: (1) direct compensation (often referred to as base pay), (2) merit pay, and (3) benefits. The motivational effect of wages is often debated, but within the scope of this discussion, employers continually look for better methods of materially rewarding people for the work they perform. This acts as a catalyst for improved productivity and a better motivational tool. Each form of compensation is introduced as a motivational tool. Benefits are introduced in this fashion and are used to motivate or entice persons to work for their company. The predominant focus on wages today is that of merit pay, where only expected and above expected performance is rewarded above a base level.

One of the greatest challenges for the HR department today is finding and devising benefit packages that employees find attractive and that are affordable to the company. One of the most expensive components of any benefits package is health insurance. As the cost of health care continues to rise rapidly, it becomes increasingly more difficult for companies to find insurance carriers with reasonable premiums. Companies are looking for innovative methods to solve this dilemma and must be sensitive to both the needs of the employees and the profitability of the company. Each company must weigh the advantages and disadvantages of this move and proceed with the path that is best for the organization. HR professionals also look for a range of benefits that help employees meet personal goals and concerns. It should be duly noted, as in other HR areas, the overriding principle in compensation is one of fairness and equity.

Health and Safety

Organizations are obligated to provide employees with a safe and healthy work environment. Requiring them to work with unsafe equipment or in areas where hazards are not controlled is a highly questionable and often a costly practice. It is also the responsibility of managers to ensure that employees are safety conscious and maintain good health. Preventative safety is one of the best ways to avert an unsafe environment for the employee and often the customer. Both managers and the HR specialist are involved in health and safety practices in an organization. HR specialists coordinate programs, develop safety-reporting systems, and provide expertise on investigation, technical, research, and prevention methods. Managers must investigate, coach, monitor, and observe employees practicing safety in the functional areas of the operation. Communication and good record keeping is vital in this area as it is with any area of the business.

Legislation

Probably the largest responsibility of the human resource department is knowing the laws of employment. But not only do they need to know about the laws, they need to make sure that every member of the organization is aware of these laws. In managing their employees, organizations must comply with many laws, regulations, court decisions, and mandates arising from the social legislation, most notably after 1960. Personnel departments had to become much more professional and more concerned about the legal ramifications of policies and practices enacted by their organizations. All management and supervisory personnel must continually be updated and coached with regard to the legalities of the ever-changing fabric of our work environment.

Sweeping federal legislation that forever changed the standards for employment in the United States was passed under the Johnson administration. The act that provided the impetus for this change was the Civil Rights Act of 1964. This act prohibits discrimination on the basis of race, color, religion, sex, or national origin and has become the cornerstone piece

of legislation protecting workers and their rights. See Table 12.1 for other legislation.

Key governmental agencies generally affect many HR activities. The HR professional must be familiar with many of these agencies and their functions. Among the more important ones to be familiar with are the actions of the Equal Employment Opportunity Commission (EEOC); Occupational Safety, and Health Administration (OSHA); the Immigration and Naturalization Services; the Department of Labor (DOL); and the various state and city equal employment commissions and human or civil rights commissions. If the individual entrusted with the legalities of employment fails to maintain an awareness of current laws and regulations, either through an HR department or individual actions, organizations may find themselves faced with costly lawsuits and significant fines. Much of this can be avoided by constantly monitoring the legal environment, by complying with changes, and by careful management of employees.

HR Is Involved in Every Supervisory or Management Position

The human resource department works in concert with all management at every level. Typically, the HR department is known for hiring employees. An example of how the HR department works with everyone is that they may be responsible for recruiting prospective employees, performing initial interviews, completing reference checks, and completing the appropriate paperwork. However, the manager or supervisor of the department where this employee will work makes the final decision regarding the hiring of an individual. This is not the only area that must employ a combined effort, and from this, you can see that the HR department and all managers must work closely together to achieve the employment goals of the organization.

There are differences in the HR relationships between a small and a large organization. In a small organization, there is no formal HR department. Those responsibilities are relegated to the operational management or ownership. Here the organization's management staff is responsible for all the HR functions along with all the other management functions relegated to their duties. Managers in a unit of a multiunit chain find themselves responsible for the

TABLE	12.1 Federal Legislation Affecting Employment Standards

LEGISLATION	IMPLICATION
Equal Pay Act of 1963	Men and women working for the same organization must be paid the same rate for comparable jobs
Title VII of the Civil Rights Act of 1964	Bars discrimination on the basis of race, sex, religion, color, and national origin
Age Discrimination in Employment Act of 1967	Prohibits employment discrimination on the basis of age against people 40 years old or older
Vocational Rehabilitation Act of 1973	Required all employers holding federal contracts of $25,000 or more to employ "qualified" individuals with disabilities and to make reasonable accommodations as needed
Pregnancy Discrimination Act of 1978	Employers cannot stipulate the beginning and ending dates of a pregnant employee's maternity leave
Retirement Equity Act of 1984	Required companies to count all services since the age of 18 in determining vesting in retirement benefits
Immigration Reform and Control Act of 1986	Designed to regulate the employment of aliens in the U.S. by verifying citizenship status on all employees
Americans with Disabilities Act of 1990	Forbids discrimination against people with disabilities—expanded the list of included disabilities (see Act of 1973)
Family and Medical Leave Act of 1993	Required employers with 50 or more employees to offer 12 weeks of unpaid leave for a 12-month period for birth, adoption, care for an ill parent/spouse/child, or for medical treatment

day-to-day functions; however, an HR department at corporate headquarters backs them up. In the latter instance, the management staff must play a more active role in HR activities due to the distance from the corporate HR staff. Looking at this example more closely, we observe that the selection procedure, in this multiunit situation, finds management responsible for all selection functions such as recruiting, interviewing, completing reference checks, making the final decision, and completing the paperwork. The HR department at the corporate office plays more of an advisory role and is responsible for the upkeep of the appropriate files and keeping unit managers aware of current accepted hiring practices as well as legal issues. As you can see from this example, it is critical that all management personnel have a thorough understanding of the functions involved in the management of human resources.

Summary

Much of what has been discussed in this brief overview of HR essentials is procedural in nature. Hospitality organizations are dynamic entities as are the individuals we seek to hire and to represent our organizations. Companies must be positioned to meet the needs of their employees every day. There can be no exception to this imperative. If your company does not provide and care for the employee, and consequently the customer, in meeting their expectations, then failure is eminent. Longitudinal studies indicate a direct relationship with a hospitality businesses failure with that of poor management. The numbers of annual failures are staggering with a clear majority of these failures pointing to poor management practices. There is always someone else out there who is able, willing, and ready to meet the challenges presented through the human resource functions.

The source of strength for successful companies is their ability to assess their surrounding and to adapt and change. In fact, a proactive posture generally accompanies these successful organizations. They are the industry leaders who remain in the forefront representing the most successful hospitality businesses in the world today. The future is very dynamic, and you have a wonderful opportunity to be a part of all the excitement and promise that is yet to come. Don't forget we are a people business, and we must take care of all the people that work for and utilize our places of business.

RESOURCES

Internet Sites
The Society for Human Resource Management: www.shrm.org
The International Association for Human Resource Information: www.ihrim.org
Workforce Management: www.workforce.com
U.S. Department of Labor: www.dol.gov

ENDNOTES

1. Woods, R. H. (2006). *Managing Hospitality Human Resources,* 4th ed. Lansing, MI: American Hotel and Lodging Association.
2. Ibid.

Review Questions

CHAPTER 12

1. What is human resource management?

2. Who typically does the actual hiring of employees?

3. Why should all managers have a fundamental knowledge of human resource management?

4. Define the following:
   a. Job analysis

   b. Job description

   c. Job specifications

   d. Job design

5. What is the difference between job descriptions and job specifications?

6. What is the goal of the selection process?

7. Why do a growing number of companies today have you apply online?

8. Describe an effective recruiting tool that you have seen used in the hospitality industry.

9. What are the challenges of staffing?

10. Identify the training cycle.

11. Discuss the importance of the Civil Rights Act of 1964.

12. Please give five reasons for management to complete employee evaluations.

13. Why is it important for an employee to be evaluated on a timely basis?

14. What is a progressive discipline policy?

15. What are three different forms of compensation?

16. Describe a challenge that a company may face when designing benefits packages.

17. What is the Americans with Disabilities Act?

18. What role does a manager play with regard to health and safety?

19. Please list two ways a company can take care of their employees.

20. What methods can be used to help ensure that management is selecting the right person for the position?

Law and Ethics

Christian E. Hardigree, University of Nevada, Las Vegas
S. Denise McCurry, Gordon and Rees

LEARNING OBJECTIVES

- To have a working knowledge of how the legal system can apply to the hospitality industry.
- To be able to recognize various areas of law and how they may affect operations.
- To understand how the actions and/or inactions of employees, independent contractors, and/or managers can create legal liability for a business.
- To recognize ethical situations and dilemmas that must be addressed by a hospitality entity.

CHAPTER OUTLINE

The Basics of Hospitality Law: Why Is the Law
    Important to Us?
    The Legal System
    Sources of Law
The Legal Process
    Basic Concepts
    Claims versus Litigation
    The Role of Risk Management
    Alternative Dispute Resolution
Basic Duties and Rights of Hospitality Businesses
Illustrations of How the Law Can Affect
    Hospitality Operations
Ethical Considerations
Summary

KEY TERMS

Answer
Cause of action
Complaint
Defamation
Defendant
Discovery

Ethics
Negligene
Plaintiff
Statute of limiations
Torts

The Basics of Hospitality Law: Why Is the Law Important to Us?

Whether we know it or not, we are faced with the law every day in virtually everything we do. When you drive to school or work, you are required to drive no greater than the speed limit. When you stop at a fast-food restaurant to buy breakfast, you exchange currency for a food product—one that is legally required to meet minimum standards for fitness for human consumption. What you are served must also comply with the description on the menu. When you enter the business place of another (whether it is a public university, a private college, a restaurant, a coffee shop, etc.), you are required to adhere to certain standards of conduct, and the owner of the establishment is entitled to engage in certain acts (perhaps ejecting a patron who fails to adhere to those standards of conduct). In some form or another, the law surrounds us every day.

When we look to the hospitality industry, we must consider in what ways the law impacts the industry, its standards, and how we operate our businesses. This would apply to hotels, motels, restaurants, amusement parks, golf courses, spas, casinos, bed-and-breakfast establishments, and so on. All the different areas of hospitality are affected by the legal system. Similarly, many aspects of the "industry norm" are established by previous legal cases, which required certain standards. This chapter will introduce you to those standards and some of the legal concepts that affect our system today.

The Legal System

When assessing the law and our legal system, one must first question what the "law" is and why it is in place. Essentially, our society has put forth a body of rules by which we expect our society to conduct itself, a form of societal control through standards of conduct. If someone does not meet the set standard, then they can be held responsible. Sometimes we see people imprisoned in jail when they fail to meet certain standards, like driving while intoxicated or robbing a store. Other times, we see a court impose a monetary award against an individual or company to assess the amount of "damage" that the other party suffered as a result of failing to meet the societal standard. Ultimately, it is through this series of legal requirements and norms that we have structure to our society.

The legal system is upheld through an interconnected web of courts at various municipal, state, and federal levels. Some courts deal with only specific areas—like traffic court only deals with traffic citations. A state civil court may adjudicate a variety of issues, ranging from criminal issues like murder to civil issues like product defect litigation or negligence claims. The federal system also adjudicates different types of cases, but has certain jurisdictional requirements that must be met to hear the case. The U.S. Supreme Court typically only hears issues involving the U.S. Constitution or issues that have differing applications among different states. It is important to understand that we have different sources of law that affect us every day.

Sources of Law

The law is comprised of parts that stem from various sources. Federal and state constitutions, state and federal statutes, local charters and ordinances, court opinions, administrative rules, regulations and decisions, certain legal opinions, and various other legal pronouncements and declarations combine and interrelate to form the laws that govern our society. Some sources of law are common law, statutory law, constitutional law, administrative law, and public policy.

Common law is the area of law that is primarily developed through case law and the legal decisions made by judges. Common law traces its heritage back to England, where it originated in the Middle Ages. Common law strives to bring consistency and equal application of the law to matters that involve similar facts. Once a ruling has been made by a court regarding a specific set of facts, all future matters involving the same or similar facts are bound by the prior court ruling under the concept called "stare decisis"—"let the decision stand." Unless there is some persuasive rationale to change previous court decisions, then previous decisions are precedent and continue to be followed. An example of common law would be the concept of "respondeat superior"—an employer is responsible for the acts of an employee within the scope of employment. If a waitress poured a pitcher of beer on a patron at the bar, the bar is responsible for the acts of the waitress if they occurred in the course and scope of her employment (i.e. while she was working and serving drinks).

Statutory law is written that has been established primarily through the legislative process. State statutes are a typical example of statutory law. Statutes can exist at different governmental levels, federal, state, city, county, and municipality. When determining whether a statute exists that covers a specific area, one must consult various statutory sources. Sometimes there will be statutes that contradict themselves, in which case the court may be asked to interpret which statute is controlling of the issue. An example of statutory law would be the requirement that an employer pay an employee a certain minimum wage under the Fair Labor Standards Act.

Constitutional law is the body of law that governs the distribution and exercise of governmental power. Constitutional law is typically codified (reduced to writing) in a country or nation's constitution. Constitutional law usually governs the human rights or civil liberties of nation's citizens. For example, the Fourth Amendment of the U.S. Constitution guarantees people the right to be free of illegal search and seizure by the government—which means that the hotel operator is limited in giving police "permission" to search a hotel, as a guest has a right of privacy in the hotel room during the time they are a guest (that right is diminished if they are no longer a guest).

Administrative law regulates the powers and procedures of public agencies. Administrative or public agencies issue rules and regulations to enforce state or federal statutes. For example, the workers' compensation benefits and unemployment benefits are regulated through administrative law. The Environmental Protection Agency creates administrative laws that they enforce for issues affecting the environment. The Equal Employment Opportunity Commission creates and enforces rules and regulations relating to discrimination in the workplace. Different administrative agencies may create and/or enforce administrative law in an effort to expedite the legal process.

Public policy is the law or actions undertaken by a governmental body to address issues that affect the public at large as opposed to a specific private individual's issues or concerns. For example, in most states, it is against public policy to terminate the employment of an individual who is serving on jury duty. The public has an interest in having individuals serve on juries and not be concerned whether they will be fired from their jobs. This is different than a person who states they cannot serve on a jury because they may have an exam to study for; this would be a private issue and not one that a government would take action on.

As you can see, the different sources of laws create a web of legal requirements that impact the hospitality industry.

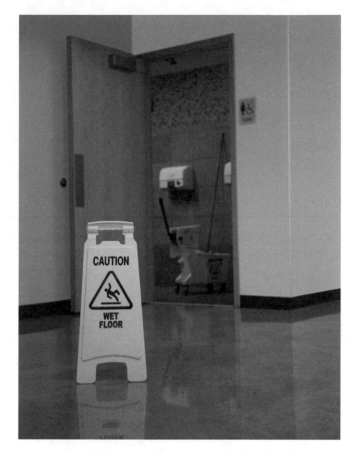

A person may sue a hotel for negligence if they believe they suffered an injury because the hotel did not uphold their duty.
© 2011 by Martin Haas. Used under license of Shutterstock, Inc.

The Legal Process

Basic Concepts

This chapter focuses primarily on civil law as opposed to criminal law. Criminal law is enforced by local, state, and federal agencies. This area of law is established to punish citizens for the crimes they have committed. The remedy is the enforcing agency incarcerating or limiting the freedom of the offending individual. Civil law is the adjudication of disputes between individuals. The primary remedy sought in civil cases is monetary damages.

The courts are utilized in hearing the disputes involving both civil and criminal matters. In the courtroom the judge makes any determination involving questions of law, whereas the jury bases their findings only on questions of fact. For example a judge would determine that running a red light is against the law, but the jury would consider if the light was red at the time the individual drove through it by listening to the facts presented by the witnesses to the accident.

In a civil case, the plaintiff is the alleged injured party. In a criminal case, the plaintiff is the state or federal government, usually through a district attorney or an attorney general. The defendant in a civil case is the party who is accused of causing injury to the plaintiff, and in a criminal matter, the defendant is the individual who is accused of breaking the law.

In a civil case, the plaintiff seeks a remedy from the court by initiating a lawsuit. This is accomplished through filing a complaint. A complaint is the document in which the plaintiff explains the facts and the claimed injuries, along with the legal theories under which they seek to be made whole. Once a plaintiff has filed a complaint, they must deliver or formally "serve" the complaint on the defendant. Once the defendant has been served, he/she has the obligation to file a response that admits or denies the allegations contained in the plaintiff's complaint. This document is called an "answer" and must be filed within a specific time frame from the date they were served. If they fail to file their answer within the time frame, the defendant will automatically lose the lawsuit. Once the defendant files their answer, the plaintiff and the defendant have the opportunity to ask questions and requests documents from the opposing party. This exchange of information is called "discovery." The written questions that one party to a lawsuit sends to the opposing party are called "interrogatories," whereas the request for paperwork is called a request for production of documents. The parties to a lawsuit can also conduct an oral interview of witness and the opposing party, this is called a deposition.

At the conclusion of discovery, the parties will begin to prepare for trial. After the trial, there may be opportunities to appeal. The process of litigation is very time consuming and can be very costly. Under the U.S. system of law, each party typically bears the burden of paying for their attorney and the costs associated with the lawsuit, even if they are deemed to be the winning party.

Claims versus Litigation

Due to the costs associated with litigation and the time that it takes to get a case to trial, many cases may be handled during a claims process or through alternative dispute resolution, such as mediation or arbitration. This may help the parties expedite any disputes.

The Role of Risk Management

Many disputes are resolved informally at the risk management level. Many large hotels and chain restaurants may have in-house attorneys available to handle cases as they arise, but most hospitality businesses do not. Rather than incurring the expense of hiring an on-staff attorney, or in-house counsel, many facilities simply identify an individual or create a department to handle claims made against the property. Sometimes the people in charge of the claims department have a legal background, perhaps even a law degree, but more frequently, they are individuals who have simply worked in the business for many years in different departments. Many such claims departments, or Risk Management departments, conduct audits and are proactive in identifying problem area and resolving them prior to guests incurring injuries. For example, if a Risk Management department notices frequent slip and falls in the pool area, they may recommend applying a more slip-resistant surface to the pool decking. Most companies that do conduct internal audits prior to an incident will undertake a cost/benefit analysis when assessing potential liability of a property. They assess whether the costs associated with fixing a hazard are too costly in comparison to the likelihood or risk of injury and/or lawsuit. For example, it may cost a restaurant $180,000 to fix cracks in the front walk area. A small restaurant may feel that the cost for fixing the cracks is too high given the minute risk that someone will trip and suffer injury. Sometimes facilities will simply ignore dangers, hoping that no one is injured and/or sues.

Facilities that do engage in proactive risk assessment typically find that they can better quantify, access, and manage risk, as well as improve the performance of their personnel. Certainly it makes sense to avoid situations that may create liability rather than simply reacting to lawsuits or claims after they have been filed. However, because it is difficult to quantify the savings to a facility, and the fact that risk management/claims departments are non-revenue-generating areas of an organization, they tend to be underfunded, understaffed, and frequently underappreciated.

Alternative Dispute Resolution

Pursuing a dispute through the courts is an expensive endeavor, and many individuals choose instead to have their matter heard through some form of alternative dispute resolution. The two main forms of alternative dispute resolution are arbitration and mediation. The parties who decide to resolve their dispute through either arbitration of mediation can mutually decide to make the determination of the arbitrator or mediator binding on the parties. Both of these processes involve employing the services of a neutral third party to hear the facts and evidence presented by each side. The fundamental difference is that an arbitrator acts more as a judge and makes a determination based on the facts and evidence presented by the parties. A mediator acts more as a facilitator between the parties and seeks to have the parties reach an agreed on resolution to their dispute. Because the parties are agreeing to the process for dispute resolution, they have more control over keeping the costs low and determining their own timeline for resolving disputes. Frequently, an arbitrator's decision is released within a few weeks of the arbitration. And issues subject to mediation are typically resolved, if they can be, at the time of the mediation.

Basic Duties and Rights of Hospitality Businesses

Restaurants, hotels, motels, nightclubs, and all businesses that receive and offer services to guests have certain duties imposed on them by law. In general, hospitality businesses have a duty of reasonable care or a duty to keep or maintain their premises in a "reasonably safe" condition. This does not mean that a hospitality business guarantees the absolute safety of its guests, only that the business must act as any other similarly situated business would in providing for the safety of their guests. For example, if the majority of hotels within a specified area have security officers patrolling their parking structures then it would be "reasonable" for other similar hotels to provide patrolling security. In fact, if a guest were injured in a parking area that was not patrolled by security, the hotel could be found to have breached their duty of reasonable care and be found liable for the guests injuries. Hospitality business in meeting their duty of reasonable care should undertake certain actions to maintain their premises in a reasonably safe condition. Regular inspections of guest areas will allow a business to determine what areas of their business may contain hazards that could harm a guest. The business then can either fix the hazard and make the area safe or warn the guest of the hazard. For example:

> Hilda is a porter at the Blue Note Hotel. Part of her job duties is to empty trash containers and keep the floors in the lobby clean (inspection). Hilda notices that a guest has spilled some soda (hazard) on the floor, and she places a warning cone next to the spill (warning) while she goes to get a mop to soak up the spill. She returns to the spill a short time later and mops up the spill (make safe).

Guests of a hospitality business also have certain rights and duties. When a guest checks in to a hotel they have the right to enjoy their room without interference from the hotel for the time period of their reservation. This is what is called a "revocable license," the guest has a license to utilize their room as long as they do not engage in conduct that would allow the hotel to revoke their license or evict the guest. Disorderly conduct, criminal activity, or a refusal to pay are all examples of conduct a guest could engage in that would allow the hotel the right to evict a guest from the premises. This is different than the rights of a tenant in an apartment or home, as they have a property right to be on the property that can only be revoked through the process of eviction.

Similarly, patrons in a restaurant or nightclub have a license to be there, which can be revoked for some limited reasons. "No shirt, no shoes, no service" signs are effectively giving notice to a patron of some of the requirements for being served in the restaurant. Nightclubs can have dress codes, so long as the codes do not discriminate on the basis of gender, ethnicity, and so on.

Hospitality businesses do have the affirmative obligation to eject people who are engaging in criminal conduct on the premises. So a hotel would have the obligation to eject suspected prostitutes, drug dealers, and so on from their premises, so long as they have a reasonable belief that the individuals are engaging in criminal activity, their actions are protected. Conversely, no business has the right to discriminate on the basis of areas protected by law. Violation of an individual's civil rights is actionable and can land a hospitality business into a lawsuit. For example, many states have made "ladies night" deals and specials illegal either through legislation or through court opinions.

Illustrations of How the Law Can Affect Hospitality Operations

There is no specific area of law called "hospitality law" that is used specifically to address our industry. Instead, the area of hospitality law is really segments of various other areas of law, including property, torts, contracts, etc. To illustrate this, the following are recognized areas of law and short descriptions of how this area may apply to the hospitality industry.

Property Law: This area typically looks that the use of real property (land). In hospitality, we typically see this relating to zoning issues for businesses.

Environmental Law: This area typically looks at the impact that a business has on the environment. In hospitality, this could be anything from the use of EPA-approved cleaning products and pesticides to the proper disposal of hazardous materials such as kitchen grease.

Torts: This area of law is a broad area with different legal theories that typically deal with personal injury claims. In hospitality, this could be anything from a fight in a nightclub between a patron and the bartender (an intentional tort) to a bellhop accidentally running over a guest's foot with the luggage cart (negligence). Other torts affect the industry as well, including defamation (saying something untrue about someone that has a negative effect on their reputation), privacy torts (whether the employer has a right to monitor e-mail or texts sent on a work computer or phone from a private account), or strict liability (whether the hotel is responsible when one of the wild animals in the magic act attacks a guest). The area of torts is very broad and has numerous applications to the hospitality industry.

Contract Law: This area includes all types of contracts, including common law contracts and sales contracts. In the hospitality industry, this would include everything from purchasing food and beverages to sell, hiring acts or entertainers, guests booking rooms, and sales associates booking meetings/events.

Intellectual Property Law: This area includes all elements under copyright, trademark, patents, and trade secrets. In the hospitality industry, this would affect whether a facility could play UFC fighting on their televisions in the bar area, use privately purchased CDs to play on the sound system, protect the use of names and menu items/ingredients, and so on. Intellectual property is a very specialized area that typically requires an attorney who specializes in these matters.

Constitutional Law: This area includes issues relating to the U.S. Constitution and the various state constitutions. In the hospitality industry, we predominately see this in regard to the Equal Protection of individuals and the Fourth Amendment right for police to engage in search and seizures on a hospitality businesses property. For example, if someone robbed a bank and ran into a hotel to hide, the police may want to conduct a room-to-room search for the bad guy. Whether they have that right may be a constitutional question.

Evidence: This area of law relates to what evidence is allowed to be used at trial. In the hospitality industry, it helps to understand what evidence must be retained for future use.

Employment Law: This area of law affects all businesses, including the hospitality industry, as relates to the hiring, discipline, and termination of employees. This includes the Fair Labor Standards Act, Title VII of the Civil Rights Act, the Pregnancy Act, the National Labor Relations Act, and the American with Disabilities Act.

Ethical Considerations

The hospitality industry is one of the fastest-growing multibillion-dollar industries in the world, one dependent on rendering good customer service and retaining customers. One of the ways to ensure that customers continue to frequent a business is for them to feel as if they have been treated fairly and with respect. Conducting your business in an ethical manner is one way to assist in maintaining good customer relations. Business ethics strives to balance honest and fair operations versus maintaining a profitable business. You are probably aware of some businesses that have suffered because of ethical violations, the prime example being Enron and more recently the activities of certain mortgage lending companies. These businesses failed to operate in an ethical manner with devastating effect. The federal government has reacted to the ethical shortfallings of businesses by passing certain regulations. One of these regulations is known as Sarbanes-Oxley. Sarbanes-Oxley set new regulations for the management of U.S. public companies and public accounting firms. Let's consider a few scenarios:

1. You notice that your coworker takes home notepads, pens, and office calculators. Do you report their behavior?
2. A guest is injured when the bed collapses in her guestroom. The hotel is aware that the bed frames are old and have had six others collapse injuring guests but has decided not to order 4,000 new beds but just fix them as they collapse. Do you let the guest know? Do you report the actions to an outside agency?
3. A front desk manager decides not to rent a room to someone who is transgendered. This is not against the law.
4. The law requires that only have to pay your employees $7.25 as minimum wage. Do you decide to reduce pay and maintain current employment numbers or lay off employees to maintain a higher pay rate, taking into consideration that your employees have families to support.
5. A guest checks in at midnight and angrily requests a suite. You know that there are none available, but you overhear a front desk clerk promise that they can get one in the morning.

Some basic questions you should ask when making a business decision to determine if the decision is ethical:

1. Would you reach a different decision if money was not involved?
2. Are my personal goals or values effecting my decision?
3. How would I feel if my decision was published in the newspaper?
4. Am I proud of the decisions that I am making?

Summary

The hospitality industry is a very complex and multi-faceted business. Many different laws affect the hospitality industry. Although many people believe that teams of lawyers are guiding the everyday operations, the reality is that most litigation arises as a result of the front-line employee or manager's actions. Thus, it is important that anyone considering a career in upper management have a working knowledge of the legal process. Hospitality businesses should endeavor to be proactive in their dealings to limit their legal exposure. As you continue on your journey through the hospitality industry, keep in mind the legal limitations and pitfalls that may define your career. And when in doubt, always contact an attorney who is licensed in your jurisdiction.

Review Questions

1. Explain the difference between mediation and arbitration.

2. Jose is suing the Rockin' Hotel for negligence when the hotel's shuttle bus driver closed the shuttle van door on Jose's foot, breaking it. Jose files his complaint in the appropriate court, having it properly served on the hotel. The hotel fails to file an answer. The court will now do what?

3. What are three sources of the laws that are required to be followed by businesses in the hospitality industry?

4. What are the limitations of litigation?

5. Why is it important to consider legal limitations and ethical limitations to business decisions?

CHAPTER 14

Physical Plant Management

Robert A. McMullin, East Stroudsburg University

LEARNING OBJECTIVES

- To be introduced to the importance of the physical plant.
- To understand the value of curb appeal.
- To understand the importance of communication between hospitality managers and independent contractors and corporate and property facility personnel with regard to property repairs.
- To be exposed to human resources issues of the facilities department.
- To understand the financial relationship between repairs and cost.
- To be introduced to engineering systems, types of maintenance repairs, security, and the Americans with Disabilities Act.
- To be able to develop the need and importance of facilities management and the relationship to guest satisfaction.

CHAPTER OUTLINE

KEY TERMS

Alternating current (AC)
Americans with Disabilities Act (ADA)
Amperes
Capital projects
Contract maintenance
Curb appeal
Engineering systems
Furnishings, fixtures, and equipment (FF&E)
Guestroom maintenance

Heating, ventilation, and air conditioning (HVAC)
Life cycle costing
Preventive maintenance (PM)
Property operation and maintenance (POM)
Refrigerant
Routine maintenance

The hospitality industry and education places great emphasis on service, marketing, and profitability to be competitive. However, one salient facet of the industry that is often overlooked is the "curb appeal" or attractiveness of the physical operations. Potential guests like to see a picture of the facility before they make a decision, and the traveling public can be fickle in choosing to patronize a hospitality entity. Quite often, they judge the quality of the potential experience based on what they think of the visual appeal. Along with the physical attractiveness of the facilities, physical operations can enhance guest satisfaction. How clean and well kept the property is also reflects on the perception of the guest. Therefore, learning and understanding the physical plant operations are imperative for hospitality management. The maintenance and design of a good working property can affect the service you deliver, or how your facility is marketed, ultimately having a great impact on profitability.

Primarily, the physical plant is comprised of landscaping, grounds, exterior and interior building structure, building systems, furnishings, fixtures, and equipment (FF&E). Landscaping and exterior appeal sets the tone of attractiveness of a hospitality facility. Many hospitality organizations spend great sums in marketing to guests, but the greatest hook is visual appearance. Hospitality properties should have clean, bright, and well-lit signage to allure travelers along with attractive landscaping.

However, other elements of the physical plant that are experienced by guests include plumbing, electricity, heating, ventilation, and air conditioning (HVAC). Managers of hospitality properties need knowledge and experience in understanding the effects of the physical plant and the actual outcomes to guests if equipment fails. In addition, management needs to be able to communicate with contractors, maintenance, and/or engineering staff to effect proper repairs without jeopardizing the guests' stay.

Manager Roles and Responsibilities

The scope and depth of the knowledge a facility manager must have depends on the type of property and size. Budget and economy lodging operations have relatively small and simple physical plants, whereas convention, resort, and luxury properties may resemble small cities. Other hospitality enterprises like restaurants and country clubs may rely on the property's general manager's communications with independent contractors or corporate personnel to repair their facility. Therefore, depending on the facility, there are many different backgrounds a physical plant manager must have.

The role and responsibilities of the hospitality facility manager or maintenance engineer typically includes detailed knowledge about the following areas:

1. Systems and building design
2. Building and system operations
3. Guestroom furnishings and fixtures maintenance
4. Equipment maintenance and repair
5. Equipment selection and installation
6. Contract management
7. Utilities management
8. Waste management
9. Budget and cost control
10. Security and safety
11. Contractual and regulatory compliance
12. Parts inventory and control
13. Renovations, additions, and restorations
14. Staff training
15. Emergency planning and response

The aforementioned responsibilities present challenges for many hospitality facilities managers or maintenance engineers. Each skill level varies depending on work experience and background. For example the facilities manager may have to work with various contractors when the property decides to renovate or restore its facility.

In many hospitality situations, the facilities manager will have some detailed technical background from contracting firms, trade or technical schools, or other similar related employment. Although a technical background in plumbing, electrical, or HVAC equipment is good, they may have little conceptual knowledge of the hospitality industry. This can create problems with communication as the different hospitality departments attempt to communicate their problems and facilities managers try to understand so that they can fix the problems. In some cases, it feels like each department is speaking a different language, and in some ways they are. This can place an additional burden on the management staff and lodging property because the facility management needs to work closely with the executive housekeeper, front office manager, and food and beverage manager.

Bridging the communication gap is an important task for the general manager of a property because the property can lose its attractiveness.

In addition to working closely with other departments, the facilities manager must understand the financial relationship between maintenance, repair, and cost. For example, the facility manager needs to track energy costs while trying to find ways to decrease this expenditure. This position requires the need to analyze records, such as work orders, equipment data cards, equipment history records, architectural plans, and instruction and/or repair records. The facility manager needs to evaluate the cost of a repair while remaining committed to bring costs within a budget. In accounting terms, the actions of the facility manager are reported on the line item of the income statement called property operations and maintenance (POM). The challenge for the facility manager is to improve the quality of the physical plant while using minimal financial resources. Meanwhile the facility manager has to study the relationship of how equipment is used and consumption of energy usage from utility bills like electric, gas, and water. Therefore, the facility manager must work closely with the property controller, too. If the facility manager can maintain the same level of property efficiency while finding ways to reduce costs, this would have a positive effect on the hospitality property's financial statements. In addition, a clean, well-kept property is more attractive to potential guests, and there will be fewer problems. As a result, it will improve guest satisfaction.

Another significant financial responsibility of the facility manager is the evaluation of capital projects. These projects require a major cash outlay when either replacing or acquiring new equipment. The facilities manager, along with other key hospitality management, must judge the initial cost, durability, safety, and energy consumption of capital equipment. There are other accounting concerns like depreciation and tax implications. The process of judging the selecting and analysis of capital projects are called life cycle costing, which considers the following:

- **Initial costs**—for example, cost of the item itself including costs of installation, interconnection, and modification of supporting systems or equipment.
- **Operating costs**—for example, costs of energy or water to operate the equipment and supporting systems or those systems affected by the equipment; maintenance labor and supplies or contract maintenance services.
- **Fixed costs**—for example, insurance, depreciation, and/or property tax changes resulting from the equipment or system.
- **Tax implication**—for example, income taxes and tax credits such as investment, tax credits, and depreciation deductions.[1]

Engineering Systems

Management in the hospitality industry needs to understand the basic design and operations of the various engineering systems. This improves the communication between the facility manager and the rest of management. Having direct daily communication is imperative to relay any information on malfunctioning equipment so it can be repaired, while not disturbing the patrons or interrupting other management in completing their own tasks. The basic elements of the engineering systems include several areas.

Management should know the basic operations of water and wastewater systems, refrigeration systems, heating, ventilation and air-conditioning systems, or site power production, and safety and security systems, so he/she can intelligently explain what needs to be accomplished by the facilities management team.

Water and Wastewater Systems

Water supply is necessary for food and beverage and lodging establishments. Management should be familiar with the operation of backflow devices, which prevent water from reentering a building. Other relevant systems include a storm sewer system for the disposal of rainwater and a sanitary sewer system for the removal of waste products. Another key system for restaurants is a grease separation or grease trap. Grease needs to be separated from wastewater to prevent water backup.

Refrigeration Systems

Hospitality managers should be knowledgeable about refrigeration systems. In the compressive refrigeration system, undesired heat is picked up in one place and carried to another place, where it is dumped or disposed. In many lodging establishments individual heating and air conditioning units are in each room. These are self-contained units that need to be maintained on a regular basis for guest comfort. Heat pumps work on a similar process except the unit is outside the room. This is a favorable way of heating and cooling for residential properties. The major components of the refrigeration cycle are

1. Refrigerant, which is a fluid with a low boiling point that starts as a liquid, absorbs heat, and becomes a gas, and then is placed under pressure to become a liquid again.
2. The evaporation is the section of the circuit in which the refrigerant evaporates or boils to soak up heat.
3. An expansion value allows the refrigerant to soak up heat, allowing pressure to be lowered, aiding the refrigeration cycle.
4. A compressor is a pump supplying the power to move the refrigerant through the system.[2]

Heating, Venting, and Air-Conditioning Systems

Heating, ventilation, and air-conditioning (HVAC) systems provide levels of comfort based on heating, cooling, and humidity for guests, staff, and management. The key components of an HVAC system are pipes (hollow cylinder or tubular conveyance for a fluid or gas), ducts (any tubular passage through which a substance especially a fluid is conveyed), pumps (a machine or device for transferring a liquid or gas from a source or container through tubes or pipes to another container or receiver), thermostats (converts the temperature into a signal that is sent to the HVAC unit conditioning the space), and valves (devices that regulate the flow of gases, liquids, or loose materials through structures, such as piping or through apertures by opening, closing, or obstructing parts of passageways). Systems can be decentralized and operate as individual units or be centralized as one system working collectively.

Electrical Systems

Some hospitality properties operate an on-site power production, but most operations have electricity delivered by local utilities. In either case, you should have a familiarity of electrical systems because you may experience brownouts (partial loss of electricity) or blackouts (total loss of electricity) that could disrupt your electrical service. Furthermore, management needs to understand electrical utility rates for cost control. Why should I be familiar with this? The utility is responsible for providing power at a correct voltage and frequency. The utility provides power through an electric meter that measures the rate and amount of power consumed, which generates the electric bill. The measure of the use of electrical energy is the watt. Amperes measure the rate of electrical flow through a device or appliance. The volt is the unit of electrical potential. Heating, ventilation, and air-conditioning (HVAC) systems should provide suitable temperature and humidity levels for guests, staff, and management. The HVAC system is an infrastructure of pipes, ducts, pumps, thermostats, valves, and pressure sensors. These systems can be decentralized and operated as individual units, or centralized as one system working collectively. Hospitality industry properties are supplied with alternating current (AC) from the local electric utility. If you do not have sufficient current, your property may experience lights flickering or reduced illumination. Why do I need to know this? The goal of the facilities manager is to provide a suitable level of guest comfort but reduce electrical use.

Safety and Security Systems

Safety and security systems are another key responsibility of management. The entire management staff should be committed to a safe and secure environment in protecting guests, staff, and management. This can be accomplished by communicating safety and security needs at management staff meetings. There are far-reaching issues in the time, training, and financial investment of safety and security systems. One of the major concerns in this area is protecting people and assets. Guests should be made aware of their surroundings and encouraged to use all protective devices a room has installed. Most hospitality lodging establishments have two or three locks in each door. Guests should be informed that all should be used along with a door port viewer to prevent room invasions by potential criminals. Guests should be informed never to open doors to strangers and always contact the front office with any concerns.

Negligence in this area could result in legal situations. Hospitality management should know the operations of fire protection equipment, including detection, notification, suppression, and smoke control systems. In knowing these procedures, hospitality employees can aid in the deterrence of fire emergencies. Another key is security systems such as electronic lock systems, closed-circuit television, elevator controls, and exit alarms. These procedures aid in protecting the guests from unwanted intruders and safely evacuating the guests if an emergency arises. Procedures should be developed in case of emergencies. Each hospitality property should have plans for terrorist acts, bomb scares, robberies, and extreme weather situations such as blizzards, hurricanes, tornadoes, and floods.

Maintenance

Regular Maintenance

Hospitality buildings are heavily used 24 hours of every day, seven days a week by guests, staff, and management. Each facility should have budgeted funds to reinvest in their property. Equipment will wear down, break down, and become obsolete. Management should have a tier plan to keep the property running efficiently.

Funds must be budgeted for reinvestment because equipment wears down, breaks down, and become obsolete. © 2011 by Ariadna de raadt. Used under license of Shutterstock, Inc.

- Routine maintenance is the general everyday duty of the facility staff, which requires relatively minimal skills or training. Examples of these duties include picking up litter, emptying trash cans, raking leaves, and shoveling snow.
- Preventive maintenance, sometimes referred to as PM, requires more advanced skills of the facility personnel. Examples of PM include inspections, lubrication, minor repairs or adjustments, and work order investigation.
- Guestroom maintenance is an activity applied to guestrooms of a lodging establishment. This is a form of prevention in ensuring guest comfort. Usually trained facilities personnel will remove several rooms a day from the rooms inventory and inspect them for the following:
  1. Change filters in HVAC systems.
  2. Test operation of TVs, electronic equipment, plumbing, and electrical equipment.
  3. Ensure the guestroom is free of any maintenance issues.[3]

When a facilities manager plans, he/she must take into consideration scheduling regular maintenance, which requires advanced planning, significant amount of time to perform, specialized tools and equipment, and coordination of the departments affected. Each task should be assigned as part of each employee's schedule every day so that it does not get lost or forgotten when problems occur.

Emergency Maintenance

Emergency and breakdown maintenance occur when equipment fails based an unforeseen occurrence like flooding or thunderstorms. Hospitality properties cannot prevent equipment breakdown, but they can use preventative maintenance procedures to possibly keep breakdowns from occurring. Having contingency plans can aid when breakdown occurs. For example, when there is a power failure, backup electrical generators can keep the guests calm so that they can get to safety. Especially the day of a big banquet, the kitchen staff does not want to find out the refrigeration unit died, and everything is slowly defrosting without a backup refrigeration unit available. Or during a heat wave, guests and staff will not appreciate the facilities staff if there are no additional air-conditioning units when one fails. Therefore planning for common emergencies is necessary. With natural disasters like hurricanes, flooding, and snow, one cannot plan every detail. However, a disaster plan should be developed to prepare as carefully as possible. Many hotels and convention centers have been rethinking their disaster plans as the year 2005 brought problems to all parts of the country. It is now becoming a major part of planning for all hospitality organizations.

Contract maintenance is necessary for certain equipment needs when repair and the skill level is beyond your facility staff. Some can be on retainer where they promise to handle emergencies as they happen for an annual fee, such as repair of refrigeration units where a repairman must come out. Cases for this type of contract might be washers and dryers for housekeeping or computer systems. Others contract for specific visits on a routine basis such as pest control. Some contractual arrangements can be available to assist in emergency or breakdown situations.

Electronic lock systems protect guests. © 2011 by Zdorov Kirill Vladmirovich. Used under license of Shutterstock, Inc.

Security

Generally in the lodging industry we welcome guests to our properties and have them lower their guard, relax, and feel at home. However, it is not always possible to know when a person is a welcome guest or a pretender. Without security measures, strangers could go up the elevators and break into rooms or worse. Yet lodging facilities are a public building, and so guests need to be aware of safety measures as well. Many establishments provide "Traveler Safety Tips" on check-in or in the room.

However, in addition to the customer's awareness, equipment can be in place to increase security. For example, guestrooms should be equipped with phones to enable guests to place emergency phone calls. Many hotels put phones by the elevators or in hallways to make sure a guest can have access. The facilities staff should install guestroom doors that self-close and lock automatically. Doors should be equipped with deadbolts, view ports, security chains, or bars. Guestroom windows and sliding glass doors should be able to lock. Windows and sliding doors should only be able to open, but not wide enough for an intruder to enter. In many cases, a simple bar that fits into the floor track of the sliding glass doors ensures safety.

Guests should be encouraged to use in-room safes or safety boxes available at the front desk. This provides an extra level of security for guest valuables.

All lodging facilities should have a key control system for both manual and electronic keys. When keys are lost, stolen, or not returned, the lock system should be evaluated. One approach to key control is referred to as the "five Rs."[4]

- **Rationale**—Criteria used to develop the keying schedule and to identify who will have various levels of access.
- **Records**—Involves guest information with regard to occupancy, status, and access.
- **Retrieval**—Actions by staff to recover keys from employees and guests.
- **Rotation**—Involves moving locks from room to room as a preventative security plan.
- **Replacement**—As keys are lost or locks compromised, replacement is necessary.

Historically, older lodging properties with manual locks need to follow the aforementioned program. Even electronic locks have been comprised, which means the system should be evaluated from time to time.

Hospitality management and facility staff should work together to provide the highest means of safety and security to the guest and their own staff. This provides a safe environment for all.

Americans with Disabilities Act

An important consideration in the hospitality industry is the Americans with Disabilities Act (ADA) of 1990. This act spells out reasonable accommodations to make for people with disabilities. Most people think that the ADA is only for people with physical handicaps or sensory impairments. However, think about which other people could use some help. How about your grandmother who is fine, but a ramp instead of steps would make it easier for her to gain entry into a building or a railing by the bathtub would make it easier to get out. Or, you break your leg and have a cast, wouldn't it be easier to use some of the wheelchair equipment? So this act requires a percentage of rooms to have special equipment, but many people have special circumstances when an ADA room would be appropriate.

With vans that are equipped to allow wheelchair entry, wider parking spaces are needed to accommodate someone exiting from the side of the van. For people with hearing and visual impairment, this act covers emergency situations like visual and audible alarms like strobe lights. In addition, many believe that complying with ADA standards is very expensive. However, many accommodations have simple inexpensive alternatives. Do you have two or three stairs but no ramp? Use a temporary metal ramp that can be folded and stored nearby and then put in place for the occasion. Some hospitality facilities will hire consultants to evaluate their facility to ensure their compliance with ADA laws.

Summary

The facilities staff is a critical department of a hospitality enterprise. The way the property looks, how it works, and the comfort of the guest is critical. Many of these factors will ensure repeat business and guest satisfaction. If measures are not taken to ensure guest comfort and safety, you may find yourself in financial and legal problems.

RESOURCES

Internet Sites

PM Engineer: www.pmengineer.com

International Facilities Management Assoc.: www.Ifma.com

FM Data: www.fmdata.com

Buildings Magazine: www.buildings.com

Burnham Boilers: www.burnham.com

American Solar Energy Society: www.ases.org

Green Globe 21: www.greenglobe21.com

National Fire Protection Association: www.nfpa.org

Water Web: www.waterweb.org

Water Online: www.wateronline.com

Electric Power Research Institute: www.epri.com

Air Conditioning and Refrigeration Institute: www.ari.org

Laundry Today: www.laundrytoday.com

Associated Landscape Contractors of America: www.alca.org

National Gardening Association: www.garden.org

American Institute of Architects: www.aia.org

Suggested Readings

American Hotel & Lodging Association (Producer). (1995). *Curb appeal: Creating great first impressions* (Videotape). Available from the American Hotel & Lodging Association, P.O. Box 1240, 1407 S. Harrison Road, East Lansing, MI 48826-1240.

Borsenik, F. D., & Stutts, A. D. (1991). *The management of maintenance and engineering systems in the hospitality industry* (3rd ed.). New York: Wiley.

Palmer, J. D. (1990). *Principles of hospitality engineering.* New York: Van Nostrand Reinhold.

Stipanuk, D. M. (2002). *Hospitality facilities management and design* (2nd ed.). East Lansing, MI: Education Institute of the American Hotel and Lodging Association.

Usiewicz, R. A. (2004). Physical plant management and security. In R. A. Brymer (Ed.), *Hospitality & tourism, An introduction to the industry* (11th ed., pp. 147–156). Dubuque, IA: Kendall/Hunt Publishing Company.

ENDNOTES

1. Usiewicz, R. A. (2004). Physical plant management and security. In R. A. Brymer (Ed.), *Hospitality tourism* (pp. 148–149). Dubuque, IA: Kendall/Hunt Publishing.
2. Stipanuk, D. D. (2002). *Hospitality facilities management and design,* 2nd ed. East Lansing, MI: Educational Institute of the American Hotel, Lodging Association, p. 231.
3. Ibid., p. 32.
4. Ibid., pp. 152–156.

Review Questions

1. Why is maintaining your hospitality facility so important?

2. What comprises the physical plant?

3. What is curb appeal? Discuss why this affects your properties image.

4. What are the responsibilities of the physical plant manager or maintenance engineer?

5. What is the relationship between the general manager and maintenance engineer with regard to the physical property?

6. What is the financial relationship between repair, guest satisfaction, and cost?

7. Name and discuss the engineering systems.

8. Name and define the three types of maintenance.

9. What is life cycle costing? Why is it important?

10. Why is security so important to a hospitality facility?

11. What is the importance of the Americans with Disabilities Act?

PART FOUR

Hospitality Career Menu

Lodging Segments

Sherie Brezina, Florida Gulf Coast University
Marcia Taylor, Florida Gulf Coast University

LEARNING OBJECTIVES

- To understand the different types of lodging available.
- To understand how lodging segments are classified.
- To understand the common and unique characteristics of each lodging segment.
- To understand the target guest market for each lodging segment.
- To understand the services and amenities typically provided in each lodging segment.

CHAPTER OUTLINE

Lodging Segments
  Classic Full-Service Hotels
  Limited-Service Hotels
  Long-Term/Extended Stay Hotels
  Bed and Breakfast Hotels
  Resorts
Other Lodging Segments
  Vacation Ownership and Rentals
  Casino Hotels
  Convention and Conference Hotels
  Boutique Hotels
  Senior Service and Residential Hotels
  Airport Hotels
  Motels

KEY TERMS

Bed and breakfast
Boutique hotel
Classic full-service hotels
Conversational currency
Limited-service
Long-term stay
Luxury hotel

Recreational amenities
Resort cruise ships
Resort hotel
Revenue per guest usage
Seasonality
Spa resort
Vacation ownership/timeshare

Lodging Segments

The lodging industry is characterized by an array of lodging alternatives to meet the demands of people traveling for business or leisure. At the core, lodging provides a place for one to sleep. Beyond the basic product, typically a room with a bed, the mix of all other products provided to satisfy guests, food and beverage, room, quality, standards, service, amenities, and parking are variable and determine the lodging category. Lodging properties are classified in numerous ways. The most common classifications are by price or rate (budget, midscale, luxury, boutique), location (urban, suburban, airport, destination), room type (standard rooms, suites, vacation condo units), market (business or leisure), size (mega resort, large, medium, small), and key attraction or amenity (spa, golf, convention, casino).[1]

Regardless of classification, all lodging segments share these common characteristics:

- The tangible product is rooms with beds for the traveling public to sleep.
- The product is perishable and consumed on site, meaning if it is not consumed or sold for the day, the revenue is lost and cannot be recovered.
- Lodging is labor intensive, with the traveling public willing to pay for services provided by people to meet their needs.
- The level and quality of hospitality courtesy and services distinguishes the lodging property.

Luxury hotels offer amenities for all senses, highly personalized service, and a focus on local culture. © 2011 by iPhotos. Used under license of Shutterstock, Inc.

- Buildings and grounds must have continuous maintenance and upkeep.
- Common laws of inn keeping apply emphasizing safety, security and cleanliness.[2]

This chapter describes the key lodging segments, the unique characteristics, services, and target guest market of each segment.

Classic Full-Service Hotels

The classic full-service hotel is best defined in the context of historical standards of accommodation and service tradition developed through experiences and refinement up to present times.[3] The full-service hotel market may be classified midscale, upscale, or luxury according to the services and amenities offered, the pricing structure, and location. Classic full-service hotels in urban areas of commerce cater to transient business travelers' needs of time and efficiency. The amenities and location of full-service hotels make them also appealing to vacation and leisure travelers. Classic full-service chain hotels represented in this segment can include Hilton, Hyatt, Marriott, Ramada, Sheraton, Intercontinental, Le Meridian, Westin, Holiday Inn, Ritz Carlton, Loews, Radisson. and Four Seasons.

Midscale—Also referred to as midpriced hotels, they are attractive to guests because of the rates, which are slightly higher than limited service hotels and below luxury hotels. They offer the basics in full service such as food and beverage outlets, including room service and uniformed guest service. They appeal to the largest segment of travelers, but cater mostly to business and individual travelers and families. Because they offer fewer services, they appeal to guests desiring some hotel services, but not the full range of luxury services offered by an upscale hotel. They are located in cities and suburban areas. Hotels in midscale classification can include Holiday Inn, Radisson Inn, Courtyard Inn, and Ramada Inn.

Luxury/Upscale Hotels—Luxury hotels are the ultimate lodging experience. The meaning of luxury or upscale is subjective and, in the hotel industry, constantly evolving. Common to understanding the product is providing extraordinary experiences that exceed customer expectations, and in many instances ultimate luxury conveys creating lifelong memories.[4] Although a small hotel segment in terms of number of properties, these hotels enjoy high-profile status within brands and customers. They are luxurious properties with an emphasis on service. Services and amenities offered include larger rooms, plush bath towels, upgraded amenities, and multiple food and beverage facilities, including fine dining or signature restaurants. Standard to luxury hotels are turndown service, valet service, 24-hour room service, concierge service, a swimming pool, and spa. Luxury hotel rates are high, which is justified by the level of personalized service offered and the ratio of employees to guest, which usually averages at least two employees per guest. This high ratio enables the hotel to offer an extensive variety of amenities and unique services.[5] Examples of brand hotels in the upscale category can include Marriott, Hyatt, Doubletree, Westin, and Omni. Brand hotels in the luxury category can include Marriott Marquis, Jumeirah, Ritz-Carlton, Four Seasons, Hilton Towers, and Forte hotels.

Limited-Service Hotels

The first limited-service hotels—Motel 6, Days Inn, and La Quinta—were built in the 1960s as an alternative to full-size hotels. They were able to offer low prices by not having the amenities of the full-size hotels, such as restaurants, lobby, and meeting space. Today limited service hotels, as the name implies, provide a limited number of services to the guests—a clean room, at a low price, in a secure environment. The idea is to meet only the basic needs of guests. Limited service hotels size varies between 50 and 150 rooms, although some of the newer properties are larger, with 200 or more rooms. The size of the rooms are usually smaller than full-service hotels, but some limited-service hotels are suite hotels, and therefore offer more space than a traditional hotel.

In addition they use modular and prefabricated construction materials, which keep the building costs low. This makes it more profitable at lower occupancy levels. Not only does this allow guests a less-expensive alternative, but it also creates a segment that is more affordable to purchase and hence attractive to first-time hotel buyers. The entry barriers to the economy segment are relatively low; less than $2 million, with minimal equity requirements, for a 40- to 50-room economy property. As a result, this segment experienced tremendous growth historically and is now considered the fastest-growing segment of the lodging industry with the largest number of rooms.

Limited-service hotel category is divided into three different segments and offers three different levels of limited service:

- Budget/economy hotels offer low-priced, clean, and safe rooms in convenient locations.
- Midscale limited service is priced higher than the economy level and offers amenities just below full-service hotels.
- Upscale limited service without food and beverage, the highest priced segment in the category, offers a higher level of comfort, such as upgraded décor and furnishing and hot breakfast.

Staffing is dependent of the number of rooms and the additional amenities. The role of the general manager is usually dependent on the size of the property and the level of service.

Long-Term/Extended Stay Hotels

Long-term stay hotels, also called extended stay, are defined as a lodging facility where all guestrooms include a kitchenette and provide clean comfortable, inexpensive rooms that meet the basic needs of the guests staying for business, leisure, or personal necessity. They are designed to offer a home-away-from-home atmosphere. The guests' rooms are apartment-style with living and dining area and a separate bedroom. The bedrooms, living, and dining are spacious, and the kitchen is fully equipped with dishes and kitchenware. In addition, limited housekeeping services, grocery shopping services, business services, self-service laundry and valet, continental breakfast, manager's reception, and limited exercise and recreational facilities may be provided. Rooms are rented by the day, week, or month. The more nights a guest stays at the hotel, the lower the rate typically. The typical long-term stay guest is business traveler on extended assignments, individuals relocating between jobs, corporate trainees, consultants, construction crews, occasional leisure travelers who are visiting relatives/friends, and families needing temporary housing.

The concept emerged as an alternative to the more traditional lodging for business and leisure travelers who needed a place to stay for seven or more days. Between 1995 and 2003, the number of rooms in the segment grew over 400%. The popularity and growth of this segment has continued, due in part to a significantly higher occupancy averages within other segments. The number of rooms represents approximately 5% of total hotel rooms in the United States. Further, marketing properties within this segment is unique. Direct mail, advertising on Internet sites, such as rent.com and homebuyers.com, are common. Marketing the property is more akin to leasing apartments than selling hotel rooms.

Bed and Breakfast Hotels

Bed and breakfast hotels, or B&Bs, offer an alternative lodging experience to the traditional hotel and limited-service hotels. They were first introduced in Europe and experienced explosive growth in the United States in the 1970s. Today, it's been estimated that the industry has grown to over 20,000 bed and breakfast hotels in the United States, catering to more than 40 million guests. The average B&B has nine guest rooms, but two-thirds have less than eight guest rooms, and one-third have fewer than four guest rooms. B&Bs are usually independently owned and operated, with the owner and his/her family living on premises. However, some Web sites refer to three different categories of B&B facilities:

1. **Bed and Breakfast**—small lodging establishment in a private residence, with one to seven guest rooms.
2. **Bed and Breakfast Inn**—larger and more commercialized facilities with 8 to 15 rooms.
3. **Bed and Breakfast Hotel**—16 to 30 rooms and operates more like a hotel, but only serve breakfast

B&B facilities vary, but typically offer an intimate, relaxing atmosphere. © 2011 by Andrew Gentry. Used under license of Shutterstock, Inc.

B&B guestrooms offer variation in size, attractive appointments, intimacy, in a relaxing home-away-from-home atmosphere. No two B&Bs are the same. Each room is decorated to match the architecture and era of the building or to match a particular theme. They are smaller than regular hotels, are personal in nature, have a quiet private atmosphere and typically provide extraordinary personalized service—catering to needs of the individual guests. Although breakfast is traditionally the only meal provided, at some B&Bs afternoon tea is served, and dinner is optional—served at the discretion of the owners. The addition of full-scale, gourmet or specialty restaurants and cooking classes for their guests has become the main attraction to some B&Bs.

With the increase in the number of B&Bs came an increase in competition. Traditionally B&Bs cater to the leisure market, so occupancy is highest on the weekends and holidays. The typical B&B guests are described as the older, affluent, well-educated travelers, who seek shorter vacations relatively close to home. They are looking for variety in accommodation—not the location—and stay an average of 2 to 3.6 nights. There is a move toward catering to the business market for meetings and the occasional business traveler, which helps the midweek occupancy. Wedding groups are also a major market because of the quaintness of some facilities and attractive locations.

Resorts

Resorts are the fusing of traditional food, beverage, and lodging hospitality facilities with recreational amenities that offer activities to guests. The variety and complex nature of the food, beverage, lodging, and recreational amenities found at resorts demand sophisticated management practices to be successful.

Resorts can be characterized in terms of:

- Location relative to the primary market—how far guests travel and by what means, car, airplane, or train
- Primary amenities, setting, and climate
- Mix of residential, lodging, and community properties[6]

Location is critical to both destination and non-destination types of resorts. The surrounding scenery, environment, or close proximity to the region's natural or man-made attractions providing recreation offerings are the experiences that motivate people to travel and stay at resorts. Resorts, particularly those referred to as mega resorts, are associated with specific types of recreational amenities and are identified by an activity such as golf, tennis, skiing, mountain climbing, fishing, health, wellness. Premium facilities for sports, exercise, gaming, equestrian, and entertainment activities create unique reputations and images for resort destinations. In many instances the resort is the destination because of the recreation amenities it offers.

At most resorts in the United States, across the country, high season is usually a 90- to 120-day period. Weather and climate dictate what is considered "high season," depending of the nature of the recreational activity that drives guest demand. Much marketing effort is given to boost occupancy levels during shoulder season. Full capacity is the norm during season. It is in the off season that a good marketing strategy can bring needed guests to the resort, extending the year and the profitability of the resort. Resort hotels often extend their season and fill the property in the months on either side of high season called the "shoulder season," with group business.

Resort guests have always been and continue to be more sophisticated consumers and have higher expectations of service and quality standards. Resorts cater to repeat guests, annually or several times a year. Often the yearly traditions and festivals attract and keep guests returning time after time to the resort. This must be incorporated with new offerings that keep the experience fresh for the guest.

The time and money that guests spend at a resort is discretionary, meaning freely chosen. Because of this, resorts are affected by demand elasticity to a much greater extent than traditional commercial hotel properties. This means management strategies must be always knowledgeable of economic, political, or social changes that may affect the resort's projected revenues and expenses in the short and long term.

Resort hotels attract guests that are seeking relaxation and an array of recreational and leisure activities. These properties are also popular choices to host business meetings because the property and location have marketing cachè, and the self-contained environment provides everything needed for a successful meeting, including recreational activities with few outside distractions to pull the attendees away from the business meeting. Resorts offer dedicated function space for meetings and events.

Resorts are found in all size categories from a few rooms or bungalows up to hundreds of rooms, suites, or housing units.

- Small resorts with 25 to 125 lodging units are often specialty "boutique" resorts catering to a small upscale market niche.
- Midsize properties of 125 to 400 rooms are typically chains and located in megaresort areas offering more space and amenities than the traditional commercial brand hotel.
- Large resorts have more than 400 rooms and are often located in primary resort locations offering ski facilities, beach frontage, theme parks, gaming, spa, golf, or a combination of these amenities.[7]

Further, resorts often offer a combination of facilities, including spa/wellness centers and residential single or multifamily homes known as multiuse resorts. The recreational amenities are available to all owners and visitors to the resort.

Residential Resort Lifestyle Communities— Second-Home Developments

Fee simple, individually or family owned attached, detached, or multifamily homes are often found in resort second-home development communities. These are best combined with primary and retiree residences to provide a mix of full- and part-time residents. These resort communities may be characterized by high-rise condominiums on beachfront locations, midrise low-density residential communities near lakes or ski areas, single-family developments with golf courses and a clubhouse, or large planned communities with a variety of housing types and recreation activities. For property owners, resort living becomes a lifestyle.

Spa Resort

The spa resort is distinct from the spa found at a resort that is part of many amenity offerings available to guests. Sometimes referred to as a destination spa, the spa resort accommodations and amenities are designed to target the spa guest, providing treatments and health and wellness programming. The spa resort markets a distinct and affluent niche, providing luxury, pampering, and programming to guests. The spa resort may not be open to outside guests. Memberships are sometimes sold to use spa facilities.

Other Lodging Segments

Vacation Ownership and Rentals

Shared ownership or timesharing was introduced to the United States in the 1970s. The term *timeshare* is defined as "the right to accommodations at a vacation development for a specified period each year for a specified number of years or for perpetuity."[8] Owners of timeshares purchase a time period, or fraction of a unit in the resort development, either by a lump sum payment or financed over a number of years. Timeshare owners pay a yearly maintenance, management, and operation fee. Many timeshares allow the purchaser to exchange or trade the timeshare through exchange companies. Over time the timeshare option has evolved from a set week that was purchased, to the addition of floating week options and most recently the more flexible option of vacation club points, which are purchased and can be redeemed at resorts within the brand or a vacation time period.[9]

The development of the timeshare concept grew out of the desire to finance property development of hotels and resorts. Timeshare units that can be sold prior to development have a much quicker return on investment (ROI) for the project's investors than traditional long-term finance options.

In the past few years most major hotel companies have developed timeshares. Marriott, Hyatt, Hilton, and Disney got into the timeshare business. Having well-known brands involved has helped to bolster consumer confidence in the timeshare product. Although some brands have recently backed away from further expansion of vacation ownership developments or sold their interests, the timeshare concept continues to evolve, offering a wider range of products and choices for consumers.

Condo hotels have become very popular with major hotel brands over the past few years The condo hotel has marketing appeal to the buyer as an investment and upscale vacation option, to the developer in securing investment funding upfront and to lenders for minimizing investment risk. Condo hotels combine hotel style amenities such as public spaces, housekeeping, spa privileges, beach, golf, tennis, and skiing access with the lodging appeal of a condominium unit. The condo hotel touts all the comforts of home, in a hotel resort atmosphere with none of the upkeep associated with owning a second home property. Structure and time options vary; however, each unit is individually owned, and the owner has a

specified right to occupy the unit. When not in use by the owner, the unit is part of the hotel's rental program and is booked and rented to guests who want to stay at the property.[10]

At many resorts and lodging properties the distinction between hotel rooms, timeshare units, and condo hotels is becoming blurred. The consumers' expectation is that resort lodging includes the availability of units with full kitchens, separate bedrooms, bathrooms, living rooms, and patios. Management of resort timeshare units or condo hotels is particularly complex. The manager often responsible to three or four stakeholders, the developer selling the units, the owner of the units, the owner of the hotel or shareholders, the timeshare association board, which governs the timeshare community, and the guest who is renting the unit.

Current demographic and vacation trends suggest that the timeshare and condo hotel concept is filling a market need for people desiring a resort or second-home experience. This consumer does not want the financial or maintenance responsibilities of year-round ownership because they only plan to spend a few weeks or long weekends on vacation. With the flex point system, vacations are not restricted to one location, and the desire to experience new places is appealing to many people. The United States dominates the timeshare market worldwide. Despite economic highs and lows, the long-term outlook for vacation ownership segment is positive.

Casino Hotels

As the gaming industry continues to grow around the world, casino hotels have proliferated to accommodate the gaming public. Most casino hotels offer full-service accommodations, several food and beverage offerings, entertainment, and shopping opportunities. In recent years casinos have developed opulent megahotel resorts with 1,000s of rooms. In addition to a large casino gambling space for the gaming consumer, large casino hotels usually have dedicated meeting facilities to market the hotel to conventions and large groups, meetings, and associations. For additional information on the unique characteristics of the casino hotel industry and entertainment, refer to the chapter on Casinos.

Convention and Conference Hotels

The large- and small-group meeting and convention market is a significant economic contributor of revenue to host destinations and meeting venues. Hotels designed to attract and serve this market are found in all major cities. Convention hotels range from 300 to 2,500 or more rooms. Conference hotels target smaller groups and usually have 300 rooms or less.

These hotels either have their own exhibition ballroom space or are located in close proximity to a large meeting exhibition (trade show) center, typically found in urban centers. The facilities offer ample function and entertainment event space, breakout rooms of varying size, up-to-date technology, and audiovisual equipment to support many simultaneous meetings and large capacity dining facilities. Reliable transportation to and from the nearby airport and area attractions as well as on-site parking and concierge services are found at convention and conference hotels. The marketing and services of these hotels is oriented to group business. The acronym for the targeted guest group business activity is MICE or meetings, incentives, conventions, and exhibitions.

Boutique Hotels

The first boutique hotel, the Bedford Hotel in San Francisco, was opened in 1981. Today, boutique hotels can be found in most major cities in places such as Europe, Asia, and South America. The growth of this segment is associated with travelers' search for a more unique or special hotel. Boutique hotels can be independently owned and operated, or they may belong to a group or collection of properties. They are located in major cities, usually in upscale/elite neighborhoods, and are traditionally housed in older, renovated buildings. Today, there are over 25,000 boutique hotels worldwide. The popularity has sparked the interest of major chains that are entering the boutique hotel market, building prototypes. The concept behind boutique hotels and also associated with the popularity of the segment is growth in the interest of history, art, culture, and design.

Boutique hotels are small uniquely designed hotels with 100 rooms or less and are described as contemporary, designed-led hotels, which offer unique levels of personalized service and high-tech facilities. Other descriptions of a boutique hotel are Avante-garde, intimate, charming, distinctive, cutting edge, trendy and classic, and with incredible attention to details and a high level of personal service. The majority of boutique hotels are sometimes described as small luxury hotels offering fewer amenities than luxury hotels. In boutique hotels the emphasis is on styling and style. This distinguishes them from other hotels because each hotel has a unique design, with

a specific focus on style. The rooms are usually furnished in a theme, stylish and/or inspirational. Some boutique hotels do have a dining room, and a majority offer bars and lounges. Those without food and beverage services are in areas with a wide variety of restaurants in close proximity.

Boutique hotels target customers from early 20s to 50s, with mid-to-upper-income averages, who are creative, fashionable, and hip and those who are looking for something different. Most guests will stay in a boutique hotel because of the uniqueness of the hotel more than the services offered.

Boutique hotels' services ranges from two to four stars, with majority at the four-star level, offering services on a personal level. They are known for offering a more unique guest experience than the typical large, corporate, and chain hotels. Boutique hotels distinguish themselves by providing personalized accommodation and services.

Senior Service and Residential Hotels

Senior service or senior living hotels, sometimes referred to as life care facilities, are designed for the affluent seniors and targeted to the specific residential and lifestyle needs of the fifty plus age group. These are typically marketed to active seniors and provide varied daily leisure programming activities and health and medical facility access. Residents can buy or rent small studios, one- or two-bedroom apartments with kitchens and have the daily convenience of hotel services. Meals may be provided as well as concierge services. Though a small part of lodging, this segment has gained renewed interest in the past few years, as affluent retirees prefer hotel living convenience to home ownership responsibility. Major hotel chains have entered this growing market segment, operating and managing senior housing facilities.[11]

Airport Hotels

Airport hotels provide guest rooms and meeting and hotel service facilities near airports. Airport hotels target the traveling public and are in high demand during the workweek, when airport traffic volume is highest. Airport hotels have added meeting rooms and conference facilities over the past few years to accommodate the needs of industrial park businesses that have developed around the airport. The convenience and cost efficiency of holding a meeting or staying overnight at the airport hotel is appealing to the busy business executive or salesperson. These hotels provide a crucial service to the traveling public in times of foul weather, overbooked or delayed flights, and air travel shutdowns.[12]

Motels

Motels are basic room accommodations, built along highway corridors to provide overnight rest stops for the traveling public. In recent years the motels that have been added to the market are managed by reputable lodging franchise chains and have customized the design and amenities of the motel to have consistent quality standards. The guest target market has expanded from the roadside leisure traveler, to the traveling businessperson and local meetings market. The provision of a clean comfortable room, parking, limited exercise facilities, a pool, and often a limited-service restaurant at reasonable rates, make the motel segment popular.

RESOURCES

Internet Sites

American Hotel & Lodging Association: www.ahla.com

American Resort Development Association: www.arda.org

B & B Industry Reports Healthy Figures, August 2009: http://www.innkeeping.org/news/28875/BB-Industry-Reports-Healthy-Figures.htm

Barsook, D. (2010). With the term boutique thrown around, we ask what is a true The Boutique hotel?: Interview with—Frances Kiradjian for the Hotel Yearbook 2010 Hotel Yearbook. Retrieved July 15, 2010, from http//:dbarsook@boutiquelodging association.org

Boutique and Lifestyle Association: blla.org

hotel.org

Anhar, L. The Definition of Boutique Hotels—HVS International. Hotel, Sales and Marketing Association International: www.HSMAI.org

http://www.hospitalitynet.org/news/4010409.search?query=lucienne+anhar+boutique+hotel. Retrieved July 15, 2010.

Small but *exclusive property* that caters to the affluent clientele with an exceptional *level of service at premium prices.* Retrieved on July 19, 2010, from http://www.businessdictionary.com/definition/boutique-hotel.html

http://www.hotelmotel.com/hotelmotel/ArticleStandard

International Resort Managers Association: www.resortmanagers.org/resort_links.htm

Weiner, Escalera, K. Top ten luxury travel and lifestyle trends 2008, http://www.hotelmarketing.com/index.php/content/article/071204_top_ten_luxury_travel_...

STR Global, 2010: http://www.strglobal.com/

ENDNOTES

1. Gee, C. Y. (2010). *World of resorts, from development to management* (3rd ed.). Educational Institute of American Hotel & Lodging Association, 23.
2. Ibid., 24.
3. Ibid., 5.
4. Greenwood, G. (2007). *How do you define luxury.* Arabian Business.com. (June)
5. Kasavana, M. et al. (2008). *Managing front office operations* (6th ed.) Lansing MI: Educational Institute.
6. Ibid.
7. Ibid., 10–11.
8. American Resort Development Association. (1997). *The United States timeshare industry: Overview and economic impact analysis.* Washington, DC: American Resort Development Association, 5.
9. Ninemeier, J. D., et al. (2008). *Discovering hospitality and tourism: The world's greatest industry* (2nd ed.). Upper Saddle River, NJ: Pearson Education, Inc., 170.
10. Baughman, M. A. (1999, May). New points system points industry in right direction. *Hotel and motel management,* 22.
11. Gee, C. Y. (2010). *World of resorts, from development to management* (3rd ed.). Educational Institute of American Hotel & Lodging Association, 19.
12. Walker, J. R. (2006). *Introduction to hospitality* (4th ed.). Upper Saddle River, NJ: Pearson, Prentice Hall, 149–150.

Review Questions

1. How are lodging segments classified?

2. Explain the difference between bed and breakfast, limited-service and long-term-stay facilities.

3. Describe the different target markets for bed and breakfast, limited-service and long-term-stay facilities.

4. Explain the difference between midscale, upscale and luxury lodging.

5. What are the advantages of being a four-season resort?

6. Explain the appeal of the timeshare or vacation ownership/club to the purchaser.

7. Why are cruise ships called "floating resorts"?

8. What fundamental needs are resort guests seeking?

9. How do resorts differ from traditional hotels?

10. Identify several trends that are impacting the lodging Industry.

CHAPTER 16

Hotel Operations

Michael Collins, Coastal Carolina University
Taylor Damonte, Coastal Carolina University

LEARNING OBJECTIVES

This chapter will provide students with a thorough understanding about how a hotel operates to effectively fulfill the needs of its customers while simultaneously generating a profit for the hotel's investors. Specifically, students will be able to:

- Outline the priorities and focus of a successful hotel management team.
- Describe the various divisions and operating departments within a hotel as well as each department's role in achieving the hotel's business objectives.
- Draw an organization chart that illustrates the structure of a hotel's management team.
- Explain how each department contributes to a property's ability to meet or exceed the expectations of the hotel's guests as well as the hotel's profitability.
- Explain how information technology assists in the successful management of a hotel operation.

CHAPTER OUTLINE

The hotel industry is an exciting and challenging industry that provides a variety of rewarding career opportunities for hospitality industry professionals. This chapter will provide an overview of how a full-service hotel is successfully managed and operated.

To provide the wide range of facilities and services, full-service hotels employ a diverse team of hospitality professionals to ensure that the guests'

needs are fulfilled and that the business is successfully operated. Hotel management must focus on the following three key constituencies to achieve the hotel's business objectives: hotel guests, employees, and investors. Hotel guests must be a primary focus of hotel managers and associates. Without satisfied guests, the source of a hotel's revenue, a hotel cannot possibly operate profitably; however, without investors, a hotel would not exist. Ultimately, a hotel is a real estate investment. Consequently, a hotel's success, from a business perspective, is dependent on its ability to generate a significant return for the hotel's owners. To operate profitably and meet the objectives of the hotel's owners, a hotel requires a dedicated team of productive, customer-focused employees that consistently meet or exceed guest expectations. As a result, the role of hotel management is to ensure that the needs of these three key constituencies, as illustrated in Figure 16.1, are fulfilled.

Successful hotel managers are extremely employee focused because they realize that internal service quality ultimately drives customer satisfaction and employee productivity, which in turn drives profitability. The hotel industry is a very labor intensive industry, and customer experiences are determined, in large part, by the moments-of-truth, or interactions, that occur between hotel employees and guests. Consequently, hotel managers that focus on fulfilling the needs of their associates and driving employee satisfaction levels will enjoy higher levels of employee productivity, which lower operating costs, and a higher level of guest satisfaction, which drives revenues, resulting in higher profitability—the

difference between revenues and costs. As J. W. "Bill" Marriott, Jr., Chairman and CEO of Marriott International, Inc., states, "Take care of your employees and they will take care of your customers," which is essential to profitability.[1]

Organizational Structure

Full-service hotel operations are organized into two primary operating divisions: the rooms division and the food and beverage division. These two operating divisions are supported by an administrative team, sales and marketing professionals, and an engineering department. The organizational structure of a typical full-service hotel is illustrated in Figure 16.2.

Rooms Division

The rooms division includes all areas of the hotel operation related to providing overnight accommodations to guests. This includes the guest services department, housekeeping department, and laundry operation. The rooms division is typically managed by a rooms division manager or assistant general manager, although in smaller hotels (under 400 rooms),

FIGURE 16.1 Management Focus

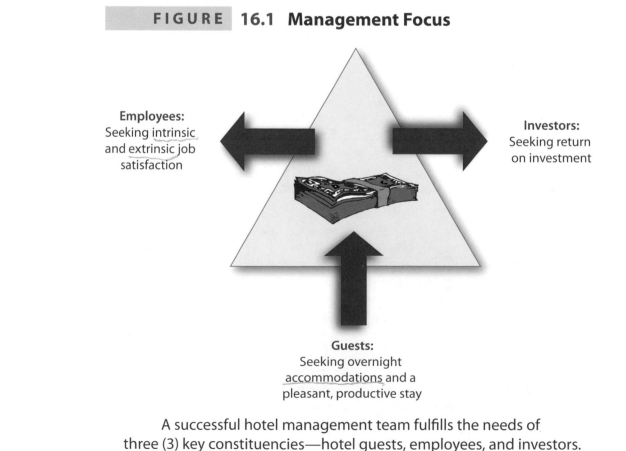

Employees:
Seeking intrinsic
and extrinsic job
satisfaction

Investors:
Seeking return
on investment

Guests:
Seeking overnight
accommodations and a
pleasant, productive stay

A successful hotel management team fulfills the needs of
three (3) key constituencies—hotel guests, employees, and investors.

FIGURE 16.2 Organizational Structure of a Full-Service Hotel

Operating Divisions		Support Departments

Rooms Division

Guest services department
  Bell services
  Guest transportation
  Front desk
  Night audit
  Concierge
  Communications

Revenue management

Housekeeping department
  Guestroom services
  Public area cleaning
  Turndown services
  Laundry operations

Food & Beverage Division

Outlets department
  Three-meal restaurant
  In-room dining
  Specialty restaurant

Catering department
  Catering sales
  Meeting/convention
    services

Banquet department
  Banquet services
  Meeting/convention
    setup

Beverage department

Culinary department
  Garde-manger
  Outlet food preparation
  Banquet food preparation
  Pastry
  Stewarding

Sales & Marketing

Individual business travel
Group sales
Advertising
Public relations

Administrative & General

General management

Accounting
  Income audit
  Accounts receivable
  Accounts payable

Human resources
  Employment
  Training & development
  Benefits & compensation

Security & loss prevention

Engineering & Maintenance

Guestroom & building maintenance
Major equipment maintenance
Energy & utility management
Sustainability

the general manager of the hotel may directly oversee the departments within this operating division or a director of operations may oversee both operating divisions (rooms as well as food and beverage). The guest services department, which is also frequently referred to as the front office, includes the front desk personnel, door and bell staff, telephone operators, concierge staff, and often the revenue management or reservations department. Some hotel management organizations choose to locate the revenue management function within the sales and marketing department because this department is responsible for maximizing hotel revenue and also serves as the interface between the sales department and the rooms division. The housekeeping department includes the heart-of-the-house areas of the guestroom operation, which includes the guestroom attendants, public area attendants, turndown attendants, and laundry operation.

Guest Services (Front Office) Operations

The primary responsibility of the guest services department is to build positive, mutually rewarding relationships with the hotel's guests by engaging in friendly, efficient, and productive interactions with the hotel's clients. Doormen and bellmen are typically the first to greet all guests arriving at a hotel and the last to wish the guest a fond farewell as they depart the property. Consequently, the bell services team makes a significant impact on the guests' perceptions of their experience at the hotel. Guest service agents provide registration services at the hotel's front desk and assist in maintaining guest accounts. Guest service agents are a central information source for hotel guests and must be aware of all events taking place within the hotel as well as the local area. Finally, guest service agents check guests out as guests settle their accounts on departure. In large hotels (over 400 rooms), the guest service agents may be supported by a communications staff or PBX operators that answer all incoming telephone calls, log all guest requests, follow up with the appropriate departments as well as the guests in an effort to ensure the timely fulfillment of these requests, and coordinate the delivery of all messages, mail, and packages that are received for guests by the hotel.

Night auditors work the overnight shift, typically from 11 P.M. until 7 A.M., and perform all the duties of a guest service agent during their shift, although in larger hotels they are often supported by an additional guest service agents. In addition to performing guest services, night auditors also update guest accounts each night by charging guests the appropriate room and tax rental charges for their accommodations. They also perform a number of additional accounting functions, such as producing daily revenue reports, posting banquet charges to group accounts, reconciling credit card receipts, and rolling the date in the point-of-sale and other information technology systems during the early morning hours when guest traffic at the front desk is minimal.

The concierge staff provides a wide variety of assistance, advice, and support to hotel guests regarding area activities. Concierges must be well versed in entertainment activities, cultural sites, local attractions, and area restaurants; a well-connected concierge also has close relationships with popular restaurants and attractions and can often obtain guest access to these facilities on short notice.

Revenue Management (Reservations)

A guest's interaction with the hotel often begins with a call to a hotel's reservation sales agents, unless the reservation is booked online or through a travel intermediary such as a travel agent. Reservation sales agents are responsible for assessing guests' needs and then selling accommodations to the guests that fulfill the guests' requirements at the appropriate guestroom rate. Hotels offer rack rates that are available to the general public as well as a variety of discounted rates for which a guest must qualify; guests will be accommodated at a group rate if they are staying at the hotel as part of an organization that has negotiated a group sales contract with the hotel. The revenue manager is responsible for overseeing the activities of the reservation sales agents as well as the availability of the various guestroom rates and the sale of guestrooms through various online (Internet) distribution channels. The revenue manager also provides

updated hotel occupancy forecasts each week that are critical for the proper scheduling of hotel personnel. Consequently, the revenue manager has a significant impact on a hotel's profitability because he/she is responsible for maximizing revenue as well as forecasting, which impacts labor costs—typically a hotel operation's largest variable expense.

Housekeeping Operations

The housekeeping department is responsible for maintaining the cleanliness of the hotel property and to ensure that guestrooms are stocked with appropriate guest supplies. The housekeeping operation is managed by the director of housekeeping or executive housekeeper. Obviously, maintaining a clean facility is critical to ensuring guest satisfaction. Guestroom attendants are responsible for the daily cleaning of guestrooms with support from the housemen. Public area attendants maintain the cleanliness of the public areas of the hotel, including the lobby, meeting room prefunction areas, exercise facilities, swimming pool deck, and public restrooms. Many upscale and luxury hotels may offer evening turndown service, in which the bed linens are turned down, the curtains are drawn, used bathroom linens are replaced, soft music is turned on, and the guestroom lights are dimmed. During this process, a card from the hotel staff and specialty chocolates are placed on the guests' pillows to wish them a pleasant night's rest.

Housekeeping management also oversees the laundry operations in a full-service hotel, which can be large and sophisticated, processing thousands of pounds of laundry on a daily basis. Because the laundry operation also services all food and beverage linen, an appropriate portion of the department's costs are allocated to the food and beverage division, with the bulk of the expense absorbed by the rooms division. If an adequate linen par is not maintained, the productivity of housekeeping and laundry associates will plummet, which will negatively affect profitability because housekeeping labor is the rooms division's largest variable cost.

Food and Beverage Division

The food and beverage division provides meals and beverage service to guests as well as meetings and convention support services to in-house groups. Food and beverage operations can be extremely complex, and because contribution margins (the difference between revenue received for a product or service and the direct costs associated with providing the product or service) on food and beverage services arc much lower than in the rooms division, it is often the most challenging division to successfully operate. The food and beverage division is typically managed by a director of food and beverage, assistant general manager, or director of operations, who may also oversee the rooms division. Outlined next is a description of the role that each department within the food and beverage division plays in meeting and exceeding guest expectations.

Food and Beverage Outlets

Food and beverage outlets refer to any retail outlet within the hotel that provides prepared food and beverage services to guests on request; this includes the three-meal restaurant, specialty restaurant(s), bar(s) or lounge(s), snack bar(s), coffee kiosk, and the in-room dining (room service) operation. The various outlets employ hosts, hostesses, food servers, cashiers, expediters, bartenders, and bussers, as appropriate, to efficiently provide quality, efficient food and beverage services to hotel guests and other outlet patrons. Menus are designed to provide both comfort foods that allow guests to feel at home, as well as specialty items that are traditionally found in the property's specific destination or that support a specialty restaurant's theme. Many hotels include at least one outlet that offers a buffet during high volume meal periods, particularly breakfast, in an effort to expedite service. Breakfast is typically the highest volume meal within the context of a full-service hotel. In-room dining (room service) is usually operated, in large part, as an extension of the restaurant, although it offers a unique set of challenges that must be overcome.

Catering Sales Department

The catering sales department is staffed by catering sales managers and meeting and/or convention services managers. Catering sales managers work with clients that are interested in planning meals and events in a hotel's meeting space that do not include a significant block of overnight guestrooms (groups requiring more than 10 guestrooms per night are booked by the sales department); these events might include retirement or holiday parties, award dinners, wedding receptions, and other corporate and social events. Because guestroom revenue has a much larger contribution margin than catering revenues, hotel management is very selective regarding the catering

Food and beverage services usually generate the second-highest amount of revenue in a hotel and lodging business. © 2011 by dusko. Used under license of Shutterstock, Inc.

revenue it will accept. Catering-only events are generally booked during times when demand for meeting space by groups that will require overnight accommodations, in addition to meeting space, is anticipated to be very weak or when hotel rooms are anticipated to be sold out and a portion of the hotel's meeting space remains available. Meeting or convention services managers, also part of the catering sales team, manage all the operational details and sell food and beverage services to groups that have contracted through the sales department to hold their meeting or convention at the hotel. As with revenue management, some hotel operating companies place the catering sales department within the sales and marketing department because they are responsible for maximizing food and beverage revenues received from a contracted group, which is a sales and marketing function.

Banquet Department

The banquet department ensures that meeting rooms are properly set to the clients' specifications and that scheduled breaks, planned meals, and events are properly served and executed. Convention or meeting services housemen are responsible for setting up all meeting rooms as well as breaking down and cleaning the meeting rooms following an event; much of this activity takes place overnight while the meeting rooms are not in use. Banquet servers are responsible for all aspects of the meal service within a hotel's meeting space. Many convention and meeting guests will require audiovisual services, including projectors, video monitors, microphones, and amplifiers.

Most hotel operators contract this service out to a subcontractor that pays the hotel a commission.

Beverage Operations

The control and distribution of alcoholic beverages within a hotel operation presents customer service, cost, and liability concerns. Consequently, this responsibility is typically assigned to one specific manager—either a dedicated beverage manager, in a large property, or one of the outlet, restaurant, or assistant banquet managers. The beverage manager receives all beverage deliveries and stores all alcoholic beverages in storage space that has tightly controlled access. Banquet bars are issued based on anticipated consumption just prior to the scheduled event, as outlined in the banquet event orders, and then inventoried on return to the liquor storeroom so that actual consumption can be determined and the group charged appropriately. The beverage manager is responsible for staff training relative to the safe serving of alcohol, which represents a potential liability for the hotel operator.

Culinary Operations

The executive chef is responsible for food production within the hotel. Typically, the executive chef is assisted by two or more sous chefs, which oversee cold food preparation, outlet food preparation, banquet food, and bakery and pastry items, as well as an executive steward. The *garde-manger* oversees preparation of all cold food items including salads, dressings, vegetable crudités, deli trays, etc. in addition to preparing *mis-en-plas* items for use in hot food preparation. The outlet sous chef oversees the food production cooking line that produces food for the restaurant(s), in-room dining, and lounge, whereas the banquet sous chef is responsible for banquet food preparation. The executive steward ensures the cleanliness of the kitchen as well as all dishes and serviceware in addition to making certain that banquet food is delivered to the meeting room service areas for the banquet servers to serve while it is hot and fresh.

In developing menus, the executive chef works closely with the director of food and beverage, the outlet manager, and the director of catering, as appropriate, to ensure that guests are provided with a variety of attractive, nutritious menu options while at the same time making certain that a manageable number of ingredients need to be maintained in the food inventory to produce the various menu items. Food preparation is very labor intensive. Although today's chef must have strong culinary skills, a chef must also be an effective manager. Managing food and labor costs, and a wide variety of employee issues including employee training and development, are critical to a chef's ultimate success.

Sales and Marketing

The sales and marketing department is responsible for driving revenue by attracting meetings, conventions, and individual guests to the hotel. The director of sales and marketing oversees a team of account executives and sales managers that are each responsible for contracting business in specific market segments. A group is typically defined as a client that requires a minimum of 10 guestrooms or more for any given night. Sales managers obtain leads from a variety of sources, including the local chamber of commerce and convention and visitors bureau, as well as the chain's national sales offices, and then follow up on these leads by assessing the clients' needs and preparing a proposal to provide the prospective clients with the appropriate array of services (e.g. guestrooms, meeting space, meals, and audiovisual services) that meet the specific needs of the client. Proposals are typically reviewed, each morning, by the general manager, director of sales and marketing, and revenue manager to ensure that they meet the targeted revenue goals of the hotel for the dates specified in the proposal prior to be sent to the client.

The director of sales and marketing also oversees the local advertising and public relations activities of the hotel. Property specific advertising may be placed in feeder markets to drive leisure business and locally to generate leads for the sales team; however, the bulk of hotel advertising, for brand-affiliated hotels, is controlled and placed by the chain to build brand awareness. Many hotels also engage in a number of public relations activities, such as hosting charitable events, in an effort to cultivate a reputation of being a good corporate citizen.

Administrative and General

The general manager of the hotel is responsible for the overall success of the property. He/she is ultimately responsible for all areas of the hotel's operation and serves as the interface between the hotel and the corporate office, the franchise organization (if applicable), and the hotel's investors. The general manager's administrative assistant often serves as the clearinghouse for all customer feedback, including guest surveys and guest correspondence. Following up on guest feedback, internally with the appropriate hotel personnel and directly with the guest, is critical to maintaining a strong guest focus among the hotel's staff and a positive reputation with the hotel's clientele.

Accounting

The hotel's controller oversees the accounting function. The accounting office is responsible for accounts payable, the timely payment of invoices from suppliers; accounts receivable, the preparation of invoices and collection of payment from meeting and convention groups; financial reporting, the timely and accurate production financial documents including monthly profit and loss statements as well as the balance sheet; and cost control, maintaining purchasing controls coupled with the daily reporting of revenues and projected expense levels. In many hotel organizations, many accounting functions, particularly the accounts payable and receivables functions, have been centralized in corporate and regional offices in an effort to reduce payroll costs.

Human Resources

The director of human resources is responsible for overseeing employment, training and development, and compensation and benefits. Due to the labor-intensive nature of the hotel industry, most large hotels (over 400 rooms) employ a human resource management team that assists hotel managers in the hiring, coaching, counseling, and development of the hotel's associates. A full-service hotel will typically employ 0.75 to 1.00 full- and part-time employees per guest room, depending on the service level provided coupled with the amount of meeting space and exact number of food and beverage outlets (e.g., a 400-room full-service hotel will employ 300 to 400 associates); a hotel also typically employs approximately one manager or supervisor for each 10 associates. Ultimately, departmental managers are responsible for coaching, evaluating, and training the employees that they supervise; however, a property's human resource professionals will ensure compliance with labor laws and regulations and the timely completion of employee evaluations in addition to assisting managers with recruiting associates, compensation issues, and other human resource issues. The human resource department also assists with benefits administration and manages workers' compensation and unemployment claims.

There are a variety of ways hotels and lodging facilities can be owned and operated. © 2011 by haveseen. Used under license of Shutterstock, Inc.

Security and Loss Prevention

Hotels maintain substantial inventories of operating equipment, televisions, food, alcoholic beverages, guestroom supplies, personal care items, linen, china, glassware, and silverware. The front desk and food and beverage outlets also collect, at times, large amounts of cash. Expensive artwork and furnishings are found throughout an upscale hotel property. In addition, a hotel is accessible through a variety of entrances, and a busy hotel has a steady flow of guests, meeting attendees, and employees in and out of the facility throughout the day and late into the evening. As a result, it is important that a hotel has a loss prevention plan and a team of loss prevention professionals that circulate the hotel to minimize the loss of such items. The department of loss prevention also ensures that appropriate emergency procedures are in place to ensure the safety and well-being of hotel guests and associates. Loss prevention officers are most concerned with the loss of a customer. As a result, loss prevention officers are cross-trained to fulfill many guest service functions.

Engineering, Property Operations, and Maintenance

The director of engineering or chief engineer oversees the maintenance of the hotel. Hotels typically employ a range of specialized technicians within the engineering department, including carpenters, electricians, HVAC (heating, ventilation, and air-conditioning) technicians licensed to work with

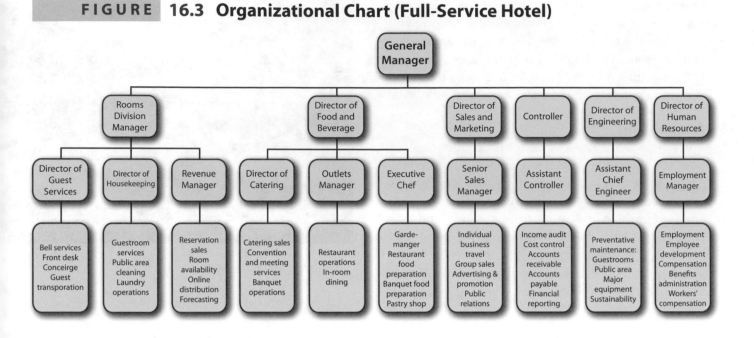

FIGURE   16.3 Organizational Chart (Full-Service Hotel)

refrigerants, a kitchen equipment mechanic, painters, and plumbers, in addition to shift engineers that handle any guest concerns or immediate needs. Because a hotel is a real estate investment, hotel operators have a responsibility to ensure that the value of the investment is protected through an aggressive preventative maintenance program; a strong preventative maintenance also ensures a positive guest experience. Preventative maintenance programs are in place for both the guestrooms as well as the hotel's major equipment

Utility Management and Sustainability

The director of engineering chairs the energy management and sustainability committee in a full-service hotel. This committee is charged with the responsibility of determining strategies that may be employed to reduce utility expenses or improve the sustainability of the hotel's operation. Hotel operations take a number of steps to reduce the hotel's consumption of the earth's resources, including the use of sophisticated energy management systems and motion or heat sensors to shut down or cycle equipment in an effort to reduce energy consumption. In addition, hotels recycle partially used bars of soap

and shampoo, food scraps, cooking oils, and many other items in addition to glass, aluminum, cardboard, and paper. Hotels guests are encouraged to reuse guestroom linen as well, which reduces the use of laundry chemicals and lowers housekeeping and laundry labor costs.

Management Structure

The senior management team at a full-service hotel property is often referred to as the Executive Operating Committee (EOC); this committee is comprised of the rooms division manager, director of food and beverage, director of sales and marketing, controller, as well as the director of human resources, and is overseen by the general manager. In some organizations, the executive chef also serves on the EOC. The next level of management is comprised of the department heads; this includes the director of guest services, executive housekeeper, revenue manager, director of catering, food and beverage outlets manager, and executive chef (if not serving on the executive operating committee). A typical full-service management structure is illustrated in Figure 16.3.

ENDNOTE

1. Marriott, Jr., J. W., Brown, K. A. (1997). *The spirit to serve: Marriott's way.* New York: HarperCollins Publishers, p. 34.

Name _____   Date _____

Review Questions

1. Briefly describe the priorities and focus of a successful hotel management team.

2. List the various divisions and operating deparments within a hotel.

3. Describe each department's role in achieving the hotel's profitability.

4. Draw an organization chart that illustrates the structure of a hotel's management team.

5. Explain how each department contibutes to a property's ability to meet or exceed the expectations of the hotel's guests.

6. Explain how information technology assists inthe successful management of a hotel operation.

Food Service Segments

David Rivera, Jr., East Carolina University

LEARNING OBJECTIVES

- To understand the difference between commercial and noncommercial food service establishments.
- To understand the different types of food service available within the commercial sector.
- To understand new types of food service operations emerging within the commercial sector.
- To understand the different types of food service available within the noncommercial sector of the food service segment.
- To examine future trends within the food service segment.

CHAPTER OUTLINE

Examination of Commercial and Noncommercial
  Food Service
Food Service within Commercial Operations
Noncommercial Food Service Operations
Summary

KEY TERMS

Casual dining restaurant
Commercial food service
Hybrid restaurant
Noncommercial Institutional Food Service

Quick-service restaurant (QSR)
Restaurant
Upscale restaurant

Examination of Commercial and Noncommercial Food Service

There are many different types of operations within the food service sector of the hospitality industry. The initial breakdown of the food service sector within the hospitality industry can begin with the separation of food service into commercial and noncommercial establishments. Commercial operations typically operate with the premise that they will be a revenue-generating establishment. Food service outlets whose primary goal may not be to generate revenue are typically referred to as a noncommercial establishment or an institutional (on-site) operation. A breakdown of this segment within the hospitality industry may be seen in Figure 17.1. The typical commercial establishment is referred to as a restaurant. Noncommercial establishments are typically separated into two types of classifications referred to as either self-operated or contract food service.

Food Service within Commercial Operations

Commercial operations within the food service segment of the hospitality industry are typically broken down into three basic categories. These categories are quick-service, casual dining, and fine dining or upscale restaurants. Quick-service (fast-food) restaurants are also sometimes referred to as limited-service restaurants. The primary function of fast-food restaurants is to provide a limited number of food items to customers in a very short period of time. In

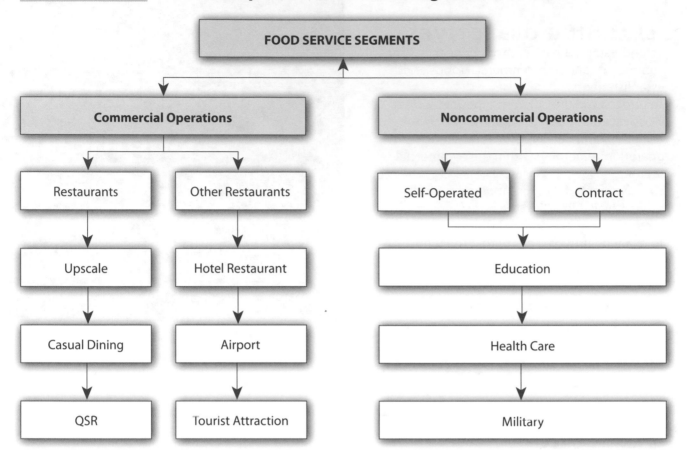

FIGURE   17.1 Example of Food Service Segment Breakdown

this type of establishment, customers typically order their food at a counter or through a drive-thru and pay for their food before consuming it. These types of establishments target individuals who are looking for a meal at a value and have a limited amount of time to spend.

Casual dining provides a relaxed atmosphere without a high price tag. © 2011 by Phil Date. Used under license of Shutterstock, Inc.

Another type of commercial food service establishment is casual dining restaurants. Casual dining restaurants were initially created to cater to the needs and want of the middle class looking to enjoy the activity of going out to eat and being served without the high price tag associated with upscale or fine dining restaurants. Casual dining restaurants are exactly as their name implies. They promote a casual relaxed atmosphere to dine in. Some casual dining restaurants may revolve around a certain theme such as seafood (Red Lobster) or Italian food (Olive Garden). Other examples of casual dining restaurants include TGI-Fridays, Outback, Steak and Ale, and Ruby Tuesdays, just to name a few.

The third restaurant type is fine dining or upscale dining. Fine dining establishments are also sometimes referred to as white table cloth restaurants. At these establishments, a high level of service is delivered and expected by the patron. The restaurant décor itself helps to deliver the feeling that a superior dining experience is about to be delivered by the staff and experienced by the customer. With this level of service delivery, the price tag associated with upscale dining restaurants is rather expensive. It is not out of the realm of possibility that the bill for this dining experience exceeds $100 per person.

Expanding further within the commercial operations segment, food service establishments may also be broken down into different areas besides the three basic classifications we've covered. These different areas include, but are not limited to, food service within hotels, country clubs, airports, cruise ships, convenience or grocery stores, and tourist attractions such as zoos, museums, sporting events, and theme parks.

Hotel food service is slightly different than typical restaurants in that they often operate with extended hours to serve the customers staying on property. They may also have different levels of menus and have a special limited menu to meet the needs of guests looking to order room service. The profit margin of hotel food service establishments is also typically lower than that of a typical restaurant.

Food service within the country club also has its own specific set of challenges. Country clubs have the task of running various types of food service from snack cart outlets to higher end or upscale restaurant type service. Other considerations that are often present in a country club are special events that add specific instructions such as a wedding or other type of party, to special-event buffet setups. The overall types of food service concepts that are available in a country club include a grill, an upscale type restaurant, a banquet department to handle the special events, and a snack bar or cart of some kind.

With airplane companies decreasing the availability of food service onboard their aircraft, airports have made adjustments in their food service availability. Each airport across the United States does things very differently; however, one can find that airports are offering a variety of quick-service and casual dining restaurant options in their terminals. Restaurants at airports are also experiencing a change in their operations due to new security restrictions. They also may be experiencing an increase in customer usage because of the security guidelines put in place at many airports that require passengers to arrive at least two hours before their flight times. This increase in time at the airport allows passengers more time to eat, so airports are making a wider variety of foods available for passengers to either eat while they wait or to take with them on the plane as they travel.

Fine dining is superior "white table cloth" dining. © 2011 by Martin Maun. Used under license of Shutterstock, Inc.

Dining on cruise ships also offers variety in food service choice. Typically, cruise ships are known for their all-you-can-eat option and wide variety in those options. These dining options are typically associated with an all-inclusive package that many cruise ship tours offer. On cruise ships one may find various types of themed restaurants such as Italian or Chinese food options, as well as find a variety in terms of dining style (casual to upscale dining).

Other dining options within the commercial food service segment that are not within the scope of the traditional three types of restaurant options include food service at various types of tourist attractions. One may find that food service at certain types of tourist attractions resemble cafeteria-style food operations that rival the best fine dining establishments in the country. Walt Disney World in Lake Buena Vista, Florida, is a great example of an establishment that offers all types of food service options in one location. Food service at Disney ranges from snack carts located throughout the theme park to very special high-end dining. This model is also being followed by many sporting arenas. The newly built Yankee Stadium in New York City has snack locations located throughout the stadium, while also offering commercial restaurant establishments that are available throughout the year.

Another food service outlet that is gaining in popularity is the convenience store. Typically one may think of the convenience store to grab a quick bite such as a hot dog and grab a soda or to just purchase gas. However convenience stores such as Wawa and Sheetz are offering made-to-order food items that are putting them in direct competition with traditional restaurant concepts. These establishments are also making premade fare daily to meet the needs and wants of the diverse consumers that patronize these establishments daily. The differing levels of food service offered at these types of establishments can range from simple snack machines to very large stores that offer a restaurant option for dine in or takeout.

New Types of Food Service within Commercial Operations

As times and preferences have changed among consumers, there has been an emergence of different types of food service outlets. A popular type of outlet that has grown over the last decade is the hybrid food service establishment concept. A typical hybrid concept one might find in the food service sector of the hospitality industry is often referred to as the fast-casual restaurant. This concept has combined the quick-service and casual dining restaurant. An example of this type of establishment is Steak 'n' Shake restaurants. In this type of restaurant you will find that if you want to be seated by a hostess and attended to by a server, this level of service is available to you. However, if you want the same type of food, but do not want the casual dining experience offered by Steak 'n' Shake, one may either go through the drive-thru or go to the Take Home a Sack counter. The idea behind this concept is that you can get a high-quality food product served with the speed and efficiency of a quick-service restaurant.

Another type of hybrid concept that is emerging and gaining in popularity is the cinema-eatery. This is a combination of a movie theater and a restaurant. These establishments provide the latest movies, while at the same time providing quality food that is not traditionally served in movie theaters such as steaks, made-to-order hamburgers, and shrimp cocktails. These establishments have reported that they have meal tabs that run between $10 and $15 per person.[1]

Noncommercial Food Service Operations

Noncommercial or on-site food service establishments include a wide variety of organizations such as hospitals, schools, college and universities, correctional facilities, and military operations. Hospital food service operates for both patients and their visitors such as family and friends. Besides the food that is served to patients, who may have special dietary needs, you will find that there are food outlets that range from a small food cart to cafeteria-style dining. Another form of noncommercial food service revolves around educational establishments such as K–12 schools and colleges and universities. The food made available at the K–12 level may not be as sophisticated as the food provided at colleges and universities because of various food programs put in place at this level. College and university food service, however, is always changing to meet the needs and wants of the students, faculty, and staff that are at the university or college where the food service is being offered. Companies such as ARAMARK and Compass Group operate on college campuses and work to generate a profit, so they offer many different types of food products and food service styles that are similar to traditional restaurant operations.

Military food service is another type of noncommercial operation. Military food service has seen a change over the last decade to cater to the preferences and trends that have also become evident in commercial establishments. The types and presentation of food has changed to make individuals enlisted in the military feel as if they are in a casual dining food service establishment. There has also been a growth on military bases of partnering with commercial establishments to offer more food options. These trends have also altered the food service in correctional facilities. Many correctional facilities are serving food that meets certain nutritional guidelines. Food service in correctional facilities also is being delivered in different ways to include self-serve salad, dessert, pasta, and pizza bars. Food safety and sanitation is becoming more evident within correctional facilities, and outdated cooking methods are being replaced with new state-of-the-art equipment.[2]

Summary

The food service sector of the hospitality industry has continued to be one of the fastest-growing and most exciting areas of the hospitality industry. If one is looking for a career that will offer excitement and an opportunity to deliver great unforgettable experiences to customers, then a profession within the food service sector of the hospitality industry may be the career direction for you. The food service sector has many different opportunities in many different areas for people with very different personalities and management styles. The level of expectation customers have of managers changes depending on which type of establishment in the food service sector you choose. However, the basic concepts and responsibilities of a food service provider are the same, no matter which type of establishment within the food service segment you choose. Being prepared is an essential component for management success in the food service sector of the hospitality industry.

ENDNOTES

1. Ruggless, R. (2007). Growing theater-restaurant hybrids target dinner and a movie dollars. *Nations Restaurant News.* Retrieved September 10, 2010, from http://www.nrn.com/article/growing-theater-restaurant-hybrids-target-dinner-and-movie-dollars

2. Gregoire, M. B., & Spears, M. C. (2007). *Food service organizations: A managerial and systems approach* (6th ed). Upper Saddle River, NJ: Prentice Hall.

Review Questions

1. What is the difference between commercial and noncommercial food service establishments?

2. What are the three different types of restaurants discussed in this chapter?

3. What is the difference between the different types of restaurants (quick-service, casual, and upscale dining restaurants)?

4. What are some types of noncommercial food service outlets discussed in this chapter?

Restaurant Operations

Joseph M. Scarelli, Niagara University

LEARNING OBJECTIVES

This chapter will provide students with an understanding of how a fine dining restaurant operates, and the responsibilities and challenges managers face. Specifically, students will be able to:

- Describe the various departments and positions within a restaurant.
- Create an organizational chart illustrating the structure of a restaurant's management team and employees.
- Identify functions and responsibilities associated with management positions.

CHAPTER OUTLINE

Management Priorities
Organizational Structure
    Front of the House
    Back of the House
Management Responsibilities

The food service industry is an exciting industry that provides many rewarding career opportunities to those in search of a challenging and fast-paced career. The subject of restaurant operations is a broad subject, with many different incarnations of restaurants to discuss. As you learned in earlier chapters, there are different ownership types: independent operations, corporate-owned chain operations, and franchises. Within those ownership types there are many styles of restaurants, which were discussed in Chapter 17. These styles include fine dining, casual, fast-casual, quick-service restaurants (QSRs), catering operations, and noncommercial operations. This chapter will focus on the structure of a typical upscale or fine dining restaurant. Many of the other types of establishments have similar structures to fine dining, with variations or fewer specialized positions.

Management Priorities

It takes more than just a quality product to succeed in the restaurant business. Those in management positions must remain focused on keeping costs within the operating budget, as restaurants typically have a low profit margin, and close attention must be paid to all financial matters to operate profitably. In addition, managers are concerned with maintaining the standards of the restaurant, both of the food and the service quality. Further, they must anticipate and keep up with changes in the marketplace. Failure to maintain standards or keep up with changes would result in a loss of the customer base, the source of revenue for the restaurant.

Organizational Structure

Fine dining restaurants are organized in two operating areas: the back-of-the-house (BOH) or kitchen operations, and the front-of-the-house (FOH) or the dining room and all nonkitchen areas. The general manager oversees both areas, and both areas must communicate and work seamlessly with the other for a restaurant to succeed. The staffing system is largely based on the brigade system developed by Escoffier,[1] where each worker or station is assigned a specific set of tasks. Within this organizational structure, each

The two great challenges of managing a restaurant are labor and perishable products. © 2011 by Christy Thompson. Used under license of Shutterstock, Inc.

position is training for the position above, giving the opportunity for advancement. This structure is illustrated in Figure 18.1.

Front of the House

The maître d'hôtel, usually shortened to maître d', is responsible for the overall management of service. This person is the host who greets guests on arrival and often handles reservations. In addition, the maître d' trains service personnel, works with the sommelier to select wine, and may work with the chef to develop the menu. During service the maître d' is the liaison between the front and the back of the house, communicating with the chef and sous chef as necessary. The sommelier, or wine steward, is in charge of selecting and purchasing wine for the establishment, as well as the proper receiving and storage of the wine. In addition, he or she will assist guests with choosing a wine and serve the wine to the guests. The sommelier may also be in charge of all alcoholic beverage purchasing for the establishment.

The headwaiter is responsible for service in a particular area of the dining room. In smaller operations, this position is not as necessary, and the role will be assumed either by the maître d' or the captain. The captain runs one area of the dining room. His or her role is to explain the menu and any specials to the guests and take their orders. If there is tableside cooking or food preparation to be done, it will be done by the captain. The captain also oversees the front and back waiters.

Front waiters assist the captain. They provide utensils and plates when needed and bring the food when it is ready. Back waiters are responsible for the most basic of customer needs. They fill waters, bring bread and butter, clear dirty dishes from the table, and doother general tasks.

Variations on this structure are seen in more casual operations, where positions and duties have been combined. In a typical casual dining restaurant, the host/hostess will take reservations, greet guests upon arrival, and seat them. The waitperson explains the menu, takes orders, brings out the food, and clears the table. Occasionally this person is assisted by a food-runner or bus person. An assistant manager or FOH manager is usually present to oversee the operation.

Back of the House

The executive chef is in charge of all kitchen operations. This person designs the menu; hires and trains the kitchen staff; is responsible for purchasing and portion/cost control for the kitchen; and sets presentation, safety, and sanitation standards for the kitchen. This person is also often the "star attraction" for the establishment. Although they often make appearances in the dining room and speak with guests, often their reputation alone is enough to draw customers to sample their creations.

Below the executive chef is the sous chef, literally the "under chef." The sous chef participates in the preparation of food during service, organizing and supervising the operations of the kitchen. This person also usually takes on the role of the aboyeur, or expeditor. The role of this person is to call orders to the other cooks, tell each one when to begin cooking or "fire" each dish, bring all the items together to go out to the table, and direct the front waiter as to the proper destination.

Working under the sous chef are the various chefs de partie, or station chefs. There are many various station chefs, and in a large operation all might

FIGURE **18.1 Organizational Structure of a Fine Dining Restaurant**

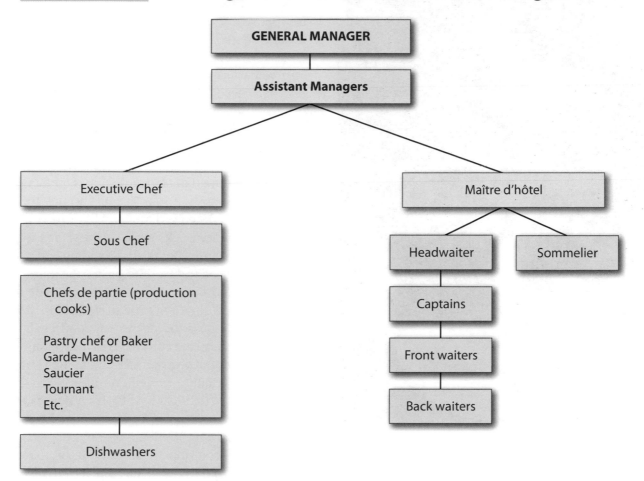

be present: the saucier (sauté/sauce station chef), poissonier (fish station), grillardin (grill station), friturier (fry station), rôtisseur (roast station), potager (soup station), légumier (vegetable station), entremetier (combines potager and légumier), garde-manger (pantry station), boucher (butcher station), tournant (swing cook), pâtissier (pastry chef), boulanger (bread baker), and confiseur (candy and confections chef).

In smaller operations, not all of these positions may be necessary. In such a case, duties are combined so that fewer chefs are necessary to accomplish all the tasks. For example, the garde-manger, who is responsible for all cold food preparation such as salads and dressings, may also be responsible for appetizers or perhaps plating desserts. The various chef positions for meats may be combined and delegated to chefs according to cooking style or equipment. The division of labor and delegation of responsibility are decisions made by the executive chef and sous chef, based on the needs of the operation.

Finally, there are the dish persons, who are responsible for providing the chefs with clean cookware throughout service, as well as ensuring the cleanliness, appearance, and sanitation of all china, silver, and glassware for the guests. These persons are also responsible for keeping the kitchen clean throughout service, removing garbage, and cleaning floors. There are two schools of thought on the cleaning of the kitchen after service is over. Some managers feel that by having the cooks responsible for the cleaning of the kitchen and its equipment that they develop a sense of pride and ownership, thereby taking better care of the equipment and taking more pride in their work. Others would rather hire a cleaning service to come in after hours or have the dishwashers (the lowest-paid employees in the kitchen) clean up at the end of the day. These managers would rather not have their highly paid cooks remain "on the clock" to perform such a menial task as cleaning. Again, this decision will be made by the managers based on what they feel is best for their operation.

It is the attention to detail that may make or break any restaurant operation. © 2011 by withGod. Used under license of Shutterstock, Inc.

Management Responsibilities

The general manager is responsible for the day-to-day operations and decision making for the restaurant. This person is the contact for everything having to do with the restaurant, including marketing activities, suppliers, lawyers, accountants, contractors, insurance, and bankers. The manager knows the ownership's long-term goals and works to accomplish those, as well as relay information between owners and employees. This person, being the key holder to the establishment, usually puts in the most hours.

The general manager is accountable for everything in the restaurant and is therefore involved in every aspect of it. This person develops the operating budget and is responsible for operating within that budget. He or she is responsible for one of the most important tasks in the restaurant: cost control. Cost control is the term for the measures and standards put in place to ensure that the establishment is profitable. A major component to cost control in the restaurant is the purchasing of food, beverage, and nonfood products. It is crucial that purchasing is done properly because it has the potential to affect all areas of the operation. The correct product must be purchased at the correct price and at the correct time. It must be received as ordered and properly placed into inventory until needed. If an error occurs during any part of the purchasing function, the restaurant may see food costs rise or quality suffer because of product spoilage while in storage or because of running out of a product. Beyond the purchasing function, the manager must ensure that standard recipes are being followed, portion sizes are correct, inventories are being properly rotated, and pilferage is not occurring.

The manager tracks all sales and is responsible for keeping records, both for accounting and tax purposes. He or she tracks food costs (the amount the restaurant paid for the food as a percentage of the selling price of the food) and periodically analyzes the menu to assess the performance of each menu item. This practice, referred to as menu engineering, determines how many of an item the restaurant typically sells and how much profit is derived from that item each time one is sold. If an item is underperforming, the manager will have to make changes to increase the contribution margin of the item (how much profit it contributes), increase the amount sold, or remove it from the menu and replace it with a more profitable item.

The manager is responsible for hiring, training, managing, disciplining, and firing employees. In addition, he or she also creates the schedules and tracks labor for payroll and labor cost analysis purposes. The manager is also responsible for revenue collection, as well as most other financial matters, such as paying bills to suppliers, utilities, and perhaps rent.

Fortunately for the manager, some of these duties can be shared among other managers and typically become the responsibility of those they directly affect. For example, the executive chef usually assists the manager in developing purchasing specifications for the food, does the purchasing of food items for the kitchen, and is responsible for the freshness, safety, and availability of the inventory. The chef also assists in the hiring of kitchen help and is responsible for training them. The sommelier purchases the wine and is often also responsible for purchasing (alcoholic) beverages as well as training bar staff and servers on beverage service. The maître d' might be given the responsibility of ordering nonfood items and is involved in the hiring and training of the serving staff. The general manager is ultimately responsible for all of these and therefore monitors these functions closely.

The life of a restaurateur is not for everyone. The hours are long, and the job is difficult. It requires someone who happily serves others, works well with employees and the public, is well organized, and can coordinate many activities simultaneously. Despite technological advances, the restaurant industry is labor intensive. Managing a restaurant is also more difficult than other areas, due to its typically low profit margin. However, for those who undertake the challenge, the career can be extremely rewarding, with rapid advancement possible and salaries competitive with other industries.

ENDNOTE

1. Labensky, S., & Hause, A. (2007). *On cooking: A textbook of culinary fundamentals* (4th ed.). Upper Saddle River, NJ: Pearson Prentice Hall.

Review Questions

1. Describe the traditional path for career advancement within restaurant operations. What are some variations to this path?

2. What is the title of the person who is in charge of the Front of the House (FOH)? Back of the House (BOH)? What position is second in the chain of command in both of these areas of operation—FOH and BOH?

3. List the traditional work positions of front line employees in both the FOH and BOH.

4. Briefly describe 4 to 5 duties of the restaurant manager. Select one, and further explain why it is important to the overall success of the restaurant operation.

5. What is menu engineering?

6. Describe how menu engineering practices influence a restaurant's profitability.

Bar and Beverage Operations

Kirsten Tripodi, Fairleigh Dickinson University

LEARNING OBJECTIVES

To enable first year hospitality students to:

- Become familiar with bar and beverage terminology.
- Become familiar with career opportunities in bar and beverage management.
- Understand the importance of responsibility regarding the sale of alcoholic beverages.
- Appreciate the profitability and cost factors involved in beverage sales.
- Gain an understanding of trends in beverage management.

CHAPTER OUTLINE

Management Responsibilities
    Legal
    Cash
    Theft
    Licensing
Products
    Wine
    Fortified Wine
    Beer
    Coffee and Tea
    Spirits
    Brandy and Cognac
    Aperitifs
    Cordials and Liqueurs
    Bottled Water

Career Opportunities
    During School
    After Graduation
Profitability
    Cost Control
    Pricing Trends
Future Issues
Summary

KEY TERMS

BYO
Cellaring
Core competencies
Corkage
Cost control
Common law
Dram shop legislation
Duty of care
In-house training
Inventory reconcilations

Liability insurance
Mini bar
"On the floor"
POS terminal
Price points
Profitability
Shot
Social responsibility
Sommelier
Spirits

The *Merriam Webster On-Line Dictionary* defines a bar as, "a counter at which food or especially alcoholic beverages are served."[1] Bar and beverage management is considered by many to be one of the most interesting, challenging, and profitable areas of hospitality management. Many types of hospitality operations have a bar or beverage operation as part of their offerings for their guests or members. For the introductory hospitality student, the career possibilities are both varied and full of opportunity.

Bar and beverage operations are connected to entertainment in many ways. Indeed, the act of going to a bar is a form of social entertainment. Many bars offer entertainment, which may be as simple as darts, or as complicated as full-blown live entertainment productions of world-famous artists. The bar business has a glamorous side, which can be enticing. Often, a lot of cash is changing hands, and for tipped employees, there is certainly a great deal of money to be made. Contact with entertainers and interesting promotional possibilities are perks. Due to the unique nature of alcoholic beverages, the legal implications and the control issues involved in its sale make this area of hospitality uniquely challenging. Success given these challenges is a sign to future employers that you have exhibited all the skills of a great hospitality manager in a fast-paced and competitive environment, that is to say, it is a great proving ground.

Management Responsibilities

Legal

As a host in your home, you would never put a guest into a situation in which they might hurt themselves or someone else. This responsibility is the same for the guest/host relationship in a hospitality business situation. Serving alcohol changes that relationship to enhance the level of responsibility. As business owners and managers, we have a social responsibility not only to our guests, but also to society at large regarding the serving of alcohol.

In addition to the social responsibility and the guest/host relationship, there are legal requirements regarding the service of alcohol. Hospitality businesses in the United States are subject to a Duty of Care for guests and the public, which has evolved under the common law from the Inns of England in the Middle Ages.[2] Dram Shop legislation refers to the legal onus on the provider of the alcoholic beverage.

In the event of an injury that was caused by an intoxicated person, alcohol is considered to be so reality altering that the person is not held responsible for their own actions. The results of the actions of an intoxicated person are rather the legal responsibility of the provider of those beverages.

Many companies take this responsibility very seriously. In addition to in-house training, many have opted for additional training by experts in responsible alcohol service. Generally, these programs include certification for employees who have passed an exam of some sort. Using a recognized program of this sort can mean substantial savings in terms of liability insurance, as the insurer recognizes that the business has taken steps to train employees to be aware of the consequences and legal ramifications of irresponsible alcohol service. At the end of this chapter, you can find a list of resources for just such additional training.

Cash

A business that involves cash is full of opportunities for employees to make costly mistakes or to be less than honest. Checks and balances must always be in place, and managers must be aware and proactive whenever possible. There are techniques for controlling costs which range from computer-regulated shots that cannot be activated unless a sale is rung into an interfaced POS terminal, to enforcing the proper use of measured portions (shot glasses or measured pourers), to management vigilance. From a marketing standpoint, guests in certain types of establishments may be adverse to some of the more mechanized controls.

Theft

Regular inventory reconciliation is a commonly used technique for controlling costs. The drawback of using this method is that it is reactive rather than proactive, which is to say that it can only detect a problem after it has occurred. Security systems and surveillance equipment can also be used to reduce theft via pilferage or overpouring. It is important that these systems work together and work well in combination with the management team's vigilance. There can be no substitute for awareness and constant training for all members of the staff. The nature of the inventory makes it inviting. Who wouldn't want a nice bottle of champagne in their refrigerator for a special occasion, especially one that did not cost anything? The unauthorized taking of inventory constitutes theft. This is referred to as pilferage if the item is stolen for consumption by an employee. Managers must also be aware that there are more ways for employees to steal. Overpouring (using more than the recipe amount of the alcohol for a beverage) constitutes a loss for the business and is theft. Tipped employees can be encouraged to add more to a beverage in return for a bigger gratuity. Left unchecked, tipped employees can even give drinks away. In many instances these businesses employ companies to "shop" the establishment. The Secret Shopper Services range from theft and cash handling identification to a full report on the particulars of service standards for a company versus the execution of those standards during a particular visit. Often these companies will provide support to the establishment in the event of a termination or further legal action as a result of their reported findings.

A competent manager will also be aware that employees who are completely honest can cost a business profit through sloppiness (waste) and poor training (poor knowledge of recipes and standards).

Licensing

In the United States, alcohol sales are regulated by individual states, which often allow municipalities to issue licenses and determine laws so long as those laws exist within the confines of any existing state regulations. In most states, background checks are completed regarding persons applying for such a license to determine that those persons are of acceptable character.[3] The number and locations of licenses are often stipulated per municipality. In some states or municipalities there is a certain distance that any establishment must be from churches and schools. Quite often, liquor licenses are very expensive and can be suspended or revoked for a number of violations. Once revoked, it sometimes cannot be replaced, and the business will suffer. Serving minors or the already intoxicated can cause a licensing problem, but so can paying your bills late or failing to keep adequate records regarding sales and purchases of alcoholic beverages. The rights to a license must be protected at all times by the owners, managers, and staff of an establishment serving alcoholic beverages.

Opportunities to BYO (bring your own) beverages do exist in many venues. Corkage fees can also be charged by an operation that holds a license to sell alcoholic beverages, should a guest prefer to bring their own selection of beverage into the establishment. Of course in a BYO situation, the legal responsibilities vary from municipality to municipality.

Licensing regulations and requirements may vary from state to state, and even from municipality to municipality in the United States; therefore, the prudent beverage manager will always have a copy of those regulations on premise for reference and will be familiar with them.

Products

Many different products are sold in beverage operations. As with sales positions in any other industry, the most knowledgeable salespersons can offer the best information and service to their guests. In bar and beverage operations it is our bartenders, servers, and cocktail servers who represent the enterprise to the guest and do the selling. Training and information cannot be overemphasized. In every type of operation it is of key importance that the sales staff be well informed of the product, including how it should be handled and served. Guests who are ordering an aged, single-malt whiskey, which can be quite pricey will have high expectations, as will the draught beer drinker at a sports-themed bar.

Wine

Wine is an alcoholic beverage made from fermented grapes. It is sold around the world and has gained in popularity in the past two decades. Wines vary from "dry" to "sweet." Dry refers to the absence of sweetness. Wines can also be distinguished by the grape from which they are made or the year the grapes were grown and harvested (vintage). A varietal is a wine that is made primarily from one grape. In general, white wines are made from white (green) grapes and are usually served cold. Red wines are made from red grapes and are served at room temperature. Particular years in certain geographic locations are either ideal, or less than ideal for the harvesting of these grapes. An ideal year will create a better wine, which can demand a higher price. Truly ideal vintages (years) age well, which means that the wines can get better with age, if stored properly. Depending on the quality of the vintage and the wine, at a certain point the wine will deteriorate, so it is important for collectors and beverage managers who are responsible for aging (cellaring) to be very knowledgeable about the products they are responsible for.

As you might expect, sparkling wines have gas (bubbles) and a different cork to manage that carbonation. Sparkling wines made in certain regions around the world may carry the name of that region,

Bars serve an assortment of beverages; most are alcohol. © 2011 by alex saberi. Used under license of Shutterstock, Inc.

as does Champagne and Asti, or they may be referred to as sparkling wines. They are served chilled and often offered for celebratory occasions.

Blush wines are a light pink color and are served chilled.

Fortified Wine
Sherries, ports, marsalas, and madieras are wines that have brandy added to them. They are usually offered alone in a glass after dinner. These alcoholic beverages are also popular as commonly used ingredients in cooking.

Beer
"Beer is a generic term for all alcoholic beverages that are fermented and brewed from malted barley, hops, water and yeast."[4] Beer is the largest-selling alcoholic beverage in the world. Beer is served ice cold in the United States, but many draught beers from the United Kingdom are meant to be served at room temperature. Beer is served in bottles or on draught (tap). The bottles take up a great deal of space and can add significant cost or recycling issues to the beverage manager's day. Draught beer is more profitable, but the systems and storage required can be costly to add if not planned for when the establishment is being built or renovated.

Microbreweries have managed to survive changing economic conditions and have changed the beer industry in ways that mimic the wine industry.

Boutique brewers offer many styles of beer that are quite sophisticated and appeal to a more discerning palate at a premium price.

Coffee and Tea
Coffee is a brewed beverage that has gained in popularity in the past 10 years. An entire industry has developed around this beverage, which was offered as regular or decaf only not so long ago. Cafes, storefronts, and retail operations feature some derivation of this nonalcoholic beverage served at a substantial profit. Tea houses and cafes specializing in teas and chai are growing in popularity.

Spirits
There is usually a selection of each category of spirits available at different price points in most establishments. House brands are sometimes referred to as well brands because they are positioned in the well or speed rail for maximum efficiency (close reach for the bartenders); these are the least expensive and are sold when no brand name is specified. Call brands, premium brands, and super premiums represent the alternatives to the house brands in increasing order.[5] Mixed drinks or cocktails often include a spirit. When the drink is simply a spirit and a mixer (soda or juice most often), the drink can be referred to as a highball.

White spirits are defined by the fact that they are colorless. This group of spirits includes vodka, gin, rum, and tequila. Brown spirits include whiskies of differing types. American, Canadian, Irish, Scotch, and Bourbon are all examples of these whiskies or brown spirits. These are made from grain, potatoes, sugarcane, agave, rye, wheat, peat, and rice. "After the process of distillation was discovered, it was inevitable that man should use the product closest at hand, easiest to obtain, and least expensive for distillation."[6]

Brandy and Cognac
Brandy is the general term for the distilled spirit of grapes. Often served after dinner, these beverages are made around the world. Cognac and armagnac are brandies that are made in a particular geographic region of France. These are generally served alone in a glass at room temperature, or even warmed a bit to enhance the guest's experience.

Aperitifs
Aperitifs are served to stimulate the appetite. These beverages are either spirit based or wine based and can be served chilled or at room temperature.[7]

Cordials and Liqueurs

These sweet alcoholic beverages are served after dinner, often at room temperature, but sometimes over ice (on the rocks).

Bottled Water

Health trends have had a huge impact on the bottled water market. A nonalcoholic, healthy alternative beverage, waters (both sparkling and still) have led the trend in nonalcoholic beverages. Less than 30 years ago, it was virtually unheard of for water to be paid for in a hospitality establishment. Today, bottled water has reached a point in popularity where it has become a multi-billion-dollar industry.

Career Opportunities

From attractions management to travel and tour operations every chapter in this book is connected to bar and beverage operations in some way. Attractions such as Disneyworld and beach destination resorts generally offer alcoholic or some type of nonalcoholic beverage service for their guests. Beverage service is usually available in private clubs for their members. Full-service hotels have lounges, restaurants, banquet and meeting facilities, room service, and minibar operations. Restaurants also have available alcoholic and nonalcoholic beverages for their guests, as do most noncommercial food service operations. Corporate dining rooms and catering operations usually include beverage service, as do the vendors in airports and stadiums. It is hard to imagine a successful casino or cruise line that would be not able to provide alcoholic beverages. Various methods of transportation from airlines to trains and even charter buses proffer beverages of all kinds.

During School

For many students and indeed for hospitality students, bar and beverage operations are a great way to earn money while you're still in school. Work schedules can often be made flexible to accommodate class schedules, and gratuities can help to defray the cost of tuition or add to spending money. Bar backs, bartenders, mini bar attendants, and cocktail servers, as well as baristas, are the entry-level line positions usually available. These positions require some knowledge about serving differing types of beverages. Bartenders and bar backs are usually found behind a "front bar" in view of guests, which often has seating for guests. There are also service bars, where only employees of the establishment can order drinks for the guests in the restaurant, lounge, or room service. Bartenders mix the drinks and are sometimes referred to as mixologists. Bar backs support the bartenders by leaving the bar to restock supplies; this way the bartenders can always be available to guests. Cocktail servers are out "on the floor" in a lounge environment; they order drinks from the bartender, which they then bring to their guests at the table. Minibar attendants restock the in-room refrigerators, which have beverages and snacks in higher-end hotels. These attendants are responsible to report the guest usage so that the guest can be properly charged. Baristas are found in a coffee bar or juice bar. Both types of nonalcoholic beverages have grown in popularity and availability in the past 10 years. Companies such as Starbucks and Jamba Juice lead this part of the industry.

The beverage industry is dynamic and provides many, and varied, employment opportunities. © 2011 by erics. Used under license of Shutterstock, Inc.

Customer service skills honed in this type of establishment in conjunction with the knowledge of the beverages served are useful skills to fall back on for the rest of your life. Particularly for hospitality students, this is a challenging beginning to a rewarding career.

After Graduation

Entry-level supervisory positions in the area of beverage management can be found in virtually all of the types of operations in hospitality. In a large hotel or casino, there might be several layers of management after that initial position. In smaller operations a beverage career can successfully morph into a food and beverage career for a more mature, full-service manager, who will have more comprehensive management responsibilities. High-end wines are usually sold in full-service restaurants that employ wine consultants (sommeliers), who are experts. These sommeliers work for the establishment ordering the wine and managing the wine list, and they are tipped for their advice to the guests as well as salaried employees. Sommeliers are highly specialized experts who usually hold a credential that identifies them as such.

Beverage management is a long-term career for a select few. The demands of the late night hours are more conducive to younger managers. There are several core competencies that are critical for success in beverage management. Cleanliness, friendliness, awareness of potential problems (inventory and cash control), and knowledge of products and services are all important. Having a great eye for detail and great interpersonal communication skills are a must in this part of the industry.

Profitability

Cost Control

"A beverage list (covering beer, wine, and distilled spirits) must be given the same careful thought and attention to detail and market trends that is involved in the planning of a food menu."[8] Balancing the size of the inventory with the needs of the guests can be a difficult task. Research and awareness of what is available and the market to which the establishment caters is essential. Increasing inventory (either levels or variety) means that more of the operation's funds are tied up in the storeroom and not immediately earning money. Preventing loss and theft require constant vigilance, control systems, and proper pricing techniques.

Katsigris and Porter, in their book, *Pouring for Profit,* identify several necessary steps to controlling costs and profit in beverage management. Budgeting for profit, pricing for profit, establishing product controls, and establishing cash controls are all vital parts of the control process, which require an in-depth understanding of the operation at hand, the market, the product, and security.[9]

Pricing Trends

"The well-known fact that the price of two martinis in the average bar will buy a whole bottle of gin or vodka at the liquor store, if you wish to drink at home, is indicative of what the bar business is all about."[10] The price of a drink is determined by the cost of the drink. This means that the recipe for the drink and the cost of each individual ingredient must be considered. Mixers, such as juices and sodas, cost significantly less than alcohol, so the cost of the bottle divided by the portion of the bottle used will determine the bulk of the cost for most drinks. The price is then based on the profit margin that a facility requires to cover its overhead costs and the profit that the owners desire. This must also be balanced with the demands of the market.

Beer, particularly draught (on tap) beer, can cost less than $.25 for a 16 oz. portion (pint), and sell for $1.50 to $5.00 depending on the establishment. Wine is often marked up two and one-half times at the low end (house brands) to one-half times for a high end wine. Recently there has been a trend toward limiting the markup for wines to a more acceptable level, given that the public is more aware of the pricing of wines at retail than ever before.

Future Issues

In his book, *How to Manage a Successful Bar,* Christopher Egerton-Thomas asserts, "[T]he future trend is fairly easy to guess. The health industry will not go away. Countries that are not traditionally wine suppliers are getting into bold, massive, well-organized stride in their search for world markets."[11] It certainly seems as though the trend toward health has changed the beverage industry forever. After the controversial *60 Minutes* segment on the relative health of the French people and their diet, many medical journals have reported on the health benefits of wine in moderation. Water and nonalcoholic beverages, particularly those made with fresh fruits and vegetables, have gained in popularity and are not likely to decline in a health-aware market. As the population ages, these trends are likely to expand, rather than contract.

The newest trends in the beverage industry concern sustainability. We are aware as never before of the limited resources of our planet, and this translates in the beverage industry in very interesting ways. Awareness of where a product comes from and how it is processed is growing. Organic beverages and local specialties are gaining in popularity for health reasons as well as to limit the carbon footprint of product that has traveled a great distance.

Packaging is constantly changing in response to waste concerns. In some establishments, purified and carbonated water is produced on property, and the bottles are cleaned and sanitized for reuse.

Biodegradable packaging is preferred, but compostable and recyclable packaging is preferred.

Summary

This chapter presented an overview of bar and beverage management. Many hospitality programs offer one or more courses in this exciting area of the hospitality industry. Hopefully, this introduction will inspire you to learn more, both while you are a student and afterward.

Bar and beverage management is an exciting and sometimes glamorous area to specialize in the hospitality industry. Due to the nature of the products (often alcohol), managing this type of hospitality operation can be more challenging than others in many ways. Management positions are available opportunities in virtually every type of hospitality operation.

RESOURCES

Internet Sites

Responsible Alcohol Training Sites

ServSafe Alcohol offered by the Educational Foundation of the National Restaurant Foundation: http://www.servsafe.com/alcohol/
TIPS (Training for Intervention ProcedureS): http://www.gettips.com/

Non-Alcoholic Beverage Companies

Jamba Juice: http://jambajuice.com/
Starbucks: http://www.starbucks.com/default.asp?cookie%5Ftest=1

Credentials

American Sommelier Association: http://www.americansommelier.org/
The Court of Master Sommeliers: http://www.mastersommeliers.org/

Information about Beverages and Mixology

Bar Business Magazine: http://www.barbizmag.com/subscribe
Mixellany.com: http://www.master.mixellany.com/Welcome.html
Drinkology.com: http://www.drinkology.com/welcome

References

Barth, S., Hayes, D., & Ninemeier, J. (2001). *Restaurant law basics.* New York: Wiley.
Egerton-Thomas, C. (1994). *How to manage a successful bar.* New York: Wiley.
Jeffries, J., & Brown, B. (2001). *Understanding hospitality law* (4th ed.). Lansing, MI: Educational Institute of the American Hotel & Lodging Association.
Katsigris, C., & Porter, M. (1983). *Pouring for profit: A guide to bar and beverage management.* New York: Wiley.
Lembeck, H. (1983). *Grossman's guide to wines, beers and spirits* (7th ed. rev.). New York: Charles Scribner's and Sons.
Lipinski, B., & Lipinski, K. (1996). *Professional beverage management.* New York: Wiley.
Merriam-Webster's on-line dictionary. (n.d.). Retrieved January 22, 2006, from http://www.m-w.com/dictionary/BAR

ENDNOTES

1. *The Merriam Webster On-Line Dictionary,* n.d.
2. Jeffries & Brown, 2001.
3. Egerton-Thomas, 1994.
4. Lipinski and Lipinski, 1996, p. 191.
5. Egerton-Thomas, 1994.
6. Grossman, 1983, p. 325.
7. Lipinski and Lipinski, 1996.
8. Lipinski and Lipinski, 1996, p. 288.
9. Grossman, 1983, pp. 305–331)
10. Egerton-Thomas, 1994, p. 7.
11. Ibid., p. 135.

Review Questions

1. Why is it important that alcohol is considered to be a drug?

2. What are some steps that a responsible company can take to ensure that alcohol is being served responsibly?

3. What are the benefits to being socially responsible regarding the service and sale of alcoholic beverages?

4. What is the most effective sales tool for beverages?

5. Given so many "harsh realities" to balance the glamour of the beverage business, why do you suppose that it remains a popular career path for hospitality graduates?

6. Why do you suppose nonalcoholic beverage establishments were included in this chapter?

7. What are some current trends that may give us a clue as to the future of this segment of the industry?

8. How can a beverage manager stay abreast of changes in the industry that can affect their business?

Culinary Arts

Keith Mandabach, New Mexico State University

The Culinary World

Ratings for television food networks and cooking shows featuring glamorous chefs appear to have increased interest in cooking or culinary careers. The programs certainly have piqued viewers' curiosity about becoming a chef and dedicating their life to the culinary world. Readers are cautioned that as glamorous as the shows make the chef appear, the individuals that star on television did not instantly become the famous "chef." They worked long hours, studied, and trained to reach the positions they are in today.

Successful chefs formally apprenticed, attended a culinary school or college, trained under qualified chefs, and/or any combination of the four. They certainly spent a great deal of time and effort mastering the basic culinary skills including knife skills and the correct methods to operate kitchen equipment. Each chef learned the correct methods of kitchen preparation, including sautéing, frying, roasting, poaching, and broiling. In addition, these individuals understood and applied the principles of menu planning, recipe modification, food sanitation/safety, culinary human nutrition, and the science of cookery. Before one becomes a chef, one must be a cook, preferably a great one, and that is not always an easy task.

A great professional cook who aspires to become a chef must develop skills that supplement one's ability beyond simply following the steps outlined in a recipe. Cooking involves organic material (food products) with individual chemical and cellular structure (similar to the way each snowflake is unique) that also change over time. Complex factors also affect the process. These might include altitude, humidity, temperature, acidity, water chemistry, gauge or thickness of cooking pot or pan, regulation of cooking temperature, cooking techniques, and storage methods for the food. As one masters the art of preparation, one must utilize effective critical thinking skills to produce a tasty, attractive end product (something that people will enjoy eating).

A chef is also a business manager, and thus one must develop one's leadership skills and master the use of the technological systems. Chefs utilize computer systems in menu planning, recipe development, marketing, purchasing, inventory control, cost control, scheduling management, accounting, and human relations. In our computer savvy world, the computer system is utilized in every facet of the operation. Knowledge of business skills is as important as the technical skills a chef possesses. No matter how well one cooks, if the restaurant is not profitable, it will not stay in business. The chef must anticipate food trends and the public's changing tastes. Most important a chef must enjoy the work, for chefs work long hours, holidays, and weekends. This requires a unique dedication to the profession and a passion for making people happy. To those whose hearts are in the profession, the rewards are fantastic. Chefs feed the world, and it is an honored profession.

The culinary world will continue to grow and is a solid career choice. Within the United States, the industry employs 12.8 million people today and is expected to add 2 million new jobs in the next decade according to the National Restaurant Association's[1] Restaurant Industry Forecast. On a typical day in 2007, the restaurant industry posted average sales of nearly $1.5 billion. On an inflation-adjusted base, restaurant industry sales were expected to increase 5% in 2007, which equal 4% of the U.S. gross domestic product.

The culinary world is an ingredient of the economic and social development of the world's cultures. American professional cookery is an excellent example of how global and diverse our dining industry has become. Novice culinarians should realize that the ever-changing cuisine is part of the world's industrial, trade, and transportation growth. It will continue to change. As the world has become global in perspective, the modern culinary world's acceptance of foods from all cultures is essential for success.

Career Opportunities

There are a wide variety of career opportunities and places to work where a culinary professional will find satisfying work in five related industry career areas: commercial food service operations, culinology, culinary education, on-site dining, and media chef. Each area has its own rewards, and all are connected and require the acquisition of technical (cooking) and managerial skills. Commercial food service includes all forms of restaurants, hotels, clubs, bars, catering, sports venues, food markets, and ships. Most culinary careers begin in this discipline. Many of our premier chefs and restaurant owners work in cutting-edge independent establishments in this segment. The work is very intense because the public is demanding. Usually the owner and/or chef will be involved in everything from purchasing the freshest ingredients to production and service on the line. It is hard work, and to be successful in this world, one must have the stamina and vision to satisfy the public with every plate that is served. Some dining companies also operate in these markets and, although it is a huge business, it is a small world. To get a job in this area, one must have a contact or friend or find a way to get "in" because everyone wants to get a job in the "best" place. Networking and reputation are important in all areas of the culinary world.

Large national chains (Chili's, Red Lobster, Olive Garden, Bennigan's, etc.) provide career paths for aspiring culinary managers in casual dining. Instead of chefs, most companies have culinary or kitchen managers. Clear-cut formulas are provided for management and for food service. Research teams in the head office develop proven recipes, and the computer systems are usually state of the art. Quick-service restaurants also offer financial rewards that many upscale facilities do not.

Culinary careers in hotels, clubs, and resorts are often very similar in the way they operate, and it is not unusual for a chef to move from one area to the other. In this segment, the chef manages multiple-leveled restaurants, catering, and room service. Because of the multiple venues a chef must manage, communication and the ability to see the entire operation are two keys to success. In addition, chefs are often required to play public relations roles with guests, members, and the corporate officers. It is also important to understand the practicalities of budgeting, and computer skills are a must. Careers are often grown in this segment either through a corporation or mentor, and if one makes solid contributions on the way up the ladder, career success is possible.

Catering is hard work, requires a certified inspected kitchen, and is a tough business to break into. The personal chef either works directly in a client home cooking all the meals or serves a variety of clients by bringing in ready-made food. There is also increased demand for culinary classes, and catering chefs and personal chefs have responded by offering fun cooking classes to the public. Food markets, or what were once called grocery stores, are one venue that is increasingly hiring culinary professionals. These establishments showcase their chefs and pastry chefs. They now offer "food to go" at the level of a fine dining restaurant quality. Bars and associated businesses traditionally provided only minimal food service, but with the growth of sports and gentlemen clubs, demand for culinary professionals has increased.

On-Site or Noncommercial Food Service

Commercial properties by their very nature require 24-7 attention, and for this reason a popular career path is to move into the on-site dining segment.

Once labeled noncommercial or institutional, those working in this area might provide food to employees at an office building or manufacturing plant, manage the dining services of an educational facility, carefully supervise the food of health-care operation, or integrate high-quality food service in the life of a retirement community. In addition opportunities in on-site dining also include producing healthy food for those incarcerated in detention facilities, managing food service operations for the military, or coordinating events and food for a religious facility. This area also includes planning and delivery of food for sporting events, including the Olympics, sports stadiums, recreational facilities, and camps.

Culinology

For many who find their love of food and innovation challenged by the repetitive nature of commercial food service, on-site dining, or those who begin their culinary careers as food scientists, an alternative might be culinology. This term describes those involved in a variety of capacities in food product development,

---

Vignette

Tips from Successful Chefs

Chef Ronald Kuralt is Executive Chef and Dining Services Manager of Corporate Services in Columbus, GA, an on-site dining operation. Kuralt feels his work in on-site dining is a good fit for his talents. He utilizes his culinary leadership skills managing within the system provided by Sodexho. The position also offers many opportunities to showcase his culinary expertise and shine in special events and parties. Chef Kuralt chose this business because he enjoyed the hard work and the team effort it takes to serve great food.

- There is always going to be a need for trained culinary professionals.
- Work in the business, determine if you really love it, then go to a good culinary school.
- Remember school does not teach you everything you need to know about cooking, and it certainly does not make one a chef.
- Develop a career plan focused on continuous learning.
- Job changes contribute to learning, but do not change jobs too often.
- Working for a quality hotel company or chain allows one to move and learn and not have to quit a job.
- Build a network of contacts to promote your career.
- Learn how computerized systems help to complete your daily purchasing, scheduling, sanitation, and food production duties.
- The support of wives, significant others, as well as family support can be a major positive force in many chefs' careers.

production, manufacturing, marketing, and distribution. The term was coined in 1996 by the Research Chefs Association to describe research chefs and food scientists (technologists). However all those involved in the development and distribution of food product now fall under this umbrella of culinology. The field embraces those involved in product, recipe, and menu development and innovation, food manufacturing, technology system (computer) development and application, purchasing, procurement, and media (television, newspapers, magazines, Internet).

Chef Educator

All chefs must teach and train their staffs, and thus many at some time consider careers in education. For whatever reason, the number of culinary schools has more than doubled in the last 10 years. In addition to traditional private and community college culinary schools, a variety of opportunities exist for chef educators. High school culinary arts programs hire experienced culinarians. Four-year universities are also expanding food service offerings, and public and private training programs addressing special needs are also growing.

Media Chef

The celebrity chefs featured on television programs and in the media are the most visible spokespersons for this growing field, and their success has provided a growing opportunity in this area. Most are successful chefs who begin their media careers in culinary competitions, appearing on local news programs, online performances and blogs, performing in-person demonstrations at stores, donating their time and culinary skills to charity events, or writing a cookbook for print or the Internet. They are celebrities in their local areas, and opportunities continue to expand. The American Culinary Federation has offered "how-to" seminars on this topic at national and regional meetings, and they are always well attended. In addition to having outstanding culinary skills, the media chef must understand the medium he or she is working in. Communication skills, performing skills, writing, and charismatic qualities are all important to media chef success.

Strategies to Build a Culinary Career

The Culinary World Is Hard Work

Getting started in a culinary career is a daunting prospect, and aspiring culinarians might research the topic by reading stories and strategies in three great books: *Becoming A Chef*,[2] *If You Can't Stand The Heat*[3] and *So You Want to be a Chef: Your Guide to Culinary Careers*.[4] After your reading, the first step is to land an entry-level position and find out if

Vignette

Tips from Successful Chefs

Chef Gary Needham has worked in every segment of the industry except on-site dining. He has been a pastry chef, bakery operator, line cook, sous chef, and chef at restaurants, hotels, and resorts. He has appeared on a variety of television programs, radio, and print. He also worked in research and was the chef owner of the award-winning Silver Oak Bistro in Washington, NJ. Chef Gary likes to simplify his advice to aspiring culinarians:

- Find out if you love the business before you spend the money on school.
- Listen to your clientele, they will tell you where you are as a chef.
- Be true to who you are as a chef.
- Don't try to please everybody's palate: Just your own.
- Create a daily mantra for yourself. Mine is "Keep it fresh, keep it good."
- Enjoy cooking and talking to customers and staff—they are all your extended family.
- This business is hard work but very rewarding when you bring happiness into peoples' lives through a good meal.

Vignette

Tips from Successful Chefs

Chef E. J. Harvey, the chef/owner of the Seagrille, part owner of The Band of Thieves Restaurant and the Nantucket Chowder Company on Nantucket Island, MA, says his favorite parts of his day are the beginning and the end. His day usually starts with the organizing and planning the food production for the day. He starts the bread dough and the mixing and baking the bread provides him with a real sense of love. Creating the stocks, then the finished soups and sauces for the operation and getting the staff set up for the busy day's business is also a tranquil time. The end of the day provides time for reflection and satisfaction. Every day his team successfully serves large numbers of customers a wide array of food. His wife Robin is his partner and manages the front of the house of the restaurant. After it is over, the spirit of camaraderie that is evident in his team makes the hard work worthwhile, and he kicks back and reflects in the shadows of the day. Chef Harvey is also an avid runner who just completed his first Boston Marathon. He believes

- The culinary profession is constantly changing.
- All students should work in the industry before attending culinary school.
- Develop a palate by tasting a wide variety of foods, and do not prejudge a dish before you taste it.
- It is important to travel and experience different countries, cultures, and their cuisines because the word *fusion cuisine* is more than a word.
- Finally, don't expect to graduate from school and be handed a top job.
- You must work hard and earn the respect of the people around you as well as keep your sense of humor.
- Be a professional, and remember that manners are important.

the career is right for you. The most common question students ask is, "What entry-level position is the right one?" This is a difficult question to answer but similar to new cooks asking, "When will the cake be done?" With a cake, one sticks a toothpick into the center of the cake. If it comes out clean, one knows it is done. In finding the right job, the job interview is the toothpick, if it does not come out clean, don't take the job.

Almost all entry positions require a variety of hours, and one must accept the fact that weekends and holidays are normal workdays in the industry. Kitchens are also hot places to work, and entry-level positions will often have little of the glamour of higher level positions. Expect washing dishes, cleaning tasks, and uncertain schedules as your daily routine. But no matter how menial, the right entry-level job is one that you are proud of and provides ample learning opportunities. Sanitation and safety are essential behaviors/skills in any kitchen. Follow the adage "Clean as you go" not just in your work

space, but also in your personal appearance, and be careful to avoid accidents. Kitchens are energized workplaces, and one must take care to behave appropriately and respect coworkers/ bosses, come to work on time, be ready to work, ask questions if you do not understand assignments, and master whatever tasks are assigned to you.

Chef Harvey says, "My goal was always to become a chef and I never lost sight of it no matter how many gatherings, holidays, or family events I missed. But I never put my family off. We might have Thanksgiving dinner on Friday, but we always celebrated. I set out to be a successful chef and I carried that vision to my family and to the community. It would mean nothing to me to be successful if I did not have the respect of my community and the people around me most importantly my family. I have been blessed with a very supportive wife and children. Without them it might have been very easy to lose my focus and thus my success."

Getting started in a culinary career is daunting, but will be worth it for many. © 2011 by ally. Used under license of Shutterstock, Inc.

Culinary School, College, Apprenticeship, Certification

Many individuals might have taken a culinary job to earn money for school or to support their families and then decide to formally train to advance their careers. Educational choices include culinary schools, colleges, and formal apprenticeships. The American Culinary Federation has a list of accredited programs and has detailed standards that list skills that must be mastered for the program to grant a certificate or degree. Almost all the programs require work experience that range from 400 to 1,600 hours.

Students should carefully investigate their options and consider local community college programs in addition to the high-profile culinary programs. The first public culinary school in the United States was founded in 1929, and America has a strong history of community or technical colleges offering certificate (800–1200 hours) and associate two-year degree programs. Programs of this type have had great success at national culinary competitions.

Two-Year Associate Degree and Certificate
The highest profile private culinary schools are the Culinary Institute of America (CIA), Johnson and Wales University, The Schools of Culinary Arts at the Art Institutes, and Le Cordon Bleu Schools, and all have more than one campus. Other smaller quality private programs are the New England Culinary Institute and Kendall College. Whether large or small, public or private, the objectives of these programs are to provide high-profile quality culinary education, and all require internships. Some require work experience prior to enrolling. Costs at private schools are significantly higher than public programs, and thus it is wise to have had experience in the industry prior to enrolling and investing big dollars in an education.

Certification and Accreditation
Some culinary schools are accredited by the college accrediting agencies, and some are accredited by trade school agencies. Coursework from schools with trade school accreditation usually will not transfer to accredited academic degree programs, so it is wise to find out what kind of accrediting agency granted the diploma before enrolling. The American Culinary Federation (ACF) inspects and certifies culinary programs in the United States, and a list is included on their Web site. This is a voluntary program, and schools that are trade school accredited can be certified as accredited by the ACF if they complete the standards required. In addition, *Peterson's Guide to Culinary Schools* publishes a list of culinary schools available both online and in print.

College Two- and Four-Year Management Programs
These are usually part of hotel and restaurant management two-year or four-year degree programs at community colleges or universities. Most emphasize food service or restaurant management and are both public and private. Almost all have a variety of cooking classes in the curriculum. Many students who advanced to college directly from high school complete a four-year management degree, intern in culinary positions, and then go directly into culinary positions, culinary school, or apprenticeship programs after graduation. For those who have completed a four-year degree and have experience in the industry, CIA Greystone has a specific program designed for four-year graduates.

Bachelor Four-Year Culinary Arts Degrees
Currently there are over 20 accredited bachelor degree programs. Nicholls State, University of Nevada Las Vegas, Walnut Hill College, the Art Institutes, CIA, Johnson and Wales, St. Louis University, Kendall College, and SUNY Cobleskill are a few of the best-known programs. All offer intensive culinary degrees with the general education components that allow them to grant a bachelor's degree. These programs were designed in response to industry demand and provide the quality of an intensive culinary degree with a stronger business and general education component.

Apprenticeship Programs

This method of training has historically been the world's standard culinary training method. The ACF apprentice program is modeled after the European system and was approved formally in 1971. Individuals work in establishments under approved chefs, attend educational sessions, and rotate through the varied work experiences for a two- or three-year period. The first step is to the ACF Web site, find your local chapter, and contact the president or apprenticeship chair. Not all chapters have apprentices. The ACF Web site also lists which programs are involved in apprenticeships. Sometimes the apprenticeships utilize the local community college to provide the educational component, and the chef at your school might also have information. The key to finding the right apprenticeship is finding the right chef and property. This is a systematic method of training. Apprentices are provided an overview of the industry, trained in sanitation and safety, and imitate chef demonstrations of basic knife cuts or cooking tasks. Eventually, the student or apprentice will complete the competencies required and complete the program. To graduate apprentices must successfully complete both written and hands-on tests and acquire the Certified Culinarian, or CC after their name, from the ACF.

Certification

This certified culinarian is part of the larger certification process. Because culinary education and skill development are lifelong processes, the ACF has a program in place to certify one's skill and experience. One is never certified as a chef on graduating from school and must gain experience and skills. Many individuals with no formal culinary education have very successful careers and rise to positions as chefs. Whether one has a formal education or just on-the-job training, Certification documents and one's culinary accomplishments provide potential employers a standard to measure a chef's professional competence. After documenting experience/skills, passing stringent exams and hands on tests, certification at a variety of professional levels is awarded from the ACF. An excellent strategy for building a culinary career would be to investigate skill requirements and strive to master skills and requirements for certification. The first step to achieving certification is to visit the ACF Web site and review the educational and experience requirements and tests necessary for certification at a variety of levels, including Certified Master Chef (CMC), Certified Master Pastry Chef (CMPC), Certified Executive Chef (CEC), Certified Executive Pastry Chef (CEPC), Certified Culinary Administrator (CCA), Certified Culinary Educator (CCE), Certified Chef de Cuisine (CCC), Personal Certified Executive Chef (PCEC), Certified Secondary Culinary Educator (CSCE), Certified Working Pastry Chef (CWPC), Certified Sous Chef (CSC), Personal Certified Chef (PCC), Certified Culinarian (CC), or Certified Pastry Culinarian (CPC). *The Soul of a Chef: The Journey toward Perfection* by Michael Ruhlman[5] provides a fascinating description of the master chef certification exam and details the challenges chefs face when they attempt to reach the highest level.

Other Options

There are a variety of Web sites for organizations that serve educational functions, networking opportunities, job sources, as well as social organizations. All stress the importance of improving the professional image of the culinarian. In addition to the ACF, other organizations also provide opportunities to enhance your career. The National Restaurant Association (NRA) also has a certification program, as does the International Food Service Executives Association (IFSEA). NRA holds the premier restaurant show in the world (currently in May in Chicago) and is the organization to join for restaurant chefs. IFSEA is primarily an on-site and military organization that provides outstanding support within their organizations. The Club Managers Association also provides excellent networking opportunities for its chefs. There are two personal chef organizations, and the International Association of Culinary Professional offers support for personal and media chefs. In the culinology field, the Research Chefs Association provides certification opportunities and networking. For educators, Foodservice Educators Network International (FENI), Center for Advancement of Foodservice Education (CAFÉ), the ACF, and International Council of Hotel, Restaurant, and Institutional Educators all provide support and certifications for culinary educators.

Summary

The culinary arts field is an exciting and growing career path. The history of the profession is tied to national and economic growth and has been heavily influenced by French and European chefs. Immigrant chefs, trained in Europe, were the dominant force in American cuisine. These professionals adapted American ingredients and began the process of blending the ethnic variety that was American into the food they served. They formed professional associations that promoted training in the culinary arts. Aspiring culinarians have a variety of career choices and educational paths. Before going to culinary school, it is good idea to work in the industry and learn through on-the-job training. While the culinary world has long hours and hard work, the rewards are many for the right person.

RESOURCES

Internet Sites

Schools

The Art Institutes Schools of Culinary Arts (all campuses): http://www.artinstitutes.edu/culinary/

Culinary Institute of America: www.ciachef.edu

Culinary Institute of America at Greystone: http://www.ciachef.edu/california/

John Folse Culinary Institute: http://www.nicholls.edu/jfolse/

Johnson and Wales (all campuses): http://www.jwu.edu/

Kendall College Culinary: http://www.kendall.edu/Academics/CulinaryArts/tabid/70/Default.aspx

Le Cordon Bleu International (all campuses): http://www.cordonbleu.net/International/English/dp_main.cfm

Le Cordon Bleu USA: http://www.lecordonbleuschoolsusa.com/

New England Culinary Institute: http://www.neci.edu/home.html

Peterson's Guide to Culinary Schools: http://www.petersons.com/culinary/

Networking and Support Organizations

American Culinary Federation (ACF)
800-624-9458
www.acfchefs.org

American Dietitic Association (ADA)
800-877-1600
www.eatright.org

Educational Institute of the American Hotel and Lodging Association
517-3724567
www.ei-ahla-org

American Institute of Wine and Food (AIWF)
800-274-2493
www.aiwf.org

American Personal Chef Association (APCA)
800-644-8389
www.personalchef.com

Asian Chefs Association
415-531-3599
http://www.acasf.com/

Assocation for Career and Technical Education (ACTE)
800-826-9972
www.acteonline.org

Black Culinarian Alliance (BCA)
800-308-8188
www.blackculinaries.com

Canadian Culinary Federation
905-773-4277
http://www.ccfcc.ca/en/

Club Managers Association of America (CMAA)
703-739-9500
www.cmaa.org

Confrerie de La Chaine des Rotisseurs
973-360-9200
www.chaineus.org

Foodservice Educators Network International (FENI)
312-849-2220
www.feni.org

Healthcare Foodservice Managers
212-297-2166
http://www.hfm.org/index.html

International Association of Culinary Professionals (IACP)
502-581-9786
www.iacp.com

International Caterers Association (ICA)
888-604-5844
www.icacater.org

International Food Service Executives Association (IFSEA)
702-838-8821
www.ifsea.com

National Association of College and University Food Services (NACUFS)
517-332-2494
www.nacufs.org

National Restaurant Association (NRA)
The National Restaurant Association Educational Foundation (NRAEF)
202-331-5900
www.restaurant.org

Research Chefs Association (RCA)
404-252-3663
www.culinology.com

School Nutrition Association (formerly the American School Food Service Association)
703-739-3900
www.schoolnutrition.org

Society for Foodservice Management (SFM)
502-583-3783
www.sfm-online.org

United States Personal Chef Association (USPCA)
800-995-2138
www.uspca.com

Women Chefs and Restaurateurs (WCR)
877-927-7787
www.womenchefs.org

Women's Foodservice Forum (WFF)
855-368-8008
www.womensfoodserviceforum.com

The World Association of Cooks Societies
http://www.wacs2000.org/index.php

References

Dornenburg, A., & Page, K. (2002). *Becoming a chef.* Hoboken, NJ: Wiley.

Gilsen, W. (2006). *Advanced professional cooking.* Hoboken, NJ: Wiley.

Kim, K. (2006). National Restaurant Association announces record sales projected in year ahead for nation's largest private sector employer. *Nation Restaurant Association* at http://www.restaurant.org/pressroom/pressrelease.cfm?ID=979

National Restaurant Association. New Mexico Restaurant Association at http://www.restaurant.org/pdfs/research/state/new mexico.pdf

National Restaurant Association. *The Cornerstone Initiative* at http:///www.restaurant.org/cornerstone/index.html

Root, W., and Rochemont, R. (1976). Eating in America. New York: Morrow.

ENDNOTES

1. National Restaurant Association. (2007). Industry research at http://www.restaurant.org/research/
2. Dornenburg, A., & Page, K. (2002). *Becoming a chef.* Hoboken, NJ: Wiley.
3. Davis, D. (1999). *If you can stand the heat: Tales from chefs and restaurateurs.* New York: Penguin Putnum.
4. Brefere, L. M., Drummond, K. E., & Barnes, B. (2008). *So you want to be a chef: Your guide to culinary careers.* New York: Wiley.
5. Ruhlman, M. (2001). *The soul of a chef: The journey toward perfection.* New York: Penguin Putnam.

Review Questions

1. Describe at least three skills that make a chef successful.

2. What are three major contributions of French cuisine to the culinary world?

3. What forces are contributing to growth of today's global cuisine?

4. Describe two behaviors that will contribute to your success in your first job.

5. Please describe at least six areas of the culinary world where one might build a career.

6. List at least two formal approaches/strategies to improve your skills and knowledge and which approach you think would be best for your career.

7. Why is it important to get experience before beginning your culinary education?

8. What is certification, and why is it important?

Food, Wine, and Distribution Services

Donna Albano, The Richard Stockton
College of New Jersey
Michael Scales, The Richard Stockton
College of New Jersey

LEARNING OBJECTIVES

- Describe career possibilities in the hospitality distribution services industry.
- Identify and explain trends affecting the hospitality distribution services industry.
- Describe elements unique to each segment of the hospitality distribution services industry.
- Describe the role of a distributor sales representative in the hospitality distribution services industry.
- Explain the purpose of hospitality industry trade shows and expositions.
- Identify the size and scope of the hospitality industry's linen needs.

CHAPTER OUTLINE

Food and Beverage
    Food Distribution
    Food Service Design
    Liquor Distribution
Equipment and Supplies
    Linens
    Furniture, Fixtures, and Equipment (FF&E)
    Technology
Trends in Distribution Services
Summary

KEY TERMS

Distribution services
Furniture, fixtures, and equipment
Peripheral careers
PMS
POS
Purchasing

The distribution services industry is the vast network of peripheral companies that help hospitality enterprises get their products and services from creation to consumption. Some of the careers in distribution services include purchasing agents, information technology, accountants, human resources, warehouse managers, delivery drivers, food inspectors, and street sales. Many of these positions require salespeople to meet face-to-face with hospitality operators weekly or more often. The sales representatives also provide information on cost-cutting ideas, introduce new or improved products, and assist in menu development. It is typically the personal interaction that creates a working relationship between the hospitality industry and its vendors.

As you can see, there are many career possibilities in distribution services. The hospitality industry utilizes thousands of goods and services in daily operations. Distribution services are the backbone of the hospitality industry. This chapter introduces you to those career choices and opportunities in the hospitality industry, as many expand beyond the popular segments of lodging and food and beverage operations.

Food and Beverage

Food Distribution

Food items are delivered daily to operations throughout the world. Price, quality, and quantity of food products are determined by chefs and kitchen managers each day. From the hotdog vendor at the ball game, to the fine dining restaurant, to hospitals and schools, all these operations must purchase food products for mass production. Many food vendors seek out former restaurant managers and employees with knowledge of food products and operations to fill positions in this industry. Food distributors (also known as vendors or purveyors) supply fruits and vegetables; meats and poultry; seafood; dairy products; coffee and beverages; bread and baked goods; dry, canned, and frozen products; and everything else needed for the food service operator.

Food product suppliers work directly with farmers, meat and poultry packaging plants, fish and seafood houses, dairies, and food processing plants. Many are small businesses that may carry a certain type of food. Dairy products and fresh baked goods and breads are normally delivered to restaurants and food service operations every day. These are sometimes considered standing orders in which the

operators receive the same quantity of food products each day. Fresh produce (fruits and vegetables) distributors typically purchase products daily from a central distributor and act as an intermediary delivery directly to the food service operators for a profit. Some seafood distributors operate the same way, whereas many purchase large amounts of fish and butcher or fillet the fish on premise to be delivered daily. Meats and poultry are also often butchered on premise according to the food service operators' specifications. Meats and poultry products are generally delivered three to four days a week. Dry, canned, and frozen food products as well as coffee and beverages can be delivered once or twice a week.

Some food distributors carry a full line of food products, including produce, meats and poultry, seafood, dairy products, coffee and beverages, bread and baked goods, and dry, canned, and frozen products. Sysco, one the largest food service distributors in the United States, provides a full line of food products along with food service equipment, paper products, and cleaning supplies. Sysco also provides services to food service operators in kitchen design and cost-cutting consultation. U.S. Food service and Sysco are two companies that employ sales representatives and are considered "total suppliers."[1] These companies supply everything from brand-name products to equipment and supplies.

Many chain food service operations and multi-unit operations purchase products exclusively from system distributors. System distributors are commonly owned by the same corporations that own the chain food service operations. This allows the chain operation to control the quality and consistency of products and also enables the organization to purchase in large volume at reduced prices.

Food Service Design

Another emerging peripheral career opportunity under the food and beverage sector of the hospitality industry is food service design. Because the food service industry is unique, an integral relationship exists between equipment, planning, productivity, and presentation of the final product. This relationship has the capacity to affect the interior and architectural design of the project. To provide effective services, a food service consultant must be prepared to participate in all aspects of the project.

Consulting firms like JEM Associates in New Jersey provide successful conceptualization and implementation of food preparation projects. They

Corporate Profile

U.S. Foodservice

U.S. Foodservice is one of the leading broad-line food service distributors in the United States, with yearly revenues exceeding $17 billion. The company distributes food and related products to over 250,000 customers, including independent and multiunit restaurants, health-care facilities, lodging establishments, gaming, cafeterias, schools and colleges, and government. U.S. Foodservice markets and distributes more than 43,000 national, private label, and signature brand items and employs more than 27,000 food service professionals.

Today, as the twenty-first century unfolds, U.S. Foodservice:

- Markets and distributes more than 43,000 national, private label, and signature brand items across America
- Supports over 250,000 food service customers, including restaurants, hotels, health-care facilities, cafeterias, and schools
- Employs more than 27,000 food service professionals
- Embraces a customer base of independent and chain businesses[2]

provide a full range of services from menu development through staff education, ensuring a successful turnkey product for new or retrofit installation. Their clients include large and small corporate and private clients in casino resorts, schools, correctional facilities, retirement communities, health care, industrial food procession, and mass production facilities. A food service consultant provides services through the design and construction phases until the business is on stable footing.

Liquor Distribution

Many restaurants sell alcoholic beverages in addition to food. Wine, beer, and spirits are typically purchased on a weekly basis. From fine wines to kegs of beer the distribution of alcoholic beverages starts with the producers and ends on the guests' palates. The liquor distribution industry supplies these products to the hospitality industry. Although state, county, and local laws dictate sales of alcoholic beverages, most liquor distributors operate the same way.

Liquor distribution sales representatives work closely with wine producers and distributors. A liquor sales representative typically attends wine tasting and training seminars to properly represent the products they sell. These sales representatives often pass along this knowledge to restaurant, club, bar, and catering operators with the hopes of getting

the wines they represent included on the operations wine list. It can be a very competitive industry.

Wine pairing is another very important way liquor distributors provide a service to the hospitality industry. Many sales representatives work with restaurateurs to pair wines with food menu items. For this position a sales representative must be familiar with not only domestic and international wines, but also liqueurs, beers, and spirits. This segment of the industry offers other positions in purchasing, accounting and finance, warehouse management, and marketing.

Promotions are also a big part of liquor distribution. A huge part of selling these products is getting guests to try them. Many bars and restaurants will work with sales representatives and the marketing department to promote certain alcoholic beverages on specific nights, giving away free or reduced price samples just as the food industry does in grocery stores. These promotions may also include entertainment, product logo giveaways (such as tee shirts, caps, and key chains), and interactive games.

Equipment and Supplies

All food service operations purchase nonfood products from vendors. Everything from a broiler oven to a mop handle to paper towel rolls must be purchased for the efficient operation of a food service operation. This industry offers thousands of products that help operators maintain their workplaces. The equipment and supply industry works directly with food service operations, from supplying kitchen equipment to new businesses to providing paper and cleaning products to existing hospitality enterprises. Many suppliers also offer consulting advice in areas such as kitchen design and layout, equipment, menu design, and sanitation needs. How many juice glasses will a new restaurant with 300 seats need? How can I budget for dishwashing detergent next year? Should I purchase a conventional or convection oven? This industry provides expertise in answering these questions.

One company that specializes in providing equipment and supplies is Edward Don & Company. Edward Don & Company is a leader in food service equipment distribution. The company provides food service equipment and supplies to restaurants, government institutions, hospitals, hotels, and schools. Edward Don & Company also offers bar and fountain supplies, catering and cooking equipment, tableware, tables and chairs, paper goods, cleaning products, sanitation supplies, and 12,000 other products. The company distributes its products nationwide. Edward Don also designs and builds full-service kitchens for the food service industry. The company, owned by the Don family, was founded in Chicago in 1921.[3]

Another organization in the food service equipment industry is Restaurant Equipment World, Inc. Restaurant Equipment World, Inc. is a world leader

Purchasing requires technical knowledge of products and market dynamics that affect prices and supply. © 2011 by StockLite. Used under license of Shutterstock, Inc.

of online restaurant equipment sales, installation, design, and export. The company owns and operates a network of 175+ product-specific Web sites with a database of more than 20,000 catalog items with photos. Restaurant Equipment World, Inc. has been in business for over 28 years, and their site features REX—the restaurant equipment search engine.

Food service equipment distributors also provide products for daily use. Particularly paper goods such as take-out cups and containers, toothpicks, lobster bibs, aluminum foil, cocktail napkins, and toilet tissue, to name a few. These sales representatives also sell cleaning products including dishwashing detergent, bleach, hand soap, and degreasing products. Career opportunities in this industry include accounting/finance, administration, customer service, human resources, marketing, operations, information technology, and sales. Sales positions include management and nonmanagement positions in street sales, national accounts, and project managers for food service equipment division.[4]

The vast majority of distributor sales representatives earn income based on some combination of total sales collected and percent of gross margin on products sold. Like other sales positions in and outside the hospitality industry, the more they sell, the more they earn. Many distributor sales representatives receive additional financial incentives if they achieve certain company goals: increasing average order sizes or sales of a particular product, maybe upping sales of private-label items. To create ongoing relationships, distributor sales representatives are expected to provide useful information and present products to hospitality managers while letting the managers make decisions. It is the steady long-term customers that will make distributor sales representatives successful.[5] Distributor sales representatives are generally provided a geographical area in which to sell their wares. These areas are typically referred to as territories. The sales representatives provide service to existing customers while constantly trying to acquire new customers in their territories. This is an extremely competitive industry that requires skilled professionals with impeccable personal and organizational skills. These individuals must also be self-motivated and driven. Much of their time is spent alone traveling the territory and working with technology, specifically e-mail and cell phones, taking and placing orders to meet daily deadlines.

Linens

With the demand for upscale services growing at a rapid pace, the purchasing, receiving, issuing, storing, and cleaning of linens, towels, tablecloths, and uniforms has become an intricate component of creating a favorable guest experience. Linen, ranging from very luxurious to normal, is used by various hospitality operations depending on their requirements. In addition to purchasing laundry, hospitality operations have several choices when it comes to how they handle the laundry as well. Many peripheral industries are related to the rental and cleaning of hospitality laundry. Guestrooms, restaurants, banquets, fitness centers, and employees all create soiled linens, towels, tablecloths, and uniforms. Although many lodging properties in the United States operate an on-premise laundry, many others have their laundry cleaned and processed by outside contractors. Linen is a very important part of a hotel's image. Lodging customers measure quality as the sum of many little things, all of which are important.

Furniture, Fixtures, and Equipment (FF&E)

Purchasing furnishings, supplies, and equipment is a function that can be performed by a corporate-level purchasing department, a purchasing manager or agent at a hotel, or performed by a third-party purchasing agent. The Internet has made the job of purchasing easier and faster, but someone or some team must still ensure that the materials purchased are the right quality and quantity. In hospitality, there are three distinct types of purchasing. Two areas—operating supplies and disposables and food and beverage items—are purchases that can be performed through computerized programs. Purchasing these standardized products is migrating toward business-to-business Internet purchasing. Purchasing furniture, fixtures, and equipment requires a different process. Because almost every item is nonstandard or custom-made, cost-effective FF&E purchasing demands professionals who fully comprehend the variables and use expertise to create the best value.

There are other intangibles that a purchasing professional addresses. Verifying that the manufacturer has liability insurance can save the hotel owner millions of dollars in potential liability claims. Coordinating time and routing of freight by balancing cost, construction and installation schedules, and packaging can save money. Purchasing is an administrative function requiring technical knowledge about the products being purchased and the market dynamics that affect prices and supply.[6] A career in purchasing

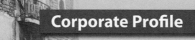

Corporate Profile

AC Linen

Located in the heart of "Always Turned On" Atlantic City, AC Linen is the current name of a laundry operation that has been around since the late 1890s. This facility now does some work for each of the city's 12 gaming halls in the Atlantic City casino properties. It is one of the largest commercial laundries on the Eastern seaboard. The ACLS also operates state-of-the-art laundries in Norwich, Connecticut.

In addition, Atlantic City Linen Services (ACLS) Management Group consults other commercial plants and various industries (hotel chains, health-care facilities, etc.) on design and operation of laundry facilities.

This operation is housed in a 14 million, 63,000 square foot complex that is energy efficient, computerized, and fully automated. As the casino gaming and nongaming hospitality industry continues to grow in the Atlantic City region, AC Linen plans on continued growth to service the marketplace.

AC Linen washes and dries about 100,000 pounds of laundry each day, and its daily load includes about 25,000 sheets and 30,000 bath towels. Laundry is processed around the clock, guaranteeing a one-day turnaround for the casino hotels. The facility is open 24 hours a day, 7 days a week.

The current facility operates at about 40% to 50% of its capacity, and the company has the ability to add more washers and dryers as its customer base grows. The company employs more than 200 workers and boasts annual revenues of $12 million.

food and beverage for a hotel or restaurant would require some experience in food production and management as well as knowledge of how a kitchen operates. Keeping aware of market trends and new products is also important. Knowledge of grading criteria, labeling, and standards of quality is also important. A purchasing agent is required to judge if a fair price is being quoted by a distributor and match orders to purchase specifications. Learning how to deal effectively with suppliers and master the managerial aspects of purchasing is necessary if you are interested in a career in the purchasing department of hospitality company. A skilled purchasing agent knows how innovative purchasing techniques can contribute to profits, efficient operations, and guest satisfaction.

The FF&E industries that students can consider include audiovisual and entertainment equipment, exercise equipment, badges, food service and preparation equipment, banquet equipment, bar equipment, electronic message displays, flooring supplies, luggage carts, housekeeping carts, guestroom case goods, chinaware, cleaners, decorative accessories, energy conservation equipment, Internet services, key control systems, maintenance equipment, safety products, vending machines, and much more.

Technology

The hospitality industry utilizes many systems and technologies to serve guests more efficiently and effectively. Information technology helps hospitality

The beer industry has become extremely competitive within the past few years. © 2011 by Oliver Hoffmann. Used under license of Shutterstock, Inc.

businesses reach their goals of delivering exceptional guest satisfaction. Hospitality information technology can range from computers and hardware to telephone systems and software. Hospitality industry technology systems range from electronic mail to global or international information systems, hotel information technology systems, energy management systems, call accounting systems, guest reservation systems, security systems, sales and marketing systems, and restaurant and food service information technology systems. More emerging technological trends being utilized by the hospitality industry is applicant tracking systems, key control, and yield management software. This automation helps make hospitality operations as efficient as possible while enhancing the guest's experience. If you have an interest in a career in technology in the hospitality industry, a number of jobs are available in implementation of systems, product development, and Web design.

Trends in Distribution Services

When working as part of the distribution systems industry, it is important that professionals stay abreast of the many trends that affect the hospitality industry. The following trends will no doubt affect hospitality operations in the near future.

More than half the nation's restaurants and bars are now smoke-free by law, and as many as 70% are estimated to be that way by the year's end.[7] These laws are passing whether restaurants and bars want them to or not. Membership and involvement in organizations like the National Restaurant Association and the American Hotel and Lodging Associations help keep you on top of public policy and legal matters that affect the hospitality industry. National issues in the hospitality industry include ADA, minimum wage, terrorism risk insurance, credit card acceptance, food safety, immigration reform, and the smoking ban.

Menu trends will include an increase in ethnic cuisines such as Thai, Mexican, and Caribbean. There will also be an emphasis in displaying ingredients such as whole grains, antioxidants, and other healthful aspects of food. Antioxidant-rich white tea will become an ingredient in many desserts, whereas other desserts will be based on single-origin chocolates from Ecuador, Venezuela, and Madagascar. Exotic tropical fruits will also be prominently featured on many menus.

David Kasinetz

*"I would not have the success I have today if it
were not for my restaurant management background."*

David Kasinetz is a sales manager for Advanced Hospitality Systems. He first worked for Darden Restaurants as a manager for Red Lobster upon completing his bachelor of science degree in Hotel and Restaurant Management from Widener University. David also studied business administration at The Pennsylvania State University. After several years he went to work for Pepperidge Tree Restaurants in Philadelphia. As technological changes began to occur in the restaurant industry, David followed his long-time interest in computers and made a career change to Comtrex Systems Corporation as a sales consultant. David excelled in selling point-of-sales (POS) systems to food and beverage establishments. He left Comtrex for Advanced Hospitality Systems in 1997, where he has continued to be on the forefront of food and beverage technology. David admits, "I would not have the success I have today if it were not for my restaurant management background." His experience gives him the unique ability to work with clients on issues and concerns adapting and customizing POS systems for food and beverage operations. Mr. Kasinetz says his daily activities involve traveling; attending trade shows; conducting software demonstrations; preparing return on investments analyses; hiring, training, and managing a sales and administrative staff; and creating innovative marketing materials.

Required Skills—Excellent communication skills, enjoy public speaking, computer skills, MS Office applications, must be a great listener, salesmanship.

Required Knowledge—Understanding of hotel and restaurant operations, basic computer networking concepts.

Highlights of Job—I enjoy travel and attending trade shows and every day meeting new and interesting people and helping them increase their profits.

Recommendations—Most high-paying sales jobs are commission based. Do not expect to have great success immediately. It takes a few years to build a pipeline of prospects, but eventually you will reap the rewards. Learn as much as you can while working in operations. Pay attention to food and beverage cost/labor cost, be detail oriented, and enjoy the hard work. Restaurant management will prepare you for different opportunities down the road. It's invaluable experience.

Restaurant patrons wish to become more educated while dining out. This will require menus to include more information about nutritional content, origins of food products, and unique and innovative ingredients.[8]

Some restaurant operations, including Subway, are experimenting with more "eco" friendly stores. This includes adding recycling bins, utilizing recycled paper goods, and switching to cutlery and plastic drinking cups made of polypropylene instead of polystyrene, which uses less oil in its production. Subway estimates that that change alone will save 13,000 barrels of oil annually.[9]

The beer industry has changed in the past few years as new products and market placement have become extremely competitive within the industry. The beer industry markets their products directly against their competitors. Many producers have also expanded their product lines by creating products to increase the market of beer drinkers such as low carbohydrate beer, low alcohol and no alcohol beers, flavored beers, and alcoholic ciders, lemonade, and iced teas known as "hard" beverages. Imported beers have always been popular in the United States; today many of the most popular imported beers have increased their television marketing. Microbreweries have also become more prominent and appealing to the market as an upscale beverage as compared to the mass production breweries, taking marketshares away from the large breweries. One mass producer of beer is attempting to emphasize beer's social value by marketing the art of the brewing process and the selection and use of natural ingredients, much as winemakers do.[10]

The National Restaurant Association announced award-winning kitchen innovations in 2006 including the MooBella Ice Cream System. A new creation that utilizes the space of a typical vending machine and produces real ice cream in 96 varieties, made to order in 45 seconds, as well as a refrigerator that improves food safety management by combining a thermometer and a programmable timer that emits a 70 decibel alarm when the current temperature of the food drops below 41°F/°C or time expires. The timer retains data for proof of HACCP compliance.[11]

Keeping abreast of trends in hospitality information technology is important for managers and businesses to stay competitive and to deliver the best service product possible. iConnect employs thin technology, desktop applications, a 15-inch flat screen monitor, multimedia sound, and a full-size mouse and keyboard, making it familiar and easy to use. Guests can surf the Internet and access e-mail accounts, but there are plenty of mind-blowing benefits as well. Installed in all 1,406 guestrooms, Gaylord Palms Resort & Convention Center, located near Walt Disney World theme parks in Kissimmee, Florida, is the first to offer this complimentary technology. With a click of a mouse, guests can send requests for fluffy pillows, arrange for valet services, peruse restaurant menus, or send an intrahotel message 24/7. Technologically delivered services are not a value-added amenity but a necessary attribute of today's core hotel product.[12]

Summary

You can see that the distribution services industry is a vast network of companies that offer services and product that keep lodging, restaurants, and attractions profitable and efficiently running. As an aspiring hospitality management professional, it is critical that you understand and appreciate the role that the distribution services industry plays in the big picture of the hospitality industry.

RESOURCES

Internet Sites

www.usfood service.com
www.don.com
www.ihmrs.com
www.aclinen.com
www.apics.org
www.restaurant.org
www.tsea.org
www.posamerica.com

References

JEM Associates at http://www.jemassociates.com

Mcyntyre, P. (2007). Industry should clean the air, reconsider its opposition to smoking ban legislation at http://www.nrn.com/article.aspx?id=346564

ENDNOTES

1. Pavesic, D. V., & Magnant, P. F. (2005). *Fundamental principles of restaurant cost control.* Upper Saddle River, NJ: Pearson Prentice Hall.

2. U.S. Food service at http://www.usfood service.com/html/index.html

3. Edward, D. at http://hoovers.com/Edward-don/--ID_44487--/free-co-factsheet.xhtml

4. Edward, D. at http://www.don.com/aboutdon/joblistings.aspx

5. Restaurant Biz at http://restaurantbiz.com/index.php?option=com_content&tast=view&id=13282&itemid=93

6. Pavesic, D. V., & Magnant, P. F. (2005). *Fundamental principles of restaurant cost control.* Upper Saddle River, NJ: Pearson Prentice Hall.

7. *Nation's Restaurant News,* 2007.

8. *Sun Times* at http://www.suntimes.com/output/news/cst-nws-eattrends16.html

9. *Wall Street Journal* at http://online.wsj.com/article/SB119560391050099871.html?mod=dist_smartbrief&mod=dist_smartbrief

10. Wharton School of Business http://knowledge.wharton.upenn.edu/article/1363.cfm

11. National Restaurant Association at http://www.restaurant.org/show

12. Angelucci, P. (2005). How can I serve you? The delicate balance of hotel staff and technology working together at http://www.hospitalityupgrade.com/hospitality/client/hu/articles.Nsf/77b53cfa89355b148525688c00608311/30fc24a37ebc03278525703600690a29?OpenDocument

Review Questions

1. How would you define distribution services in the hospitality industry?

2. What is meant by "peripheral career opportunities"?

3. Liquor distribution includes beer, wine, and _____.

4. What is wine pairing?

5. Edward Don & Company is a leader in what industry?

6. Why are breweries adding new products such as low carbohydrate beer, nonalcohol beer, and hard cider?

7. With restaurant patrons wishing to be more educated during their dining experiences, restaurants will be pressured to provide menus offering information about _____, _____, and _____.

8. Equipment distributors play a role in the daily operations of food service operations. True or False?

9. What is the career opportunities outlined in this chapter?

10. What are some trends that will affect hospitality operations?

CHAPTER 22

Facility Layout and Design Consulting

Ken Myers, University of Minnesota, Crookston
Gail Myers, Suite Harmony Corporation

LEARNING OBJECTIVES

- Explain the role of the many professionals involved on a design team.
- Describe what "universal design" is and how it affects the planning and design of a hospitality establishment.
- Explain the design considerations and how those considerations work together in creating the desired environment.
- List organizations that rate hotels and restaurants on specific criteria and how hospitality establishments can use these criteria as they plan design projects.

CHAPTER OUTLINE

KEY TERMS

Acoustical engineers
Aesthetics
Architects
Color
Commercial kitchen designers
Contractors
Electrical engineers
Environmentally friendly
Flow

Function
Health inspector
Hospitality manager
Interior designers
Interior plantscapers
Style
Sustainable design
Universal design

Hospitality Design Fundamentals

It all begins with the concept. Every aspect of layout and design is driven by a central idea that will make your establishment an exciting place. Whether the concept is a Southern-style barbeque restaurant, a Far Eastern–inspired spa, or a historical building turned hotel, every choice of lighting, piece of furniture, choice of linens, and even exterior signage will signal to potential guests who you are.

The design and layout of the property also sets the stage for guest expectations and behaviors. Do you want guests to wear suits and ties? Do you want guests to stay a long time or move in and out quickly? Do you want your guests to have romantic memories of your establishment or do you want them to remember you as a hot, trendy new property? Elements like color, traffic flow, and music can all communicate strong messages to the guests. You control those messages by proper use of layout and design.

Layout refers to the placement of furniture and equipment within spaces that guides the traffic patterns of both people and product. Design refers to the placement and selection of your building and the specifications for the colors, fixtures, walls, ceiling and floor treatments, furniture and equipment, lighting, and all the accessories. The best interior designs will create a synergy through the combination of all the elements while adhering to applicable building codes. Creating ambience, providing for safety, buffering sound, and increasing efficiency and comfort for the guest—these are some of the goals of layout and design in the hospitality industry.

In this day of online restaurant reviews, hotel reservations, and general entertainment planning on the Internet, layout and design now plays a key role in consumer choice because it can be available to them before they ever take a step inside the establishment. Further, many travelers today are influenced in their choice of lodging and restaurants by various rating systems. Rating systems for hotels rank criteria they have established with layout and design specifics for the exterior, public areas, guestrooms, bathrooms, and hotel amenities in addition to service. Other rating services examine restaurant quality with criteria covering ambiance, lighting, traffic flow, and general comfort, in addition to the quality of the food and service.

Hotels must actually plan the rating they wish to achieve well in advance of construction because revisions in layout and design after the hotel is built can

be costly. For example, one hotel chain saved money by installing vinyl bathroom flooring that resembled tile, only to find later that they met all of the four star criteria except for that flooring. Most highly rated hotels have wide corridors and spacious bathroom layouts. If not considered in the initial planning, these elements are difficult to impossible to change once the hotel is built.

Function, flow, and aesthetics are the important factors in making a decision about how a hospitality facility should be planned and maintained. Yes, guests need a comfortable bed to sleep on (function), but is the layout arranged so that they can get to the bathroom in the night without tripping on a chair, or escape to a nearby stairway in case of fire (flow)? In addition, is the bed well appointed with dust ruffle, extra pillows, and coordinating bed linens (aesthetics)? Guest perception is always the first consideration in function, flow, and beauty. Just any bed serves the function of a place to sleep but quality hotels are concerned about upgrading function to achieve a higher level of comfort. Radisson Hotels have been switching some of their conventional mattresses to the "Sleep Number Bed"; a specific brand name that consumers recognize and associate with increased comfort. Some luxury hotels are offering a more customized approach to function that allows guests to choose from a selection of pillows: goose down or foam, firm or soft. How a person sleeps directly influences their perception of the hotel in the morning. An appropriate traffic flow pattern is essential in a family dining establishment. For example, guests expect they will not have to take their kids through the bar to get to the restroom. Aesthetics or beauty plays a primary role in touching the emotions of people. A café seems a little more upscale—a little more pleasant—if there are flowers on the table. A well-designed and aesthetically pleasing environment keeps the guests coming back.

It is hard to place an order of importance on function, flow, and aesthetics. Once again, guest perception and expectations play a part in the layout and design choices. Great food served on picnic tables that are squeezed into a small space where elbows touch, where waitstaff have a hard time maneuvering, and the noise of pots and pans blends in with loud music may be acceptable at an outdoor barbeque, but will leave a bad taste in the mouths of guests at most restaurants. Guests who walk in the door may expect adequate aisles, private space, and a low noise level so that they can hear conversation and enjoy comfortable seating.

Interior design is much more than selecting carpet or wall coverings to meet fire codes. The elements of interior design can be used to imaginatively create theatrics, special effects, or historic restoration. When you walk into a restaurant, whether it is freestanding, at the casino, or on a cruise ship, interior excitement is created by the materials on the wall, ceilings, and floors; the psychological effect of color; and the level and type of lighting. A jazz club may use bold and unique color combinations, small halogen track lighting, and contemporary furniture to promote its "on the edge" feel. The flow-through of the concept should enter into every design detail including, the furniture, the menu, and the centerpiece. Even the switch plate covers are preplanned to become part of a total design concept.

Hospitality facilities are known to remodel every 5 to 7 years. No matter how old or new, the design of the inside of the building affects every aspect of the comfort and enjoyment of guests. In fact, design involves the stimulation of the five senses. How does the food smell in conjunction with the flowers on the table, the aromatherapy, and the smell of wood or leather? How does the texture of the carpet or the flooring work with the wall covering, the texture of the tablecloth and linens, and the ceiling materials? Is the room acoustically balanced so that guests can hear the music playing and hear the conversation of the partner next to them, without hearing the conversation of the next table? Do the guests feel soothed by the colors so that they are encouraged to linger over many courses, or are the colors passionate and brash encouraging a fast-food approach? We will leave the sense of taste and the blend of exquisite flavors to the chef, but when it comes to artistic taste for the environment, the interior designer reigns. Do the styles mix: the furniture, the waiter's uniform, the china, glass, and silver? When one of these factors is different from the rest, a discord is created, which results in guests feeling that something is not quite right. It may not be enough to make them leave, but it can be a reason to select another restaurant next time without them even being aware of why. Can a remodel of the layout increase business by adding more seats? Will a new layout train customers to stand in line, to order at a particular place, to become part of the flow of service? A green carpet creates a pathway to the registration desk when bordered by a contrasting color

A well-designed and aesthetically pleasing environment keeps guests coming back. © 2011 by Caruntu. Used under license of Shutterstock, Inc.

such as white marble. A key ingredient in making design decisions is whether all these aspects of the décor blend together into a consistent whole.

These questions are answered with careful planning and a project design team that follows through from developing the very concept of the hospitality establishment to making that concept a physical reality. Add to that the responsibilities of health and safety standards required by building codes, analyzing specifications of products for use and wear, planning for the efficiency necessary for any services that are provided, and of course, close attention to a budget, and you can begin to understand the knowledge required by a design team.

Professionals Involved in the Design Team

Architects: These professionals prepare and review plans for the overall construction. Qualified architects will have an AIA (American Institute of Architects) appellation.

Interior Designers: These professionals design interior spaces involving materials, finishes, colors, space planning, and layout. This person may be employed by the architects or may have their own design firm. The interior designer in this case should be a commercial interior designer, as residential design is very different. A qualified applicant will have an ASID appellation. See American Society of Interior Designers Web site.

Electrical Engineers: They design all the electrical systems. They may have to prepare and stamp electrical plans to obtain building permits and are usually employed by the architects.

Contractors: They are the builders of the project. The general contractor will appoint a construction manager who will oversee specialty sub-contractors needed for the project. Specialty contractors include tradespeople like cabinetmakers, carpet and tile installers, and painters. Contractors are hired by bid and recommendation and are licensed by the state.

Acoustical Engineers: They offer advice and planning for acoustic or sound issues and suggest materials to solve noise problems or enhance sound. They are usually employed by the architects.

Interior Plantscapers: They advise on the proper selection and positioning of plants as well as their maintenance, and are generally hired by recommendation.

Commercial Kitchen Designers: They provide planning and drawings for commercial kitchens as well as specifying equipment. They will begin with the menu and the number of seats to make appropriate determinations of the kitchen layout and design. Often these kitchen designers are freelance or are employed by equipment sales companies. There is no professional appellation here, so check for appropriate hospitality background and equipment knowledge.

Health Inspector: Inspectors are employed by the state and interpret state codes. They will inspect existing facilities and must review and approve plans for new or remodeled food preparation areas, service areas, and restrooms. In addition, they will want to approve selections of interior finishes and equipment.

Hospitality Manager: This essential part of the team represents the owners of the facilities. They coordinate the design team and keep them on track with the concept and budget. They will be the final decision maker and/or represent investors, developers, or board members of the company. The manager will follow every detail of the plan. The manager may involve other company personnel, including the purchasing agent.

Once you have a well-defined concept and you have selected your design team, you can begin on the new or remodel project. Every project is different and will require a different combination of members, depending on what is to be accomplished.

Design Considerations

Each area in the hospitality establishment has different design considerations and priorities. In some areas safety and function come before beauty. In some areas pure drama is the most important element. The right interior design for your concept can allow guests to perceive the value of your services as much greater than the competition. A hotel lobby that uses plush carpet, incandescent lighting, and a fireplace may be perceived as a better value than a similar hotel lobby down the street that uses a loop carpet, cool fluorescent lights, and vending machines, even though the room prices of both hotels are comparable.

Some specific design considerations are as follows.

The Guest Room

The design of the guest room influences the perception of all the hotel's facilities. Guests spend more time in their room than anywhere in the hotel. Rooms should accommodate the physical needs and comfort of a diverse group of people. Layout considerations include planned spaces to accommodate the five functions of a guest room: sleeping, bathing, grooming, dressing, and entertainment activities. Some guest rooms also become a workspace. Trends for guest room design include increased comfort and spa-like details such as elaborate showerheads and featherbeds. More options for work and play include universal adaptors and docking devices for PDAs, MP3s, portable DVD players, and phones, which many guests bring with them. Room design can be more fluid than other areas in a hotel as accessories can be changed frequently.

Food/Beverage Service Areas (dining areas, bars, and meeting rooms/ banquet areas)

Design concepts in these areas portray to guests the type of service offered and even the pricing. Crystal chandeliers may cue guests about menu prices and even their attire in this setting. Design characteristics for fast food include easy maintenance, elements that encourage fast turnover, and lots of energy (see Table 22.1). Some restaurants soften the hard edge of fast-food design by adding plants, skylights, and play areas. Contrast this environment with tableside dining where there are often barriers for privacy and a high level of comfort that makes guests want to stay. Theme restaurants are not just about food but also about creating an experience. Theatrical food and beverage areas allow guests to "see the show" from all areas. Open kitchens may be part of the show as are animatronics, displays, actors and acrobats, or plasma screens. Trends for food and beverage areas run from casual and trendy European styling to the nostalgic craze from the '40s and '50s. Lots of props add to the ambiance. Multitasking in a restaurant, including eating, drinking, and socializing, has now expanded to include entertainment, games, and Internet surfing all while you're still at the table or bar.

A restaurant's design conveys the type of service offered and even the pricing. © 2011 by Sergey Chirkov. Used under license of Shutterstock, Inc.

Kitchen/Food Production Areas

The kitchen square footage is planned at one-third to one-half of the dining area square footage. Ignoring this rule can cause a restaurant to fail as adequate space is needed for the manufacturing processes surrounding food. Workstations are established based on the menu, salad station, grilling station, and so on. Tasks are analyzed and placed in efficient adjacencies. For example, baking areas can be next to roasting areas so that ovens are accessible to both. Areas to be considered are hot foods, cold foods, beverage, service, warewashing, storing and receiving, offices, and employee areas. Health and sanitation requirements will dictate some of the placement and the materials used for walls, floors, and so on. Equipment selection and traffic patterns in the kitchen and to the dining room are important decisions that will affect success. Management in the hospitality field is well aware that even service and food quality are largely affected by the layout and design of the kitchen and related production and storage areas. Trends include more color and design attention being paid to these areas, as guests can often see them from dining rooms or actually dine in the kitchen on special VIP tables.

TABLE 22.1 Fast Service Design versus Table Service Design

FAST SERVICE RESTAURANT	TABLE SERVICE RESTAURANT
Bright warm colors	Soft peaceful colors/trendy special effects
Bright overhead lighting	Low-level lighting with some lighting specifically for mood or atmosphere
Short seat depth and upright back on chairs	Long seat depth/angled back
Nonpadded or partially padded seating	Thickly cushioned seats and back
Hard surface low-cost floors	Multisurface flooring including carpeting, tile, wood
Limited noise reduction	Finishes chosen to reduce noise including wall fabrics, linens, carpets, ceiling treatments
Line stanchions, condiments stations, open beverage dispensers for self-service	Wide aisles to accommodate waitstaff, tableside cooking, tray stands

Common Areas (corridors, elevators, stairways, lobbies, public restrooms)

The hallways in any hospitality establishment are not only the primary circulation areas, but also the escape system. The design should actually point the way to an exit, a cashier station, or a restroom, in the form of directional cues including wallpaper patterns, handrails, colors, and signage. Illumination of the walls and floors is also of primary importance as long, narrow dark hallways trigger negative emotional responses. Trends include hallways wide enough to provide niche seating areas as accommodation for those guests with reduced strength and endurance.

The number of seats in a restaurant will dictate the number of restrooms that are needed. Good restroom design is a way to communicate goodwill to guests by adding colorful tiles, easy-to-clean wall coverings that are aesthetically appealing, flowers, and makeup areas. Certainly, the appearance of cleanliness is part of good design. Some restrooms offer cloth hand towels as part of a luxury appeal.

Lobbies communicate the identity of the establishment to guests as well as provide adjacencies to all other public areas. Guests are encouraged to socialize, transact business, and linger. Typically there are changes in materials, lighting, and signage in lobby areas as directional cues to other main areas of the hotel. Trends for design include mixing a multitude of textures such as glass, wood, and even concrete with fabrics, leathers, and metal. Custom designs are often used in flooring such as logos created with tile or carpet, exotic lighting, and high ceilings. Lobby areas are often opened up to bar areas or entertainment areas to draw guests into the establishment.

Mechanical Equipment and Special Systems

The internal workings of the facility are usually unseen by the guests but are essential to their needs and comfort. Architects and technicians are involved in planning security systems, audiovisual equipment and use, as well as telephone and computer accessibility for the guests and for the business of the hotel. Mechanical equipment planning and maintenance is also essential. Plumbing, electrical, and HV/AC systems (heating, ventilation, and air conditioning) must be efficient and meet environmental standards for the health and safety of everyone. Sprinkler systems, elevators, and fire extinguishers are inspected periodically to make sure they are working correctly.

Air quality in a hotel or restaurant can make or break what should be a pleasant experience even if the food and furnishings are of the highest standards; sewer smells, kitchen grease, or mildew would be offensive and would ruin the occasion. One new restaurant was constantly filled with smoke, as their hood system in the kitchen was inadequate. Potential diners, enticed by a unique concept and a great menu, were uncomfortable with an atmosphere that was environmentally unfriendly and left guests smelling badly when they left. Hood systems, air exchange systems, and exhaust fans must be properly sized, installed, and maintained to create the desired environment.

A Friendly Design Approach

The design industry is moving in a friendly direction: people friendly and plant friendly. As professionals in the hospitality industry, we have the opportunity to make every guest comfortable and preserve our environment at the same time.

Universal Design

The importance of access to the environment for all physically challenged people began to be regulated in 1990 with the American with Disabilities Act. The act listed specific regulations that affected building codes and new construction all over the country, which as a result affects the design of every hospitality establishment. Increased awareness of the growing aging population of the baby boomers and the variety of physical challenges affecting the entire population caused those in the design industry to develop products that would allow accessibility to all kinds of people, including adults, children, and the elderly. The term "Universal Design" was used to convey the idea that products (furnishings, hardware) and architectural changes could be made to make life easier for all people, whether or not they have a disability. Some of those design changes today include barrier-free/accessible rooms and lobbies, lever faucets and door handles, 34- to 36-inch door openings, grab bars in restroom stalls and shower areas, water fountains at different height levels, and self-flushing toilets. Although hotels are required to have a certain percentage of handicapped rooms to be ADA compliant, the concept of Universal Design is that of inclusion so as to have all rooms as barrier free and accessible as possible. Some efforts to create universal accessibility are as simple as wider aisles in a restaurant or full-size mirrors in restrooms.

Sustainable Design

Strategies for reducing consumption involve design practices that are environmentally friendly. Governments, other businesses, and guests expect the hospitality industry to be environmentally conscious, yet the competitive environment requires us to be luxury conscious. How do we accommodate both worlds and still be accountable for our planet? Luxury says no to low-pressure showerheads but environmentally friendly design says yes to dual flush toilets. Guests still dictate what amenities they are willing to leave home for. Some environmentally friendly design aspects include using eco-friendly fabrics and organic bedding and regional building materials and resources including local artists and local stone. Green design can be as simple as installing windows that open to let in the fresh air and durable goods like glass and porcelain instead of paper. Major recycling methods involve using dishwater and shower water to water gardens and landscaping (assuming soaps are biodegradable), or minor methods like putting recycling bins in restaurants or guest rooms. There are organizations that rate hospitality establishments on their "green" efforts. Two such organizations are the Audubon Green Leaf™ Eco-Rating Program, which advises and rates hospitality establishments on their sustainable design efforts and Environmentally Friendly Hotels organization that allows the guest to be involved in the rating.

Summary

The entire interior design industry is committed to making the hospitality experience more efficient, more beautiful, more exciting, and more profitable. Your layout and design choices communicate to the guest your commitment to their enjoyment and pleasure. Good design will keep guests coming back.

RESOURCES

Internet Sites

American Institute of Architects (AIA): www.AIA-online.org

American Society of Interior Designers (ASID): www.asid.org

The International Facility Management Association (IFMA): www.ifma.org

Three links for AAA Diamond Criteria:

   http://www.aaanewsroom.net/Main.asp?SectionID=&SubCategoryID= 22&Category ID=9&

   http://www.aaanewsroom.net/Main.asp?CategoryID=9&SubCategoryID=22&ContentID=62&

   http://www.aaanewsroom.net/Main.asp?CategoryID=9&SubCategoryID=22&ContentID=63&

Mobil Stars Criteria: http://www.mobiltravelguide.com/mtg/

Travelocity: http://svc.travelocity.com/info/info_popup/0,,YHOE:EN%7CRATINGS,00.html

Yahoo Travel: http://travel.yahoo.com/

Audubon Green Leaf™ Eco-Rating Program: http://www.auduboninternational.org/programs/greenleaf/?gclid=CKHm1bj-0I8CFSXOIgodQyjFzw

Environmentally Friendly Hotels: http://www.environmentallyfriendlyhotels.com

Review Questions

1. What is the role of the architect, interior designer, electrical engineer, contractor, acoustical engineers, interior plantscapers, the commercial kitchen designer, the health inspector, and the hospitality manager in a design project?

2. List the five functions of a hotel guest room.

3. Why is the design of a guest room considered more fluid than other areas in a hotel?

4. If the size of a restaurant's dining room was 2,500 square foot, how many square feet would you expect the kitchen to be?

5. What term is used to convey the idea that product and architectural changes can make life easier for all individuals?

6. What are two organizations that rate hotels and restaurants on specific criteria?

7. How frequently do many hospitality establishments remodel?

8. How can design affect the guest room, food and beverage areas, and common areas of a hospitality establishment?

9. Compare and contrast how design considerations may affect guests at a fast service versus a table service restaurant.

10. What are environmentally friendly methods that can be used by the hospitality establishments in their design?

11. What are ways that we can satisfy the desire for both luxury design and sustainable design?

Real Estate in Hospitality

Karl J. Mayer, University of Nevada, Las Vegas
John M. Stefanelli, University of Nevada, Las Vegas

 LEARNING OBJECTIVES

- To familiarize the student with an important and dynamic sector of the hospitality industry—the real estate area.
- To understand the importance of real estate.
- To understand the variety of career choices that are available for those students who wish to focus on hospitality real estate.
- To identify the skills, background, and experience required to effectively engage in the real estate field.
- To distinguish which hospitality programs offer specific classes in real estate at the present time.

CHAPTER OUTLINE

Typical Hospitality Real Estate Positions
    Company Real Estate Representatives
    Appraisers
    Real Estate Sales
    Vacation-Ownership Sales
    Business Opportunity Sales
    Site Analysts
    Financial Positions
Desirable Background for Hospitality Real
    Estate Positions
    Your Future in Hospitality Real Estate

 **KEY TERMS**

Appraiser
Broker
Real estate representative
Support staff
Vacation-ownership firm

Typical Hospitality Real Estate Positions

One of the advantages of working in the hospitality industry is the availability of a wide array of career options. Hospitality real estate offers a number of interesting and worthwhile career opportunities. Several hospitality firms employ real estate specialists, including market analysts, location analysts, and lease negotiators. However, you do not have to be employed by a hospitality company to work in this field. For instance, you could be an independent appraiser or work for a lender, private investor, or real estate brokerage firm.

Several career options in real estate relate directly or indirectly to the hospitality industry. Persons wishing to work in this area may find employment with real estate departments in multiunit hospitality corporations, appraisal firms, real estate brokerages, vacation-ownership firms, business brokerages, site selection firms, and lending institutions. The skills needed to perform well in hospitality real estate are very diverse and depend on the specific area of emphasis that a person chooses. These skills are identified and discussed later in this chapter, but first, the wide variety of positions that are available in hospitality real estate will be considered.

Company Real Estate Representatives

Many large multiunit hospitality corporations employ a real estate director and one or more real estate representatives. These persons are usually responsible for the following activities:

1. Performing location analyses (i.e., evaluating real estate sites to determine whether the company should construct new businesses in these locations)
2. Evaluating existing business locations from the perspective of acquiring and managing the business that is situated there
3. Working with a hospitality company's franchisees (if the firm franchises its business) to assist with site selection decisions, provide design advice, or help coordinate the activities of the company's internal resources with the franchisees
4. Working with a variety of external agents; for example, negotiating lease or purchase agreements with brokers and/or owners
5. Interfacing with the company's legal, construction, operations, and financial personnel.

Although the Internet has allowed company real estate representatives to perform more efficiently from the corporate office, these representatives nevertheless typically travel a great deal. It is not unusual for them to be on the road four days a week. Such extended travel, however, is necessary to evaluate a site properly. Real estate, by its very nature, is a highly localized business opportunity, even for very large national or international firms. If insufficient time is spent researching a location, the company may make a rash decision. Because location is a critical factor influencing a hospitality property's success, it is very important to make solid, well-informed site-selection decisions.

Appraisers

Real estate appraisers are employed to render estimates of value. They are trained to value various assets, including real estate (i.e., land and buildings); furniture, fixtures, and equipment (FFE); collectibles and artifacts; and going-concern businesses.

Commercial lenders, investors, sellers, insurance companies, contractors, attorneys, accountants, pension funds, and other entities with a financial stake in a hospitality project engage appraisers. For example, before a commercial lender, such as a bank or savings and loan, can lend money, it must have the collateral (i.e., assets) appraised by an independent appraiser it selects. A hospitality firm that needs to borrow money to build a new property must pay the cost of the appraisal needed to satisfy this regulatory requirement.

Some appraisers specialize exclusively in the hospitality industry. The major one, *Hospitality Valuation Services* (HVS), was founded in 1980. Currently, HVS has 11 offices in the United States, including New York, San Francisco, Miami, Dallas, Chicago, Atlanta, and Denver, as well as offices in Mexico, Canada, London, Hong Kong, China, Brazil, and five other countries. Although its array of client services has expanded in recent years, HVS's major focus is the appraisal of lodging properties.

It is unusual, however, for individual appraisers to specialize in hospitality because there may be insufficient work available to make it a full-time job. Generally speaking, appraisers tend to specialize in a particular category and not in a particular industry. For instance, a business valuation specialist who appraises restaurants will also typically appraise related businesses, such as taverns, liquor stores, bakeries, and food marts.

In other cases, appraisers may be part of a larger consulting practice. The firm *Ernst & Young* is representative of these types of appraisers and has consultants who are specifically designated to serve the hospitality industry through its Real Estate, Hospitality and Construction Services Group. Besides their appraisal work, these firms also conduct a wide variety of other assignments designed to assist their client companies.

In addition to appraisal assignments, appraisers usually counsel clients. For example, a motel owner may hire an appraiser to estimate the most likely sales price for the property. He or she may also ask the appraiser to suggest things the owner could do to make the motel more attractive to potential buyers. In this role, the appraiser is required to draw on his/her considerable expertise in the real estate field to make sound recommendations to the property owner.

Last, over and above an appraising or counseling role, some appraisers also get involved with real estate sales, property management (such as overseeing a shopping center complex), and loan brokerage (such as helping clients search for and secure the most favorable debt financing available). It is important to note, however, that in all aspects of appraisal work, it is essential for appraisers to render objective, unbiased advice and to avoid any situations that might be possible conflicts of interest between themselves and their clients. To do otherwise would severely impair their reputations.

Real Estate Sales

Although property owners are free to sell their properties without help from other professionals, most prefer using a third party to represent their interests. The same is true for potential buyers. Thus, brokers play a valuable role by serving as an intermediary in a real estate sales transaction.

Several brokerages specialize in the sale of lodging properties. For example, there are consortiums of brokerages in the United States that account for a majority of all lodging properties sold nationwide.

A brokerage office may also specialize in the sale of restaurants, taverns, liquor stores, and other similar hospitality businesses. In large cities, it is not unusual to find offices that deal exclusively with the sale and purchase of restaurants or with tavern operations.

Persons working in a sales office generally are in business for themselves; that is, they are independent contractors. Their livelihood depends on the amount of property sold, in that their main (and most

The role of real estate agent continues to evolve with the impact of technology and the growth of the Internet. © 2011 by EdBock-Stock. Used under license of Shutterstock, Inc.

often, only) source of income is sales commissions, which are generated when deals are concluded. Some sales associates represent sellers, and some represent buyers. Few represent both parties in a transaction because doing so may be a conflict of interest.

Although sales commissions are their primary source of income, some sales associates prefer to operate as independent consultants. In the typical sales transaction, the seller pays the commission, which is then divided among the relevant sales offices that helped consummate the deal. However, some salespersons work strictly for hourly fees and are paid regardless of the outcome of a transaction. In effect, they sell their time and are compensated accordingly.

A day in the life of the typical real estate sales associate finds him or her showing property to potential buyers, shopping and analyzing other properties in the market, gathering pertinent data, suggesting appropriate sales and purchase strategies, recommending alternative financing arrangements, estimating the most likely sales prices, organizing and completing deal-related paperwork, negotiating contract terms and conditions, and shepherding the deal to ensure that it stays on track and is finalized.

The role of a real estate sales associate is continuing to evolve due to the impact of technology and growth of the Internet. The Internet is making it possible for companies to circumvent intermediaries and "go direct" to potential buyers and sellers on a worldwide basis. Although many aspects of being a real estate sales associate will not be affected by these developments, students who are interested in this area should carefully explore the impact of these trends on the future of working in a real estate sales position.

Vacation-Ownership Sales

A vacation-ownership firm is in business to sell long-term vacation packages to guests. They sell "slices of time," in that they normally sell a guest the right to use a vacation apartment, hotel room, or condominium for a specified time period per year (usually 2 weeks) for several years (usually 7 to 20 years) at a specific property in a specific location. Alternatively, they can also purchase "points" from a vacation-ownership firm that allow them to take future vacations in various locations in exchange for using a specified number of the "points" that they own each year.

Guests who prepay for these vacations usually have the option of swapping their time at one location for comparable time at other vacation locations that are part of a time-share exchange network. Normally the guest pays a small fee for this exchange privilege.

In most cases, the prepaid vacation is an economical alternative to paying for vacations every year. Usually the guest needs to pay only a relatively modest maintenance fee each year to defray the cost of routine repairs, necessary remodeling, and so forth. In addition, the guest will pay local property taxes on a proportionate basis—normally, these annual tax payments are also fairly modest amounts.

At one time these "time-share operations" had a seedy reputation. Most of them were high-pressure sales operations that generated numerous consumer complaints. However, although a few of these boiler-room operations probably still exist, the industry is now generally considered to be quite legitimate. This is due primarily to the involvement of major lodging firms in the field such as Disney, Hilton, Marriott, Carlson, and Starwood. Their participation has legitimized the industry. In addition, other large firms, such as Fairfield Resorts, Bluegreen, and Royal Resorts, have specialized in providing high-quality time-share properties for guests. Today, this sector represents a major growth area in the hospitality field. It offers excellent opportunities for hospitality students who are interested in the variety of careers available in vacation-ownership sales. For those uninterested in sales, there are also many positions available in vacation-ownership operations, such as housekeeping, maintenance and engineering, and property management.

Business Opportunity Sales

A business opportunity is an ongoing business located in leased real estate facilities. The owner typically sells the business's furniture, fixtures, and equipment (FFE); its leasehold improvements (i.e., interior finishing of the leased premises); the business name and reputation; and perhaps some other types of assets, such as inventory or a valuable liquor license. The business opportunity purchase usually includes everything except the real estate.

A business opportunity brokerage is very similar to the typical real estate brokerage. Although business brokers do not normally sell real estate, they do sell businesses that must be transferred to buyers. In effect, the work performed by business sales associates parallels almost exactly that performed by most real estate sales associates. However, like the role of the real estate sales associate, this intermediary role will likely continue to evolve due to the development of new technology and the growth of the Internet, so students should be mindful of the potential impact of these trends on future careers in this area.

Site Analysts

Some research firms, real estate brokerages, and business brokerages provide location analysis for persons or firms unable or unwilling to do the work themselves. These companies typically maintain computerized databases that can be adapted to suit any need or answer any question. Their reports help clients make sound real estate and business decisions.

Some hospitality firms prefer to contract out this type of work to independent firms because it is more economical than maintaining their own real estate divisions. This concept is known as outsourcing. However, even those large hospitality companies that have real estate divisions are apt to use an outside firm on occasion because it is not always feasible for them to study every potential site, especially if a site is in a market where the firm does not have any existing properties under management.

Financial Positions

Many lending institutions are active in hospitality finance. These lenders provide the discretionary capital that allows new properties to be conceived and developed, or existing properties to be refinanced. The major players include the following organizations:

1. Life insurance companies that specialize in financing lodging properties

2. Pension funds that invest in lodging properties or lend to them
3. Banks and savings and loans that make real estate and business loans to qualified hospitality operators
4. Government agencies (such as the Small Business Administration) that make direct loans or guarantee loans made by a third party
5. Leasing companies that will construct a property and/or provide all necessary equipment and lease these assets to a manager/operator (especially in the gaming or restaurant sector of the hospitality industry) on a rent-to-use or a rent-to-own plan

Lenders must qualify potential borrowers. Before recommending a loan, the lender must ensure that there is a high probability that the money will be repaid in a timely manner. Lenders must perform "due diligence," which means that they must evaluate a borrower's creditworthiness, character, reputation, capacity to repay, business skill, and collateral. These evaluations require that a skilled financial professional is involved in the decision to extend credit to a borrower.

Lenders who are heavily involved in hospitality finance may employ real estate experts on their own staffs to perform these functions. For example, DePfa Bank AG (Deutsche Pfandbriefbank) is a German-based institution that has a specialized hotel financing team. This team has financed first-class hotels all over Europe and the United States, including properties such as the Plaza Hotel in New York City and the Adam's Mark Hotel in Dallas. In other cases, a lending institution may outsource these tasks to appraisers or consulting firms on an as-needed basis. Whichever approach is taken, it creates an opportunity for you to build a hospitality real estate career in a financial position.

Desirable Background for Hospitality Real Estate Positions

If these career opportunities seem exciting, you should begin to prepare for them now. It is never too early to select the right college courses and work experiences most likely to give you an edge when applying for this type of work.

These positions are very academically oriented, in that a great deal of research, writing, and computer skills are needed to be successful in a hospitality

Hospitality real estate positions are academically oriented, requiring research, writing, and computer skills. © 2011 by Stephen Coburn. Used under license of Shutterstock, Inc.

real estate position. You should take college courses designed to develop and enhance these skills.

You should also take a basic real estate course, real estate investments course, and real estate appraisal course. These classes will give you the best perspective of the industry, as well as highlight the various career opportunities that may exist in your local area. The next section of this chapter discusses which hospitality programs presently offer such courses.

Accounting and finance courses are also necessary for success. At the very least, you should take the basic accounting and financial principles classes. Generally, however, additional finance courses are necessary to acquire the techniques needed to prepare the types of research projects that you will encounter.

Computer literacy is a must. You should be very familiar with word processing, database, and spreadsheet software. In addition to working with your own computer files, you must be able to use the computerized databases most offices subscribe to. For instance, a real estate sales office usually subscribes to a computerized multiple listing service (MLS). Sales offices also typically use services that provide demographic data and updated lists of lenders and their current loan terms and conditions. The number of service firms offering these data has expanded significantly in recent years to meet the industry's ever-increasing demand for information. Also, geographic mapping software is now available, offering detail that can be used to examine a potential site on-screen before ever leaving the office for a site inspection.

Computer literacy is also needed to efficiently access information available on the Internet. In recent years, there has been an explosion of real estate information that can be downloaded from Internet sources. This information could include local market data and reports, national economic trends and conditions, financing availability and terms, or federal and state guidelines for site development activity. Thus, a broker, appraiser, or real estate director can now obtain a great deal of pertinent information without ever leaving the office. However, because real estate is inherently a localized business opportunity, there is no substitute for on-site visits by a trained real estate professional.

Many real estate positions require licensing or certification, or both. For instance, if you want to be an appraiser, you will likely need a state license as well as certification from a nationally recognized appraisal association.

Finally, you should acquire a reasonable amount of operations experience before tackling one of these staff positions. If you want to work in a hospitality company's real estate division, you should have a basic understanding of how the firm's food, lodging, or gaming units are operated and managed. This provides the perspective needed when wrestling with decisions that can make or break your employer's bottom line.

Your Future in Hospitality Real Estate

Currently seven leading programs offer at least one real estate course (Cornell, Michigan State, UNLV, Penn State, DePaul, University of Central Florida, and Florida International University) as a part of their hospitality programs. Further, Cornell, Michigan State, and DePaul appear to be the only three hospitality programs that also offer a specialization, or concentration, in this area. Students who are serious about a career in hospitality real estate may want to carefully consider their choice of a program and select one that offers a real estate curriculum, either in the hospitality program itself, or in a related business program at the university.

This chapter introduced you to the opportunities that are available for hospitality students who have an interest in real estate. Real estate is a vitally important aspect of most sectors of the hospitality industry, and those students who decide to pursue a career in this area will find it to be a rewarding and challenging career option. They would be well advised to take full advantage of the quantitative courses that are available in the hospitality school in which they are already enrolled. Alternatively, they may choose to attend one of the hospitality programs that offers either specific real estate courses or a concentration in this unique and exciting area.

RESOURCES

Internet Sites

Hospitality Valuation Services: www.hvsinternational.com

Ernst & Young: www.ey.com/global/content.nsf/International/Industries_-_REHC

Fairfield Resorts vacation ownership: www.fairfieldresorts.com

Real estate terms and definitions: www.realestateabc.com/glossary

Review Questions

1. List the typical hospitality-related real estate positions that are available to you.

2. What are the functions of a real estate director and the real estate representatives who work for large, multiunit hospitality corporations?

3. Discuss the importance of having real estate representatives make well-informed site selection decisions when working with hospitality companies.

4. What functions are performed by real estate appraisers? Who would typically hire an appraiser? How do most appraisers handle areas of specialization?

5. Explain the concept of "independent contractor" as applied to persons working in real estate sales. How are these people usually compensated?

6. List what is typically included in a business opportunity purchase. What is the function of the business opportunity brokerage?

7. What types of businesses may be involved in conducting a site analysis?

8. What is a vacation ownership firm? How has the vacation ownership industry been legitimized?

9. List the types of organizations that are most active in hospitality finance and are major lenders in this industry.

10. Discuss the impact that the Internet is having on the careers of people working in hospitality real estate positions.

11. Describe the type of skills and experience that would be beneficial for someone seeking a career in hospitality real estate.

Golf Management

Don Farr, Florida State University

LEARNING OBJECTIVES

- Learn about "golf the game" and "golf the business."
- Value the economic impact that golf has on the economy.
- Comprehend the key management positions in golf and their job descriptions.
- Become familiar with how to manage the golf operation.
- Gain knowledge of the different types of golf facilities.
- Discover the various career opportunities within the golf industry.

CHAPTER OUTLINE

KEY TERMS

Equity clubs
Etiquette
Featherie
Golf club head
Golf club shaft
Golf management companies

Municipal golf course
Official rules of golf
PGA professional
Royal and Ancient Golf Club of St. Andrews
USGA handicap

Golf, the Game

Little is actually known about the exact origin of golf, but most historians agree that the game was introduced to the world over 550 years ago by the Scots. Regardless of the actual origin of the game, over the past 500 plus years golf has grown into a sport that nearly 30 million Americans enjoyed last year alone, with a direct impact on our national economy of 76 billion dollars while providing an excess of 2 million jobs.[1] Golf is a game, but it is also an industry that provides meaningful employment to millions of people, generates billions of dollars toward our economy, and allows all players of different abilities to challenge themselves against what the greatest amateur of all time, Bobby Jones, called "old man par."

There are multiple reasons why some call golf "the greatest of all games" played on the most spectacular arenas nature can provide. Golf is a game where you can compete against yourself, or using a certified USGA handicap, compete equally against

Many golfers enjoy the sport well into their 60s, 70s, and sometimes 80s. © 2011 by bikerderlondon. Used under license of Shutterstock, Inc.

other players of various skill levels. Golf is played outdoors in harmony with the environment; every course is unique with different yardages, different degrees of difficulty, different topographies, and placed in different settings around the world. There are mountain courses, seaside or "links" courses, desert courses, and courses that meander through the rivers and forests of every locale. They are homes to local wildlife, endangered species and deciduous plants and foliage. A round of golf can truly be an experience that one will appreciate for a lifetime.

Most golf courses have 18 holes and vary in length from about 5,500 to 7,300 yards in length, although

there are several 9-hole and executive golf courses that are much shorter and cater to senior citizens and beginning golfers. There are usually three or four different sets of tee markers for championship players, average players, senior golfers, and women, all designed to make the game more enjoyable for the different skill levels of golfers. Some of the amenities at a typical golf facility include a practice area with a driving range and practice putting green, a pro shop where golf merchandise can be purchased or rented, a halfway house located on the course that serves food and beverages, and a dining room or grill. Many country clubs and resorts also have tennis courts, swimming pools, caddie shacks, and multiple dining options.

Golf, the Business

The business of golf is almost as old as the game itself; ever since their became a market for golf balls and golf clubs in the early 1500s, club and golf ball makers have been looking for ways to improve the game and sell their latest equipment. Today the golf industry has a direct economic impact nationally of 75.9 billion dollars and a total U.S. impact of 195 billion dollars annually.[2] It is estimated that over two million people are employed in the golf industry with total wages of over 61 billion dollars.[3]

When most people think about the golf industry, they think about Titleist, Nike, Taylor Made, Callaway, and other large manufacturers of golf equipment. In reality, all these equipment firms added together only

FIGURE   24.1   2005 U.S. Golf Economy

MULTIPLIER IMPACTS ON NAITONAL ECONOMY, 2005						
INDUSTRY	DIRECT	INDIRECT	INDUCED	TOTAL OUTPUT ($ MILLION)	TOTAL JOBS	TOTAL WAGE INCOME ($ MILLION)
Golf Facility Operations	$28,052	⟶		$81,231	913,161	$25,932
Golf Facility Capital Investment	$3,578	⟶		$4,872	38,749	$1,498
Golfer Supplies	$6,151	⟶		$7,126	71,149	$2,164
Media, Tournaments, and Associations	$1,682	⟶		$5,403	57,656	$1,871
Charities	$3,501	⟶		—	—	—
Real Estate	$14,973	⟶		$39,933	317,570	$12,276
Hospitality/Tourism	$18,001	⟶		$56,549	668,120	$17,444
TOTAL	$75,938	⟶		$195,115	2,066,404	$61,183

account for about 6.7% of the total golf industry in the United States. Of all the industry segments that directly affect our economy, the operations of the nearly 19,000 golf facilities make up the largest amount of revenues at $28 billion. As an example let's use a typical semi-private golf club in the heart of Florida. Some of the usual revenue sources include

- Green fees—the fee nonmembers of the club must pay to play golf
- Cart fees—the fee a golfer must pay for the use of a golf car
- Membership dues—monthly fees golfers must pay to be members of a club
- Initiation fees—a onetime upfront fee a golfer must pay to become a member of a club
- Guest fees—the fee a member must pay for a nonmember guest to play at the club
- Golf lessons
- Golf club rental fees
- Food and beverage revenues

Many golf facilities have additional revenue opportunities such as equity fees, locker room fees, caddie fees, tournament fees, and other miscellaneous income sources.

Another segment of the golf industry that contributes billions of dollars to our national economy is travel and tourism as it relates to golf travel and vacations. With nearly 40 million golf travelers spending an average of $452 per trip, including air travel, lodging, car rental, and food and beverage,[4] the direct economic impact of this core group is slightly above $18 billion annually. Many of these travelers choose moderately priced golf packages they find through discount Internet searches,

whereas others spend up to $400 per round of golf at top-rated resorts. Although the great majority of these travelers are men, *Golf Digest* magazine ranks resorts like Pine Needles in Southern Pines, North Carolina, The Boulders Resort and Spa in Carefree, Arizona, and Amelia Island Plantation in Amelia Island, Georgia, as facilities having found a niche catering to female golfers.[5]

Real estate is another core area that has a positive impact on the economy, $14.97 billion, in the United States in 2005. Nearly 1.7 million homes are currently built on or near a golf course, and they resell at double the speed, and on average at a 70% higher sales price, than those homes in subdivisions without golf courses. Golf course real estate is not just being purchased by avid golfers, 60% of all golf course residents don't even play golf on a regular basis.[6] Golf course construction and renovations, infrastructure improvements, clubhouse redesigns, and irrigation installations add an additional $4.87 billion to the economy.

Key Managerial Positions

Two million jobs employing over $60 billion people, $195 billion in total societal impact, larger than the newspaper and motion picture industry; all created to support the 500 million rounds of golf we play in America each year. Golf is more than a game; it is a community that helps collect $3.5 billion for national and local charities annually, it is a fraternity of athletes with a diversity of skill, and it is a flourishing industry that is expected to continue to grow substantially worldwide over the next several years.

FIGURE **24.2 Career Opportunities**

Head golf professional	Director of golf
General manager	Corporate executive
Teaching professional	Tournament director
Golf course ownership	Golf course development
Golf course architecture	Golf course superintendant
Broadcasting/journalism	Association management
Manufacturer representative	Rules official
Education	College golf coach
Tour player	Merchandiser
International	

The general manager (GM) is the senior employee at most golf facilities and is usually responsible for the entire operation. His direct reports include the head golf professional, golf course superintendant, food and beverage manager, and the accounting department. Most GM's at golf properties have a strong food and beverage background with a good understanding of finance. They have a minimum of a four-year degree, seven years in the club industry and should be active members of the Club Managers Association of America (CMAA). However, as financial accountability becomes even more important at the high-end private club level, and jobs are becoming scarcer, many PGA professionals and golf course superintendants are learning the required skills of becoming general managers. There are currently 1,222 PGA members who are serving as their club's GM.

At most golf operations it is not the general manager's responsibility to make policy; this is usually performed by the board of directors or corporate managers. It is the GM's responsibility to communicate these policies to department heads and to ensure they have the resources needed to achieve the goals of the facility. General managers must be strong leaders, problem solvers, and visionaries. They do not have to be experts in all areas of golf; they do need to have a general understanding of the industry and allow their team of experts to make decisions based on the objectives of the company.

The head golf professional or director of golf is usually the "face" of the club. He is in a very public position, always in front of the members or the guests. Golf professionals are usually very extraverted, are approachable, and posses a passion for great customer service. Depending on the size and type of the facility, the golf professional has a range of responsibilities.

Because golf is the primary revenue stream at most golf facilities, the professional must have a basic understanding of finance. He works with the general manager on setting the golf operation budget, controls labor costs for his department, manages the tee time reservations, and must work closely with the golf course superintendant on a daily basis monitoring possible course issues that may need addressing. Other responsibilities of the golf professional and his staff include merchandising, tournament management, golf instruction, monitoring the pace of play, outside golf car services, properly marking the golf course for ground under repair and hazards, rules officiating, and maintaining the appropriate number of golf rounds needed to allow the club to attain its financial goals.

There are two paths to becoming a PGA golf professional: the PGA/PGM Apprentice Program and the PGA Golf Management University Program. In both programs you must pass a PGA Playing Ability test to prove you are an accomplished player, you must pass all levels of the PGA/PGM curriculum, and you must fulfill the employment or internship requirements. In addition to the PGA requirements, if you choose to attend one of the 20 certified PGA University programs, you must also meet the academic requirements of that university. Both programs generally take a minimum of four and one-half years to complete before you earn membership to the PGA of America.

There are currently 22,472 PGA of America members and 5796 apprentices.[7] Of the 28,000 plus members, less than 1,000 are female, showing both a need and an opportunity for the membership to become more diverse.

FIGURE **24.3 Management Team**

FIGURE **24.4 Golf Shop Team**

The golf course superintendant is the behind-the-scenes department head whose success or failure greatly affects everyone affiliated with the golf course. He is responsible for supervising the golf course maintenance associates, preparing and adhering to the maintenance budget, and most important, ensuring the health and playability of the turf grass. Like most managers in the golf industry, the superintendant's job performance relies greatly on the decisions made by his superiors; unlike most, his job performance is also at the mercy of nature. Combating drought conditions, extreme heat, excessive rain, damaging wind, turf grass disease, insect infestation, and seasonal flooding are all a part of golf course superintendent's day.

The golf course superintendant must also arrange agronomic tests and soil samples, prepare reports for the management team and environmental agencies, and maintain the buildings, roadways, lakes, irrigation systems, and maintenance equipment. He must maintain a positive working relationship with governmental turf grass, chemical and fertilizer authorities, his vendors, and his colleagues, always willing to share advice to ensure a healthy eco-friendly environment.

Many golf course superintendants have a bachelor's degree in agronomy or turf grass management, have a chemical application license, have a commercial driver's license, and are certified by the Golf Course Superintendants Association of America, (GCSAA). They must also have an extensive knowledge of irrigation systems, fertilizer applications, heavy equipment, and other golf course supplies. They need to be an expert in managing soils, winter and summer grasses, and all areas related to a successful turf grass program. It is also important that the Superintendent is an avid golfer, understanding and being able to communicate course conditions and preventative maintenance steps to the management team and membership.

The fourth element of the management team is the food and beverage (F&B) manager. Whether a golf facility has a small F&B or a large F&B element, the success of the department is vital to the attraction and retention of its members and guests. The F&B manager must hire, train, and motivate his team of associates. He is responsible for compliance with all local, state, and federal liquor and food safety laws. He must provide a diverse menu that meets the needs of his customers while achieving the profit goals of the company. At many facilities he must be able to manage several different food venues, including fine dining, casual dining, weddings, banquets, bar food, halfway house, and even beverage cart foods and drink.

The F&B manager must operate and control the department. He must understand food costs

FIGURE 24.5 **Food and Beverage Team**

and other pertinent financial indicators; he should be proficient in the use of computer spreadsheets, word processors, and database management. The manager should be extraverted, willing to meet and great guests, an accomplished leader, and familiar with all areas of the business. His primary objective is to provide consistent food at all the facility's venues for all the patrons while achieving the department's financial goals.

The golf operation, like all hospitality industries, relies on their team of managers to work together to achieve the goals and objectives of the company. They must communicate with one another often because their jobs are so intertwined. The golf professional relies on the golf course superintendant for a playable golf course allowing him to sell more tee times, which means more dollars to the club. The food and beverage manager relies on these additional rounds of golf; each round produced $10.38 in food and beverage revenue for resorts and $27.62 for private clubs in 2007. In fact, each round of golf at a resort was directly responsible for $85.52 in revenues, whereas each round at a country club produced revenues of $101.15.[8] The golf course superintendent relies on these additional revenues to provide funds for special course projects, wages, and new equipment. The golf facility leaders are truly a team; when one succeeds, all team members benefit; when one falls short of expectations, they all come together to find solutions.

Golf Facilities

Private Clubs

There are two types of private country clubs, equity and nonequity. Both types of clubs provide goods and services to their members; both clubs probably have similar amenities. They have dining areas, swimming pools, tennis courts, and of course a golf course. The primary differences between the two types of clubs are ownership and governance; equity clubs are owned and governed by their members, whereas nonequity clubs are privately owned and usually managed by the owner or a management team under the supervision of the owner. Equity clubs are not-for-profit clubs, whereas nonequity clubs tend to be profit oriented. Both equity and nonequity clubs have several membership categories:

- **Full member**—All members of the family have full rights and privileges to all club amenities and services.
- **Social membership**—Membership is usually limited to dining privileges.
- **Nonresident**—Membership requirement demands that the member lives outside a specific geographic location.
- **Junior membership**—Membership places a maximum age limit on individuals within this category. Maximum allowable ages can vary between 17 and 35.

- **Legacy membership**—A legacy member is one who was willed or gifted his membership by a previous member. He is still responsible for paying monthly dues and a transfer fee.

All truly private clubs are in existence for the sole use of their members and their members' guests. With the exception of a few board-approved Monday golf outings, you must be a member or a guest of a member to play golf, dine, or enjoy any of the other services the club provides. The Honorable Company of Edinburgh Golfers is the first known club, formed in 1744 in Scotland. The first North American club, Royal Montreal, was actually formed in Canada in 1873. Today there are over 10,000 private country clubs in the United States. Augusta National GC, Pine Valley GC, and Shinnecock Hills GC are the three highest-ranked private golf courses in the country according to their 2009/2010 rankings.[9]

Resorts

Resorts are usually located in destination areas and include a variety of amenities such as golf, skiing, water sports, and spas. Resort golf is usually expensive compared to other accessible facilities, but playing during off seasons and later in the afternoon can reduce the financial burden on players. The primary target market for resort golf is travelers who will stay at their hotel, dine in their restaurants, and play golf on their courses. Most resorts also allow golfers staying at other local hotels and residences play at a premium fee. A trend that is growing due to recent economic conditions is for resorts to form memberships at their facilities. These members would pay initiation fees and monthly dues providing a revenue stream for the properties.

Semiprivate Clubs

Semiprivate clubs have both members and nonmembers play their golf course. Many clubs that were private have recently changed their bylaws and have become for-profit facilities, allowing them to attract outside golf. As a member of a semiprivate club, you are able to enjoy most of the advantages of membership while having your dues and other fees supplemented by the nonmember revenue generated from their green fees.

Daily Fee Courses

Daily fee courses can be further categorized by the amount they charge patrons for a round of golf. High-end daily fee courses may charge between $75 and $125 for green and cart fees, whereas lower end courses typically charge between $35 and $75. The condition of the golf course, the added services, and the overall design of the course is oftentimes superior at high-end daily fee courses. Most true daily fee courses rely solely on transient golf because of the lack of a membership base.

Municipal Courses

Municipal courses are operated similar to the daily fee courses, with the primary difference being they are owned by the government. University courses and city courses are examples of municipals. Although they are government owned, many municipal golf facilities are managed by a management company and not by the government themselves. Bethpage State Park, host site of the 2002 and 2009 U.S. Open Golf Championships, is one of the most famous and prestigious municipal courses in the country.

There are nearly as many different types of facilities as there are courses themselves. Private clubs can range in their initiation fees from $1,000 to $200,000 or more. You can find specials on daily fee courses for as little as $15 per round or pay $400 per round plus a caddie fee. For golfers who like the exclusivity of their own course, private clubs are perfect. For golfers who like to play different golf courses and meet new people, then daily fee or resorts should be their choice. There are also executive courses for seniors and beginning golfers, par 3 courses, and for entertainment purposes, miniature golf. Whatever the skill

The demand for golf-related housing is a driving force in golf course development. © 2011 by iStockphoto/Thinkstock.com.

TABLE 24.1 Top Golf Management Companies

COMPANY	HEADQUARTERS	MANAGED COURSES
Troon Golf	Scottsdale, AZ	197
ClubCorp	Dallas, TX	130
Billy Casper Golf	Vienna, VA	111
American Golf Corp	Santa Monica, CA	116
KemperSports	Northbrook, IL	99

level, time restraints, financial limitations, or preferences of a golfer, there is a golf course built for them.

Trends

Because of the recent decline in play from 2007 to 2010, several golf course owners had to close their doors permanently, whereas others chose to hire large management teams with the expertise and resources needed to prosper in a down economy. As the industry starts its recovery, more struggling public, resort, municipal and private clubs will forgo the traditional route of managing their own facilities and hire these experts to lead them into the next decade.

The management companies listed in Table 24.1 own or operate over 600 golf facilities collectively and look to add to their portfolios in the upcoming years.

Although the growth of the game of golf has stagnated here domestically, it continues to grow in popularity abroad, particularly in Asia. China is one of the fastest-growing markets with more than half of their 300 golf courses having been built in the past 10 years. The average initiation fee for a private club in China is $53,000, whereas the daily fee courses average $161 per green fee.[10] In 2006 South Korea, a country one-sixth the size of the United States, had 32 players on the LPGA Tour. As players from foreign countries continue to perform well in the LPGA and PGA events and the popularity of the game increases due to media exposure, more foreigners will pick up the game, purchase equipment, and join clubs; international employment opportunities will increase.

Summary

Golf is a game that has been described by some as "the greatest game on earth" and by others as a "good walk spoiled." What is not debatable is the hundreds of billions of dollars that is directly and indirectly added to our economy, the $3.5 billion raised for charities, and the two million jobs created, simply to support the wants and needs of those who enjoy the game of golf. As the golf business is expected to grow for the next several years it will be important for managers in all industries to understand the impact golf has on the lives of millions of people across the world.

RESOURCES

Internet Sites

Professional Golfers Association of America: pga.com
United States Golf Association: usga.org
Ladies Professional Golfers Association: lpga.com
PGA Tour: pgatour.com
Golf Course Superintendants Association of America: gcsaa.org
National Golf Course Owners Association: ngcoa.org
American Society of Golf Course Architects: asgca.org
National Golf Foundation: ngf.org
National Amputee Golf Association: nagagolf.org
National Alliance of Accessible Golf: accessgolf.org
Club Managers Association of America: cmaa.org
Executive Women's Golf Association: ewga.com
American Junior Golf Association: ajga.org

ENDNOTES

1. PGA of America at http://pgalinks.com
2. PGA of America at http://pgalinks.com
3. Ibid.
4. Ibid.
5. Golf Digest Magazine at http://golfdigest.com
6. Golf Inc. Magazine at http://golfincmagazine.com
7. PGA of America at http://pgalinks.com
8. Ibid.
9. Golf Digest Magazine at http://golfdigest.com
10. Golf Inc. Magazine at http://golfincmagazine.com

Review Questions

1. What are several attributes of a golf course that ultimately result in each golf course being unique?

2. What is the economic impact of the buisness of golf in the United States?

3. List the usual revenue sources of a typical golf course operation. Select three, and briefly describe aspects of each.

4. Describe the relationship between the game of golf and the travel and tourism industry.

5. What is the title of the person in charge of golf operations?

6. List 5–7 of the traditional work posiitons often found in a golf operations department.

7. Briefly describe each type of golf facility.

8. What trends are occurring related golf within the United Stastes? Outside of the U.S.A.?

Sports and Entertainment Centers

Molly J. Dahm, Lamar University

LEARNING OBJECTIVES

- To describe the historical origins of sports and entertainment services.
- To identify the advantages of downtown entertainment districts.
- To discuss the development of festival market-places and urban entertainment districts.
- To explain the strategic link between urban entertainment centers and sports/events centers.
- To discuss venue management and the services provided by key venue management companies.
- To identify key mega events and their link to sports and entertainment complexes.

CHAPTER OUTLINE

Origins of Sports and Entertainment Services
Festival Marketplaces and Entertainment Centers
Urban Entertainment Centers and Districts
Venue Management
Mega Event Services and Management
The Future and Careers

KEY TERMS

Festival marketplace
Location-based entertainment
Mega event

Tourist bubble
Urban entertainment center
Venue management

Many of you will likely choose to work in the hospitality industry because you want to be around people while they're having fun. You want to be where the excitement is. What could be more exciting than managing the Field House or the Golf Club at the world-famous Chelsea Piers in New York City, supervising concessions or novelty sales at Camden Park, home of the Baltimore Orioles, directing activities at the Verizon Center in Washington, DC, or helping to feed athletes at the 2012 London Olympics? All these opportunities are available when you venture into a career in sports and entertainment centers or venue management.

In major and second-tier cities around the world, sports and entertainment complexes offer a focal point for urban development and/or revitalization. Thus, you may find yourself working for a public entity like the New Jersey Sports and Entertainment Authority (NJSEA) at the Meadowlands in East Rutherford, New Jersey, or for a private entity like SMG (formerly known as Spectator Management Group), which manages services at locations such as the Long Beach Convention and Entertainment Center in Long Beach, California, and Reliant Park and Astrodome in Houston, Texas. And opportunities are not limited to the United States. For instance, Burswood Entertainment Complex, on the outskirts of Perth, Western Australia, features a casino, restaurants, a sporting events dome, a convention center, and a theatre.

Origins of Sports and Entertainment Services

People have long traveled to central locations to attend sporting events and enjoy accompanying entertainment. The birth of sport venues and what has come to be termed *mega event entertainment* began with the Greek Olympic Games in the fifth century BC (Markerink & Santini, 2004). Other historical examples include gladiatorial events at the Roman Colosseum, jousting tournaments in Medieval Europe, and the initiation of team football, baseball, and soccer competitions in the late nineteenth century. Beyond the sporting events themselves, visitors seek peripheral entertainment as well as lodging and dining services. Today, events such as the Summer Olympics and the World Cup are international in scope, generate millions of dollars in revenue, take place over extended periods of time, and demand extensive collaborative planning and management expertise, as well as providing the impetus for infrastructure development, and employ thousands of people.

The development of sports and entertainment complexes in the United States follows the ebb and flow of efforts to maintain a vital and vibrant downtown district in cities. In the mid-twentieth century, urban residents, responding to increased housing and transportation options in areas outside the city versus reduced property values and higher crime rates in central urban environments, fled downtown areas and settled in the suburbs. By the 1970s, the suburban population located in metropolitan statistical areas far exceeded the population in cities, creating what is

The Burswood Entertainment Complex features a casino, restaurants, sporting events dome, convention center, and a theatre. © 2011 by Alister G Jupp. Used under license of Shutterstock, Inc.

referred to as the "doughnut effect" (Bender, 2003). Eventually, many retail businesses followed their primary customers and relocated to more densely populated suburban areas.

Subsequent efforts to revive downtown areas attempted to capitalize on remaining identifiable advantages, namely unique cultural experiences in historical urban neighborhoods, ready access to centralized transportation via the preexisting hub-and-spoke model, expansive public parking spaces, creative municipal and private funding incentives, existing large sports venues such as stadiums and arenas, and the steady growth of the events and meetings market as well as the continued presence of downtown business workers (Bender, 2003; Turner & Rosentraub, 2002).

Festival Marketplaces and Entertainment Centers

By the 1980s, developer James W. Rouse (The Rouse Company) integrated many of these favorable aspects in what became known as the festival marketplace. Rouse successfully integrated downtown cultural districts and convention facilities with entertainment facilities, taking advantage of natural urban boundaries such as waterfronts and bridges to create a designed space that was safe and easily accessible to pedestrian traffic. One of Rouse's earliest efforts was Faneuil Hall in Boston, where a wealth of stores and restaurants surrounded the historical waterfront marketplace and attracted both local and nonresident visitors. These marketplaces featured unique specialty stores, a wide variety of food and entertainment options, and historical and architectural sites of interest and were readily accessible to downtown lodging accommodations as well as public transportation. Importantly, the marketplaces also attracted a broader, more affluent demographic.

Festival marketplaces remain successful in many cities throughout the United States. Faneuil Hall attracts 20 million visitors annually (Baedeker, 2010). Other well-known marketplaces include Pier 39 in San Francisco, California, Union Station in Washington, DC, and Harborplace in Baltimore, Maryland. Underground Atlanta in Atlanta, Georgia (see http://www. underground-atlanta.com/) is a five-block historic site that originally served as the supply depot for the Confederate Army during the Civil War. In 1970, Underground Atlanta opened as an entertainment

Faneuil Hall in Boston attracts 20 million visitors annually.
© 2011 by Jorge Salcedo. Used under license of Shutterstock, Inc.

district that featured dining areas, specialty shops, and bars. It closed down in 1980 as the city metro-rail system was constructed, during which time city leaders were successful in having the district registered as a National Historic Place. Renovated at a cost of $142 million through a joint venture between the city of Atlanta and private industry, the site reopened in 1989 with an expressed mission of preserving and revitalizing the center of Atlanta as the focal point of community life. Underground Atlanta offers a complete family experience, with specialty and gift shops, unique features and entertainment, special events, and fine restaurants. In addition, visitors can easily move from Underground to nearby attractions such as Centennial Olympic Park, CNN Center, the Georgia Aquarium, the World of Coca-Cola, and the Georgia Dome.

As festival marketplaces grew in popularity, so also did other forms of entertainment centers. Location-based entertainment sites (LBEs) are entertainment sites commonly anchored by a multi-screen cinema, combining entertainment, dining, and specialty retail. Beyond the movie theatre, LBEs typically feature themed restaurants, stores, museums, and sports arenas (Entertainment Centers, 1998). Factors contributing to the growth of these centers included increased leisure time and disposable income among consumers, a growing market seeking family entertainment, and aggressive financing incentives from both public and private institutions. In many instances, these entertainment centers have supplanted the arcane shopping center or mall in the minds of consumers because the centers add elements of fun and variety to the shopping experience. The Verizon Center in Washington, DC (see http://www.verizoncenter.com/) is an example of an LBE site that has made the obvious link to sports entertainment. The complex houses a 30-screen theater, theme restaurants, museums, and a Disney store. The arena hosts three national sports teams: the Washington Wizards and Mystics (men's and women's basketball) and National Hockey League's Washington Capitals.

Urban Entertainment Centers and Districts

In the 1990s, partnerships between retail and large-scale entertainment companies such as Sony, Paramount, and Disney created adult-oriented urban entertainment destinations known as UECs (Urban Entertainment Centers; Bender, 2003). The added expertise of successful theme park entertainment companies like Disney provided new and creative ways of integrating local attractions, shows, shopping, dining, lodging, and meeting/event space. UECs draw primarily on city tourist traffic but also serve local residents. One of the first successful ventures was the collaborative effort between Disney and New York City interests that resulted in the revamped family-oriented entertainment destination, Times Square. This world-famous destination currently attracts 37.7 million visitors a year (Baedeker, 2010).

It was a simple strategic step to link the urban entertainment center with other preexisting facilities and services and thereby market the multipurpose appeal of downtown districts. Hence, city and private developers worked together to integrate stadiums, arenas, convention centers, and other public facilities into a comprehensive and accessible destination location for sports and entertainment seekers. "Without exception, all cities turned to sports facilities to anchor development" (Turner & Rosentraub, 2002, p. 489). With these added venues, developers and municipal authorities could entice corporate investment interests with naming rights for stadiums and arenas as well as attract higher-income fans. Many argued the economic advantages of bringing professional sports franchises to the city (Coates & Humphreys, 2003; Lentz & Laband, 2008), although economic downsides to the ventures were duly noted (Baade & Sanderson, 1997).

Urban entertainment centers have thus expanded to become urban entertainment districts or mega-developments, extensive destinations that appeal to and serve many different customers. Judd (1999) referred to this safe, stylish, planned entertainment environment as a "tourist bubble." Various forms of public transportation provide tourists ready and affordable access to a host of entertainment options. And the relative proximity to a full range of downtown lodging accommodations makes such destinations ideal for meeting and event attendees. In many instances, urban entertainment districts offer a dense collection of services directly accessible to convention and conference centers, thereby providing the means and capacity to host thousands of tourists at one time.

Chelsea Piers Sports and Entertainment Complex in New York City is a 28-acre "waterfront sports village" located in Manhattan on the Hudson River. The complex offers a wide variety of sports venues including The Golf Club; The Sports Center Health Club and Spa; a state-of-the-art training center called the Blue Streak; the year-round ice skating Sky Rink; a bowling center; a maritime center; film, television, and photographic Silver Studios; and the Chelsea Piers Fieldhouse, which includes a gymnastics training center, a 28-foot rock climbing wall, basketball courts and batting cages, two indoor turf fields, a Kids Gym, and special sports facilities designed for young toddlers. Chelsea Piers Sports and Entertainment Complex epitomizes the success of the urban entertainment vision.

An international example of a UEC is the Burswood Entertainment Complex located on the Swan River near Perth, Western Australia. It is operated by Crown Limited, one of Australia's largest gaming and entertainment management companies. The complex includes a casino, nightclubs, bars, restaurants, two luxury hotel properties, a convention center, a theatre, and the Burswood Dome (sports/event arena). Although not directly located in a downtown area, the complex is convenient to the Burswood Train Station so that visitors have quick and easy access to downtown Perth.

Venue Management

When urban entertainment centers expanded in size, area, market, and purpose, they frequently attracted companies that specialized in providing managed services to leisure and recreation sites such as stadiums and arenas or to convention and conference centers. Traditionally in these companies, operations management was grouped in a division called Attractions or Leisure Services, largely focused on providing food and beverage services. Although there were similarities between managing services in a national park or racetrack and a stadium, there were some distinct differences. The result for many companies was a revised organizational structure, which separated off-site attractions management often associated with natural resources from meeting, event, and entertainment management. Meanwhile, ARAMARK's Sports and Entertainment Division accommodates the full range of facilities, from convention centers and stadiums to amphitheatres, racetracks, and parks and resorts.

As mega entertainment districts grew in scope, companies such as SMG, ARAMARK, and Delaware North expanded their managed service offerings to market their expertise under the guise of venue management. For these companies, there were also real economic advantages to managing a complex of venues versus individual properties. For example, there are many "dark days" in stadiums, arenas, and meeting sites. Events may take place on Thursday through Sunday with no activity the balance of the week. It is often difficult to maintain a fully qualified staff in this type of environment, not to speak of securing adequate numbers of part-time staff to appropriately serve crowds numbering in the thousands. Operational efficiencies can be more easily achieved when resources such as personnel can be utilized across multiple venues.

In the past, management services primarily included oversight of facilities and/or delivery of foods and beverages/concessions. Recent growth has provided opportunities to expand managed services to include housekeeping and maintenance, uniform and laundry, operations planning, programming and design, cash management and budgeting, security, parking, landscaping and property maintenance, and additional retail services. Property owners and investors, as well as municipal authorities, respond positively to contracting with companies like SMG to provide complete or partial managed services. SMG, Delaware North, and ARAMARK, as well as other venue management companies, have even expanded into gaming (casinos and racetracks), lodging and resort, and meeting services. In addition, venue management often takes the form of special event management. Venues are often called on to accommodate unique, one-time events, ranging from customized weddings to film openings to religious revivals to the Olympics, or even to facilitate an event in an unusual site. Ensuring quality services for such unique experiences is a challenge that these management companies welcome.

SMG (see http://www.smgworld.com/), a venue management company based out of Pennsylvania, was founded in 1977. Its very first client was the Louisiana Superdome in New Orleans. At the Superdome, SMG provided food and beverage services through what would eventually become their food services division, Savor Foods. Since that time, SMG has expanded its client list as well as its services. Separate company divisions operate in the United States, Europe, Asia, Mexico, and Latin America, and management services span convention centers, stadiums, arenas, theaters, and special-use sites such as the Aquarium of the Pacific in Long Beach, California. SMG also manages the Long Beach Convention and Entertainment Center, a waterfront multipurpose complex that houses two theatres, extensive meeting space/exhibit halls, and a sports arena. As with other UECs, it provides direct pedestrian access to downtown shopping, dining, and lodging.

Delaware North Companies (see http://www.delawarenorth.com/) is a family-run venue management company that offers a host of managed service options, include real estate management, event management, and security services. The company operates in the United States, Canada, the United Kingdom, and Australia/New Zealand. Delaware North's operating divisions provide management expertise in food services, retail, resorts and hotels, special events and catering, sports venues, parks and attractions, and gaming. In fact, the Jacobs family (founders of Delaware North, are the owners of the

National Hockey League Boston Bruins. The company provides management services at TD Garden, Sports and Entertainment Arena (see http://www.tdbanknorthgarden.com/), home to the Boston Celtics, Boston Blazers, and of course, the Boston Bruins.

It is impossible to present an overview of sports and entertainment complexes and urban entertainment districts without discussing the Xanadu Meadowlands project (see http://visitmeadowlands.com/complex/) in New Jersey. Direction of this huge development project falls to the New Jersey Sports and Exposition Authority. The massive sports, shopping, and entertainment complex comprises the New Meadowlands Stadium, which is home to both the National Football League's New York Giants and the New York Jets, the 20,000-seat arena, the IZOD Center, Meadowlands Racetrack, and the original Giants Stadium. There are further plans to add a minor league baseball stadium, a 17-screen Movie Experience, a Snow Park, live entertainment theatre, and office space. Railway lines directly access Hoboken and New York's Penn Station. The Complex is slated to host two upcoming mega events—the 2012 Superbowl and the 2018/2022 FIFA World Cup. Currently, ARAMARK provides many of the venue management services for the complex.

Mega Event Services and Management

We cannot leave the subject of sports and entertainment centers without addressing mega event services. Urban entertainment districts as well as sporting facilities—or planned development of these complexes—are often selling points for cities that bid to host one of the premiere mega sporting events. Among the most important are the Olympic Games (particularly the Summer Games), the FIFA World Cup, major league baseball's World Series, and football's Superbowl. Cities, venue management companies, and host governments work closely with international and national organizations to successfully host these events, coordinating myriad services over an extended period of time. Strategic planning for these events often starts as much as five years in advance of the event itself.

As previously noted, ARAMARK Corporation (see http://www.aramark.com/) is one of the leading venue management service companies. A particular area of expertise for ARAMARK is the provision of services during the Olympic Games. ARAMARK has been integrally involved in providing food and other services to athletes, officials, and media in 15 different Olympic Games, including plans to provide those services for the 2012 Olympics. During the Beijing Olympics in 2008, ARAMARK served three and a half million meals to over 28,000 people using approximately 7,000 employees (Mickle, 2008). ARAMARK proudly promotes its "Olympic Heritage," the ability to plan and implement services on such a scale. The company has developed mega event expertise over the 40-plus years it has been serving Olympics customers.

The recent 2010 FIFA World Cup in South Africa was considered a major tourism success by organizing authorities, who projected that overall tourism arrival would attain at least 10 million in 2010 (South Africa's Tourism Boost, 2010). Venue management services for this month-long event were provided at 10 different stadiums across the country, not to speak of the peripheral entertainment services required. Organizers of such mega events look not only at the direct impact of tourist spending but also at infrastructure improvements and additions, as well as worldwide market exposure that should have positive economic effects for years beyond the event itself.

The Future and Careers

The current revival and development of downtown entertainment districts and the continued passion that America and other countries have for all kinds of

sporting events has served to brighten the future for sports and entertainment complexes. Certainly, the herculean efforts to complete the New Meadowlands Stadium and its associated venues attest to the interests of civic authorities, venue management services, and consumers at continuing to provide a centralized, accessible, and safe environment in which customers of all types can be entertained. As previously noted, such projects take advantage of preexisting infrastructure such as transportation systems and parking, cultural attractions, and financial incentives. Revitalization and/or development efforts represent a significant long-term investment in metropolitan growth.

Career opportunities in the sports and entertainment managed services industry are numerous and varied. The more traditional routes of working in this industry involve working for one of the major venue management companies such as ARAMARK or SMG. Entry points for employment would include food services in the form of concessions or catering services, sales and marketing, lodging services, maintenance, or human resources. You might also access this industry by working for one of the civic authorities in positions such as box office sales, event booking, or facilities management. Retail management provides another avenue of career growth. And finally, you may wish to work with an organization such as the Olympic Federation or FIFA in any number of event planning or operational capacities. Whichever path you choose, you will definitely find yourself in a fun, exciting, and challenging career.

RESOURCES

Internet Sites

http://www.faneuilhallmarketplace.com/
http://www.underground-atlanta.com/
http://www.verizoncenter.com/
http://www.chelseapiers.com/
http://www.burswood.com.au/
http://www.smgworld.com/
http://www.delawarenorth.com/
http://www.tdbanknorthgarden.com/
http://visitmeadowlands.com/complex/
http://www.aramark.com/
http://www.smgworld.com/executive_profiles.aspx
http://www.london2012.com/get-involved/

References

Baade, R. A., & Sanderson, A. R. (1997). The employment effect of teams and sports facilities. In R. G. Noll & A. Zimbalist (Eds.), *Sports, jobs, and taxes: The economic impact of sports teams and stadiums* (pp. 92–118). Washington, DC: The Brookings Institution Press.

Baedeker, R. (2010). America's top 10 tourist attractions. *Forbes Traveler.com.* Retrieved from http://travel.yahoo.com/p-interests-25465855

Bender, J. S. (2003). *An examination of the use of urban entertainment centers as a catalyst for downtown revitalization.* Unpublished master's thesis. Virginia Polytechnic Institute and State University, VA.

Coates, D., & Humphreys, B. (2003). Professional sports facilities, franchises and urban economic development. *Public Finance and Management, 3*(3), 335–357.

Entertainment centers. (1998, September). Retrieved from http://www.specialtyretail.net/issues/sept98/entertainmentpg2.htm

Judd, D. (1999). Constructing the tourist bubble. In D. Judd & S. Fainstein (Eds.), *The tourist city* (pp. 35–53). New Haven, CT: Yale University Press.

Lentz, B. F., & Laband, D. N. (2008). *The impact of college athletics on employment in the restaurant and accommodation industries.* North American Association of Sports Economists (Working Paper No. 08-03). Retrieved from http://college.holycross.edu/RePEc/spe/LentzLaband_CollegeAthletics.pdf

Markerink. H. J., & Santini, A. (2004). The development of stadiums as center of large entertainment areas: The Amsterdam arena case. *SYMPHONYA Emerging Issues in Management, 2.* Retrieved from http://www.unimib.it/go/Home/Italiano/Symphonya-Emerging-Issues-in-Management/2004-Issue-2-Sport-Management-and-Global-Markets

Mickle, T. (2008, August 12). *Aramark serves record number of Olympic meals.* Retrieved from http://www.sportsbusinessdaily.com/beijinggames/entries/2008/aramark-serves-record-number-of-olympic-meals

South Africa's tourism boost. (2010, June). Retrieved from http://www.fifa.com/worldcup/news/newsid=1256029/index.html

Turner, R. S., & Rosentraub, M. S. (2002). Tourism, sports, and the centrality of cities. *Journal of Urban Affairs, 24*(5), 487–492.

Review Questions

CHAPTER 25

1. What are some examples of historical forerunners of sports and entertainment events?

2. Explain how the economic health of downtown areas affected the development of sports and entertainment centers.

3. How is a festival marketplace different from an urban entertainment district?

4. If you were presenting a proposal to a development company about the advantages of creating an urban entertainment district, what advantages would you identify?

5. Explain how sports centers became associated with urban entertainment centers. Give an example.

6. Visit a sports and entertainment complex Web site. Describe the location and the range of services offered. Identify nearby attractions and accommodations.

7. Based on this chapter, explain what type of environment and facilities are included in a "tourist bubble."

8. What are the managed services offered by a venue management company? Give an example of one company that provides these services.

9. What is an example of a mega event? What makes a mega event unique?

10. Visit the Web site for the 2012 London Olympics. Track the planning and development stages. Identify and list the venue sites. What managed services should be offered at these sites?

Attractions Management

Ronald J. Cereola, James Madison University
Reginald Foucar-Szocki, James Madison University

LEARNING OBJECTIVES

- Define an attraction.
- Explain how attractions benefit local economies.
- List the ways attractions are classified.
- Describe the characteristics for each classification of attractions.
- Classify examples of attractions according to their product offering or benefits they provide.
- Apply your knowledge of why people travel and attractions to match and select appropriate attraction products.

CHAPTER OUTLINE

What Are Attractions?
    Attractions Promote Travel to Destinations
    Attractions Help Satisfy Needs
    Attractions Are Economic Engines
How Are Attractions Classified?
    Status
    Origin
    Life Span or Time-Oriented
    Ownership and Purpose
Attractions: Product Attributes
    Topography
    Culture and Heritage Attractions
    Planned Play Environments
    Events
    Industrial Attractions
    Infrastructure
Summary

KEY TERMS

Amusement parks
Attractions
Cultural tourism
Economic growth
Events
Gaming
Grand tour
Heritage tourism
Industrial attractions
Life span
Man-made attractions

Museum
Natural attractions
Nonprofit organization
Origin
Planned play environments
Secondary attraction
Shopping
Status of attraction
Theme parks
Topography

What Are Attractions?

Attractions Promote Travel to Destinations

Go to *Google.com,* type "*attractions*" in the search box, select the *image* function, and click search. Look over the various pictures presented to you in the next few pages, and you are likely to see pictures of Disney World and other theme parks such as Six Flags, natural environments such as Bryce Canyon and San Diego ocean beaches, cultural landmarks in the form of Scottish castles, adventure experiences on the Jurassic Coast Railway, and Southern California hot-air balloon excursions. Venturing further into the Web pages, you will see pictures of assorted museums, mountains and lakes, themed mega resorts and hotels such as NYNY in Las Vegas, and even a few proverbial "biggest ball of twine" roadside stops. Consider for a moment the diversity of the items that appeared on your computer screen. What do they all have in common? They are places, activities, and experiences sought out by leisure travelers. Some are wildly popular, whereas others may be just interesting stops along their way to the final destination. They are in the vernacular of the hospitality industry "attractions." *Attractions are the places we visit and the things we do while we are traveling for leisure.*

Attractions Help Satisfy Needs

Attractions are the lifeblood of tourism. Families take vacations to theme parks, or the shores of Southern California to enjoy the ocean, the mountains of Vermont and New Hampshire for recreational skiing, and to Washington, DC, to visit the capital monuments and museums. Attractions are an integral part of the need satisfaction that fuels the desire to travel. Whether the need is belongingness (family vacation in Disney), physiological (rest and recuperating at the shore), or self-actualizing (visiting cultural and historical sites of Washington, DC), it is an attraction that the traveler will seek out to help fulfill that need. In short, attractions assist in satisfying the needs that motivate travel.

Attractions Are Economic Engines

They provide economic benefit to the region in which they are located. The money spent for the theme park admission may only be a small percentage of the leisure traveler's expenditure, but then consider all the other amounts the traveler will spend on lodging, food and beverage, souvenirs, rental cars and other forms of transportation, guided tours, and ancillary activities as well as shopping in local stores and malls. These expenditures provide economic benefits such as employment for the local residents, who in turn use their wages to generate additional economic activity. Without the attraction, these jobs might not exist. In addition to providing employment, attractions also support local governments when they generate income, sales, and excise taxes. A visitor to Maui can visit Haleakala (ha-lee-ah-ka-la), an extinct volcano that rises through the clouds, over 10,000 feet above sea level. Although the volcano is part of the National Park System, local tourism entrepreneurs have flourished around the attraction. There are bike rental stores and guided tour packages starting on the mountain just outside the park limits. (As of October 10, 2007, the National Park Service suspended bike tours within the park for 60 days while it investigated several fatal biking accidents.[1]) While guided tours are being limited by the Park Service, the more adventuresome can still purchase everything they need at one of the local shops and go it alone at their own pace. There are also guided excursions 3,000 feet down into the crater itself, either on foot or by horseback, as well as helicopter and airplane tours, balloon rides, and ATV excursions all centered on the volcano.

All these activities are available through local businesses and generate economic benefits to the providers and their employees as well as to the community. The fees and taxes they generate circulate through the local economy. Without an attraction such as Haleakala none of these tourism business opportunities would exist nor would the economic benefits that they generate.[3]

How Are Attractions Classified?

The most common methods of classification are status (importance or interest to the traveler), origin, life span, ownership, profit orientation and product attributes.[4]

Status

Attractions are often broadly characterized as either *primary* or *secondary* attractions. A primary attraction is essentially the main reason a visitor travels to the destination and spends several days. As a result, primary attractions are usually supported by extensive ancillary facilities: lodging, food and beverage, transportation, extensive retail, and other hospitality services. An excellent example of a primary

Vignette

Living in Eco Harmony

Economics and **Eco**tourism are not necessarily mutually exclusive. Attractions often provide local residents an improved quality of life through increased economic opportunities from business activities that support tourism. Often these business opportunities are criticized as occurring at the expense of the surrounding ecosystems. Companies such as Kauai Backcountry Adventures have learned to use the surrounding ecosystem as part of their business plan, while at the same time being sensitive to the impact on the land. The mission of Backcountry is to provide ecotourism activities that preserve the environment, history, and culture of Hawaii. To that end they offer zip line and tubing adventures to a broad range of individuals.

Visitors opting for a zip line adventure soar over the rainforest and traverse mountain sides while attached to a cable strung high above the forest floor. They are able to enjoy the awe and beauty of the rainforest with minimal intrusion upon the forest floor.

The less adventurous might try the tubing adventure down irrigation ditches and tunnels of a sugar plantation that were hand dug by the workers in the 1870s, all the while enjoying the majesty of Kauai's coastline, valleys, and mountains. The company restored the irrigation system covering over 17,000 acres of pristine land after sugaring ceased in late 2000.

Both the zip line and tubing adventures are accompanied by certified guides explaining the island's history, culture, flora, and fauna.[2]

attraction is Disney World in Orlando, Florida. Visitors, especially families, make the trip and stay for several days. They purchase multiday passes to the Disney theme parks and may stay in one of the many Disney-owned properties, eat at Disney food outlets, use the Disney transportation system, and shop for their needs at Disney retail outlets. Because Disney World has tremendous drawing power, significant non-Disney-owned hospitality facilities have developed around the theme park and have contributed to the growth of the Orlando area in Florida.

In contrast, a secondary attraction is of lesser importance to the traveler and might be considered simply something nice to do while on the way to or in the area of the primary attraction. Again, using the Orlando area as an example, there are many secondary attractions like Gatorland, which even advertises itself as the "best half day attraction minutes away from Sea World, Walt Disney World and Universal Studios."[5]

Origin

Attractions may be classified according to whether they are *natural* or *man-made*. Natural attractions are those that occur in nature without human intervention. They include mountains, coastlines, lakes,

islands, forests, deserts, rain forests, and other landforms and seascapes. Man-made attractions owe their very existence to the intervention of humans. Examples of pure man-made attractions are theme parks, shopping centers, sports and entertainment facilities, festivals, casinos, and museums. Often, human intervention combines with nature to create a mixed origin attraction such as the Hoover Dam constructed on the Colorado River, which created Lake Mead. The surrounding area, referred to as the Lake Mead National Recreation Area, is a premier inland water recreation area managed by National Park Service and encompasses over 1.5 million acres of land with 700 miles of shoreline. The area generates over 500 million dollars directly for the local economy and is within a day's drive of more then 23 million people from Los Angeles, California, to Phoenix, Arizona, making it one of the fastest-growing tourism destinations in the country.[6] Some natural attractions are made more accessible by man-made attractions that are constructed on or about the natural formation, such as the rain forest cable tours available in Costa Rica and other parts of the world. In these locations various forms of cable transportation and other viewing facilities have been constructed to permit visitors access to the natural attraction that would otherwise be relatively inaccessible to the visitor. The excitement of traveling along the cable itself has become one of the "things to do" for visitors to the area.[7]

Life Span or Time-Oriented

Attractions can be classified according to their life span or whether they are *relatively* permanent or temporary. Natural attractions such as lakes, mountains, and other landforms and seascapes are permanent attractions. However, permanent attractions can also be man-made such as an amusement park, a zoo, or a historical monument. Although these attractions can be demolished and moved, they are relatively permanent in comparison to temporary attractions, which are short lived or can be easily relocated. Examples of temporary attractions are concerts, conferences, trade shows, parades, award shows, certain sporting events like the Super Bowl, and festivals. Permanent attractions are sometimes referred to as *site* attractions, whereas temporary attractions are referred to as *event* attractions.

Ownership and Purpose

Approximately 85 percent of all recreational land in the United States is under *public ownership* managed by the federal and state governments for the benefit of the public at large. The National Park Service, part of the Department of the Interior, manages the majority of federal lands under the auspices of the National Park System, which includes parks, monuments, and preserves. The world's first national park—Yellowstone—was created in 1872, at which time Congress set aside more than one million acres as a public park for the benefit and enjoyment of the people.[8] This American invention marked the beginning of a worldwide movement that has subsequently spread to more than 100 countries and 1,200 national parks and conservation preserves. Today there are more than 388 units in the national park system encompassing more then 83 million acres.[9] These units are variously designated as national parks, monuments, preserves, lakeshores, seashores, wild and scenic rivers, trails, historic sites, military parks, battlefields, historical parks, recreation areas, memorials, and parkways. All represent some nationally significant aspect of the American natural or cultural heritage.

The federal and state governments own and manage a significant portion of natural attractions, but *private ownership* accounts for the overwhelming number of man-made attractions. Major corporations such as Disney, Universal, and Six Flags own and operate theme and amusement parks; MGM Mirage operates mega gaming resorts in Las Vegas, Nevada; and Simon Malls provide shopping opportunities throughout the United States.[10]

Closely aligned with ownership is the purpose for which attractions are operated, either as *nonprofit* or *profit-seeking* entities. Generally, nonprofit entities that own man-made attractions, such as museums, or natural attractions, such as nature preserves, do not have tourism as their primary goal. Rather, their interest is that of preservation of the natural environment or a historical, cultural, or religious consequence. Profit-seeking entities, on the other hand, are seeking to provide a return on investment to the private owners. There is a delicate balance for both types of owners. Profit-seeking entities cannot engage in unrestrained use and development without fear of the public backlash resulting from spoiling the environment or encouraging unrestrained commercial development of the surrounding area. In addition, it would not be in the long-term interest of the private owners to exhaust or physically depreciate the attraction through overuse, thereby shortening its useful life. For nonprofits the balance is between their preservation goals and generating sufficient revenues to maintain the attraction, while at the same time permitting public access at an acceptable level. The National Park Service faces this very same dilemma. How do they provide the widest array of access to the public while at the same time avoiding the overcrowding that would destroy the natural beauty of the environment, which is the very reason visitors come to the parks.

Attractions: Product Attributes

We can also categorize attractions based on what the attraction has to offer to the tourist as leisure activity. Common classifications include topography, culture and heritage, planned play environments, and events and entertainment.

Topography

The topography of an area is significant as an attraction and has an added benefit to the tourist in that scenery is free. Topography attractions consist of three areas of interest: *landforms, wildlife,* and *ecology.*[11]

Landforms such as beaches, mountain vistas, and deserts can all be visually appreciated free and in many instances be utilized for little or no dollar costs to the traveler. Often, because climate is closely aligned with topography, these attractions experience heavy seasonal demand. The beaches of Florida are in "high season" when the northern states are in their winter season, whereas, despite their ability to make snow, the ski slopes of the West and New England are largely dependent on a snowy winter for a successful ski season. The challenge for these seasonal attractions is to manage the heavy demand during peak season and to create additional off-season activities to create demand during slow times.[12] Each year thousands of individuals travel to California's Sequoia National Park[13] to take in the majesty of giant sequoia trees or to the California Redwood Coast[14] to view the giant redwoods.

In addition to scenic beauty, topography is closely tied to recreational activities as well as wildlife viewing and ecological activities. In recent years concern for the environment has created a heightened awareness of the effects of tourism on the natural environment.[16] Efforts to control access and the types of tourism activities centered on natural attractions have been implemented by federal and state governments in the United States as well as by their counterparts around the world.[17] At the same time this heightened awareness has created environmentally friendly or ecotourism opportunities centered on natural attractions. A prime example of this is the whale-watching excursions that permit visitors to Maui, Hawaii, to see and hear the humpback whales during the annual migrations in December and January.

Culture and Heritage Attractions

Since the early days of mankind, travel has been closely linked to culture and heritage. The preservation for future generations, of artifacts and sites, in

Landforms such as beaches, mountain vistas, and deserts can be enjoyed by tourists free of charge. © 2011 by Yuri Arcurs. Used under license of Shutterstock, Inc.

particular those associated with a peoples' origins, religion, war, and art, as well as science and myth, are commonplace among the world's cultures. Cultural attractions are very popular among travelers. In fact, most U.S. adult travelers attend a cultural activity or event while on a trip. Most often attended are performing arts events and/or museums.[18]

Museums

Visitors are attracted to museums out of both curiosity and for education. The Grand Tour, a root of modern tourism, was a long, arduous, albeit cultural journey through Paris, Venice, Florence, and Rome, and a capstone educational experience for the elite of the sixteenth century. Today a visitor can approximate the experience by visiting the plethora of museums around the world, such as The Metropolitan

Vignette

Walk the Sky

The Glass Bridge of the Grand Canyon Skywalk, located on Hualapai Indian Tribal land, extends 65 feet over the edge of the Grand Canyon's West Rim. Since its opening on March 27, 2007, more than 200,000 visitors have paid the $25.00 fee to walk across the glass floor and peer 4,000 feet into the abyss of the canyon to the Colorado River below. The glass floor is designed to support the weight of 71 fully loaded Boeing 747s and withstand 100 mph winds and an 8.0 magnitude earthquake. Visitors are given shoe covers to prevent the highly polished glass floor from being scratched.[15]

Museum of Art[19] or The Museum of Natural History[20] both in New York, wherein many great works reside. In addition to exhibits, awaiting the visitor of museum attractions are programs and events, which include lectures, performances, workshops, and films. Many have been designed for children, the tourist of tomorrow.[21]

Religious Attractions

Rivaling museums in their numbers and diversity are religious attractions primarily consisting of cathedrals and churches, temples, and mosques. There are also geographic areas that consist of entire cities and the surrounding locales of religious significance, such as the Holy Land in Jerusalem, where many of the principal religious sites for Christianity, Judaism, and Islam converge; or the city of Mecca in Saudi Arabia, where millions of Muslims from around world make an annual pilgrimage. Modern tourism has its roots in religion. During the Middle Ages individuals made pilgrimages to visit religious sites, and many of the same are still visited by tourists today. Much like travelers today, these pilgrims came from every strata of society.

Historical Attractions

Often quoted, George Santayana's statement, "Those who cannot learn from history are doomed to repeat it," is at the heart of historical attractions. They are the efforts to preserve the events of the past that demand remembrance. Primarily consisting of monuments and structures such as the Pyramids of Egypt, the Statute of Liberty, Tiananmen Square, or the Great Wall of China, they also encompass area attractions of historical significance such as battlefields. A recent survey reveals that 41 percent of travelers say they visited a designated historic site such as a building, landmark, home, or monument during their trip. Three in 10 visited a designated historic community or town.[23] All too often, war provides tourism opportunities. American Civil War sites such as Gettysburg, Pennsylvania, are extremely popular, and many Civil War attractions involve battlefield reenactments (*events*), which heighten the visitors' understanding and appreciation of the historical significance as well as increasing visitor involvement.[24]

In addition to battlefields attractions, there are numerous memorials in Washington, DC, such as the Vietnam Veterans Memorial[25] whose principal exhibit is The Wall containing the names of the 58,249 men and women who gave their lives, visited by over 3 million people in 2004, as well as the Korean War Veterans Memorial.[26] Lest you start to believe that historical attractions are just about war, numerous attractions celebrate historic ideas that changed the world and in particular America, many of which are found at the National Mall in Washington, DC. There a tourist can visit the Thomas Jefferson Memorial, the Lincoln Memorial, the Washington Monument, and the Franklin Delano Roosevelt Memorial.[27] In December 2005 the National Capital Planning Commission (NCPC) unanimously approved a preliminary design for the Martin Luther King, Jr., National Memorial to commemorate the life and work of Dr. Martin Luther King, Jr., and to honor his national and international contributions to world peace through nonviolent social change. The King Memorial site is a four-acre plot on the northeast corner of the Tidal Basin and creates a visual "line of leadership" from the Lincoln Memorial, where Martin Luther King, Jr., gave his famous "I Have a Dream" speech, to the Jefferson Memorial.[28] Like museums many of these

Vignette

A Virtual Pilgrimage

Take a virtual tour of Vatican City, a tiny sovereign state within the city of Rome. It is the seat of the Roman Catholic Church, referred to as the Holy See. Every year it is visited by millions of tourists both Christian and non-Christian alike, not only because of its religious significance, but also because of the cultural aspects of its architecture as well as the great works of renowned masters such as Michelangelo, Botticelli, and Bernini. While there you can visit St. Peter's Basilica and the Sistine Chapel, as well as the Vatican Museum.[22]

monuments also include programming and special events to enhance the experience of the visitor.

Planned Play Environments

Planned play environments provide recreation and entertainment and are a significant sector of the tourism market. The ancient Greeks and Romans traveled for both theater and sport.

Sporting Facilities

Sports, recreation, and travel go together. The array of sporting and recreational attractions available to the traveler is almost endless. Fishing, hunting, cycling, mountain climbing, hang gliding, horseback riding, boating, surfing, snorkeling, and scuba diving are but a few, and for each there is a sporting attraction where one can engage in their desired recreational activity to their heart's content. Would you like to go fishing? Then try steelhead fishing in Northern British Columbia, Canada. Need a bit more excitement? Try your hand (wings) at Lookout Mountain Flight Park in Georgia,[29] where you can purchase a complete hang gliding instruction package that will have "most

students flying the mountains in less than one week." The point is that no matter what your interest, there is either a natural or man-made attraction drawing you to a destination where you can recreate.

Among the most popular sporting and recreational activities are skiing and golf. In 2003, approximately 10 million Americans spent 58 million days on the slopes of more then 500 ski resorts across the United States. About 10 percent of the United States population are snow sport enthusiasts, making the ski industry a multibillion-dollar business. Twenty-five percent of all ski excursions are multiday visits more then 500 miles from home. In the United States, the ski resorts of the Rocky Mountain West are the prime ski attractions, accounting for approximately 30 percent of all lift tickets sold in the United States.[30]

If ski and snow sports are a bit too adventuresome, consider golf. There are over 25 million golfers in the United States. Reportedly, a golf facility is the only significant sports activity that will influence a meeting planner's choice of destination.[32] In a recent year, one in eight U.S. travelers played golf while on a trip of 100 miles or more away from home.

Vignette

Rocky Mountain High

SKI magazine ranked the Vail-owned ski resorts: Vail (#2), Keystone (#11), and Heavenly (#17) among the top 20 ski resorts. The resorts and resort hotels derive revenue through a comprehensive offering of amenities, including lift ticket sales, ski and snowboard lesson packages, resort accommodations, retail and equipment rental outlets, dining venues, private club operations, and other recreational activities, such as golf, tennis, horseback riding, fishing tours, float trips, and on-mountain activities centers.[31]

Vignette

Golf's Home

Scotland is known worldwide as "the home of golf." Dutch sailors are thought to have introduced to Scotland "kolf" a game originally played by them with a stick and ball on the frozen canals in winter. It was transformed on the public links land becoming the game we know today.[34] Visitors have been coming to Scotland for golf holidays for over 100 years to play world-famous championship golf courses such as The Old Course St. Andrews, Royal Troon, Carnoustie, Muirfield, Turnberry, and Gleneagles.[35]

The ski industry is a multibillion-dollar business. © 2011 by Mikael Damkier. Used under license of Shutterstock, Inc.

Sixteen percent of travelers who played golf said that golf was the most important reason for taking the trip. Golf is a time to be among friends and a time to compete, to relax, and to do business, as well as to just enjoy the beauty of the natural surroundings.[33]

Theme and Amusement Parks

Theme and amusement parks are likely the most often recognizable attractions to the general public. Theme parks offer escape and replicate both real, as well as "unreal," places that may or may not exist beyond the gates. Amusement parks on the other hand have rides, games, and exhibitions. Today the distinction has been blurred, as both tend to contain elements of each in their offering.

According to the Travel Industry Association of America, approximately 1 in 10 (9%) trips includes a visit to a theme or amusement park, equating to over 92 million person-trips taken in the United States in 2002. Households visiting a "theme park" spend an average of $845 per trip, excluding transportation to their destination. On average, overnight theme park trips last 5.3 nights. A large share (55%) of household trips involving a visit to a theme park includes children under age 18.[36] As with many businesses of the twentyfirst century, theme parks and their product offerings have been driven by technology. Today's visitor demands an immersive, realistic, and intense experience. Universal's "Back to the Future: The Ride" in Orlando, Florida, in 1991 was one of the first to blend movie themes, IMAX technology, and computer-based motion simulation technology to meet that immersive, intense, and realistic requirement.[37] Since then, theme park and amusement attractions have become increasingly sophisticated. The Amazing Adventures of Spider-Man attraction at Universal incorporates 3-D technology and pyrotechnics into the experience.[38] Of course, not to be forgotten is the roller coaster, virtually defining the "thrill ride," having been around since the early 1900s.

Of course not every visitor to a theme park is looking for the intense experience of a thrill ride. Theme parks must continue to be family friendly by offering a wide spectrum of attractions, suitable for all ages and tastes. Universal's Seuss Landing[40] is a whimsical attraction that appeals to young and old alike and is suitable for the less adventurous. In addition to diverse product offerings, modern theme and amusement parks need to be clean, visually appealing, and family friendly.

Vignette

The Tallest Fastest Roller Coaster on Earth

The 456-ft Kingda Ka ride at Six Flags Great Adventure Park, a 1-hour drive from Philadelphia, will reach 128 mph on its 50.6-second journey. The 18 riders on Kingda Ka's four cars will feel weightless at some points as they are propelled to 128 mph in just 3.5 seconds before being shot vertically to 456 ft. After reaching the top, they will plunge straight back down while turning in a 270-degree spiral before climbing a 129 ft-high hill and returning to the starting point. A chest harness with two locking devices will be used to secure passengers.[39] If fast isn't enough, you can see the tallest, longest, and biggest drops list at http://www.coastergrotto.com/fastest-roller-coasters.jsp.

Gaming

The modern Las Vegas-style casino resort has created a hybrid between gaming and entertainment. Moving along the Las Vegas Strip, one is presented with an Egyptian Pyramid, a Medieval Castle, New York City and the Statute of Liberty, the Eiffel Tower, ancient Rome, and Venice, as well as an Arabian Oasis. All of which might be classified as an adult theme park, given the numerous adult-oriented attractions contained therein, of which gaming only happens to be one activity.

Shopping

Shopping is one of the most popular trip activities for U.S. adult travelers.[41] This should be no surprise for anyone who has visited Disney World in Orlando, Florida. As you stroll along Main Street in the Magic Kingdom and the other streets of the park, you are flanked on both sides by retail opportunities. It may be that part of the genius of Walt Disney was his disguising a retail mall within a theme park. Approximately 91 million people, or 63 percent of adult travelers in 2000, included shopping as an activity on a trip.[42] In a reverse of the Disney strategy, the West Edmonton Mall in Alberta, Canada, contains the Galaxyland Amusement park (the world's largest indoor theme park), the World Waterpark (the world's largest indoor water park), the Ice Palace, (a national Hockey League size ice arena), an exact replica of the Santa Maria (which is available for weddings and special functions), an 18 hole, par 46 miniature golf course, and the 354-room Fantasyland Hotel.[43] The West Edmonton Shopping Mall is listed in the Guinness Book of World Records as the "largest shopping center in the world." The Mall's Web page refers to the center as an "entertainment and shopping center, Alberta's *number one* tourist *attraction*."[44]

Lest you think that the West Edmonton Mall is an anomaly, consider the Mall of America, located in Minnesota, which, in addition to 520 stores, contains The Park at MOA™, which has 30 rides, including the Timberlane Roller coaster, the Underwater Adventures® Aquarium, LEGO® Imagination Center, Dinosaur Walk Museum, A.C.E.S. Flight Simulation, and the NASCAR Silicon Motor Speedway. On the MOA Web site you can plan your entire visit including air, hotel, and auto packages. The MOA even hosts meeting facilities at its Executive Meeting and Events Center.[45]

Events

Events are temporary attractions. Relative to permanent site attractions, they are generally easier and less expensive to develop, although that may not always be the case in every instance, such as with the Olympics and other large-scale events, including the Super Bowl. Events include such activities as fairs and festivals, live entertainment offerings as in the performing arts, sports exhibitions, parades, pageants, and other celebratory gatherings such as New Year's Eve, "First Night" celebrations. In many instances events give birth to site attractions. The sporting facilities specially constructed for the Olympics live on as site attractions for future sport exhibitions.

Sporting events, both professional and intercollegiate, are significant attractions for travelers. Over 75 million U.S. adults attended an organized sports event as either a spectator or as a participant while on a trip of 50 miles or more, one-way, in the past 5 years.[46] One of the fastest-growing sporting events is NASCAR stock car racing[47] NASCAR races are broadcast in over 150 countries. With 75 million fans, it holds 17 of the top 20 attended sporting events in the United States.[48]

The performing arts have always been events that attract travelers. They include theater, dance, and music of all forms. Some destinations such as Branson, Missouri, and Monterey, California, are well associated with music festivals that serve as primary tourist attractions for the area. New York City's Broadway theater district is just one of the performing arts attractions the city offers to visitors. A legendary musical performance event was the 1969 Woodstock Festival and Concert, and though planned for 50,000 people it is believed to have been attended by over 500,000 individuals.[49]

The modern-day epitome of an "event" is the Super Bowl which occurs annually at the end of January each year. The first Super Bowl, was between the Green Bay Packers and the Kansas City Chiefs. Tickets cost only $12, and the game had less than 50 percent attendance. Today, ticket costs are measured in the thousands of dollars and are difficult to come by, as the game is sold out. On average, 80 to 90 million Americans are tuned in to the Super Bowl at any given moment. Cities compete to host the game in a selection bidding process similar to ones used by the Olympics and soccer's World Cup. Entertainment has become a major component of the event. A number of popular singers and musicians have performed during the pregame ceremonies, the halftime show, or even just singing the national anthem of the United States. Among the notables have been Stevie Wonder, Paul McCartney, Aretha Franklin, The Rolling Stones, and of course the infamous "wardrobe malfunction" by Janet Jackson and Justin Timberlake in 2005.[50]

Industrial Attractions

Industrial attractions consist of operating concerns, manufacturing and agricultural, whose processes and products are of interest to visitors. For example, many manufacturing concerns provide tours of their facilities. Ethel M in Las Vegas conducts free interactive tours where the visitor can watch them make chocolate confections. You can tour the kitchen, walk through the enrobing and molding rooms, then, finally, try a free sample. Of course your tour ends in their retail outlet.[51] The Boeing Everett factory tours are conducted to showcase The Boeing Company and the Everett product line, the 747, 767, and 777 aircraft. Visitors can see airplanes in various stages of flight test and manufacture. The facility also contains conference space for 250 people, special event space for groups of up to 700 people, as well as a 240-seat theater and a 125-seat restaurant and retail space. There is also an aviation education program for children K–12th grade.[52] Virtually every state has one or more factory tours that would qualify as industrial attractions. Some charge a fee, but most are free. You can get a comprehensive listing, by state, of available factory tours on the Web at Factory Tours USA.[53]

Wine tourism is experiencing steady growth. © 2011 by Elena Elisseeva. Used under license of Shutterstock, Inc.

Wine tourism is defined as visitation to vineyards, wineries, wine festivals, and wine shows for which grape wine tasting and/or the experiencing the attributes of a grape region are the prime motivating factors for visitors.[54] Wine tourism is experiencing steady growth edged along by the growing public interest in wines. The 2004 movie *Sideways* spurred the creation of wine tours mirroring the journey of the film's two main characters through Santa Barbara, California, wine country.[55] (Note how the movie is a convergence between culture and tourism.) Napa and Sonoma in California, both major wine-producing areas in the United States, have flourishing wine tourism industries centering around vineyards and wine tasting attractions. The Beringer Vineyard is just one of many vineyards that provide tours and tasting to visitors.[56]

Infrastructure

Although the infrastructure of a destination would not be considered an attraction, any discussion of attractions would be incomplete without some reference to infrastructure. For attractions to be viable tourism components, they must be supported by roads, airports, and other transportation facilities; municipal services such as water, police, and fire protection; and medical, power, and communication resources. In addition, there must also be hospitality services to serve the travelers' needs while away from home. Hospitality services consist of lodging, food, and beverage services. Integral among all the infrastructure components, and in particular with hospitality services, are people available to work in the various supporting functions. For an attraction to be successful, the local employment base must be trained in the technical of skills of each area of service. Yet technical skills are not enough because the hospitality industry is a people industry. The workforce as well as the community at large must also have a "hospitable" mind-set; that is, they must truly care about delivering a quality experience and being warm and friendly toward visitors. They must understand that their self-interest, and that of the visitor, is inextricably intertwined in a unique partnership that creates both a high-quality experience for the visitor, while at the same time providing a high standard of living for them.

Summary

For attractions to be viable tourism components, they must be supported by the area's *infrastructure*: roads, airports, and other transportation facilities;

municipal services such as water, police, and fire protection; medical, power, and communication; resources as well as *hospitality* services, lodging, food, and beverage facilities. In addition, the people of the area must have hospitality service skills and be open and amenable to the tourism industry and genuinely friendly to the visitor.

RESOURCES

Internet Sites

American Gaming Association: http://www.americangaming.org

American Museum of Natural History: http://www.amnh.org

Beringer: http://www.beringer.com

Civil War Traveler: http://www.civilwar-va.com/

Disney Theme Parks: http://disney.go.com/home/today/index.html

Google: http://www.google.com

Factory Tours USA: http://factorytoursusa.com

Gatorland: http://www.gatorland.com

Mall of America: http://www.mallofamerica.com

Martin Luther King National Memorial: http://www.mlkmemorial.org/

National Park Service: http://www.nps.gov

Maui Mountain Cruisers: http://www.mauimountaincruisers.com/

NASCAR: http://www.nascar.com

National Football League: http://nfl.com/

Olympic Movement: http://www.olympic.org/

Pacific Whale Foundation: http://www.pacificwhale.org

Travel Industry Association of America: http://www.tia.org

The Holy See: http://www.vatican.va/

Universal Theme Parks: http://www.universalorlando.com/

ENDNOTES

1. Haleakala bike tours suspended at http://news.yahoo.com/s/ap_travel/20071008/ap_tr_ge/travel_brief_haleakala
2. Kauai Backcountry Adventures. (n.d.) at http://www.kauaibackcountry.com/index.html
3. Maui Mountain Cruisers at http://www.mauimountaincruisers.com 3a. National Park Service. NPS Haleakala at http://www.nps.gov/hale
4. Mill, R. C., and Morrison, A. M. (2002). *The Tourism System.* Dubuque, IA: Kendall Hunt.
5. Welcome to Gatorland at http://www.gatorland.com
6. National Park Service. Lake Mead National Recreation Area Strategic Plan 2001–2005 at http://www.nps.gov/applications/parks/lame/ppdocuments/ACFB12.doc
7. Hacienda Baru National Wildlife Refuge at http://www.haciendabaru.com/tours.htm
8. National Park Service. Yellowstone at http://www.ns.gov/yell
9. National Park Service. The National Park System Acreage at http://www.nps.gov/legacy/acreage.html
10. MGM-Mirage at http://www.mgmmirage.com
11. Goeldner, C. R., Ritchie, J. R., and McIntosh, R. W. (2000). *Tourism Principles, Practices, and Philosophies.* New York: John Wiley and Sons.
12. Middleton, V. T., and Clarke, J. (2001). *Marketing in Travel and Tourism.* Oxford: Butterworth Heinemann.
13. National Park Service. Sequoia and Kings Canyon at http://www.nps.gov/seki
14. California's Redwood Coast at http://www.redwoods.info
15. Walk the Sky: The glass bridge at Grand Canyon West at http://www.grandcanyonskywalk.com
16. Weaver, D. (2001). Criteria and Context. In: *Ecotourism.* Milton, Australia: John Wiley and Sons.

17. Weaver, D., and Lawton, L. (2002). *Tourism Management.* Milton, Australia: John Wiley and Sons.
18. Travel Industry Association of America. Cultural Events/Festivals at http://www.tia.org/pressmedia/domestic_a_to_z.html#c
19. The Metropolitan Museum of Art at http://www.metmuseum.org/home.asp
20. The American Museum of Natural History at http://www.amnh.org
21. The Metropolitan Museum of Art at http://www.metmuseum.org/home.asp
22. The Holy See at http://www.vatican.va
23. Travel Industry Association of America. Shopping at http://www.tia.org/pressmedia/domestic_a_to_z.html#s
24. You can explore the Civil War historic monuments and battlefield attractions of Virginia, North Carolina, South Carolina, Pennsylvania, West Virginia, and Washington, DC, at http://www.CivilWarTraveler.com
25. National Park Service. Vietnam Veterans Memorial at http:///www.nps.gov/vive
26. National Park Service. Korean War Veterans Memorial at http://www.nps.gov/kwvm
27. National Park Service. National Mall at http://www.nps.gov/nama
28. Build the Dream at http://www.mlkmemorial.org/site/c.hkIUL9MVJxE/b.1190591/k.B083/About_the_Memorial.htm
29. Lookout Mountain Flight Park at http://www.hanglide.com
30. Aron, A. A. (2004). Marketing the Thrill of Skiing, the Serenity of the Mountains, the Luxury of Travel. In: Dickinson, B., and Vladimir, A. *The Complete 21st Century Travel and Hospitality Marketing Handbook.* Upper Saddle River, NJ: Pearson Prentice Hall, 191–200.
31. Vail Resorts at http://www.vailresorts.com/Corp/index.aspx and http://www.vailresorts.com/Corp/awards-and-accolades.aspx
32. Cook, R., Yale, L., and Marqua, J. J. (2002). *Tourism: The Business of Travel.* Upper Saddle River, NJ: Pearson Prentice Hall.
33. Travel Industry Association of America. Golf and Tennis at http://www.tia.org/pressmedia/domestic_a_to_z.html#g
34. United States Golf Association. What is the origin of the word golf at http://www.usga.com/questions/faqs/usga_history.html
35. Scotland, the home of golf at http://golf.visitscotland.com
36. Travel Industry Association of America. Theme/Amusement Park Travel at http://www.tia.org/pressmedia/domestic_a_to_z.html#t
37. Lounsberry, F. (2004). The Theme Park Perspective. In: Dickinson, B., and Vladimir, A. The Complete 21st Century Travel and Hospitality Marketing Handbook. Upper Saddle River, NJ: Pearson Prentice Hall, 191–200.
38. Universal Studios. The Amazing Adventures of Spiderman at http://www.univacations.com/themeparks/IOAspiderman.asp
39. Six Flags Theme Parks, Inc. Tallest Fastest Roller Coaster on Earth at http://www.sixfl ags.com/greatAdventure/rides/Kingdaka.aspx
40. Universal Studios. Suess Landing at http://www.univacations.com/themeparks/IOAsuesslanding.asp
41. Cook, R. A., Yale, L., and Marqua, J. J. (2002). Tourism: The Business of Travel. Upper Saddle River, NJ: Pearson Prentice Hall.
42. Travel Industry Association of America. Shopping at http://www.tia.org/pressmedia/domestic_a_to_z.html#s
43. West Edmonton Mall at http://www.westedmall.com/about/wemtrivia.asp
44. West Edmonton Mall. Welcome to West Edmonton Mall's Web site at http://www.westedmall.com/about/default.asp
45. Mall of America at http://www.mallofamerica.com/home.aspx
46. Travel Industry Association of America. Profile of Travelers Who Attended Sports Events at http://www.tia.org/Pubs/pubs.asp?PublicationID=80
47. NASCAR at http://www.nascar.com
48. About NASCAR at http://www.nascar.com/guides/about/nascar
49. Woodstock Festival at http://en.wikipedia.org/wiki/Woodstock_festival
50. Super Bowl at http://en.wikipedia.org/wiki/Super_bowl
51. Ethel M Chocolates. Factory Tour at http://www.ethelm.com/jump.jsp?itemID=117&itemType=CATEGORY
52. Boeing. About Us at http://www.boeing.com/companyoffi ces/aboutus/tours/index.html. You can find out more on Boeing's factory tours at http://gown.about.com/od/attractionsWA/a/futureoffl ight.htm

53. Factory tours USA at http://factorytourusa.com/index.asp
54. Hall, C. M., Johnson, G., Cambourne, B., Macionis, N., Mitchell, R., and Sharples, L. (2002). Wine Tourism: An Introduction. In: Hall, C. M., Sharples, L., Cambourne, B., and Macionis, N. *Wine Tourism Around the World.* Oxford: Butterworth Heine-mann, 1–22.
55. Chiff.com. Sideways: The Virtual Wine Tour at http://www.chiff.com/a/sideways-wine-tour.htm
56. Beringer. Winery Tours at http://www.beringer.com/beringer/page/tours2.jsp

Name _____   Date _____

Review Questions

CHAPTER **26**

1. Define an attraction.

2. Explain how attractions benefit the community in which they are located. Provide an example.

3. For each of the following methods of classifying attractions, indicate the characteristics of each classification and provide an example for each type.

   a. Status

   b. Origin

   c. Life span

   d. Ownership

4. What are the methods for classifying attractions by product attributes? Provide an example for each.

5. What is the relationship between an attraction, infrastructure, and hospitality services in the surrounding area?

6. Revisit questions #3 and #4 and provide examples not found in the chapter for each.

7. Using *Google.com,* search the Internet for an attraction (as per the chapter introduction) and select one of the search results. Classify your choice using as many of the classification techniques described in the chapter as possible. Support your answer with a brief explanation for each.

Travel Management Companies and Tour Operators

Patrick T. Tierney, San Francisco State University

LEARNING OBJECTIVES

- To introduce services provided by travel management companies and tour operators.
- To know differences in traditional, contemporary, and electronic travel and tour agencies.
- To learn about consumer trends related to travel bookings and tours.
- To gain insights into management issues and techniques.
- To learn types of jobs in travel management companies and tour operators.

CHAPTER OUTLINE

KEY TERMS

Airlines reporting corporation
Consolidators
Electronic travel agencies
Foreign independent tour (FIT)
Global destination systems
Incentive travel houses
Outside sales agents
Preferred providers

Receptive operator
Sales commission
Ticketing fee
Tour escort
Tour operators
Travel agent
Travel management company

E xpanding demand from the domestic and international tourist and the travel industry complexity have led to an increasing desire by many travelers for highly specific travel information and a unique travel experience, help in making their travel plans, and convenient packages of travel services. Out of these needs have evolved *travel management companies,* including *electronic travel agencies,* and *tour operators.* Travel management company (TMC) is a more contemporary and accurate term for the new travel agency because it reflects less of a ticketing role and more consulting and management functions that successful agencies now provide.

According to a leading travel industry research group, Yesawich, Pepperdine, Brown, & Russell,[1] travel management companies are shifting into sellers of "complex" and "high-risk" travel products and services, such as cruises, all-inclusive vacations, multistop tours, and group packages and away from selling airline tickets. *Travel agents* within a travel management company act to match the travel desires of leisure and business travelers with the most appropriate suppliers of tourist services. Agencies do not normally own the means of production, that is the lodging facilities, restaurants, or attractions that will be used by travelers, but act as agents for the suppliers. So what do travel management companies provide? They provide information to plan an optimal trip, arrange individualized coordinated itineraries, and secure tickets for transportation, lodging, receptive services, resorts and cruise lines, and recreation attractions. TMCs still play a key role in the travel industry representing about 70 percent of the U.S. travel market sales.[2]

Electronic travel agencies, such as Travelocity, have developed from the Internet revolution and communicate entirely via Web sites and e-mail. They do not have physical locations where clients can go, but they employ extensive databases, and online booking technology and are open 7 days a week and 24 hours per day. They have taken away a significant amount of travel industry sales, especially domestic airline ticketing, and are projected to reach 40 percent of the U.S. travel market by 2007, according to PhoCusWright, a leading Internet research firm.[3]

Tour operators organize complete travel programs for groups or individuals to every continent, by all kinds of transportation modes. Perish the thought of tour operators only offering sedate sightseeing to groups of senior citizens in buses; today there are a vast array of tour itineraries and formats that appeal to youthful and mature audiences alike. Tour operators are different from travel agents and individual suppliers in that they plan, arrange, and market preestablished *packages* at a *set price* that include, to varying degrees, transportation, lodging, educational opportunities, recreation, meals, and entertainment. Many, but not all, tour companies operate substantial portions of the tour package. They make their profit from operations, markup, and/or buying other accommodations, meals, and necessary services at discount rates. They can offer competitive rates through volume buying power. The importance of the tour industry is underscored by the fact that residents of the United States and Canada spent a total of approximately $166 billion on packaged tours worldwide.[4]

Travel Management Company Operations

In 1867 Thomas Cook introduced the first hotel coupon and started the travel agency business. The modern travel agency era really began with the advent of the airline industry in the 1960s. Since that time the number, roles, and types of travel agencies have mushroomed. Some travel agencies specialize in one type of travel service, while others, as exemplified by the country's largest travel agency conglomerate, American Express, are active in multiple markets. Over 85 percent of travel agencies today are considered small independently owned businesses. Most (57%) TMCs are single-location businesses, but over half (73%) are affiliated with or buy the services of a consortium or association. The average independent TMC receives 68 percent of their revenue from leisure sales, 25 percent from business, and 7 percent from combination business and leisure buyers.[5]

Types of Travel Management Companies

Corporate Agencies

Those agencies who specialize in serving business clients, often with little or no walk-in clientele. They cater to corporations on the telephone or through e-mail, often working under contracts that provide for exclusivity but also require the return of a portion of the normal travel agent commission, or on a fee-based arrangement. They rely heavily on revenue from airline tickets, hotel rooms, and rental cars.

Leisure Agencies

Tourists going on vacation are the primary clients of this agency. Clients have traditionally gone to the agency office to discuss options and to look at brochures and videos. This business relies heavily on cruise sales, resort packages, airline tickets, rental cars, tours, and hotel room sales.

Wholesalers

These organizations sell primarily to travel agents and not to the general public. They organize and promote specific types of travel services, but do not operate the tours or facilities. Wholesalers contract with suppliers for blocks of tickets or rooms in anticipation of future sales.

Specialized Leisure Agencies

A growing trend in the travel agency business are shops that specialize in one category of leisure product, such as cruise or dive agencies, or in one region of the world. By limiting what they sell these agents can become experts on unique products, services, and destinations.

Incentive Travel Houses

These agencies develop customized programs for corporations who offer incentives for high employee productivity by providing deluxe travel rewards. They set up and administer reward contests, inform eligible staff, and contract with suppliers. Incentive agencies earn their profits from supplier commissions and management fees.

Consolidators

These are businesses that purchase large blocks of airline seats or cruise berths at a substantial discount and resell them to travel agents or the general public for a lower than normal fare. They may also have contracts with certain airlines for larger commissions on certain routes. Consolidators, also known as "Bucket Shops," advertise to the public in the travel sections of metropolitan newspapers, while others deal exclusively with travel agents.

Electronic Travel Agencies

As a result of the Internet revolution and communication advances, a growing number of companies sell travel products entirely via Web sites. There are no human travel agents to talk with, and they do not have physical locations where clients can go, but they employ extensive databases and online booking technology. Some electronic travel agencies are independently owed, like Travelocity,[6] while others are owned and/or controlled by the airlines, such as Orbitz.[7] Initially these businesses only offered airline tickets, but now they offer a wide range of travel services and have moved aggressively into booking hotel rooms and rental cars.

How Travel Management Companies Get Paid

Because TMCs do not own the facilities or equipment used to operate destination services, they are paid only when they make a sale. Payment is in the form of a commission, based on a percentage of the sale price, or increasingly payment is by an additional ticketing charge. The cost of the agent commission was built into the sales price, so in the past it did not cost the consumer more to use the travel agent than if they went direct to the supplier. Commissions historically

have been about 10 percent for airline tickets and other services, but on February 9, 1995, Delta Airlines announced it would pay travel agents no more than $25 on any one-way domestic ticket. Since then all major U.S. airlines have discontinued paying commissions on domestic flights altogether. The main exception to this no-commission policy is where the airlines and large travel agencies have a preferred-provider contract that allows for a small commission.

In contrast to the airlines, other segments of the travel industry, such as cruise lines announced at the same time it would increase its travel agent commission from 10 to 12 percent. The end result has been that more travel agencies are seeking other sources of revenue besides the sales of airline tickets, such as commissions from cruise lines, tours, resorts, and international air carriers. In fact, many travel suppliers offer agents *override commissions* of an additional 2 to 5 percent to encourage group sales or introduce new travel products or services. A large number of agencies have diversified and are starting to develop and market their own tour packages; others, like Corniche Travel, have also started an event planning company.[8]

Still other experienced agents charge *hourly fees* for the time they spend developing complex customized vacation packages. A *ticketing fee* of from $15 to $40 in addition to airline ticket price is being charged customers by an increasing number of agencies. Even electronic travel agencies are charging a ticketing fee. For example, Expedia.com has a $5 ticketing fee, but they show it in the ticket price, rather than as a separate charge. Another way to increase profits has been by reducing their operational costs through increased automation. TMCs offer their own online booking, and many use "robotics" software programs that handle automated ticketing, check for compliance with corporate travel policies, and e-mail a complete itinerary. Last, more travel agents are quoting lower fares to consumers than the public can find on the Internet by becoming or using consolidators.

Certainly one of most desired benefits of being a travel agent is discount travel to destinations worldwide. Suppliers wanting to promote new travel services are often willing to provide familiarization trips at little or no cost to agents. Airlines, cruise lines, and resorts provide very low cost tickets or ticket class upgrades. These benefits tend to make up for the rather low wages that travel agents receive, which average about $45,000 per year for an agent with three years of experience. Further, to increase profitability three-quarters of TMCs have joined consortiums, groups of agencies that combine strength to negotiate lower rates for clients and higher commissions for their agencies. A member agency is often required to use a limited number of *preferred providers* who have contracts with the consortium. With such contracts the agency must offer a fare quote from their preferred supplier first, but can sell to any supplier the consumer wishes.

Automation and Certification

Precise accurate information on schedules, availability, and rates is critical for a travel consultant to know, but the scope and amount of information on the global travel industry is overwhelming. Therefore, computerized databases are a basic tool of the travel agent. *Global Destination Systems* (GDS), such as Apollo, Sabre, World Span, and Amadeus, list over 15 million fares, a quarter of which are updated daily. These systems were started by airlines and at one time carried just airline schedules and inventory, but today they have become full-scale travel information systems that also contain lodging, tours, and attraction information. Effective data search and ticketing with a GDS are critical skills for agents.

To be able to issue domestic tickets, an agency must be approved by the *Airlines Reporting Corporation* (ARC). This organization is an association of U.S. airlines who facilitate funds transfer and ensure that travel agencies have experienced management. For sale of international airline tickets, a travel agency may also be approved by the *International Airlines Travel Agent Network* (IATAN), who has similar responsibilities to the ARC. These licensing agreements limit companies who can sell travel to legitimate businesses and help protect the consumer from fraud. Individual travel agents must show proper identification to receive travel discounts and promotions. The most accepted form of credential is a photo identification card issued by IATAN. Some travel agencies, but not all, require that their senior agents be a *Certified Travel Counselor* (CTC). The later credential, issued by the Institute of Certified Travel Agents, is awarded to persons who pass rigorous examinations and have five years full-time experience in a travel agency.

Although the full-time in-office travel agent will continue to be the backbone of any TMC, there are a growing number of *Outside Sales Agents* (OSA) who are affiliated with the company, but are independent contractors, not employees. The OSAs work at their home and provide their own telephone, and pay employment taxes, but share commissions with their affiliated agency.

Information Revolution and Travel Management Companies

Travel agencies no longer have exclusive access to myriad schedules, fares, and destination information that are found in a GDS. One of the most popular types of sites on the World Wide Web provide travel ticketing. The electronic travel agency Travelocity, for example, allows booking reservations on most domestic and international flights for a $5 booking fee. It also has content on destinations, an area where viewers can ask questions about travel providers, and a shopping "mall" with specialized travel merchandise for sale. Suppliers have also embraced the Internet as a way to lower their travel sales distribution costs. Hilton Hotels, for instance, was one of the first lodging chains to place all its properties worldwide on the Internet. Travelers themselves, especially business travelers, have gone directly to supplier Web sites, bypassing the middle organization. Obviously, this type of lower cost service is in direct competition with some of the services that both traditional and electronic travel agencies have provided. The travel management business has been undergoing a radical transformation due to changes brought on by the Internet and air carrier payment policies.

But the Internet revolution is also threatening other "middlemen," and it is leading the push toward a more direct consumer-supplier link. For example, in January 1999, Delta Airlines announced that it will require anyone not booking directly with only the Delta Web site to pay a $2.00 per ticket surcharge. Subsequently, Delta and other airlines have backed off requiring surcharges, but instead are offering lower priced "Internet only" fares to drive traffic to their Web sites. This and other technological innovation is expected to again lead to increases in the percentage of travelers booking through the Internet. However, recent research suggests that the majority of travel management companies that were able to survive the increased use of the Internet over the last five years will remain profitable in the longer run, even as use of Internet for airline ticket sales increases further.[9]

Tour Operators

The most basic functions of a tour operator are to bundle together a *package* of travel services, offer it at a fixed price, and provide some or all of the services during a tour itinerary. To develop and operate exciting and safe tour programs, the tour operator staff must have a very good understanding of what consumers desire, outstanding knowledge of destinations, keen negotiating skills to secure reasonable supplier prices, sophisticated marketing skills, exceptional guides, a strict trip budget, and a well-constructed risk management plan for each tour. They usually provide and operate transportation equipment, such as a motorcoach, van, raft, or ship. A strong consumer trend in tours is more active healthy programming, with convenience and safety. Describing exactly what a tour operator offers can be tricky because there are many types of tours. Following is a listing of the most common tour formats.

In a *group tour* clients travel with a number of individuals sharing similar interests and have the potential for substantial savings and unique opportunities. *Escorted tours* offer a professional guide who remains with a tour group for the entire package. This escort takes care of travel problems that may arise and usually is knowledgeable about the culture and natural history of the area being traversed. A fully *inclusive tour* provides everything that a traveler will need for a set price, except for shopping, gambling, and personal needs. This type of tour is the most convenient because the escort facilitates and pays for all included services.

A *foreign independent tour* or *FIT* is a travel package that normally includes some lodging and a rental car or train pass, but they are not just to foreign countries. It can also include airline tickets and specialty recreation activities, like rafting trips or attraction admissions. The traveler is independent when it comes to travel and must get from destination to destination on their own by driving a rental car or catching trains and busses.

A *fly-drive package* is a common tour in the United States and includes flights, motels, and a rental car. Mass-marketing companies, such as Pleasant Hawaiian Holidays, specialize in this type of tour. Such a package allows the traveler to enjoy volume discounts but have the freedom to travel where they wish in between specific meeting dates.

Rafting tour, Green River, Dinosaur National Monument, Utah.
© Jupiterimages/Brand X Pictures/Thinkstock.com

Types of Tour Operators

The escalating demands of sophisticated travelers and the competitive nature of the travel industry has resulted in the tour operator business becoming more specialized with many types of tour services. Some companies engage in only a narrow niche in the tour market, such as Adrift Adventures, a white-water rafting outfitter in Jensen, Utah,[10] whereas other large organizations, such as Maupintour,[11] operate tours throughout the world via multiple transportation modes. To further confuse things some air carriers and travel management companies also act as tour operators. Described next are the most well-recognized types of tour operators.

Wholesale Tour Company

Wholesale tour companies arrange and promote tour packages, but sell them primarily to travel agents or international tour operators, and not the general public. They often do not operate any portion of the tour. Marketing to the travel trade is one of the strengths of this type of firm. Revenues come primarily from markup of tours they represent.

Receptive Operator

This type of company, also called a ground operator, may meet and greet groups at airports, make arrangements for lodging, and shuttle them to the lodging at one particular destination. They also frequently offer foreign language interpreters, sightseeing tours, or step-on guides.

Specialty travel tours may be geared toward sightseeing in unique settings. © 2011 by Sergiy Zavgorodny. Used under license of Shutterstock, Inc.

Specialty Travel Tour Operators

Organizations who possess highly specialized equipment and guides for unique tours, such as diving, rafting, biking, and photography programs. Tours may be geared toward adventure and risk activities, nature or eco-tourism, skills development, or simply sightseeing in unique settings. Clients are often younger than for other tours, averaging 40 years old.

Motorcoach Tour Operators

These companies own and operate deluxe motor coaches, holding up to 52 passengers, with some costing over $250,000. Sightseeing via motorcoach is still the most popular and economical tour both domestically and internationally. Operators may provide long-distance or local tours, with and without narration. Some motorcoaches have two levels for sightseeing and sleeping onboard; others have bars, and gambling tables.

Types of Jobs with a Tour Operator

Tour Escort/Guide

The tour guide job provides exciting opportunities to enter the travel profession and for a career traveling the globe. This occupation can require the skills of a teacher, entertainer, accountant, doctor, and psychologist. Tour conductor and guide schools provide training and certification to get a start in the field. Guides lead everything from adventure travel, like rowing a raft through the Grand Canyon, to sightseeing tours in the wine country of Italy.

Operations Manager

This professional manages the logistics of equipment and staff scheduling, as well as coordination with other suppliers. This person must also be proficient in budgeting. He or she works primarily in the office and not on the road.

Tour Planner

Designing a new tour, contracting with appropriate suppliers, testing the itinerary, and costing the program are the duties of a tour planner. This person must be in touch with changing client wants and supplier status. Such a position usually involves a balance between business travel and office work.

Sales and Marketing Manager

He or she works with key trade industry and client accounts, and develops promotions directed at consumers. They must be very familiar with company services and the competition. Personal sales skills are very important in this position.

Future of Travel Management Companies and Tour Operators

Despite being battered by global changes in the marketplace, travel management companies and tour operators will continue to provide needed services to business and leisure clients in the future. Undoubtedly, there will be consolidation through attrition and independent agencies joining consortiums. Travel agencies have shifted away from their traditional dependence on domestic airline ticket sales and are looking for more profitable opportunities as consumers are better able to book flights directly and revenues from commissions decline. More agencies will rely on outside sales associates to reduce employment costs and enlarge their reach in the marketplace. The shear magnitude of travel services available and the need for expert advice will continue to push small agencies to specialize and large firms to hire agents who are experts in a segment of the industry.

Most industry analysts agree that there will be continued consolidation in the industry, but TMCs and tour operators will not disappear because they add value through personalized service and are increasingly savvy businesses. Many people with Internet hookups, simply do not have the time or desire to conduct an extensive search of the Internet, and these folks will continue to look to travel consultants for assistance with lengthy and expensive travel plans.

Others will still value the specialized expertise and time savings that experienced consultants possess. The days of agents simply being "order takers" are nearly gone, and they are being quickly replaced by true *travel consultants*. Revenue growth in electronic travel agencies will continue, and this will provide exciting opportunities for sales, programming, and operations jobs with these companies.

Tour operators will need to design new tours that cater to changing customer demands, such as family travel, more independence, and participation. Aging of the population will provide expanding opportunities for senior travel, served by new and more active tour programs. Demand for eco-tourism and other specialty travel tours are predicted to experience rapid growth. But managers will need to contend with increased access restrictions and regulations. They must develop ways to assure clients their deposits are secure and satisfaction guaranteed.

Tour operators will need to design tours that cater to changing customer demands such as family travel. © 2011 by Losevsky Pavel. Used under license of Shutterstock, Inc.

RESOURCES

Internet Sites

Adrift Adventures: www.adrift.com

American Society of Travel Agents: www.asta.org

PhoCusWright Travel Research: www.phocuswright.com

National Tour Association: www.nta.org

ENDNOTES

1. Yesawich, P. Ten trends to watch in the year ahead at http://ehotier.com/browse/news_more_.pdp?id=D721301100M

2. PhoCusWright. U.S. online travel market fueled by supplier sites, though growth slows at http://www.phocuswright.com/press/releases.php

3. Ibid.

4. *2001 Packaged Travel in North America.* (2001). Lexington, KY: National Tour Association.

5. *Travel Weekly.* Travel agencies are solo, small and selling hard at http://www.travelweekly.com

6. Travelocity at http://www.travelocity.com

7. Orbitz at http://www.orbitz.com

8. Terro, R. (2005). Anastasia's way: Corniche travel carves an artful path through the world of luxury. Luxury Travel Advisor (October).

9. Gulker, M. (2006). *Reshuffling the Retail Deck: Internet Adoption and the Profitability of Brick and Mortar Travel Agents.* Stanford, CA: Stanford Institute for Economic Policy Research.

10. at http://www.adrift.com

11. at http://www.maupintour.com

Review Questions

1. What is the name of the privately operated global ticketing system used extensively by travel agents for airline tickets? Why are these organizations so important to travel management companies?

2. An FIT package usually includes what services and products?

3. Can anyone sell airline tickets? What are two organizations that have a licensing requirement for a company to be able to sell domestic and international airline tickets?

4. What is the difference between travel agencies who are primarily order takers, in comparison to travel consultants?

5. Why have travel management companies shifted from "order takers" to travel consultants and managers?

6. Are tours just for seniors on motorcoach-based sightseeing trips? What types of tours are available in major tourist destinations?

Meetings and Events Management

Jan H. van Harssel, Niagara University

LEARNING OBJECTIVES

- To describe the development and growth of the meeting, convention, and event industry.
- To outline the programs, facilities, and services required for organizing successful meetings and events.
- To identify the industry's stakeholders, including:
    - Associations
    - CVBs
    - Facilities
    - Transportation
    - Exhibition service contractors
    - Professional meeting planners
    - Government organizations
    - Sponsors
- To describe types of conventions, meetings, and events.
- To understand supplier/buyer dynamics.
- To identify and discuss the impact of technology on meeting and event operations.
- To manage conferences and events.
- To discuss the economic impact of meetings and events.
- To discuss the linkage between sponsorships and event promotion.
- To recognize the importance of ethical behavior within the convention, meeting, and events industry.

CHAPTER OUTLINE

Economic Impact of Meetings and Events
The Supplier/Buyer Relationship
Meeting Categories
    Corporate Neetings

The Meeting Planning Function
The Meeting Planner's Job
Event Tourism
Event Management

Organization of Events
Strategic Sponsorship
Role of Events
Opportunities
Summary

KEY TERMS

Animation
Association
Catalyst
Conferences
Conventions
Convention and Visitors Bureau (CVB)
Destination Marketing Organization (DMO)

Economic impact
Exposition
Festivals
Incentive travel
International Special Events Society (ISES)
Meetings
Meeting Professionals International (MPI)

Request for Proposals (RFPs)
Sponsor
Supplier
Trade show
Venue
Virtual meeting

Meeting planners and event planners represent an important function as intermediaries in the hospitality industry. The fields are experiencing exciting changes, its economic impact is tremendous, and job opportunities abound. The jobs of a meeting planner and an event planner have overlapping responsibilities, but events and meetings do differ in their characteristics, function, and role. In simple terms, an event is a destination in search of an audience, whereas a meeting is an audience in search of a destination.

Meetings and conventions bring people together for a common purpose, and meeting and event planners work to ensure that this purpose is achieved seamlessly. Some meetings are held to conduct business, others to engage in a social ritual, some are educational in nature, whereas others are organized as fund-raisers. Events are usually more entertainment oriented, and activities organized for a special occasion are called special events. Events vary in durations from hours, to days or even weeks. Their temporary nature represents a powerful marketing draw and distinguishes events from (permanent) attractions. Conventions are a special type of meeting held in a specific location, often comprised of meetings and presentations, and a trade show or exhibition. Larger business or educational meetings without a trade show are referred to as conferences. Conferences may last a single day or several days but are held at one venue.

Economic Impact of Meetings and Events

Meetings, conventions, and events contribute significantly to the travel and tourism industry. Destinations that host meetings benefit from the dollars spent by delegates and guests and the services provided for them. One-fourth of all air travel expenditures represent passengers attending a meeting or convention. One-third of all hotel room income is represented by guests attending meetings. The economic impact of meetings, events, and incentive travel is far reaching.

The U.S. Travel Association has calculated that business travel creates 2.4 million jobs, injects more than $240 billion into the national economy annually, and generates $39 billion in federal, state, and local tax revenues. Specifically, meetings and events help create one million jobs to the American workforce in local economies across the United States. Many of these jobs support employment in the hospitality and food service industries. Meetings and events generate $27 billion in wages that are critical to local economies across the country.

Meetings and events provide $16 billion in tax revenue at the federal, state, and local levels. The meetings and event activities support over 200 local convention centers around the country. The industry segment is responsible for nearly 15 percent of all travel in the United States. The health of the meetings industry is essential to our nation's economy. In 2008, in Orlando alone, spending by visitors as a result of group meetings totaled over $3.30 billion. In the United States, meeting and convention planners held about 56,600 jobs in 2008. About 27 percent worked for religious, grant-making, civic, professional, and similar organizations, and 14 percent worked for accommodation, including hotels and motels. The remaining worked for educational services, government agencies, private industry, and in other organizations that host meetings. About 6 percent of meeting planners were self-employed.

The Supplier/Buyer Relationship

The dynamics of the meeting planning industry centers on the supplier/buyer relationship. Meeting planners who work as suppliers represent the destination or venue hosting the event. Employment opportunities include convention and visitor bureaus, hotels, conference centers, convention centers, sport arenas, cruise ships, and college campuses. Meeting planners who work for suppliers are constantly looking for opportunities to convince groups to schedule their next meeting at their locations. Supply-side businesses also include organizations that provide services for meeting and event planners. Buyers, on the other hand, are employed by organizations that plan meetings. Employment opportunities here include larger corporations, industry associations, government agencies, educational institutions, and event-planning companies. Meeting Professionals International (MPI) is the leading international organization of meeting planners, and its membership reflects the balance between planners and supplier members, as many of MPI's programming activities help create opportunities for both sides to meet and conduct business.

Meeting Categories

Meetings are organized by various groups. Categories include corporations, associations, government agencies, civic groups, and religious organizations. Marketers often refer to meeting prospects with the acronym SMERF. The SMERF market includes Social, Military, Educational, Religious, and Fraternal groups. Corporate meetings center on issues relevant to employees, customers, sales representatives, or strategic planning activities. Corporate meetings tend to center around product development and promotion, training sessions, or the brainstorming of new ideas. Importantly, meetings serve to enhance employee motivation and productivity. Associations often comprise membership organizations. Examples include professional organizations, unions, hobby clubs, and trade groups. Associations are often organized around a common interest, and the group schedules meetings to explore and discuss their common interest. Many associations have at least one annual meeting, and it often serves as the group's major fund-raiser. Many other groups hold meetings, including military organizations (reunions), fraternal organizations (Rotary), family gatherings (weddings), educational sessions (seminars), and alumni gatherings.

Corporate Meetings

Meetings that are well executed and designed to meet specific objectives greatly contribute to the achievement of goals. To a company, the benefits of successful meetings include the development of engaged employees, improvements in the corporate culture, more satisfied employees, and increased employee retention. Engaged employees form an emotional connection that comes from being involved in their work, their company, and its brand. When employees know their company values them, they are able to focus on their work instead of worrying about keeping their job, resulting in greater commitment to stay with the company. The three aspects of work that employees consider most important are (a) exciting, challenging work, (b) a chance to learn and grow, and (c) great people with whom to work. Corporate meetings address all three of these aspects. Meetings are a means to communicate company and brand message and to bring challenges to the table. By keeping them informed, employees are able to play a role in finding and creating solutions. Meetings that

A meeting is a gathering of two or more people. The purpose of a meeting varies. © 2011 by Morgan Lane Photography. Used under license of Shutterstock, Inc.

include seminars, round tables, and other educational settings address the employees' desire to learn and grow. Bringing workers together in a less formal setting away from the workplace allows them to learn more about each other, which translates into more trust and better communication. Meetings, of course, also provide settings for educational seminars, new product introductions (trade shows), and industry-specific conferences and conventions.

The Meeting Planning Function

Planners coordinate every detail of meetings and conventions, from the speakers and meeting location to arranging for printed materials and audiovisual equipment. The first step in planning a meeting or convention is determining the purpose, message, or impression that the sponsoring organization wants to communicate. Planners increasingly focus on how meetings affect the goals of their organizations; for example, they may survey prospective attendees to find out what motivates them and how they learn best. A more recent option for planners is to decide whether the meeting or convention can achieve goals in a virtual format versus the traditional meeting format. Virtual conferences are offered over the Internet where attendees view speakers and exhibits online.

After this decision is made, planners then choose speakers, entertainment, and content and arrange the program to present the organization's information in the most effective way. Meeting and convention planners search for prospective meeting sites, primarily

Independent event planners can coordinate details of meetings and events held anywhere. © 2011 by StockLite. Used under license of Shutterstock, Inc.

hotels and convention or conference centers. When choosing a site, the planner considers who the prospective attendees are and how they will get to the meeting. Being close to a major airport is important for organizations that have attendees traveling long distances who are pressed for time. The planner may also select a site based on its attractiveness to increase the number of attendees.

Once they have narrowed down possible locations for the meeting, planners issue requests for proposals (RFPs) to all possible meeting sites in which they are interested. These requests state the meeting dates and outline the planner's needs for the meeting or convention, including meeting and exhibit space, lodging, food and beverages, telecommunications, audiovisual requirements, transportation, and any other necessities. The establishments respond with proposals describing what space and services they can supply and at what price. Meeting and convention planners review these proposals and either make recommendations to the clients or management or choose the site themselves.

Once the location is selected, meeting and convention planners arrange support services, coordinate with the facility, prepare the site staff for the meeting, and set up all forms of electronic communication needed for the meeting or convention, such as e-mail, voice mail, video, and online communication. Meeting logistics, the management of the

details of meetings and conventions, such as labor and materials, is another major component of the job. Planners register attendees and issue name badges, coordinate lodging reservations, and arrange transportation. They make sure that all necessary supplies are ordered and transported to the meeting site on time, that meeting rooms are equipped with sufficient seating and audiovisual equipment, that all exhibits and booths are set up properly, and that all materials are printed. They also make sure that the meeting adheres to fire and labor regulations and oversee food and beverage distribution.

There also is a financial management component of the work. Planners negotiate contracts with facilities and suppliers. These contracts, which have become increasingly complex, are often drawn up more than a year in advance of the meeting or convention. Contracts often include clauses requiring the planner to book a certain number of rooms for meetings to qualify for space discounts and imposing penalties if the rooms are not filled. Therefore, it is important that the planner closely estimates how many people will attend the meeting based on previous meeting attendance and current circumstances. Planners must also oversee the finances of meetings and conventions. They are given overall budgets by their organizations and must create a detailed budget, forecasting what each aspect of the event will cost.

In addition, some planners oversee meetings that contribute significantly to their organization's operating budget and must ensure that the event meets income goals. An important part of the work is measuring how well the meeting's purpose was achieved. After determining what the objectives are, planners try to measure if objectives were met and if the meeting or conference was a success. The most common way to gauge their success is to have attendees fill out surveys about their experiences at the event. Planners can ask specific questions about what sessions were attended, how well organized the event appeared, how they felt about the overall experience, and they can ask for suggestions on how to improve the next event. If the purpose of a meeting or convention is publicity, a good measure of success would be how much press coverage the event received. A more precise measurement of meeting success, and one that is gaining importance, is return on investment. Planners compare the costs and benefits of an event and show whether it was worthwhile to the organization. For example, if a company holds a meeting to motivate its employees and improve company morale, the planner might track employee turnover before and after the meeting.

The Meeting Planner's Job

Some aspects of the work vary by the type of organization for which planners work. Those who work for associations must market their meetings to association members, convincing members that attending the meeting is worth their time and expense. Marketing is usually less important for corporate meeting planners because employees are generally required to attend company meetings. *Corporate planners* usually have shorter time frames in which to prepare their meetings. Planners who work in federal, state, and local governments must learn how to operate within established government procedures, such as procedures and rules for procuring materials and booking lodging for government employees. *Government meeting planners* also need to be aware of any potential ethics violations. *Convention service managers,* meeting professionals who work in hotels, convention centers, and similar establishments, act as liaisons between the meeting facility and planners who work for associations, businesses, or governments. They present food service options to outside planners, coordinate special requests, suggest hotel services based on the planner's budget, and otherwise help outside planners present effective meetings and conventions in their facilities.

In large organizations or those that sponsor large meetings or conventions, meeting professionals are more likely to specialize in a particular aspect of meeting planning. Some specialties are *conference coordinators,* who handle most of the meeting logistics; *registrars,* who handle advance registration and payment, name badges, and the set-up of on-site registration; and *education planners,* who coordinate the meeting content, including speakers and topics. In organizations that hold very large or complex meetings, there may be several senior positions, such as *manager of registration, education seminar coordinator,* or *conference services director,* with the entire meeting planning department headed by a department director. In organizations of any size, frequent meetings serve an important management function. The meeting planner is a high-profile position and is of tremendous importance to the achievement of organizational success. Often, meeting planners face the challenge of cutting costs while still meeting expectations of meeting delegates.

Event Tourism

A well-organized event can turn a place into a destination. Events are often the "pull" that draws people to a place. Events can add to the popularity of a destination and can help stimulate the further development of already existing tourist attractions. According to the Tourism Works For America report, published annually by the Tourism Works For America Council, special events are becoming ever-popular tourist attractions and, in some cases, the largest tourist attraction in a state. Not only do they serve as catalysts and deliver a distinct economic impact, but they also go beyond these in many ways. Festivals are important to communities because they help preserve the heritage of many cultures. Through celebration, demonstration, and education, artists' skills are preserved, and traditional culture is strengthened. Special events are also important because they pull a community together and provide family-oriented entertainment. In addition, special events can build up the infrastructure and add to the economic prosperity of a town or city. Major events tend to stimulate investment into the service side of the hospitality sector, especially hotels and restaurants. Sport events ordinarily lead to new or improved facilities that can be used to attract events in the future, and improvements to convention or arts centers can have a similar effect.

Mega-events can also be perceived as general economic stimulants, owing to the extensive investment and infrastructure improvements that often accompany them. Cities and governments often view events as creating employment opportunities, as a chance to rehabilitate rundown sections of towns, and an opportunity to survive (even thrive) during periods of economic uncertainty. The value of a special event, compared to other forms of public expenditure, stems from its high profile and its ability to mobilize public support. Events are indeed a catalyst for tourism. They act as a lure and increase travel. They are an energizing force. And although major events attract many participants and spectators, the associated publicity and image enhancement often induces additional visits not directly related to the event. This "induced demand" is especially evident with special events often leading to spin-off economic activity and the creation of additional employment opportunities.

Organizers and planners of events amplify uniqueness by ensuring that the experience is both special and important. Festivals and events have been around for as long as humans have celebrated their cultural achievement, but special events have a more recent origin, and the management of events is rapidly evolving as a distinct discipline within the hospitality industry. The event industry requires managers who have special skills in marketing, promotion, entertainment, programming, and communication design. Events can make a major contribution to destination development challenges and often can help "brand" a destination. Communities and their marketing organizations are paying attention and are becoming aware of the need for an annual event portfolio to help capture and communicate a destination's attractiveness and encourage repeat visitation.

Event Management

Organization of Events

Professional managers, volunteers, corporate sponsors, and nonprofit associations are all involved in events management. Smaller events can be produced without any formal organization, staff, or detailed planning. However, as events become larger or more sophisticated, traditional theories and methods of management must be applied. Event management also includes the functions of programming and event production, which combines creativity with operational skills. The event manager is the person to take on all these duties and becomes responsible for researching, designing, planning, coordinating, and evaluating events. Event professionals must be experienced, able to adapt, be creative, and demonstrate dedication and problem-solving skills. The profession of event management has many specialized fields and settings, and event planners belong to a new and rapidly growing career field, complete with professional associations, certification, and formal educational programs. The leading international professional association representing event and meeting professionals is the International Special Event Society (www.ises.com) with chapters on four continents. An event can transform an ordinary place into a successful destination, and the hotel industry has taken notice and is eager to support local events planners with financial and operational support. In fact, many hotels are realizing the versatility of the name "events" and are internally replacing the position of meeting planner with event planner.

Strategic Sponsorship

Corporate sponsors have become very important to the success of events. Without them, an event may not take place at all. Starting with the Summer Olympics in Los Angeles in 1985 (it realized a $200 million profit), event sponsorship has grown exponentially. Corporations increasingly seek to market their products and promote their image through events, and many festivals have become dependent on sponsorship revenue.

Sponsorship grants not only benefits the event, but it also helps to brand the sponsor's image. Sponsors seek opportunities to associate with events (and their causes), as this strategic partnership provides for exciting marketing opportunities. It is this symbiotic relationship between the event, the sponsor, and the event's cause that will continue to shape event tourism. In fact, it has proven difficult for events that do not adopt a cause to attract sponsors.

Sponsorable events give companies a chance to communicate with a specific audience and give events the chance to generate revenue. The sport management industry provides a good example. When title sponsors pay a premium fee to have their name as part of the event itself, it is called the *exclusive* or *title sponsor*. When the major sponsor has a predetermined portion of the entire event, it is called the *presenting sponsor. Cosponsors* share event sponsorship with one or more other sponsors. *Media sponsors* usually provide a predetermined amount of advertising support for the event. They may also provide some cash support. *In-kind sponsorship* is provided through the donation of products or services. This type of support helps to lower event expenses. It is important to consider event needs when determining what type of sponsor will be needed. In turn, the event must provide the sponsor with a "platform," a portfolio of benefits that will guarantee the sponsor publicity and visibility.

Role of Events

An event is a variety of different things to a host of different interest groups. From a sponsor's standpoint, association with the event links an organization with such things as good citizenship, community interest, health, and wholesomeness. Event organizers have to find unique ways to attract a sponsor to their event. Large corporations, especially, receive hundreds of inquiries daily for various sponsorship opportunities.

They will often only select those that stand out and will be beneficial to them. As different events have been able to attract and define specific audiences, however, it has become easier for sponsors to determine with greater sophistication the most appropriate event through which they can reach a target group with a message. For festivals and events, these trends have profound implications. Events will continue to attract a large scale of the huge leisure market, and those events that cater to those with higher amounts of disposable income can look forward to continued growth. Direct impacts arise from transactions closely related to the event, such as material, labor, and purchases made from vendors. Some indirect impacts include changes in employment levels, retail earnings, and government revenues. There are also nonmonetary benefits that occur, but these are more difficult to measure. These include increased awareness and an enhanced image of the host community.

Opportunities

Sociodemographic forces have a tremendous impact on leisure, travel, and event tourism. As the world's population grows and the demographic composition continues to change, it will affect the nature of tourism and events. Intergenerational factors, life-stage responsibilities, and cultural influences are all vitally important in explaining event preferences and demand patterns. In designing and planning events, it is essential that event professionals address these influences because they affect people's choices about how they spend their free time. Technology, too, has infused every facet of event planning and programming. New advances are transforming the way in which event managers stage events. As more technologies are introduced into the organizing and planning functions, it will advance operations and increase profit margins. Also, the use of technology at events is leading to more exciting, interesting, and successful events.

Summary

For those seeking an exciting and rewarding career in the hospitality industry, the meeting and events industry holds the promise of challenge and success. Meetings and events are divided into numerous categories, including conventions, conferences, trade shows, events, reunions, festivals, sport, and others. People meet to learn, compete, discuss, entertain, or celebrate. Jobs within this industry are available with suppliers (destinations, hotel, conference centers, and arenas) and buyers (associations, groups, corporations, government agencies). Meeting and event planners are responsible for coordinating all aspects of an event. They take advantage of the resources of the facility (venue), put to use conference services and suppliers, and meet the special needs of the group so that its goals and objectives or met.

Events serve as major catalysts for successful tourism development. They stimulate growth, create destination brand awareness, produce employment, stimulate tourism during the off season, and bring communities together. Event tourism has an extremely bright future. Amplitude of opportunities exists for this industry. With the continuation and rise of events come myriad positive effects that encompass the entire travel/tourism/hospitality industry, resulting in an economic payoff that circulates throughout the host city and surrounding communities.

RESOURCES

References

Andersson, T. & Getz, D. (2008). "Stakeholder Management Strategies of Festivals." *Journal of Convention and Event Tourism, 9*(3).

Bureau of Labor Statistics. (2010). *Occupational Outlook Handbook.* Washington, DC: U.S. Government Printing Office.

Faulkner, B. (2003). "Evaluating The Tourism Impact of Hallmark Events." *Occasional Paper No. 16. Tourism Australia.*

Fenich, G. G. (2008). *Meetings, Expositions, Events & Conventions.* Columbus, OH: Pearson.

Freedman, Harry A. & Feldman Smith, Karen. (1991). *Black Tie Optional: The Ultimate Guide to Planning and Producing Successful Special Events.* Rockville, MD: Fund Raising Institute.

Getz, Donald. (2008). "Event Tourism: Definition, Evolution, and Research" *Tourism Management, 29.*

Getz, Donald. (2007). *Event Studies. Theory, Research and Policy for Planned Events.* Oxford, UK: Elsevier.

Getz, Donald. (2005). *Event Management and Event Tourism.* Elmsford, NY: Cognizant Communication Corporation.

Getz, D. & Cheyne, J. (1996). "Special Event Motivations and Behavior." In C. Ryan (Ed.), *Essays of Experience—A Tourist Affair* (Chapter 7). London.

Goldblatt, Joe Jeff. (2007). *Special Events. The Roots and Wings of Celebration.* New York: Wiley.

Goldblatt, Joe Jeff. (1997). *Special Events: Best Practices in Modern Event Management.* New York: Wiley.

Goldblatt, Joe Jeff. (1990). *Special Events: The Art and Science of Celebration.* New York: Van Nostrand Reinhold.

Goldblatt, Joe Jeff & Waterhouse, Jodi. (1999). "Taking Advantage of the Growth in Event Tourism." *San Diego Business Journal, 20*(30).

Goodall, B. (1988). "How Tourists Choose Their Holidays: An Analytic Framework." In B. Goodall & G. Ashworth (Eds.), *Marketing in the Tourism Industry: The Promotion of Destination Regions.* London: Croom Helm.

Hartman, M. (n.d.). "Obtaining Support from your City." *Event Trends in the 90's.* Port Angeles, WA: International Festivals Association.

Hoyle, L. H. Jr. (2002). *Event Marketing.* New York: Wiley.

Horne, J. (2007). "The Four Knowns of Sport Mega-Events."*Leisure Studies, 26*(2).

Jackson, Robert & Wood Schmader, Steven. (1990). *Special Events: Inside and Out.* Urbana, IL: Sagamore Publishing.

Monroe, J. C. (2005). *Art of the Event.* New York: Wiley.

Mules, T. & McDonald, S. (1994). "The Economic Impact of Special Events: The Use of Forecasts." *Festival Management & Event Tourism, 2*(1).

Preuss, H. (2005). "The Economic Impact of Visitors at Major Multi-Sport Events." *European Sport Management Quarterly, 5*(3).

Quinn , B. (2006). "Problematising Festival Tourism; Arts Festivals and Sustainable Development in Ireland." *Journal of Sustainable Tourism, 14*(3).

Ramsborg, G. C. (2007). *Professional Meeting Management.* Dubuque, IA: Kendall Hunt.

Shifflet, D. K. & Bhatia, Pawan. (1999, September 6). "Event Tourism Market Emerging." *Hotel & Motel Management, 214*(15).

Silvers, J. R. (2003). *Professional Event Coordination.* New York: Wiley.

Skinner, B. E. & Rukavina, V. (2002). *Event Sponsorship.* New York: Wiley.

Smith, K. A. (2007) "Distribution Channels for Events: Supply and Demand-Side Perspectives." *Journal of Vacation Marketing, 13.*

Sonder, M. (2003). *Event Entertainment and Production.* New York: Wiley.

Sullivan, D. & Jackson, M. J. (2002). "Festival Tourism; A Contribution to Sustainable Local Economic Development." *Journal of Sustainable Tourism, 10*(4).

Supovitz, F. (2004). *The Sport Event Management and Marketing Playbook.* New York: Wiley.

Tarlow, P. E. (2002). *Event Risk Management and Safety.* New York: Wiley.

Van der Wagen, L. (2005). *Event Management.* Columbus, OH: Pearson.

Wilkinson, David G. (1988). *The Event Management and Marketing Institute Handbook.* Winnipeg, Ontario, Canada: The Wilkinson Information Group.

Williams, Amy. (2000). *Events as Catalysts for Successful Tourism Development.* Senior Year Honor Thesis. The College of Hospitality and Tourism Management. Niagara University, NY.

Review Questions

1. Differentiate between a meeting and an event.

2. Define "trade show" and provide an example.

3. Name several functions a meeting planner performs.

4. Name the two leading organizations in the meeting planning and event planning industry.

5. What type organizations host meetings and events?

6. For many organizations, events represent a major fund-raising opportunity. Name at least five different revenue-generating opportunities associated with event planning.

7. What benefits do sponsors bring to an event?

8. What benefits do events bring to sponsors?

9. Explain the role of events in creating a destination image (branding).

10. What current demographic forces (shifts) will have the greatest impact on future event planning challenges?

Private Club Operations

Denis P. Rudd, Robert Morris University
Richard J. Mills, Jr., Robert Morris University

 **LEARNING OBJECTIVES**

- Understand the components of the club management industry.
- Identify the function that private clubs play in the hospitality industry.
- Explain the significance and economic impact made by clubs.
- Identify future employment opportunities in the club industry.

CHAPTER OUTLINE

KEY TERMS

City clubs
Club
CMAA
Country clubs
Equity clubs
Full membership
Member

Military clubs
NCA
Proprietary clubs
Service
Social membership
Yacht club

We Serve the World

"Clubs are the training grounds, for some of the finest Restaurateurs and Hoteliers."

John H. Rudd Sr.
Senior Vice President of the Statler Hotel Corp.

Since the beginning of civilized man, archaeologists have found evidence of *clubs* throughout the world. Within the heady industrial development that so profoundly transformed the American economy and society in the decades following the Civil War, the proliferation of the new American clubs revealed the strength and social stature of their founders, most of whom were newly wealthy entrepreneurs. The new clubs provided a place where peers could meet and discuss mutual problems and solutions. As American urban centers expanded and became more industrial, the desirable residential districts were located further and further from the business and industrial centers. Busy businessmen could no longer go home for lunch. A downtown club could provide the pleasant environment and excellent noontime meal that later became an important part of the American club. Once considered the playground of the rich and famous, the club became a center for the American family and its recreational activities.

A **club** is defined as a group of persons organized or united for social, literary, athletic, political, or other purposes. People join clubs to engage in social discourses and to surround themselves with others who have similar interests. Growing steadily each year are the ever-increasing markets for private clubs. Catering to a multitude of clientele, clubs have existed for many millennia and include various interest groups, recreational activities, and organizations. With over 14,000 private clubs in the United States alone, clubs have created an atmosphere conducive to friendliness and comfort.

Fiscal Impact

The Club Managers Association of America (CMAA), the premier industry professional association for 7,000 managers of approximately 3,000 membership clubs, compiled the 2006 Economic Impact Survey. The survey reported CMAA member-managed clubs generating annual gross revenues of over $14 billion per year, with food and beverage revenue contributing $4.5 billion. Average CMAA-managed club income is approximately $5.18 million dollars.

The average club spends $1.2 million within the state as a whole, overall club operations generate $6.2 one billion for state economies around the country. A typical club pays over $150,000 in property taxes; provides over $367 million for charities, with approximately 83 percent of this money moved into local community charities; and reports an excess of $6.4 million in student scholarships.

Modern Environment

The competitive landscape has increased significantly over the past several years, placing never before experienced pressure on membership at private clubs. Specifically, industry experts have drawn a general consensus identifying the changing golf course marketplace and population demographics as key culprits.

Frank Vain, president of The McMahon Group, a consulting firm to the private club industry, says the biggest challenge is the evolving golf marketplace that "has experienced a total reversal in market composition. Going back to the 1920s, about 80 percent of the golf courses were private. Public golf was almost unheard of, and up until the 1990s, most of the existing public courses were not comparable to private courses." Vain's group now estimates that currently about 75 percent of U.S. golf courses are public and is projected to plateau at 80 percent around 2010.

Furthermore, these public facilities have grown in quality commensurate with its numeric growth. Steve Graves, president of Creative Golf Marketing, a membership-marketing firm, comments that private clubs today are in direct competition with upscale daily fee courses. "These clubs are not your typical municipal courses that we all grew up around," suggested Graves, "these courses are being built and designed by the best in the industry and offer equal and many times better golf courses than a typical private club. [Therefore] the up-scale daily fee courses present an adequate golf experience without the high monthly cost associated with being a member of a private club." Vain further accentuates the point, "Most of the new course construction has been in the high-end arena with the conditions, accessibility and slope rating that can rival the private club experience, except there are no initiation fees, dues or assessments. There is a whole generation of people growing up not having or needing a private club still able to call themselves golfers. This was simply not possible 20 years ago."

In addition, the influence of technology, ease of travel, and the transient lifestyle produced by the corporate career ladder has created a different societal need and, hence, a change in the population demographics. Leesa Mitchell, CMP, operator of Members Solutions, a consulting firm that has been involved in marketing high-end daily fee operative clubs, states,

> Many clubs have failed to change in correlation to the changing needs of our society. Many clubs are looking for the "tried and true" program to recruit and retain members. In my opinion, the fact of the matter is, those programs do not exist. Every club has a different situation, different demographic and different trend line. In recruiting and retaining members, those are the areas that many clubs have been failing to recognize and utilize in their planning. Turning a deaf ear to demographics and related trending is not the route to go and creates a challenge in recruitment and retention, as well as maintaining a positive satisfaction level of existing members.

In crisis situations, shortcuts often abound and glow with appeal. The private club industry is not immune. Graves articulates that one of the most disturbing national trends within the industry are clubs resorting to the "path of least resistance" by drastically reducing initiation fees or completely waiving initiation fees to compete. The harder path, and ultimately more fruitful, is to set member retention, recruitment, and satisfaction as the club's highest priorities. Gregg Patterson, general manager of The Beach Club of Santa Monica, California, states that because members have options with their leisure time and money, then a key realization for the club manager becomes that this is a "consumer oriented world." Patterson states, "All clubs need to find out what their members want and go after it aggressively. Every member has similar wants goods, services,

programs, facility and a sense of community but the expression of those wants change with time."

Therefore, it is of critical importance for the club manager to stay abreast of the consumers' need and want continuum. Case in point is the busier American lifestyle with children's athletic events, community functions, alternative entertainment activities, that serves to place more scrutiny on a family's discretionary dollars. Thus, a main reason for problematic retention and recruitment is lack of use of the facilities. Vain concluded that in light of this scenario, too many clubs "have failed to update their product to appeal with the growing age brackets of baby boomers."

Given the preceeding discussion, a consensus is again drawn about to the options available to success. A club manager may take a more formal route such as hiring a membership director focused specifically on retention and recruitment, utilizing third-party firms in the consultation arena, and drawing on survey information cultivated in-house or from broader industry outlets. They then use this information to tweak or remodel the product to fit the niche that is unique to each club situation.

Variety of Clubs

Although all clubs share a common bond being the fee/due-paying member, the private club industry has evolved into a vast landscape of variety. Listed and described next are some of the most common clubs in existence today.

In addition to golf, many clubs offer facilities for swimming, tennis, and more. © *2011 by Nick Stubbs. Used under license of Shutterstock, Inc.*

Country Clubs

Around 80 percent of all private clubs are country clubs, and they often provide elaborate social amenities along with their outdoor recreational facilities. Activities in a typical country club usually center on the golf course, yet many clubs also provide members with outdoor facilities for swimming, tennis, horseback riding, and other interests. Members might hold weddings, reunions, or other social events there. Recently many upscale housing projects have encouraged the building and growth of country clubs to attract neighboring communities and new residents.

There are two types of memberships at country clubs: full membership, which entitle the club

Profile

A Club Manager's Perspective

Dan Brennan, Edgeworth Club

The Edgeworth Club was formed in 1893, and under the bylaws its purpose was to promote interaction and friendship among its members and their social enjoyment, and for the purpose of furnishing facilities for athletics and other innocent sports, and the erection and maintenance of a building or buildings thereafter. Sports that were emphasized at the club were tennis, bowling, and golf. The architectural style of the Edgeworth Club is decidedly Elizabethan, which lends itself particularly to the ground on which it was built and the uses for which it was designed. The Edgeworth Club hosted the Wightman Tennis Cup matches, a prestigious international tennis event. Since then its emphasis has been on tennis and paddle tennis. The club is the principal location for charity events in the raising of funds for health associations and other organizations, as this is important part of the club personality. Similarly, the century-long tradition of the ventricle presentations involving club members in all phases of the writing, directing, and acting in these entertainments.

Entering into the year 2008 and beyond has been quite difficult for many of the private clubs nationwide. Member expectations have changed dramatically. The private club members of today have the same high expectations for service and food as they had thirty years ago, but they want it faster and more casual. Private club members of today are searching for the value in their investment and have put aside family tradition and legacy as reasons for joining a given club. The age of technology has played a large part in that. Club members are constantly on the go. They want to eat fast and be able to use their laptops or cell phone while they dine. The older established clubs across the country have been fighting that change. Many have figured out how to permit it without giving up their status.

Members want to make reservations online, they want to use e-mail for committee reports and meeting. The Edgeworth Club has been able to make the progression into the "high-tech" society. Managing a club that encourages their senior staff to be progressive with technology is quite challenging. They want to have the club at their fingertips 24 hours a day. The challenge is to purchase the right hardware and software that best fits your club. We must keep inline with the updates. What we purchase today is obsolete in 3 to 5 years. How do we ask long-term employees of 20 years to change their habits and become "high-tech"? Putting the emphasis on education has never been more important in the club industry. The Club Managers Association of America has done a wonderful job in preparing managers for the present as well as the future.

As clubs move along trying to figure out what is right for them, we also must maintain our private club status. Sometimes going to "high-tech" can open up a whole new set of problems. Does the club membership understand the privacy laws? Do they want to put the club in jeopardy of losing their private club status? What are the tax implications? It is so important to keep up with education and to hire the right person to lead your club. Hiring intelligent, well-educated, and well-rounded individuals to manage the various departments in and around the club is of the utmost importance. They are the leaders who make the club successful. No one person has ever successfully run a private club, been successful financially, and kept their job longer than three years, doing it all by themselves.

member to the full use of the facilities the club offers, and social membership, which permits the member to use specific facilities, such as the restaurant, lounge, bar, or tennis courts. Social membership sometimes requires that club members use the clubs facilities at certain times or days. Equinox Country Club in Manchester, Vermont, and the California Country Club in Whittier, California, are two examples of country clubs. In the past, country clubs were seen as the last bastions of the upper-class elite. In some cases this is still true; however, in most instances the stuffy cigar smoke and the Mayflower context are no longer used to determine whether an individual should be qualified for membership.

Yacht Clubs

Yacht clubs are 4 percent of the total clubs; these clubs are designated for establishments near or on the water and generally promote and regulate boating and yachting. The Montauk and Rochester Yacht Clubs are examples of this type of organization. Most Yacht Clubs own and operate a marina for their members, which may include the operation of a clubhouse with dining and recreation facilities.

Military Clubs

Military clubs cater to the enlisted man, the noncommissioned officer, and the officer. Military bases in the United States and overseas provide these clubs for the welfare and the benefit of the soldiers. They provide extended amenities for their club members, such as guest quarters, recreational activities, food and beverage operations, and entertainment. In the past the clubs have been run by military personnel, but recent changes in resource allocation have required the military to contract civilian firms to provide services. These facilities are located around the world and include the Bamberg officer's club in Bamberg, Germany, and the Fort Benning officer's club in Fort Benning, Georgia. An example is the 911th Airlift Wing of the U.S. Air Force. Before 1974 they had two Military Clubs on base. The NCO Club was for the enlisted members of the base, and the Officer's Club was designated for the officers of the base. Due to the downsizing in the military and the costs of running two clubs, the 911th NCO and Officer's Club became a Consolidated Open Mess (Club) in February 1974. Today's club is open to officer and enlisted members of all branches of the Armed Forces—Air Force, Army, Navy, Marines, and Coast Guard—and is currently 1,133 members strong. Being a member

of the club is a tradition at the 911th Airlift Wing. Members join the club for several reasons, but the biggest include camaraderie and a place to share military experiences with other armed services members. It is also a gathering place for the numerous retirees in the area. The 911th Club hosts several events each month for its members ranging from official functions to holiday celebrations, as well as membership nights, sports parties, meet-and-greets, birthday parties, wedding receptions, and other functions. The club offers excellent dining opportunities and does promotions with giveaways.

Professional Clubs

These types of clubs are for people in the same profession for social and business interaction. The Engineer's Club of St. Louis is a professional club that appeals to engineers from the St. Louis area, for example.

Social Clubs

Social clubs are similar to the Everglades Club in Palm Beach, Florida, concentrate on serving the social needs of members who are normally from similar socioeconomic backgrounds.

City Clubs

As the name implies, city clubs are usually located in urban communities and range from luncheon-only clubs that serve segments of the business population to fully integrated dining and athletic clubs make up about 11 percent of its clubs. Unlike most private clubs, city clubs may rent out guest rooms, organize themselves around a specialized profession, or associate with a particular college or university. City clubs fall into the following categories: professional, social, athletic, dining, fraternal, and university. The Duquesne Club has achieved the number one ranking among America's 10 thousand private clubs, according to a national survey conducted by the Club Managers Association of America.

Athletic Clubs

Athletic clubs such as the Palm Beach Bath and Tennis Club and the Toronto Cricket and Skating Club provide an outlet for working out, athletic activities, dining, and meeting. *Dining clubs* are usually located in large office buildings offering their members top-quality food service in urban surroundings. Examples include the Toronto Hunt Club and the Union Club of British Columbia.

Profile

The Duquesne Club
Scott F. Neill CCM, General Manager, The Duquesne Club

The Duquesne Club was founded as a "voluntary association" in 1873 and incorporated as "a club for social enjoyment" in 1881. Membership was limited to 300, and annual dues were $50. Only two years later, many of Pittsburgh's most illustrious citizens had been admitted, including Andrew Carnegie, Henry Clay Frick, B. B. Jones, Frank B. Laughlin, Andrew W. Mellon, Henry Oliver, Jr., and George Westinghouse. Many of their portraits can be seen hanging in the Founders Room. By 1902, membership limits had been raised to 1,100 and in 1980 members voted to elect women to membership. Today, the club has 1,457 active resident members, 465 senior resident members, and 448 nonresident members.

First situated on Penn Avenue between 8th and 9th Streets, in 1879 the club leased a brick house on its present site. Membership flourished, and shortly thereafter the club commissioned architects Longefellow, Alden, and Harlow (who later designed the Carnegie Institute) to plan the new clubhouse. The firm submitted an elegant plan in the Richardson Romanesque style reflecting the success of H. H. Richardson's Allegheny County Courthouse and Jail.

The club occupied its new quarters in 1889. In 1902, LA&H designed a matching addition, which broadened the facade and expanded the club's space. Upon completion, it was reported that the Duquesne Club was the best-appointed club in America. In 1994, the club opened a 22,000 square foot state-of-the-art health and fitness center located in the adjacent Gimbels building. This facility has been an outstanding success and offers members one of the most extensive fitness facilities in the area.

The overnight rooms of the Duquesne club are ideally located in the heart of Pittsburgh business, financial, and cultural districts. When sponsored by a member, overnight guests enjoy all the pleasures and privileges of a private club. Each of their elaborately appointed overnight rooms is designed to accommodate the business and leisure traveler. From the moment you arrive, it is their goal to provide you with personal service of the highest standard. The club's 33 overnight rooms are elegantly appointed, featuring cherry furniture, imported fabrics, marble baths, and original artwork. Overnight guests enjoy incomparable robes, luxurious cotton towels, and signature amenities. In room data or data ports, the convenience of two-line phones and high-speed Internet access provides a seamless connection to the business world. Room service, valet and evening turn-down service, complete with their legendary macaroon cookies, round out the perfect night's stay experience. Bottled water, morning newspaper, and the use of 35,000 square-foot, state-of-the-art health and fitness center are complimentary.

Dining Experience

The pursuit of excellence at the Duquesne Club is nowhere more apparent than in the preparation of its cuisine. The Duquesne Club's kitchen offers both traditional specially in any contemporary fare, all prepared with the richest and finest ingredients. A dining experience at the club may include angelfish from the Gulf of Mexico, Cobbe from the Persian Sea, white truffles from Oregon, and Elysian Fields Lamb from nearby Greene County. Hand-selected, prime cuts of beef are prefabricated on the premises, as are lamb, veal, poultry, and seafood. These ingredients are transformed into culinary masterpieces by Executive Chef Keith Coughenour and his disciplined and creative brigade of cooks and stewards.

With 325 employees, excellent facilities, central location, and perennial membership waiting list, the Duquesne Club remains one of America's preeminent and most respected private clubs and is considered a Pittsburgh treasure by its members.

The Duquesne Club just received the honor of being the number one city club in the United States.

The demands on today's club manager are greater than ever before, which requires managers to have a comprehensive set of skills and understanding of their club. Due to members' busy lifestyles today, more than ever, club directors and committees are looking to the manager to lead the organization with less and less of their involvement. The manager needs to ensure the club evolves in a direction that will keep it relevant in the lives of its current members and attract future members.

Members increasingly look to their club to provide additional services and programs for them and their families, while still offering high-quality traditional services. Many clubs are offering "Clubs within the Club" for a variety of interests such as wine, art, travel, fly fishing, etc. These additional programs add value to the membership, as well as improve member retention. However, the administration of these additional submemberships and their activities can be very demanding and time consuming for the management team.

The rewards for today's club manager are keeping pace with the higher demands, both monetarily and in terms of career fulfillment. However, the most rewarding and important aspect of being a club manager has not, and probably will not, change, and that is working with people. The club manager is the intermediary and communicator between the club's leadership, its membership, and the staff.

Fraternal Clubs

Fraternal clubs like the Elks Club and the Veterans of Foreign Wars, provide fraternal organizations with a central location for meetings, dining, and social activities.

University Clubs

University-associated clubs are reserved for the activities of faculty, alumni, and guests. The Harvard, Yale, Princeton Club of Pittsburgh, and the University of Toronto Faculty Club are perfect examples.

Club Personnel

Within club types, country clubs are the largest employers, followed by golf clubs and city clubs. Taken together, the total employment in country clubs is four times the number employed in golf clubs, and almost 10 times the number of those employed by city clubs. The ratio of full-time and part-time nonseasonal employees is almost exactly the same for both golf clubs and country clubs. Approximately 43 percent of all employees in these clubs are full time and nonseasonal. This contrasts sharply with city clubs, where 74 percent of the employees are full-time nonseasonal employees. Similar ratios were found among full-time and part-time seasonal employees in both golf and country clubs. However, among city clubs, only one-third of the seasonal employees are part time.

Legal Form of Business

Club ownership includes two categories: equity clubs and proprietary clubs. **Equity clubs** are nonprofit clubs and are the oldest form of club management;

yet, they are still the most common form of ownership today. These clubs are owned and organized by the members for their own enjoyment. The board of directors then establishes the policies and budget and does the hiring and firing of executives, such as the club manager. Any profits that are generated from the dues or club operations must be reinvested in the club's services and facilities and cannot be returned to the members.

Proprietary clubs are operated for profit and are owned by a corporation, company, business, or individual. These clubs became popular in the 1970s and 1980s and provided an expansion of club membership and stringent admission requirements. Club members purchase a membership from the club's owner(s) and have limited input and control over the activities or management of the daily operations of the club. In some cases contract organizations run the facility for the owner. The club manager reports to this organization or the owner of the facility. Depending on the type, interest, and development of all clubs, the category of ownership may vary.

Management Styles

As a student one of the most challenging experiences in life will be to choose a career. If you're looking for a career that is creative and combines business skills, human resource management, marketing, and public relations, welcome to the world of club management. It is one of the fastest-growing industries and hospitality fields and will provide you with outstanding career opportunities in the future. Club management is similar to that of hospitality management because it offers similar facilities. The largest difference is that the club,

FIGURE **29.1** **The Duquesne Club: Facility Description**

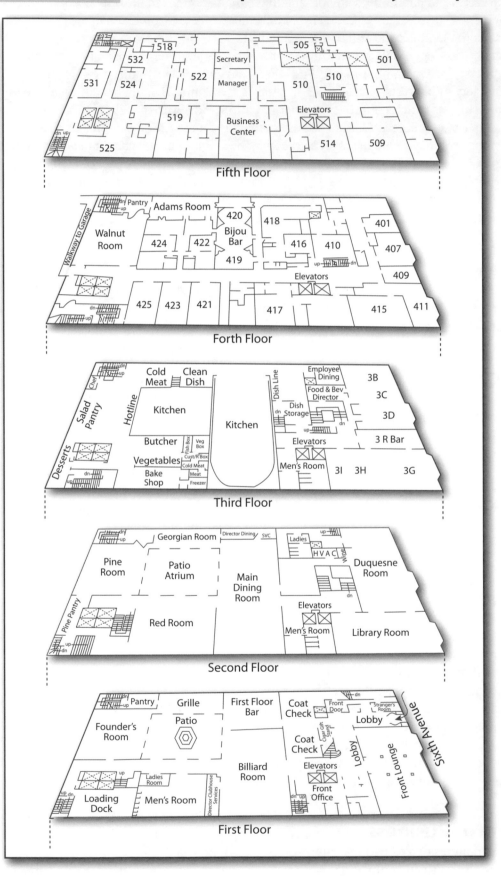

Basement: Laundry, Print Shop, Carpenter Shop, Paint Shop, Engineering Department, and Locker Rooms

unlike a hotel or restaurant, is actually looked at as being owned by the members. The member pays a fee each year, which can vary drastically depending on the nature of the club. In turn, the members feel that they are the owners of the facility. Having one boss may be difficult, but imagine having thousands! This sometimes can put the manager in a difficult situation.

The manager of a club is actually governed by a constitution and the bylaws of the club. The board of directors and club president are elected by their peers to ensure the goals and mission of the club are carried out effectively, and they create the constitution and bylaws that govern members' policies and standards. Club management structure is similar to that of company structure. There is a president, vice president, treasurer, secretary, and different committees. The manager of a club, usually referred to as the chief operating officer or the general manager, has to answer to and abide by the rules set forth by the governing body and is responsible for all areas of club operation. Although the board of directors and president may be responsible for the policy setting and implementation, it is the club manager's job to hire personnel to run the day-to-day operations of the club.

Technology

Club managers ranked the important technologies of the future in a recent study by Dr. Kasavana from Michigan State University: (1) convert the club to a wireless environment; (2) utilize e-procurement to lower transaction costs, improve pricing, enhance productivity, leverage purchasing, reduce inventory, and improve communications; (3) USO POS technology touch input and handheld terminals; handheld technology eliminates the duplication by recording the order directly into the POS device right at the table, thus saving significant time; (4) MRM data mining captures and stores member data forming a club's central focal point of its information systems; (5) ASP subscription outsourcing provides a third-party agency that manages and distributes Internet-based services. Future technologies will provide clubs with a competitive advantage through product differentiation, unique service, cost reduction, and market segmentation.

Club Continuing Education

The sprawl of the club industry, in all its variety, onto the cultural and business landscapes has served, as Perdue, Ninemeier, and Woods (2002) astutely observed, to increase the industry's sophistication, thereby prompting managers to utilize new technologies and products to offer improved services, all the while operating in an extremely competitive environment and labor market. As a result of these changing dynamics, the need for lifelong learning has emerged as a key element for individuals, organizations, and societies in maintaining their competitive position (Barrows & Walsh, 2002).

It is to this end that the CMAA and its Canadian counterpart, the Canadian Society of Club Managers, have been instrumental in keeping its members, and, thus the industry as a whole, in a learning mode. These organizations have served as a bridge to bring academia and club management together producing collaborative efforts in the valuable forms of management development/professional credentialing programs, teaching, conference participation, and applied research.

Club Managers Association of America (CMAA)

Many club managers belong to the Club Managers Association of America (CMAA). This organization is the oldest and most widely respected association representing club management professionals and is comprised of more than 7,000 professional managers from the most prestigious private country, city, yacht, and military clubs in the Untied States and around the world. In the early 1920s professional club managers recognized the impact clubs had on the American way of life and the need for a professional association of these clubs. In February of 1927 the first annual meeting of the CMAA took place.

CMAA actively promotes and advances cooperation among individuals directly engaged in the club management profession, as well as other associations in the hospitality industry. In addition, CMAA encourages the education and professional advancement of its members and assists club officers and managers through their management to secure the utmost in efficient and successful operations. The organization recognizes its responsibility to assist students in gaining a better understanding of the private club management profession and in selecting a career in this sector of the hospitality industry.

A student chapter of CMAA can be offered at any school that offers an undergraduate or graduate program in hospitality. As chapter members, students participate in professional development programs,

FIGURE 29.2 Club Demographics

CLUB TYPE AND LOCATION

- 80 percent of CMAA members' clubs are golf and country clubs.
- 13 percent of CMAA members' clubs are city clubs.
- 4 percent of CMAA members are yacht clubs.
- 65 percent are IRS classified tax-exempt-501(c)(7) organizations.

CLUB INCOME

- Gross revenues equaled $14 billion for all clubs in 2006.
- Food and beverage revenues equal $4.5 billion.
- The average club income is $5.18 million.

CLUB EMPLOYEES

- Clubs employ more than 289,821 employees.
- Club payrolls total over $4 billion.

CLUB OUTREACH PROGRAMS

- Clubs raised $367 million for charities in 2006.
- Most of CMAA's 50 chapters sponsor scholarship funds.

ECONOMIC IMPACT OF CLUBS

- The average club spends $1.05 million in the local community.
- The average club spends $1.2 million within the state as a whole.
- Overall, club operations generate $6.21 billion for state economies around the country.
- A typical club pays $150,773 in property taxes.

source: WWW.CMAA.org

site-visitation at local clubs, hands-on club operations and demonstrations, and leadership development programs. The CMAA provides its student chapters with an internship directory, which provides more than two hundred internships at private clubs around the world.

National Club Association (NCA)

The National Club Association (NCA) has served as an invaluable resource for thousands of club leaders across the country for more than 45 years. Although noted for its influence on Capitol Hill, NCA's staff of professionals is also readily available to answer members' questions and concerns about compliance, governance, and federal and state tax issues. In addition, NCA's team constantly gathers industry-specific news and trends data and disseminates pertinent information so that club leaders can focus on giving their members that unparalleled club experience.

Specifically NCA strives to:

- Provide support and information to assist club leaders in addressing legal, governance, and business concerns.
- Help clubs strengthen their financial health and protect their assets.
- Ensure recognition and advancement of club interests through lobbying and other government relations activities, seek to preserve the independence of clubs to operate.
- Assist clubs in complying with laws and regulations.

Summary

Clubs provide a unique managing experience that combines many elements of the hospitality and tourism industries. Club managers must be versatile and open to the changing needs of the club members and the world around them. The most important job of a club manager is to provide club members with a positive experience every time they attend a function at the club. If managers fail to do this, attendance and membership will drop off, and the club will cease to exist. Service is the key to a club manger's success, and service is the core of the business. Club managers must remember that they "serve the world."

RESOURCES

Internet Sites

Algonquin Club of Boston: http://algonquinclub.memfirst.net/Club/Scripts/Home/home.asp

American Club in Singapore: http://www.amclub.org.sg/

American Society of Golf Course Architects: http://www.golfdesign.org/

Ariel Sands Beach Club: http://www.arielsands.com/

Army Navy Country Club: http://ancc.org/

Association of College and University Clubs: http://www.collegeanduniversityclubs.org/

Atlanta Athletic Club: http://www.atlantaathleticclub.org/

Ballantyne Country Club: http://www.crescent-resources.com/communit/charlott/ballanty/default.asp

Bear Creek Golf Club: http://www.bearcreekgc.com/Club/Scripts/Home/home.asp

Belmont Country Club: http://www.belmontcc.org/Club/Scripts/Splash/splash.asp

Boca Raton Resort & Club: http://www.bocaresort.com/

California Yacht Club: http://calyachtclub.com/cms/index2.htm

Capitol Hill Club: http://www.capitolhillclub.com/

Cedar Rapids Country Club: http://www.thecrcc.com/

Club Managers Association of America: www.cmaa.org

Club Services: http://www.clubservices.com

ClubCorp: http://www.clubcorp.com

Country Club of Lansing: http://www.cclansing.org/

Country Club of St. Albans: http://www.stalbans.com/

Golf Course Builders Association of America: http://www.gcbaa.org/

Golf Course Superintendents Association of America: http://www.gcsaa.org/

International Association of Golf Administrators: http://www.iaga.org/

International Club Network: http://www.privaccess.com/

International Health, Racquet, & Sportsclub Association: http://csdemo12.citysoft.com/IHRSA/viewPage.cfm?pageId=2

International Military Community Executives Association: http://www.imcea.com/

Ladies Professional Golf Association: http://www.lpga.com/

Lighthouse Point Yacht and Racquet Club: http://www.lpyrc.com/

National Association of Club Athletic Directors: http://www.nacad.org/

National Club Association: http://www.natlclub.org/

Professional Golfers Association of America: http://www.pga.com/

Sanctuary Golf Club: http://www.sanctuary-sanibel.com/

The ACE Club: http://www.theaceclubonline.com/

The Virtual Clubhouse/Club Management Magazine: www.club-mgmt.com

References

Barnhart, C. L., ed. *The American College Dictionary.* New York: Random House 1990.

Barrows, C. W., & J. Walsh. Bridging the gap between hospitality management programmes and the private club industry. *International Journal of Contemporary Hospitality Management.* 14, no. 3 (2002): 120–127.

Brown, Mark M., Lu Donnelly, and David G. Wilkins. *The History of the Duquesne Club.* Pittsburgh: Art and Library Committee, 1989.

"Club Management Forum" Virginia: Club Managers Association of America, 2000. Retrieved January 2, 2001, from http://www.cmaa.org/conf/conf2000/time.htm

"Club History." Retrieved July 2007, from wikipedia.org/wiki/Club

Crossley, John C., and Lynn M. Jamieson. *Introduction to Commercial and Entrepreneurial Recreation.* Urbana, IL: Sagamore Publishing, 1997.

"Economic Impact Survey 2006." Club Managers Association of America. Retrieved June 29, 2005, from http://www.cmaa.org/EconImpactSurvey/2006EconImpactSurvey.doc

"Membership issues: Opinions on what works in today's private club industry. Retrieved July 1, 2005, from http://www.board roommagazine.com/fa59.cfm

Perdue, Joe., ed. *Contemporary Club Management.* Alexandria, VA: Club Managers Association of America, 1997.

Perdue, J., J. D. Ninemeier, & R. H. Woods. Comparison of present and future competencies required for club managers. *International Journal of Contemporary Hospitality Management.* 14, no. 3 (2002): 142–146.

"Perfect storm: What does it mean for private clubs." Retrieved July 1, 2005, from http://www.boardroommagazine.com/fa58.cfm
Singerling, James, Robert Wood, Jack Nimemeier, and Joe Purdue. "Success Factors in Private Clubs." *Cornell Hotel and Restaurant Administration Quarterly* 38, no. 5 (Oct. 1997).

"The CMAA Student Advantage: A Commitment To Your Future." Virginia: Club Managers Association of America, 1999. Retrieved January 4, 2001, from http://www.cmaa.org/ student/adv_bro/index.htm

Walker, John R. *Introduction to Hospitality,* 3rd ed. Upper Saddle River, NJ: Prentice Hall, 2001.

Review Questions

CHAPTER 29

1. What types of facilities are likely to be found at a country club?

2. What types of services are likely to be offered at a city club?

3. Describe the types of military clubs and the purposes they serve.

4. What is the mix of full-time to part-time staff at country clubs?

5. What is the mix of full-time to part-time staff at city clubs?

6. What is the mix of year-round to seasonal staff in country clubs?

7. What is the mix of year-round to seasonal staff in city clubs?

8. Define an equity club.

9. Define a proprietary club.

10. Sketch an organization chart that shows which positions report to whom.

11. What is CMAA? Visit their Web site at www.cmaa.org.

12. What is NCA, and what are the goals of NCA?

Assignment 1

Visit Club Managers Association of America's Web site, ClubNet (www.cmaa.org). This Web site offers links to home pages for numerous private clubs throughout the United States. Visit as many of these home pages as possible to gain an understanding of the variety of private clubs available as well as the quality facilities that are provided for members and their guests.

ClubNet also describes the numerous professional development opportunities available for club managers through CMAA. Peruse this section of ClubNet to better understand how professional development and learning is a lifelong pursuit.

As you look ahead and plan your career, how will you pursue professional development and continuous educational opportunities?

Assignment 2

According to an article in *Club Management* by Chris White (December 2000), the growth of the spa industry can provide opportunities for the private club sector. The spa industry has grown across the United States due to a number of reasons delineated by White (p. 94):

- Baby boomers' desire to slow the effects of aging
- The high costs of conventional, remedial health care as compared to preventive health care
- The increasing concern for the quality of the lengthening average life span
- Increasing amounts of personal disposable income

The variety of types of spas is also expanding. Spas no longer have to be the destination, resort, or cruise line spas also known as vacation spas. Day spas, which tend to cater to local clientele and offer hair salons, skin care, body treatments, and massage, are a growing segment. White emphasized in this article that the day spa market may provide enormous opportunities for private clubs, particularly involving massage, body treatments, and possibly skin care.

What is your opinion of these expanded services for private clubs? What other types of amenities might be added that would be popular with private club members? How could these services be effectively marketed to the membership? What are potential disadvantages of offering "day spa" types of services?

Assignment 3

Many clubs are increasingly experiencing quite varied demographics among their membership resulting in contrasting membership expectations and demands. For example, although clubs may still have a population of older members who have perhaps been with the club for many decades, younger members, often with children, are also a growing segment. The older members may still enjoy dressing up for an evening of fine dining, but this may not be realistic or pleasurable for a family with three young children. How does a club cater to differing member preferences? The solution of operating different facilities to cater to the preferences of all members may work for some clubs but would be too costly and unrealistic for many operations.

If you were the new general manager of a club with these dilemmas (varied member preferences/limited budget and the membership resistant to increases in dues), what would you suggest? Think of going before the club's board with at least three options to possibly increase member usage of the food and beverage facilities. What will you propose?

Casinos

Chris Roberts, DePaul University

LEARNING OBJECTIVES

- Describe the different areas of the casino.
- Understand the business nature of gambling.
- Explain the possible careers in the gaming industry.
- Identify gambling that occurs outside a casino.

CHAPTER OUTLINE

Gambling has been an ingredient of American life since before the foundation of the country. The Revolutionary War of 1776 was funded, in part, by the proceeds of a national lottery. However, the public acceptance of gambling has come and gone in waves over the years. In the early twenty-first century, public acceptance of gaming is high, with 48 states currently participating in some form of legalized gaming. Casinos operate in 27 of the 50 states. Only Hawaii and Utah do not have any form of legalized gaming.

Organization of the Casino

The typical casino is organized in a functional manner. The various departments are usually table games and slots in the casino area, the hotel, food and beverage outlets, entertainment, and shopping. Managers of each area are organized in a similar fashion. Careers are built within this structure, with most employees starting at entry level and working their way upward. The casino itself forms the heart and soul of the enterprise. It includes the front of the house, called the casino floor, where customers actually gamble at the table games or play the slot machines. It also includes the back of the house, where the accounting operations, security, and computer control systems are housed.

Front of the House

The casino floor is carefully designed to attract customers. The floor plan of the games takes into account the desired ease of movement, which can either slow customers down so they may linger and gamble, or speed them up to facilitate quick passage. A theme is often selected that is woven throughout the entire area. Color, sound, lighting, and even scents are chosen to maximize customer responses. Often the result is bold, bright, and noisy, but this is intentional. The bright lights and sounds attract attention, as does the general theme. However, although these strong attributes are used to entice the customer into the play area, softer hues, tones, and muted sounds are used further into the casino. This helps to keep the customer comfortable and continuing to gamble. If this change is not made, customers can easily become overwhelmed by the excessive noise and lighting, at which point they may leave the playing area.

The table games are arranged in what is called a pit. A pit will generally have as few as two and as many as eight tables. The tables are arranged in a

Slot machines account for 60 to 70 percent of the wins in many casinos. © 2011 by Richard Goldberg. Used under license of Shutterstock, Inc.

circle. Customers are kept to the outside of the circle. This outside area is called the playing area. Dealers, supervisors, and other support staff such as security are the only people permitted inside this circle of tables. This is primarily for security reasons so that the casino can effectively manage the cash as well as the integrity of the games.

The table games are generally located well inside the casino. Slot machines are placed near the entries to attract players. Gamblers must walk past them when desiring to play at the table games. The slot machines act as tempting devices to all customers passing by them.

A large cashier's office will be typically located either in the rear or along the side of the casino floor area. This office is referred to as the "cage" because of the iron bars placed along the front side of the office to separate customers from cashier employees. These bars are important security features to help protect the large sums of cash inside the cage. The primary function of the cage is to act as an intermediary between customers and employees inside the casino playing area and the accounting office in the back of the house. Employees in the cage will exchange cash and house chips for customers, establish credit for qualified players, manage debt collection activities, and provide the table games with sufficient cash reserves to operate.

Many casinos will also provide small cashier kiosks scattered about inside the casino play area. These kiosks are for customer convenience and can provide limited service transactions such as exchanging cash for chips.

Back of the House

The back of the casino houses the support departments, including accounting, security, human resources, marketing, and the general administrative offices. Accounting and security play key roles in the daily operation of the casino.

Accounting

The accounting department manages the immense cash holdings that flow through the casino. Virtually all transactions within the casino are made with cash. Cash is exchanged for casino chips at the cashier cage and at table games. Cash is used to gamble in slot machines. A dedicated collection box is provided for each gaming machine or table. This "drop box" is carefully labeled to record the shift and the device from which it came.

The drop boxes are collected from the casino floor by special teams of three people made up of staff from security and either the slots department or the table games department. The boxes are delivered to the counting room that is located in the back of the house. This special room is carefully monitored and protected. The cash from each device is counted and recorded so that the productivity of each game can be monitored. Counting room employees verify the count, double-checking the work of others. These employees wear special clothing designed to prevent the accidental or intentional loss of cash. Access to this room is extremely limited, even to other managers!

This department is also responsible for the standard accounting activities of any business such as payroll, accounts payable, accounts receivable, and collections. These functions are performed for the casino and any other support departments such as gift shops, restaurants, and hotels if they are owned and operated by the casino.

Surveillance and Security

These two departments have the responsibility for the surveillance of the gaming areas as well as the general safety and security of the casino property. They are separate departments to increase the protection of the business. Surveillance protects the games and uses the latest in high-resolution video cameras and computer technology to monitor all gaming activities. Each table game has a camera mounted directly over the playing area so that all transactions can be observed. Cameras also carefully monitor each section of slot machines. With the advent of digital cameras, these images can be readily stored in computer format on disk drives. This reduces the bulky storage and retrieval problems associated with videotape. It also greatly reduces the surveillance cost.

Specially trained employees monitor the video images on a 24-hour basis. Often, these employees are ex-cheaters who have been recruited to watch other gamblers that may be cheating. These employees are required to sit in darkened rooms staring at video screens for eight-hour shifts. It takes a unique personality to do well at this job.

Before the advent of high-resolution video cameras, casinos had built "catwalks" into the ceilings over the gambling area. One-way mirrors were built into the ceiling so that personnel walking above the ceiling over these catwalks could observe players as they gambled. The mirrors were often incorporated into the casino design, making them less noticeable by patrons. However, the advent of the high-tech computers and digital cameras has made catwalks unnecessary in the modern casino. Uniformed security personnel will periodically patrol the playing areas. Their presence can be a comfort to customers and a clear warning to criminals. In addition, surveillance personnel will sometimes dress in plain clothing to mingle unobtrusively with gamblers. This aids in the identification of problems before they escalate into disruptive events.

The security department is responsible for the safety and welfare of customers and employees throughout the entire facility. They focus on the physical assets of the casino rather than the games. Security patrols often walk the perimeter of the casino and throughout the hotel, restaurants, and shops to observe customer and employee behavior firsthand. Cameras are also used to monitor these areas. Their uniformed presence is frequently enough incentive to discourage crime.

Other Business Support Departments

As with other hospitality businesses, casinos require the use of human resources, marketing, and general administrative departments. The casino is labor intensive, so the human resources staff plays a major role in the hiring and training of workers necessary to operate the casino. Given the large increase in the number of casinos around the country and competition for the gambler, casino marketing departments have strengthened their efforts to attract and keep customers. Managing the entire operation requires a top management team to coordinate and oversee everything. The general office staff typically includes the casino manager, assistant casino managers to supervise the evening and late night operations, and support staff to process paperwork and answer telephones.

Management and Casino Careers

Lifelong careers can be built in the casino industry. There are many entry-level positions in the restaurants, hotels, and shops. However, to create a career in the gaming industry, the vast majority of people begin as a dealer and work their way up through the ranks. The casino career ladder leads into management positions such as pit boss, shift supervisor, and casino manager. It has been a long-standing tradition within the casino industry that to move up the career ladder, an employee must start as a dealer so that they truly learn the integral elements of the world of casinos. However, this attitude is slowly changing. The need for professional managers with subject matter expertise, such as marketing and human resources, is becoming better understood.

To become a dealer, a potential employee must attend a dealer school and become qualified to deal prior to applying for a dealer position with a casino. This is a standard industry requirement. The casinos do not train their own employees to become basic dealers. Even employees who work in a different part of the organization must attend external dealer schools if they want to become a dealer. Once certified, the casinos then spend their time training the dealers in the particular approaches they use.

Employees can become members of the slots department without dealer certification. Positions in this department include the slot hostess, slot cashier, and slot machine maintenance. The slot hostess and slot cashier positions are entry-level positions that require only a small amount of training. The hostess greets slot machine players and offers them beverages and helps to keep the playing area clean and tidy. The slot cashier walks about the slots playing area so

A casino dealer could possibly work his or her way up to a pit boss. © 2011 by Svetlana Larina. Used under license of Shutterstock, Inc.

that customers can conveniently exchange dollar bills for coins. The maintenance staff is responsible for the repair and upkeep of the slot machines. They handle both the routine maintenance as well as respond to customers who have an immediate problem with a machine while gambling. Although these positions are on the casino floor, these workers cannot become dealers without earning the outside certification provided by dealer schools. Employees of the slots department are often considered the lowest-ranking employees within the casino.

Dealers also have their internal ranking order. Blackjack, or 21, is considered the simplest table game. Therefore, new dealers are assigned to this game. When a dealer has more experience, they may then be moved to more complex games such as roulette and the variations of poker such as Caribbean Stud and Pai Gow. The game that requires the most skill is craps because of the complexity of bets and payouts as well as the pressures of managing a crowd of excited players. Craps dealers have much more status within the dealer ranks. Because of the sophisticated image and high-stakes betting developed for baccarat that attracts premium players, only the most polished and experienced dealers are assigned to this game. These dealers are often considered at the top of the dealer status ranks.

Once a dealer becomes highly experienced, he or she may be promoted to become a pit boss. The pit boss manages a group of dealers. The next step is shift supervisor. Because the casinos often do not close their doors, three shifts each day are usually necessary to staff the playing areas. Therefore, shifts of workers are needed for each job level. A shift supervisor oversees all gaming operations that happen on that particular shift.

Coordinating and managing all casino operations is the responsibility of the casino manager. The shift supervisors report to this position. In the past, the casino manager had the authority and responsibility for the entire operation, including the hotel and food service. In more recent times, that has changed. Today, the casino manager is primarily responsible for the gaming areas of the business. Other top-level managers are responsible for the hotel, restaurants, shops, and entertainment departments. Although at some casinos, these other department managers report to the casino manager, more and more these area managers all report to a central administration that has as a chief operating officer (COO) who oversees the entire operation.

Gambling Outside the Casino

Sports Betting

Sports are extremely popular in the United States and so is the sport of betting on athletic games. This includes horse and dog racing as well as college and professional sports such as football, basketball, and baseball. Unfortunately for most bettors, betting on sporting events is only legal in four states: Delaware, Montana, Nevada, and Oregon. Other states have discussed this issue, but none have permitted it to date. Delaware is the most recent, with their state Supreme Court clearing the way of constitutional issues in May 2009 (NBC Sports, 2009).

Casinos in other states do attempt to cater to customers interested in betting on sporting events. They often provide a dedicated area within the casino that provides gamblers with information on the sporting events and the odds on the outcomes and other features of the games. Although these other casinos cannot accept sport bets, they can provide their customers with links to booking agents (bookies) in the other states that can accept the wagers.

Internet Gambling

Internet casinos have emerged over the past decade as the Internet has grown in use. American casino firms would like to take advantage of this technological development but may not. Under existing U.S. law, gambling on the Internet is illegal. Therefore, firms that offer Internet gaming may not be based in the United States.

The federal law extends to the player. It is technically illegal for anyone in the United States to place a wager on the Web. However, practicalities make it extremely difficult and costly to apprehend the individual gambler. Although the technology exists to trace an illegal bet back to the computer where it was entered, it is very difficult for the law to prove who was sitting at the keyboard placing the bet. It could be a minor who cannot legally bet or be responsible for debts incurred. It may not necessarily be the owner of the computer terminal.

Prosecuting the individual gambler does nothing to stop the availability of Web-based gambling opportunities. Many of the firms that offer Internet gaming are located offshore in different Caribbean nations. For example, Antigua has established a very gaming-friendly environment. Although they do generally investigate the firms wishing to offer this service, they do not have a formal gaming commission that regulates the operation of the games themselves.

This situation makes it difficult for customers to know that the game they are playing is fair. In U.S. land-based casinos, state regulatory agencies monitor the games and help ensure they operated fairly. Online players have no such assurances, as there is little or no regulatory oversight.

Further, online players cannot be certain the Internet casino will honor their winnings. Credit cards are the most common form of establishing credit with an online casino (although the U.S. government has worked with the major American credit card issuers to stop the use of credit cards for bets by having them refuse to accept the transactions). Using this credit card method, it is very easy for the casino to receive the money for the bets placed. However, the casino firms do not often automatically return winnings back to the credit card. Instead, they establish policies that they will send large winnings directly to players. The player must then trust that the Internet casino will follow through on that promise.

If the winnings are not returned, the gambler has little or no legal recourse—especially if they reside in the United States—as the initial betting transaction is viewed as illegal. Furthermore, it may be difficult for the player to determine where the Web-based casino is located if they wish to contact them directly or if they wish to pursue legal action. This situation makes gambling on the Internet very risky for players.

The Future of Gaming

The future forecast for gaming is one of continued institutionalization. The gaming industry will suffer the usual ebb and flow cycles that all industries experience. The international dimension of modern commerce—especially the travel industry—will ensure a steady supply of customers. Further, governments have come to rely on the tax revenues of lotteries and casinos as well as the increases in local employment. Rather than face the daunting prospect of lost revenues and unemployment, states will continue to support the casino industry. Any proposed gaming regulation would be crafted with care as it will directly affect state coffers.

Undoubtedly, there will be some areas of withdrawal from the gaming industry. As scandals emerge, there will be a call for a reduction or distancing from gaming. State lotteries may be adjusted or eliminated, and casinos may be more tightly controlled. Riverboat casinos may be banned from certain ports or states. The concept of NIMBY (not in my back yard) will certainly continue as an argument against the industry. However, with entire communities supporting gaming, it is unlikely there would ever be a complete withdrawal. Las Vegas, Reno, and Atlantic City have limited other commerce of significance to sustain themselves without the gaming industry. If there is any general reduction in gaming across the country, these specialized communities will continue to operate. Gaming may, at the very least, become a geographic niche service, as it was from the 1930s through the 1970s.

Gambling in virtual casinos on the Internet will not disappear. Governments cannot completely control the operation or the content of the Web. Therefore, gambling in virtual casinos will continue to be widely available regardless of land-based casinos and any government regulation.

In conclusion, this recent surge in gambling popularity will not end in full prohibition as earlier waves of gaming have. It may dissipate to low levels of interest and use by society, but it will never completely disappear. Social acceptance may oscillate, but with softer peaks and valleys. There are simply too many jobs, dollars, and customers involved.

RESOURCES

References

Arthur Anderson LLP. (1996). *Casino gambling in America: The economic impacts.* Washington, DC: American Gaming Association.

Associated Press (Boston). (1999, March 17). Reilly opposes casino gambling.

ClearLead, Inc. (2010). Gambling Addiction—Gambling Addiction Statistics. Retrieved July 26, 2010, from http://www.clearleadinc.com/site/gambling-addiction.html

Daily Hampshire Gazette. (1998, September 10). Foxwoods pays $58 million in July. p. B1.

Elder, R. W. (1990). Opening the Mirage: The human-resources challenge. *Cornell HRA Quarterly, 31*(2), 24–31.

Ettis, M. (1997). Personal comments given during a private casino tour to a student group at the Mohegan Sun Casino, Ledyard, CT.

Hashimoto, K. (1998). Cripple Creek, Colorado. In K. Hashimoto, S. F. Kline & G. Fenich (Eds.), *Casino management: Past·present·future* (p. 11). Dubuque, IA: Kendall Hunt.

Heneghan, D. (1994, March 20). Casinos generate more than $1b in state economy. *Atlantic Free Press,* p. A1.

Lasvegas.com. (1999). Hotel-casino guide. http://lasvegas.com/travel/hotels

Michael Evans Group. (1996). *A study of the economic impact of the gaming industry through 2005.* Reno: I.G.T.

NBC Sports. Delaware Supreme Court gives OK to sports betting. (2009). Retrieved July 26, 2010, from http://nbcsports.msnbc.com/id/30982541/

Roberts, C., & Fladmoe-Lindquist, K. (1999). *Hypercompetition and mega-casinos.* Unpublished manuscript, University of Massachusetts, Department of Hotel, Restaurant and Travel Administration.

Rose, I. N. (1996). The rise and fall of the third wave: Gambling will be outlawed in forty years. In K. Hashimoto, S. F. Kline & G. Fenich (Eds.), *Casino management for the 90's* (pp. 491–501). Dubuque, IA: Kendall Hunt.

Sylvester, K. (1992). Casinomania. In K. Hashimoto, S. F. Kline & G. Fenich (Eds.), *Casino management: Past·present·future* (pp. 428–432). Dubuque, IA: Kendall Hunt.

Review Questions

CHAPTER 30

1. Discuss why public acceptance of gaming is higher in today's society than it has been historically in earlier decades.

2. Describe at least three specific characteristics of a casino's Front of the House layout and design. What is the underlying or primary purpose of the FOH casino design?

3. Within a casino's layout and design, where are the slot machines usually placed? Why?

4. What is unique about the Accounting Department within a casino/lodging property compared to the same department in other large hotel properties?

5. Describe the traditional career path into management of a casino. Is it the same today? If not, how does it differ?

6. Discuss Internet gambling. What specific criteria must exist for it to be legal? (i.e., location, player's age, etc.)

LEARNING OBJECTIVES

- Discuss benefits of cruising.
- Explain what is included in the cost of a cruise.
- Name two possible disadvantages of cruising.
- Generalize about cruise line clientele.
- Name factors that determine the cost of a cruise.

CHAPTER OUTLINE

The Cruise Industry
Changes in Cruising
The Ship Itself
   Cabins
Types of Cruise Lines
The Major Cruise Lines
Career Opportunities

KEY TERMS

Berth
Bridge
Bow
Cabin
CLIA
Deck plan
Flag of convenience

Galley
Gross registered tonnage
Purser
Space ratio
Stabilizer
Stern
Tender

Cruise Ships

Chris DeSessa, Johnson & Wales University

The Cruise Industry

Welcome aboard to the wonderful world of cruising. The cruise industry is set to reach 14 million passengers annually by 2011. The cruise industry's growth is also reflected in its expanding guest capacity. Although less than 18 percent of North Americans have ever cruised, the market generates nearly $19 billion in revenue and contributes almost $32 billion to the U.S. economy. Nearly 40 new ships were built in the 1980s, and during the 1990s, nearly 80 new ships debuted. Today, 88 new ships will have been introduced since 2000. There are plans to build 28 new ships between 2009 and 2012. Because more huge ships are being built, the competition between cruise lines is very competitive. However, because 83 percent of U.S. adults have never taken a cruise vacation, there remains an enormous untapped market.

There are many reasons for the popularity of cruises. Historically, cruise ships were for people to sit in a deck chair and eat 24 hours a day. Now, you can book a fitness cruise with spa treatments, healthy dietary cuisine, and exercise programs for everyone. Cruise lines continue to build new ships with more shopping, health clubs, casinos, and restaurants. In addition, cruise companies have expanded their choice of itineraries to include more exotic ports of call and have introduced more innovative onboard facilities such as cybercafes, multiple themed restaurants, and state-of-the-art meeting facilities to attract a more diverse clientele. So, for many, a cruise represents a vacation that allows one to do as little or as much as he/she wants.

Not all boats are large Carnival cruises that carry 3,000 people. Some are small boats that sleep four or six people, which can go up rivers to see places one cannot get to by any other means of transportation. For example, you can go to Amsterdam and hop on a schooner for 4 to 6 people and stop to check out the tulip fields, historic cities, and museums from the water. Stopping at a cheese farm that can only be reached by canal is a tasty change of pace. You can watch as the captain pays tolls by putting the money in a wooden shoe that swings out from the tollbooth operator. There are actually stoplights at major intersections, and you can watch as the crew dismantles the steering cabin to get under a short bridge. If you get bored, you can ride a bike along the canal paths. And then there are always the gourmet dinners with short educational sessions tasting different cheeses, ports, and wines. There is a cruise for every budget, age group, eating habit, and activity level. It is easy to see why a cruise is the choice for many vacationers.

Americans love to cruise. They represent about 70 percent of the people who take cruise vacations. For many, a cruise represents both value and piece of mind. Unlike a land-based vacation, the hassles of paying for meals and entertainment and deciding where to eat are eliminated. A cruise allows passengers to pack and unpack once. There is security in knowing that everything is taken care of and no money for necessities is needed once you are on the boat. On board the problem of carrying money is eliminated because on board one is part of the "cashless society," which allows the passenger to sign for

For many vacationers, a cruise represents both value and peace of mind. © 2011 by Bryan Busovicki. Used under license of Shutterstock, Inc.

extra expenses. You can relax and enjoy yourself. In addition, because there are a lot of people on the boat, you can meet new friends, have drinks, party, and know that you are steps away from your bed when it is over. The price of the cruise includes one's accommodations, all meals and in-between snacks, entertainment, lectures, social functions, movies, and the use of a ship's facilities, including entry into the casino and fitness centers. Sometimes the price also includes the price of flights to the ship and transfers (transportation between airport or hotel and the cruise port).

What is not included in the price of a cruise? Some people have the misconception that everything is included in the price. Therefore, it is important to clarify in advance what is not included. With a little common sense, most of these are obvious. Alcoholic beverages and gambling debts are not included. In addition, the following are not included in the price of a cruise: shopping, liquor, photos, health spas, Internet cafes, tipping (on some ships), phone calls, seasickness inoculations, and shore excursions.

Changes in Cruising

The concept of cruising has changed dramatically over the years. Not so long ago cruising was for the very rich or very poor. Cruise ships were divided into classes. Many of our ancestors came to America via cruise ships. Their experiences were less than joyful because they were in the part of the ship known as "steerage," which was little better than bare-bones accommodations. They were housed at the bottom of the boat with no windows or air. Their recreation deck was the only place they could get sun. The movie Titanic with Leonardo DiCaprio portrayed what it was like in steerage. It also portrayed the problem if something happened to the ship, but it did allow poor people to be able to cross the ocean. Of course, the very rich could cross the oceans in elegance cruising in first class accommodations on such famous ships as the *SS France, Queen Mary,* and the ships of the White Star Line.

Many of the early cruises were for transportation. Before airplanes, cruise ships were the main method of crossing from one continent to another. The cruise could be luxurious, but it was still basically walking around the deck, sitting in lounge chairs, and eating. So up until the 1960s, recreational cruising was considered a vacation option for senior citizens. That all changed with the creation of the hit television series *The Love Boat.* Television viewers then saw cruising as a getaway to exotic ports such as Acapulco, where romance filled the air, and passengers were pampered with dinners with the captain and adventures with fellow passengers. The series portrayed passengers as young or young at heart, adventuresome, and available. Certainly, a more exciting image was created.

Another important event that changed the image of cruising was when Carnival Cruise Lines introduced the idea of a cruise ship as a destination in itself with its introduction of "The Fun Ships." The cruise ship itself was the focal point of activities with myriad scheduled fun activities from morning until night. The ships contained everything that a small city would. A passenger can do as little or as much as he/she wants on a cruise. Most ships have pools, basketball and volleyball courts, and jogging tracks. Or, people could go rock climbing, golfing, skating, or skeet shooting. You can even go surfing in a surfing pool. On the quieter side, one can go to nightclubs, libraries, or art and photo galleries. Typically a passenger will have an opportunity to attend a Broadway-type production before or after dinner. Another option could be to attend a first run-movie in the ship's movie theatre.

The cruise lines have also introduced innovative onboard amenities and facilities, including cell phone access, Internet cafes and wireless fidelity (Wi-fi) zones, multiroom villas, and multiple themed restaurants. They could get a massage or facial at the spa or work out at a state-of-the-art health club. Clients can take a tour of the galley (kitchen) or the bridge (area where the captain and crew navigate the ship). Or, as before, they could sit in a lounge chair and soak up the sun with occasional dips in the pool. These are all included in the price of a cruise.

The Ship Itself

Ships come in various sizes. The modern cruise ship can be the height of a 10-story building and cover the space of three football fields. Currently the world's largest ship, *Royal Caribbean International's Independence of the Seas,* can accommodate 6,400 passengers. Some clients prefer large ships because of the many amenities. Others prefer the intimacy of a smaller ship. The size of a cruise ship is registered in gross tonnage (GRT). Some large ships cannot pull into ports, so passengers must be ferried to shore.

A tender is a smaller boat that will ferry passengers from the larger ship to shore. Some of the tenders can hold more than 400 passengers.

Cabins

Throughout the trip passengers will rest and relax in your cabin, sometimes called a stateroom. The cost of a cruise also depends on the location, size, and special amenities of the cabin. Cabins that have a porthole or window are referred to as outside or exterior cabins. These are more expensive. Some cabins have a porch or veranda to enjoy the scenery. Inside or interior cabins do not have a porthole or window. Beds on a cruise ship are referred to as berths. One can decide between king, queen, and twin. Many cabins have bunk bed type accommodations, which are referred to as upper/lower berths, which are perfect for accommodating children on a cruise.

On modern ships all passenger cabins are above the water line. Only the crew's quarters are below the water line. Other considerations that may affect the choice of a cabin may be proximity to elevators, stairs, and public areas and the propensity for seasickness. Like any hotel, when an elevator or stairs is next door, it is can be noisy, as people constantly are on the move.

A deck plan is a chart that displays the location of cabins and public rooms. With larger ships, you have a choice of levels of floors, depending on how close to the activities one wants to be. Each deck on a ship is identified by a name or letter. Normally the higher the deck, the more expensive the cabin. Also cabins in the middle of the ship (amidship) are more expensive. These are more preferable to passengers who are prone to seasickness because there is less ship movement in the middle of a ship. Modern-day cruise ships have winglike projections called stabilizers that are used in rough seas.

Types of Cruise Lines

The Cruise Lines International Association (CLIA) is the world's premier cruise marketing and training association comprising 21 major cruise lines and 16,500 travel agencies. Its goal is promoting the desirability, diversity, and high value of the cruise vacation experience. CLIA divides the cruise lines into three types: contemporary, luxury, and premium, depending on quality, service, amenities, and itineraries. Contemporary brands are geared to

FIGURE 31.1 The CARNIVAL DREAM Team—Carnival Cruises

Sunrise: 6:53 am • Sunset: 6:10 pm

SEA DAY

FRIDAY, OCTOBER 15, 2010

FOR YOUR INFORMATION

MEDICAL CENTER   Deck 0, Fwd
Phone: 4444   Emergencies: 911
Medical Center Hours
8:00am – 8:00pm
Doctor's Hours:
8:00am – 11:00am & 3:00pm – 6:00pm

SMOKING AREAS
Smoking is only permitted in Caliente club, Sams bar, outside ocean, plaza bar, deck 5 portside mid and Lido bar, deck 10 portside fwd & Aft. Smoking in the casino is limited and only permitted while playing at designated Slot Machines and Table Games. Cigars or Pipes are only permitted on the Lanai outside the Plaza Bar, Deck 5 Portside. Please note all Spa Suites are smoke free.

GUEST SERVICES
Feel free to visit us throughout your cruise for general information, questions, change or to report lost and found items. Open 24 hours Dream Atrium, 3 Fwd

SAIL & SIGN CARD®
You'll receive a printout of your purchases Saturday morning between 6:15am – 7:00am. If you have a cash deposit and have an outstanding balance or discrepancy, you must settle your account onboard at Guest Services tonight or tomorrow, 7:00am - 8:30am. Accounts with credit card deposit do not need to settle account

CARNIVAL'S SEASIDE THEATRE™
Live Morning Show with Josh   9:00am
Concert: U2: Vertigo   10:00am
Concert: Festival Express   5:00pm
Family Movie: How To Train the Dragon   6:15pm
Movie: Book of Eli   8:00pm & 10:15pm

Seaside Theatre™   Seaside Theatre, 10 Mid

ON AIR
Cruise Director Fun   Channel 5
Debarkation Information   Channel 6
Movie: Shine of Rainbows   Channel 22
Movie: Avatar   Channel 23

A SPECIAL THANK YOU
We sincerely hope that you have enjoyed every aspect of the service during your cruise. As a reminder, gratuities were posted to your Sail and Sign accounts. A special thanks for your gracious acknowledgement of your cabin and dining service teams. If you have enjoyed the Service and the fun in the dining room, it's thanks to your Maitre D'. Although your Maitre D' is not included in the posted amounts, it is customary to extend a gratuity. Envelopes have been provided for you in your stateroom
Maitre D' in the Scarlet Dining room is Ante
Maitre D' in the Crimson Dining room is Kris

PHONING HOME
Consult your stateroom directory for dialing instructions. Charges apply to all calls including 1-800 calling cards, credit cards and collect calls. $6.99 per minute to USA, Canada, Puerto Rico and Caribbean Islands. $9.99 per minute for international.

BOARDING PASSES
Don't stand in line, check in online, choose your seats and print your boarding passes in the Internet Café on deck 5. Please note the deadline to purchase any additional Internet minutes is tonight at 11pm. Time Plan minutes can be used until you disembark tomorrow. Printing is available for guests who wish to log on and print boarding passes. We wish you safe travels.

HELP US HELP YOU
The goal of all the Officers, Staff and Crew on board Dream is to provide you with a memorable and fun-filled vacation. If for any reason we have not met your expectations, please contact a Guest Services Associate at extension 7777. We welcome your feedback and will work to resolve any issue immediately.

CARNIVAL ONLINE
Stay in touch with the fun!
Follow us on Facebook.com/Carnival

DEBARKATION INFORMATION
For important debarkation information and procedures, please tune your stateroom TV to channel 7. There the Cruise Director will advise the fastest, easiest, and most efficient ways to disembark the Carnival Dream.

CARNIVAL WATERWORKS
Get ready to get soaked at our largest water park; every towel's worst nightmare. Fly down our twisty waterslides or make some splash art. Deck 12 Fwd 9:00am - 6:00pm

GROOVE FOR ST. JUDE™
Do good. Feel good. And help some kids – also good, right?
Grab your groove thang and sign up at Celebrations on Deck 5 for this special dance charity event taking place Friday. A $10 donation to St. Jude gets you a T-shirt and wristband. Help us save children's lives. Today at 4:30pm, Ocean Plaza.

OPEN TIMES

Fitness Center	6:00am - 10:00pm	Deck 12, Fwd
Midship Pool	7:00am - 10:00pm	Deck 10, Mid
Aft Pools	8:00am - 12:00am	Deck 10, Aft
Spa Cloud 9	8:00am until late	Deck 12, Fwd
Casino Slots	8:00am until late	Deck 5, Mid
Midship Whirlpool	9:00am -9:00pm	Deck 5
Lanai Whirlpools	9:00am - 12:00am	Deck 11, Mid
Lido Whirlpools Aft	9:00am - 12:00am	Deck 14, 15 Fwd
Serenity (Adults Only)	9:00am - 11:00pm	Deck 5, Aft
Photo Gallery	10:00am until late	Deck 5, Mid
Casino Tables	10:00am - 1:00pm	Deck 5, Aft
Future Cruise Desk	3:00pm - 10:00pm	Deck 5, Aft
Celebrations	9:30am -12:00pm	Deck 5, Fwd
	1:00pm - 6:00pm	Deck 5, Fwd
The Fun Shops—	7:00pm - 10:30pm	Deck 5, Fwd
Shore Excursions	9:00am - 11:30am	Deck 5, Fwd
	12:00pm - 1:30pm	Deck 3, Fwd
	4:00pm - 5:30pm	Deck 3, Fwd
Air Brush Artist	10:00am - 6:00pm	Deck 10, Mid
Art Gallery	5:00pm - 10:00pm	Deck 5, Mid

HELP US GREEN!FY! M/S Carnival Dream is certified by ISO14001 for the Environmental Management System. Please help us to Save Energy, Conserve Water & Reduce/Recycle Waste for a Sustainable Environment. For all environmental concerns, please contact 1-305-406-6863 (international), 1-888-290-5105 (North America), or 4ENV(4368) from your ship phone. Environmental Compliance web site: www.carnivalcompliance.com. "Carnival's goal is to be the industry leader in environmental excellence."

The CARNIVAL DREAM℠ Team

CAPTAIN: Carlo Queirolo   **CHIEF ENGINEER:** Antonio Colotti
HOTEL DIRECTOR: Donato Becce   **CRUISE DIRECTOR:** Josh Waltzman

Safety Message: Use cabin lights and keep the floor clear to prevent trip and falls.

RELAX & ENJOY A FUN DAY AT SEA

IMPORTANT:
Don't miss the last live morning show at 9:00am & be sure to get all of the debarkation information for tomorrow morning by watching channel 7 at some time today. It's not too late to sign up for the Groove for St. Jude with Josh.

BREAKFAST
5:30am - 10:30am	Continental	The Gathering, 10 Mid
7:30am - 10:30am	Lido Buffet	The Gathering, 10 Mid
8:00am - 10:00am	Open Seating	Scarlet Dining, 3 Aft
10:30am - 12:00pm	Late Risers	The Gathering, 10 Mid

LUNCH (Open Seating)
12:00pm - 1:30pm   Lunch   Scarlet Dining Room , 3 Aft

LUNCH
11:30am - 11:50pm	Deli	The Gathering, 10 Aft
12:00pm - 2:30pm	Lanai Bar-BQ	Lanai Deck 5, Mid
12:00pm - 2:30pm	Lunch	The Gathering, 10 Fwd & Aft
12:00pm - 2:30pm	Mongolian	The Gathering, 10 Aft
12:00pm - 2:30pm	Burrito Bar	The Gathering, 10 Aft
12:00pm - 2:30pm	Pasta Bar	The Gathering, 11 Aft
12:00pm - 2:30pm	Indian Tandoor	The Gathering, 10 Aft
12:00pm - 6:00pm	The Grill	The Gathering, 10 Fwd
3:00pm - 4:00pm	Tea Time	Crimson Dining Room, 3 Fwd

DINNER
Assigned Dining Guests
Scarlet Dining Room   Lobby 3 & 4 Aft
Crimson Dining Room   Lobby, 3 Fwd
Early Dining: 6:00pm   Late Dining: 8:15pm

Your Time Dining ™Guests
Allows you to dine at your leisure anytime between 5:45pm and 9:30pm   Crimson Dining Room, 4 Fwd

Tonight's dining room attire is **Cruise Casual**
Please Note: Gym or basketball shorts, flip-flops, bathing suit attire, cut-off jeans and men's sleeveless shirts are not allowed in the dining rooms.

ALTERNATIVE DINING
We are pleased to offer alternative dining venues with varied selections.

The Gathering		
6:00pm – 9:30pm		The Gathering, 10 Aft
The Wasabi Sushi Bar		
5:00pm – 8:15pm		Promenade , 5 Mid
Late Night Snacks		
11:30pm - 1:00am		The Gathering, 10 Aft

Open 24 Hours
Pizza Bar		The Gathering, 10 Fwd
Coffee, Tea & Ice Cream		The Gathering, 10 Aft
Room Service		Dial 8000

BEVERAGE SERVICE
You must be at least 21 years old to be served alcohol on board. Proper identification with birth date is required.

Today's Drink Special : "Ultimate Suntan"

Master Mixologist's Drink:
Tammy Kushner's Master Beverage, the "Tee Zee"

Margarita with Chips & Salsa
5:00pm – 8:15pm   Ocean Plaza, 5 Mid

Plaza Café
Latte, Cappuccino or Espresso. Treat yourself to a thick milkshake made-to-order or indulge with a fresh pastry.
7:00am - Midnight   Plaza Café, 5 Mid

CHEF'S ART™ STEAKHOUSE
How'd we create the ultimate steak experience? We combined a delicious steakhouse menu with our unique 'Carnival style'. USDA prime beef seasoned and charbroiled to fit your exact specifications, mouth-watering seafood entrées, gourmet appetizers and an extensive wine list. For reservations, call [1178].
There will be a fee of $30 per person.
5:30pm - 9:30pm   Chef's Art Steakhouse, 12 Aft

United States Department of Public Health has determined that eating uncooked or partially cooked poultry, meat, eggs or seafood may present a health risk to the consumer, particularly those who may be more vulnerable.

FIGURE 31.1 The CARNIVAL DREAM Team—Carnival Cruises (continued)

1. JOSH'S MORNING SHOW
Live TV Fun with Josh & George and your dedications!
9:00am ... Channel 6 & Seaside Theatre

2. GROOVE FOR ST. JUDE WITH JOSH
Do good. Feel good. And help some kids – also good, right? Grab your groove thang and sign up at Celebrations for this special dance event. A $10 donation to St. Jude gets you a T-shirt and wristband. Join your Cruise Director to celebrate your donations today!
4:30pm ... Ocean Plaza, 5 Mid

3. TOWEL FOLDING DEMONSTRATION
Like that warm, fluffy welcome in your stateroom? Join us for this fun interactive demonstration.
9:30am ... Dream Atrium, 3 Fwd

4. POWERBALL BINGO & MORE
Three sessions today with large cash prizes, multiple games and someone will win a 7 day cruise for 2.
11:00am $1199 Tax & Duty Free ... Lido Deck 10, Mid
3:45pm 5 Game Bingo ... Lido Deck 10, Mid
9:45pm "$5000 Powerball" ... Encore Theater, 3 Fwd

5. 60 SECONDS OR LESS
Join your Fun Patrol for some fast and furious fun with great prizes.
3:00pm ... Lido Deck 10, Mid

6. GLASS FIGURINE SALE
Hit up our glass figurine sale and find that perfect something to decorate your home. Pick up two nautically-inspired souvenirs for one low price.
10:00am - 11:30pm ... The Fun Shops, 5 Fwd

7. ELEMIS OXYDERMY FACIAL
Give your skin what it has been craving. Now you can fight lines, wrinkles, spots and get the radiant glow that's been eluding you. Let us pamper your skin with our new cutting-edge technology that brings Microdermabrasion and Oxygen together in one luxurious treatment. Book your appointment today!
8:00am - 10:00pm ... Cloud 9 Spa, 12 Fwd

8. WIN A CRUISE RAFFLE
Today during our three Bingo sessions grab a few tickets to hear you name called at 10:25pm and get ready to sail all over again!
10:25pm (Drawing) ... Encore Theater, 3 Fwd

9. WORK THAT BODY ART
Airbrush body art but afraid of the commitment? Airbrush body art applies in seconds, dries instantly and lasts up to 7 days! For more details ask our Tattoo Artist.
10:00am - 6:00pm ... Lido Deck, 10 Mid

10. GRAND FINALE ART AUCTION!
Join us for our last afternoon of artwork and prizes. You'll find the work of some of the most collected artists, as well as raffles and giveaways. So grab a glass of complimentary champagne with one hand and cross the fingers of your other hand – you never know, you could win a work of art!
1:00pm ... Art Gallery, 5 Aft

GET YOUR GROOVE ON

COOL MUSIC WITH IMPRESSIONS
11:45am – 1:00pm, 2:00pm – 5:00pm ... Lido, 10 Mid

COCKTAIL PIANO WITH LAURA
2:00pm – 3:00pm ... Dream Atrium, 3 Fwd
5:00pm – 6:00pm ... Sam's Bar, 5 Aft
7:00pm – 8:30pm ... Sam's Bar, 5 Aft

ROMANTIC MUSIC WITH MUSIC NOTE
5:00pm – 6:00pm ... Dream Atrium, 3 Fwd
7:15pm – 8:15pm ... Dream Atrium, 3 Fwd
9:30pm – 10:30pm ... Dream Atrium, 3 Fwd
11:15pm – 12:15pm ... Dream Atrium, 3 Fwd

FUN MUSIC WITH OSCAR
5:30pm – 8:30pm ... Jackpot Casino, 5 Fwd
7:30pm – 8:30pm ... Jackpot Casino, 5 Fwd
9:15pm – 12:15am ... Jackpot Casino, 5 Fwd

KARAOKE PARTY WITH VITALII
5:00pm – 7:00pm ... The Song, 5 Aft

FUN FAREWELL PARTY WITH THE BAND
5:00pm – 6:00pm ... Burgundy Lounge, 5 Aft

LATIN FIESTA WITH MAMBO KINGS
3:45pm – 12:30am ... The Song, 5 Aft

PARTY TUNES WITH CELEBRATION
8:30pm – 12:30am ... Ocean Plaza, 5 Mid

SING-ALONG WITH JASON
8:30pm – Late ... Sam's Bar, 5 Aft

CALIENTE CLUB OPENS WITH DJ CLYDE
5:00pm Motown Hour ... Caliente Club, 5 Aft
10:00pm – Late ... Caliente Club, 5 Aft

HIT THE JACKPOT

SLOT TOURNAMENT
It's all in the wrist! Land on the right real combinations and you could win yourself some cash and a fancy new title in our slot tournament. Must be at least 18 years of age to participate. +
12:00pm – 3:00pm ... Jackpot Casino, 5 Mid

IMPORTANT REMINDER - SLOT PLAYERS
Cash out remaining funds from your slot machine player bank from the cashier's desk tonight before the casino closes. POKER PLAYERS- Cash out your poker accounts from the cashier's desk before the casino closes tonight.

CARNIVAL YOUTH EXPERIENCE
Come by for fun activities, games, & more!

FUN FORCE SHOW
4:15pm (ages 2–11) ... Encore Theater, 3 Fwd

GLOW STICK AFTER PARTY
11:00pm (ages 12–14) ... Circle C, 4 Aft

SIGN YOUR BFF'S T-SHIRT
10:00pm (ages 15–17) ... Club O, 4 Aft

CARNIVAL LEGENDS
Hosted by your Cruise Director Josh
Starring:
Your Fellow Guests
and the Carnival Dream Dancers & Vocal Dynamics Of Simone Cattalano & Desmond Dansby
Live Music By Eddie C. & The Dream Showband
10:30pm One Show Only! ... Encore Theater 3 Fwd

GET IN ON THE ACT

GROOVE FOR ST. JUDE WITH JOSH
Do good. Feel good. And help some kids – also good, right? Grab your groove thang and sign up at Celebrations for this special dance event. A $10 donation to St. Jude gets you a T-shirt and wristband. Join your Cruise Director to celebrate your donations today!
4:30pm ... Ocean Plaza, 5 Mid

THE GENDER SHOWDOWN
Come see who the dominant gender is going to be! Males vs. Females! Must be 18 or older.
8:15pm ... Encore Theater, 3 Fwd

PLAN ON IT

DEBARKATION INFORMATION
For important debarkation information and procedures, please tune your stateroom TV to channel 7. There, your Cruise Director, Josh, will tell you the fastest, easiest, and most efficient ways to disembark the Carnival Dream.
Through-out the Day ... Channel 7 on your stateroom TV

BOARDING PASSES
Don't stand in line, check in online, choose your seats and print your boarding passes in the Internet Café on deck 5. Please note the deadline to purchase any additional Internet minutes is tonight at 11pm. Time Plan minutes can be used until you disembark tomorrow. Printing is available for guests who wish to log on and print boarding passes. We wish you safe travels.

FUN SHIP FILMS
Take your entire cruise home with you on a professional edited DVD! Show everyone the amazing time you had on the Fun Ship Carnival Dream as you relive highlights of your cruise. Order at the Photo Gallery on Deck 4, Fwd.
10:00am -11:00pm ... The Gallery, 4 Fwd

LOYALTY & CRUISE VACATIONS
Today is the last day to sign up for your Future Cruise Certificate. Place $100 deposit towards your next cruise and have 4 years to pick your sail date & destination. You will receive an onboard credit up to $200 on your next cruise! Don't miss out on this exclusive onboard promotion.
10:00am –1:00pm & 3:00pm - 10:00pm ... Promenade, 5 Aft

PUNCHLINER COMEDY CLUB
We are now offering more comedy than ever before!
PG Rated (All Ages) Comedy Specials
7:30pm - Alyn Ball, 8:30pm - Michael Macy
R-Rated (Adults Only, 18 Yrs. +) Comedy Specials
9:45pm - Alyn Ball, 11:00pm - Michael Macy
12:00am - Alyn Ball
... Burgundy Lounge, 5 Aft
Due to copyright laws, videotaping & photography are strictly prohibited.

SHOP TO IT

MIX & MATCH LAST DAY SPECIAL
Choose two of the following and save today (50 mins)
Back Massage, Scalp Massage, Mini-Facial, Foot & Ankle Massage, Hot Stones Massage.
8:00am-10:00pm ... Cloud 9 Spa, 12 Fwd

LAST CHANCE
It's your last chance to purchase the portraits you've taken all cruise. Great deals on canvases and wallet size photos. Share those memories with your friends and family back home.
9:00am –11:00pm ... The Gallery, 4 Fwd

GRAND FINALE ART AUCTION
This is it; your last chance to play games, win prizes, bid on art and drink complimentary champagne. Does that sound like something you'd want to miss? Didn't think so.
1:00pm ... Art Gallery, 5 Aft

THE FUN SHOPS
Today is your final chance for Tax and Duty Free Shopping at it's best. Today the shops have specials on everything from T-shirts to Diamonds. Don't miss the watch blowout at 4:00pm.
9:00am - 11:30pm ... Fun Shops, 5 Fwd

FRIDAY, OCTOBER 15, 2010

MORNING
7:00am Sunrise Stretch ... Cloud 9 Spa, 12 Fwd
7:30am Total Body Workout ... Cloud 9 Spa, 12 Fwd
8:00am Yoga + ... Cloud 9 Spa, 12 Fwd
9:00am Morning Show Show with Josh... ... Ch 6 & Seaside Theatre
Tour D9 Spa + ... Cloud 9 Spa, 12 Fwd
9:30am Daily Puzzle Challenge ... Ocean Plaza, 5 Mid
Towel Folding demo ... Dream Atrium, 3 Fwd
10:00am Good Morning Trivia. ... Ocean Plaza, 5 Mid
Dirtox for health & weight loss ... Cloud 9 Spa, 12 Fwd
Nike Golf Demo. ... Lido, 10 Mid
Air Brush Artist 'til 6pm ... Promenade, 5 Aft
Future Cruise Desk Opens 'til 1pm... ... Rendezvous, 4 Fwd
Friends of Bill W./ Jimmy K meet ... Dream Atrium, 3 Fwd
10:15am Bean Bag Toss. ... Deck 14, Aft
10:30am Volleyball Tournament ... Deck 14, Aft
11:00am $1199 Tax & Duty Free Bingo + ... Lido Deck 10, Mid
Pool & Deck Games
Gams of the Sea Giveaway ... Cloud 9 Spa, 12 Fwd
Puffy Eyes/Magic make-up Seminar... ... Pageturner, 4 Fwd
Herbal Remedies
11:30am Bridge Players Meet
Live Champagne Art Auction. ... Art Gallery, 5 Aft
11:45am General Knowledge Trivia. ... Ocean Plaza, 5 Mid
Music with Impressions ... Lido, 10 Mid
Look 10 years younger in 10 Minutes. ... Cloud 9 Spa, 12 Fwd

AFTERNOON
12:00pm Slot Tournament+ ... Jackpot Casino, 5 Fwd
Open Scrapbooking Session ... Ocean Plaza, 5 Mid
1:00pm Super Trivia Final Round. ... Ocean Plaza, 5 Mid
Pool & Deck Games ... Lido, 10 Mid
Bridge Players Meet ... Art Gallery, 5 Aft
Live Champagne Art Auction ... Art Gallery, 5 Aft
1:30pm Big Screen Musical Trivia Fun. ... Lido, 10 Mid
Golf Lessons Available until 4:00pm+ ... Deck 14, Aft
2:00pm Win, Lose or Draw ... Ocean Plaza, 5 Mid
No Limit Texas Hold'em + ... Jackpot Casino, 5 Fwd
Secrets to a flatter stomach ... Cloud 9 Spa, 12 Fwd
Music with Impressions ... Lido, 10 Mid
2:45pm Afternoon Trivia & Charades. ... Ocean Plaza, 5 Mid
3:00pm 60 Seconds or Less ... Lido Deck 10, Mid
... Crimson Dining Room, 3 Fwd
Future Cruise Desk Opens 'til 10pm ... Promenade, 5 Aft
3:15pm Cartoon Trivia. ... Ocean Plaza, 5 Mid
3:30pm Watch Sale & Giveaway. ... Fun Shops, 5 Fwd
3:45pm 5 Games of Bingo + ... Lido Deck 10, Mid
Slot Tournament Finals. ... Jackpot Casino, 5 Fwd
4:00pm Adult Dodgeball ... Deck 14, Aft
4:15pm Fun Force Kids Dance Show. ... Encore Theater, 3 Fwd
4:30pm Groove for St. Jude with Josh ... Ocean Plaza, 5 Mid

EVENING
5:00pm Fun Farewell Party ... Burgundy Lounge, 5 Aft
Music for Dancing ... Dream Atrium, 3 Fwd
Nike Golf Sale ... Shore Excursions, 5 Fwd
Karaoke time ... The Song, 5 Aft
5:30pm Friends of Dorothy Meet (GLBT) ... Ocean Plaza, 5 Mid
Fun music with Oscar ... Jackpot Casino, 5 Fwd
7:15pm Music for Dancing ... Dream Atrium, 3 Fwd
7:30pm PG Comedy Show. ... Burgundy Lounge, 5 Aft
Fun music with Oscar ... Jackpot Casino, 5 Fwd
8:15pm The Gender Showdown ... Encore Theater, 3 Fwd
8:30pm PG Comedy Show. ... Burgundy Lounge, 5 Aft
Sing along with Jason. ... Sam's Bar, 5 Aft
Party Tunes with Celebration. ... Ocean Plaza, 5 Mid
9:00pm Latin Fiesta with Mambo Kings ... The Song, 5 Aft
No Limit Texas Hold'em + ... Jackpot Casino, 5 Fwd
9:30pm Music for Dancing ... Dream Atrium, 3 Fwd
9:45pm $5000 Powerball Bingo+ ... Encore Theater, 3 Fwd
Uncensored Comedy show. ... Burgundy Lounge, 5 Aft
10:25pm Cruise Raffle Winner Announced. ... Encore Theater, 3 Fwd
Cash Craze Raffle Winner. ... Encore Theater, 3 Fwd
Carnival Colors Winner. ... Encore Theater, 3 Fwd
10:30pm Carnival Legends Showtime. ... Ocean Plaza, 5 Mid
11:00pm Uncensored Comedy ... Burgundy Lounge, 5 Aft
No Limit Texas Hold'em+ ... Jackpot Casino, 5 Fwd
11:15pm Music for Dancing ... Dream Atrium, 3 Fwd
12:00am Uncensored Comedy show. ... Burgundy Lounge, 5 Aft

+ Fees apply

FIGURE **31.2 Deck Plans and Ship Profile**

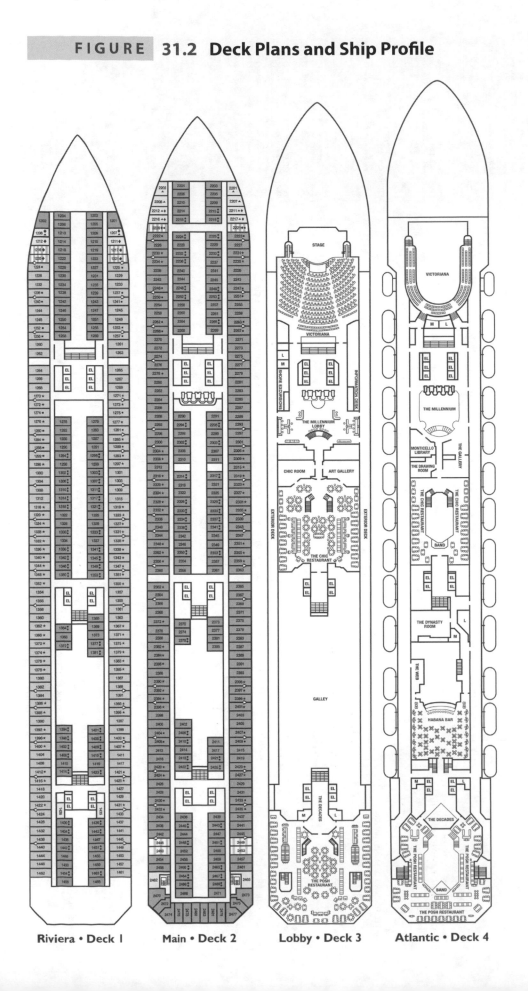

Riviera • Deck 1   Main • Deck 2   Lobby • Deck 3   Atlantic • Deck 4

FIGURE 31.2 Deck Plans and Ship Profile (continued)

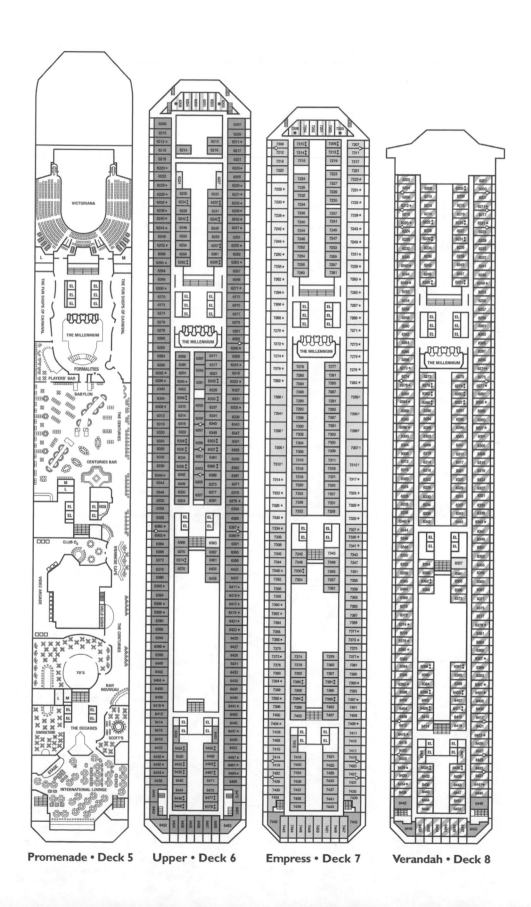

Promenade • Deck 5   Upper • Deck 6   Empress • Deck 7   Verandah • Deck 8

FIGURE **31.2 Deck Plans and Ship Profile (continued)**

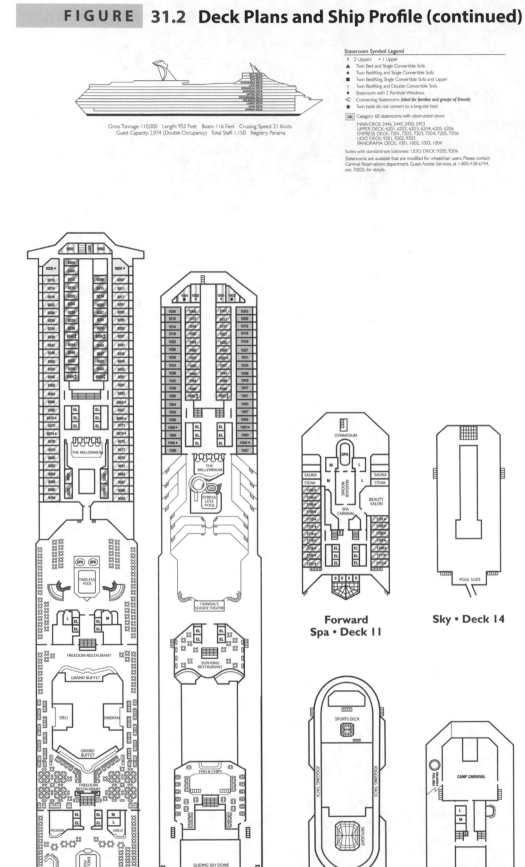

Gross Tonnage: 110,000   Length: 952 Feet   Beam: 116 Feet   Cruising Speed: 21 Knots
Guest Capacity: 2,974 (Double Occupancy)   Total Staff: 1,150   Registry: Panama

Stateroom Symbol Legend

- ⁞ 2 Uppers   • 1 Upper
- ▲ Twin Bed and Single Convertible Sofa
- ★ Twin Bed/King and Single Convertible Sofa
- ■ Twin Bed/King, Single Convertible Sofa and Upper
- † Twin Bed/King and Double Convertible Sofa
- ◆ Stateroom with 2 Porthole Windows
- ◁ Connecting Staterooms *(Ideal for families and groups of friends)*
- ✳ Twin beds do not convert to a king-size bed

6B   Catagory 6B staterooms with obstructed views:

MAIN DECK: 2446, 2449, 2450, 2453
UPPER DECK: 6201, 6202, 6203, 6204, 6205, 6206
EMPRESS DECK: 7201, 7202, 7203, 7204, 7205, 7206
LIDO DECK: 9201, 9202, 9203
PANORAMA DECK: 1001, 1002, 1003, 1004

Suites with standard-size balconies: LIDO DECK: 9205, 9206

Staterooms are available that are modified for wheelchair users. Please contact Carnival Reservations department, Guest Access Services, at 1-800-438-6744, ext. 70025, for details.

Lido • Deck 9

Panorama • Deck 10

Forward
Spa • Deck 11

Sky • Deck 14

Aft
Spa • Deck 11

Sun • Deck 12

a mass market. Many of the contemporary brand cruise lines visit the same ports. Some distinctions between luxury and premium brands may have to do with the quality of food, level of service, and number of passengers on a ship. In comparing the passenger to crew ratio between two ships, one may get a rough estimate of the level of service. Another important factor for comparison would be the cruise itinerary. Premium cruise brands may visit more exotic ports.

The Major Cruise Lines

All the larger cruise lines offer a well-packaged cruise that include a variety of itineraries, plenty of food, a variety of activities, and large-scale Broadway production shows. The lines differ in the facilities, space, food, and service. Each cruise line has its own niche.

There are also more destinations to travel and more ports to depart from. There are over 30,000 different cruises to choose from each year and about 2,000 cruise destinations in the world. Cruises can range from a day getaway cruise from Miami to the Bahamas or an "Around the World in 180 Day" cruise. The Caribbean and Bahamas continue to be the number one destinations for cruises. Other leading cruising areas are Europe, Alaska, and Mexico and West Coast.

Most Caribbean seven-day cruises depart from Miami and usually visit three ports, including a private island (where clients can enjoy water sports and beachside activities), and two to three days at sea.

One has the option of visiting the Eastern Caribbean, Western Caribbean (which is geared toward beach lovers), or Southern Caribbean. A good choice for a first-time Caribbean cruiser who is more concerned with the itinerary than the ship could be a port-intensive cruise departing from San Juan, Puerto Rico, and visiting six islands. The ship is already in the Caribbean, so it is easy to visit so many islands.

Cruises to Europe have become popular because a client only has to unpack once. Clients also like the fact that they go back each night to the familiar surroundings of their cabin and cruise ship. Alaskan cruises became very popular following 9/11 because passengers felt safer cruising in U.S. waters. Clients also have the option of taking "theme cruises." Some popular themes for cruises might be sports, music, food, wine tasting, and murder mystery. Other options include adventure cruises or expeditions to such places as the Galapagos Island, "around the world" cruises, and river cruises on such rivers as the Danube, the Rhine, and the Nile. On the Danube River tours, people can board a medium-size boat of 100 to wander through the beautiful canyons and scenic splendor through five or six different countries. One possibility is to spend three days in Budapest exploring the city split into two parts by the river. Then board the boat to explore castles, abbies, or medieval cities that are difficult to reach except by boat, biking, or hiking. The river winds past Slovakia, the Czech Republic, Vienna (where you can do a Viennese waltz to a live orchestra), ending in Prague, the current European party capital.

TABLE 31.1 Big Eight Cruise Lines

LINES	NO. OF SHIPS (MAY CHANGE BY PUBLICATION DATE)	BRIEF PROFILE
Carnival Cruises	23	Largest, most popular cruise line
Celebrity Cruises	8	Most elegant ships and spas
Costa Cruises	12	"Cruising Italian Style"
Cunard Cruises	3	Ocean liners—regularly scheduled transatlantic sailings
Holland America	13	Preserves many traditions of the past—good cooking demonstrations
Norwegian Cruise Line	11	Free-style cruising, Hawaii cruising
Princess Cruises	16	Best-known name the "Love Boats"
Royal Caribbean International	22	Good for the Caribbean and first-time cruisers

A modern cruise ship is a restaurant, hotel, resort, and activities center. © 2011 by Oleksiy Mark. Used under license of Shutterstock, Inc.

Other trends in cruising include

- Voyages to Antarctica
- Flexible and alternative dining options
- More large resort ships
- Multigenerational cruising aboard the resort-style ships
- Single parent cruising
- Widest ever variety of adventures ashore for active adults
- Zip lines on cruise ships
- Ships divided into neighborhoods—each neighborhood has a unique feel to it
- "Homeland" cruising—departing from a port closer to home

Career Opportunities

When one thinks of working for a cruise line, there are two options: working on the ship or on land. When one thinks about positions on a ship, one must realize that a modern cruise ship is a restaurant, hotel, resort, and activities center. Many of the positions offered at those land-based establishments are offered on a cruise ship.

All the cruise ships except one are registered in other countries such as Panama and Liberia. This is referred to as a "flag of convenience." When flying a "flag of convenience" of another country, the cruise line does not have to follow United States' standards in regard to taxes and minimum wage requirements. Traditionally cruise lines tend to hire residents from

less-developed countries for positions such as waiters, cabin stewards, and bartenders because residents from those countries are willing to work for less pay than Americans. Things changed in 2005 when Norwegian Caribbean Line's ship *The Pride of America* was the first oceangoing passenger vessel in nearly 50 years to sail under the American flag. As such, NCL was required to hire an all-American crew. NCL fully touts its NCL American brand.

Hospitality students with a degree can aspire to some of the better positions on a cruise ship. The top position in the rooms department is the hotel manager. The chief purser is responsible for personnel services and accounting. The cruise director is responsible for ensuring that guests are enjoying themselves. He/she is in charge of arranging activities and procuring entertainment for the ship. The chief steward is in charge of guest accommodations. These positions are similar to those in land-based operations. The top position in the restaurant side of the cruise ship is the executive chef. The food and beverage director and the maitre d' report to him. Many cruise lines promote from within, so an employee may start as a child's activities director and work their way up to cruise director. Many workers sign contracts for 6 months.

Each cruise line has policies concerning crew members fraternizing with guests. Some lines will allow its officers to mingle with the guests in selected areas. The crew does have its own deck, which consists of cabins and shared space for activities. Oftentimes the crew shares living accommodations. Working on a ship might seem glamorous but it does involve many hours of work per day. Members of the crew may get some time off when the ship is in port. At that time they may attend to their personal needs or take some time off at the beach. There are advantages to working on a ship. First of all, one gets to meet people from all parts of the world. Because the crew's accommodations and meals are taken care of, one does not have to spend a great deal of money while on the ship, so one has the opportunity to save money. The downside is that the crew is away from their family and friends for long periods of time. Because life aboard a cruise ship may not be for everyone, it may be good idea for a college-age student to seek summer employment on a cruise ship. Some larger cruise lines may hire youth activity directors for the summer. Other smaller cruise lines may hire one to act as both a steward and a waiter. Some cruise lines may have opportunities for internships during college.

On shore one can work at the company's headquarters in the areas of marketing and sales, reservations, and finance and accounting. There are also limited amount of positions working as a sales representative in major cities across the country. This position would entail visiting travel agents and groups highlighting the features and benefits of your product.

RESOURCES

Internet Sites

Carnival Cruises: www.carnivalcruiselines.com
CLIA: www.cruisingorg/
Royal Caribbean International: www.royalcaribbean.com

CHAPTER 31

Review Questions

1. What are the major departments of a ship?

2. What are the different career opportunities in the cruise industry?

3. What are the major trends in the cruise industry?

4. Please list the names of at least five cruise lines.

5. Where are the major cruise areas of the world?

6. What is the name of the organization that promotes the cruise industry?

7. What is included in the price of a cruise?

Senior Services Management

Bradley Beran, Waukesha County Technical College

LEARNING OBJECTIVES

- Define and identify the different types of senior assisted-living centers.
- Identify job requirements that are similar to other segments within the hospitality industry.
- Identify job requirements that are unique to senior assisted-living centers.
- Understand and identify define the career positions, scope, and growth potential of careers within senior assisted-living centers.
- Understand the market needs and trends of senior assisted-living centers.
- Identify specific guest needs, demands, services, and requirements and the types of centers that fill these needs.

CHAPTER OUTLINE

KEY TERMS

Assisted-living communities
At-home assisted living
Costs and reimbursement
Forms of ownership

Full-care centers/nursing homes
Growth and demand for living centers
Respite care
Support services

Baby boomers are beginning to retire and will continue to retire in large numbers over the next two decades. This group of retirees will be the healthiest, most financially well off, most independent and mobile, and longest living of any group to date. Census projections for 2010 from the U.S. Department of Commerce (2010) shows that 40 million people, or 12.97 percent of the population, are 65 years old or older, and about 97 million people, or 39.07 percent, are 45 years old or older.

Where are these people retiring? Of the 100 fastest-growing counties in the United States from 2000 through 2004, none were in the Northeast, only seven are in the Midwest, with the rest being in the West and South. The states below the Mason Dixon line— Florida, South Carolina, North Carolina, Kentucky, Tennessee, Virginia, West Virginia, Georgia, Alabama, Missouri, and Mississippi—have 60 percent of the fastest-growing counties (U.S. Dept. of Commerce, 2008). Not all the growth can be attributed to retiring seniors, but much of it is from retirees.

Who are these people? Demographic data indicates that as of the 2004 projections of the total population, of those 65 years and older, 14.57 percent are women, and 11.32 percent are men. By 2020 the split should be 17.61 percent women, and 14.46 percent men. By 2030, the expectations are 20.99 percent women and 17.56 percent men. Put another way, by 2030, 38.3 percent of the population of the United States should be retired (U.S. Dept. of Commerce, 2010).

The potential market for senior living centers is enormous. The current estimates are that there are over 36,000 assisted-living centers in the United States (A Place for Mom, 2010). Senior living centers provide many services to attract and support the needs of this population. The potential clientele has many different needs and goals for their retired years, including people who no longer have the ability and/or desire to maintain a private residence, want greater flexibility and/or fewer responsibilities during their retirement, and are looking to senior living centers to meet their residential and personal needs.

Senior living centers are filling the need of retirees by offering a multitude of services and conveniences. The services and conveniences are as minimal or as extensive as retirees' desire, depending on needs, demands, health, family and support, and financial situation. Minimal services can be limited to living space and basic interior and exterior maintenance at one end of the spectrum to full-service living centers offering restaurants and meal plans, laundry, cleaning, pharmacy and basic medical services, transportation, activities and entertainment, and more. As the level and amount of service increases, so does the cost to the living center resident.

Senior living centers can be categorized by the amount and level of service they provide ranging from at-home and independent living centers to full-care living centers.

Independent, Assisted, Full-Care, and Respite Care Living Centers

Independent Living Communities

Independent living communities are for the most healthy and independent residents. These residents typically own a car, are in good health, drive often, are quite independent, and come and go as they please. If they require any medical support at all, it is minimal and usually not much more than pharmacy support for medications.

Independent living communities for independent residents like these offer the fewest services and are the lowest cost. Typical services at this level are lawn care, snow removal, and similar outdoor maintenance. Other services often include a community center and/or recreation center and may include food services (restaurant or catered meals) and/or home replacement meals and laundry services. These centers often resemble apartment complexes. Newly built facilities are usually no more than two stories high and often look more like a small community of duplex or multiplex housing.

Independent living communities are for healthy and independent residents. © 2011 by sjgh. Used under license of Shutterstock, Inc.

One example of high-level services at the independent level is Sunrise Independent Living Communities. Services for residents include exercise and wellness programs, outings to local events and attractions, on-site entertainment, programs and activities, fine dining, landscaped grounds, barber and beauty shops, housekeeping, linen, and transportation services and more (Sunrise Senior Living, Inc., 2003).

The price for independent living communities ranges from about $1,500 per month to upwards of $3,500 per month, depending on location and the number and type of services offered and selected by the resident. The resident pays for the fees with possibly some government assistance (A Place for Mom, 2010).

At-Home Assisted Living

For some seniors who are healthy and relatively independent, the prospect of giving up their home is unacceptable, yet they need assistance in certain tasks. A small but growing area known as at-home assisted living fills this need. This service provides support for a multitude of needs such as light housekeeping, meal preparation and planning, bathing and grooming assistance, medication management, errands and shopping services, and more (Sunrise Senior Living, Inc., 2003).

Assisted-Living Centers

The typical resident of assisted-living centers either drives minimally or does not drive at all and often needs varying degrees of assistance due to various limitations such as medical, physical, or mental conditions. They are not as healthy or independent as residents of independent living centers and may be in declining health. These residents value their independence, but are not capable or comfortable living completely independently. Typically, the longer these residents stay at a center, the more services they require as they age. These centers are often set up as smaller, efficiency apartments, or as group units with a central common area and bedrooms for 8 to 20 residents with several units per center.

Assisted-living centers offer more services at a greater cost to their residents. In addition to the services offered at independent centers, assisted centers generally add or offer assistance with medications, meal preparation and/or feeding, personal care (shaving, showering, dressing, etc.), ambulatory care, and transportation services. Medical care my be on-site, but is minimal, usually provided by a licensed practical nurse (LPN) or registered nurse (RN), is often not available 24 hours per day and is generally for minor injuries, consulting, and referrals. Some assisted-living centers provide specialty care for residents with Alzheimer's and other debilitating, noncommunicable disease. Coordination with external physician and pharmacy services are provided, as the medical needs of this group are much greater than in independent living centers (Saint Barnabas Health Care Systems, Inc., 2010). Living center administration must be aware of special medical requests, such as Do Not Recessitate orders, visitation restrictions, hospital preference in case of emergency transport, personal physician information, and the like.

Services available for assisted living are usually offered in one of three ways. A resident may select from a menu of services and pay a fee based on the number and type of services selected. Another option allows a resident to select one of several service programs or packages, each offering more services at different price points. Finally, an assisted-living center may offer only one set of services at one price. In this instance, if a resident requires more services than are available, they must to move to another center to have their needs met, which is usually a transfer to a full-service center/nursing home.

At Sunrise Assisted Living Centers, services include three meals per day served in a restaurant-style setting, health and wellness assessments, scheduled transportation, activities programs, weekly housekeeping and linen service, and personalized levels of care based on each resident's needs (Sunrise Senior Living, Inc., 2003).

The price for assisted-living centers ranges from about $1,800 per month to upwards of $3,500 per month, depending on services used. Alzheimer's care is more expensive, from nearly $3,000 per month to around $4,000 per month. The resident most often pays for these costs with possibly some assistance from Medicaid (A Place for Mom, 2010).

Full-Care Living Centers

Full-care living centers are most commonly known as nursing homes. Residents are unable to live by themselves and, at best, can only provide minimal care for themselves. These residents may require feeding assistance, may be bedridden, and may need continual observation and care.

These centers provide full service for those seniors least able to care for themselves. All services are provided for these residents, which includes all

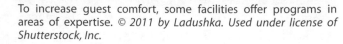

meals, housekeeping, laundry, eating, personal care, medication, and other services. Medical personnel are on staff 24 hours each day, including registered nurses (RNs), licensed practical nurses (LPNs), and certified nursing assistants (CNAs). Doctors are on call and often maintain a regular schedule. Pharmacy services are provided, and some medical testing is often available on-site.

Sunrise Senior Living nursing homes offer 24-hour nursing, posthospital care, postsurgical care, physician and pharmacy coordination, family counseling and other support services, and emotional and physical health and well-being (Sunrise Senior Living, Inc., 2003).

Nursing home prices will range from around $4,000 per month to around $8,000 per month, depending on services needed by the resident. Residents pay these costs themselves, and Medicare or Medicaid can supplement the costs (A Place for Mom, 2010).

Respite Care

Many assisted-living centers and full-service centers offer respite care as an option if there is space available. Respite care is a short-term, temporary use of assisted-living center resources and services. This care is designed to fill the needs of an individual who may need assistance in recovery from surgery, injury, or other ailment and only needs temporary assistance during recovery and rehabilitation. Respite care

To increase guest comfort, some facilities offer programs in areas of expertise. © 2011 by Ladushka. Used under license of Shutterstock, Inc.

generally lasts from one week to a few months and is usually billed by the day and/or week. Typical services for respite care can include medical and pharmacy services, physical therapy, meals, laundry and housekeeping services, and other services as needed, depending on each situation. Costs for respite care vary from about $75 to $150 per day, depending on location and level of care and services needed. Respite care fees are usually paid for through some combination of insurance, Medicare, Medicaid, and personal funds (A Place for Mom, 2010).

Market Outlook and Cost Support

Expected Demand

The 2000 census lists 1,720,500 residents in nursing homes. By 2010 it is projected that there will be 36,818,000 Americans aged 65 or older, and by 2020 the estimate increases to 54,804,000 and to 88,547,000 by 2050 (U.S. Dept. of Commerce, 2010). To meet the expected demand for senior living centers, an additional 1.25 million units will need to be built. Put another way, the construction of one unit capable of housing 600 residents must be built each week for the next 40 years to fill the expected demand. Private companies are building and/or completely renovating apartments and other buildings into senior living centers to begin to meet the demand through private investment and federal programs. To put these figures into dollars, in 2000, long-term care for those 65 and older was $123 billion and expected to double in 30 years (Senior Journal, 2004).

Government Support

Medical costs have risen drastically over the last several years, with costs for seniors accounting for a significant portion. To address and try to contain these costs and to help improve the quality of life for seniors, the federal government is also expanding the market for living centers. To reduce costs while still providing services, seniors who meet certain eligibility criteria are encouraged to consider assisted-living centers instead of more expensive nursing home care. To accomplish this, two programs have been developed. First, Medicare has developed the PACE program. PACE has options that allow qualified seniors to receive assistance while remaining in their own homes, adult day health centers, and inpatient facilities.

From the Medicare WEB site:

What Are Programs of All-inclusive Care for the Elderly (PACE)?

PACE is a Medicare program for older adults and people over age 55 living with disabilities. This program provides community-based care and services to people who otherwise need nursing home level of care. PACE was created as a way to provide you, your family, caregivers, and professional health care providers flexibility to meet your health care needs and to help you continue living in the community. PACE provides all the care and services covered by Medicare and Medicaid, as authorized by the interdisciplinary team, as well as additional medically-necessary care and services not covered by Medicare and Medicaid. PACE provides coverage for prescription drugs, doctor care, transportation, home care, check ups, hospital visits, and even nursing home stays whenever necessary. With PACE, your ability to pay will never keep you from getting the care you need. (U.S. Dept of Health, Education and Welfare, 2010)

A second program is matching government funding under the HUD Section 202 grants program. HUD provides capital advances to finance the construction, rehabilitation, or acquisition with or without rehabilitation of structures that will serve as supportive housing for very low income elderly persons, including the frail elderly, and provides rent subsidies for the projects to help make them affordable (U.S. Dept. of Housing and Urban Development, 2010).

Several Web sites and other forms of assistance in defining, identifying, and selecting a senior living center and/or determining the levels of service needed are available. One site, http://www.aplacefor mom.com (2010), offers complete and free consulting and advice to families considering senior living center alternatives.

Development and Ownership of Senior Living Centers

Religious Groups

Senior living center residents do not own their apartments. They are tenants who contract for the space and services they receive. Senior living centers have several types of ownership. Some are owned by religious orders, such as Menorah Park, which is owned by the Jewish Orthodox. Religious-based living centers are operated for members of their religion, and costs can be subsidized by the religion (Menorah Park, 2010).

Charities and Foundations

Charities and foundations, such as the Sunshine Terrace Foundation, which owns the Terrace Grove Assisted Living Center, also own and operate living centers. Like religious-owned living centers, resident fees are often subsidized to some degree. Residents generally must meet certain criteria to belong to these living centers, such as income guidelines, specific medical needs, etc. (Sunshine Terrace Foundation, 2010).

Private Businesses and Corporations

Private companies and corporations, such as Sunrise Assisted Living, Inc. provide a third type of ownership. These are usually for-profit companies supported by private investment, returning dividends, or tax deductions to investors, often through real estate investment trusts, or REITs (Harper, 2004). Government agencies also own retirement centers; however, this type of ownership is declining and most often was limited to nursing homes. As local and state governments cut costs and move toward the privatization of services, many community-/government-owned senior centers are being sold to private concerns or closed.

Individually Owned with Contracted Management and Services

All prior forms of living centers involve private groups, investors, and nonprofits as the owners and providers of services. In each of those cases, all services are contracted for, including living quarters, which are leased spaces. In individually owned living centers, private individuals own their living space, which can be anything from a free-standing bungalow, to an apartment, called apartment homes. Think of the latter as a condominium form of ownership. In these examples, the owners have all the benefits of ownership, such as complete freedom to remodel, renovate, and the like, with the tax benefits of ownership.

Assisted-living communities contract with or are operated by management companies to maintain grounds, operate a clubhouse and recreation area, coordinate activities, and more. Most of the living communities offer many of the same amenities provided by other senior living centers, such as a clubhouse, recreation center and support, medical assistance, full-service restaurant with or without a meal plan, and more. Larger operations offer the opportunity to trade or move into higher care and more services as they are needed by the resident (Senior Living Centers, 2010).

Work, Jobs, and Positions in Living Centers

The Nature of Work in Assisted-Living Centers

By their needs, characteristics, and service to residents, assisted-living centers have career tracks that share many similarities to other hospitality venues. Private clubs have a consistent, semicaptive crowd. One challenge is to create interesting and creative opportunities for members from menus to activities. Assisted-living centers have this same challenge, a consistent clientele.

Hotels and hospitals are 24-hours-a-day, seven-days-per-week operations with on-site guests or patients who may need services at any time. Assisted-living centers are in the same situation, whether it's basic needs such as heat, light, power, security, or a medical emergency.

Events planning, activities, and recreation services are part of the services to meet guest needs, along with special events, catering, and nutrition/dietetics services (e.g. nutrition counseling, menu and recipe analysis, food service consulting).

Restaurant operations and management are part of assisted-living centers, from menu planning, dining room setup, to servers, chefs, product and inventory management, food safety and sanitation, and more.

Resort operations tasks are also part of assisted-living centers, including recreation services and maintenance, grounds maintenance (e.g., golf course, swimming pools), snow removal, mowing, gardens, and walkways.

Assisted-living centers are diverse places to work. Some centers have residency requirements for managers who may receive living quarters for themselves and their families as part of their job compensation.

Service Coordination

Part of the manager's job is to coordinate multiple services from external providers for the residents. This often includes medical scheduling and doctor visits, pharmacy services, transportation, through self-operated or contracted services, nursing and other medical care, grounds and maintenance issues, ambulatory services, emergency services, including medical emergencies, natural disasters, security issues, and physical plant maintenance and repair. All this involves good planning and scheduling, contacts with different vendors, contract analysis, bidding and procurement systems, a high level of organization, and more.

Summary

In closing, senior assisted-living centers offer stable careers in a growing and high-demand field with jobs similar to those found in a broad assortment of hospitality venues. These positions tend to not have the stress and pressure of other operations, like restaurants, offer good pay and benefits, and are often overlooked by hospitality professionals as solid and stable career choices.

RESOURCES

References

A Place for Mom. (2010). *The search for senior care.* Retrieved July 26, 2010, from http://www.aplaceformom.com/

Harper, D. (2004). *What are real estate investment trusts (REITs).* Retrieved July 27, 2010, from http://www.investopedia.com/articles/04/030304.asp

Menorah Park. (2010). *Menorah Park Center for Senior Living online.* Retrieved July 25, 2010, from http://www.menorahpark.org/

Saint Barnabas Health Care Systems, Inc. (2010). *Saint Barnabas Health Care.* Retrieved July 27, 2010, from http://www.saintbarnabas.com/hospitals/nursing_homes/assistedliving/index.html

Senior Journal. (2004). Reverse mortgages can help with long-term care costs, study says. Retrieved July 27, 2010, from http://seniorjournal.com/NEWS/ReverseMortgage/4-04-15LTC.htm

Senior Living Centers, Inc. (2010). *Senior Living Centers.* Retrieved July 27, 2010, from http://www.senior-living-communities.com/

Sunrise Senior Living, Inc. (2003). *Sunrise Living Centers.* Retrieved July 24, 2010, from http://www.sunriseseniorliving.com/Home.do

Sunshine Terrace Foundation. (2010). *Terrace Grove Assisted Living.* Retrieved July 27, 2010, from http://www.sunshineterrace.com/assisted.php

U.S. Department of Commerce. (2008). *Census Bureau online.* Retrieved July 27, 2010, from http://www.census.gov/popest/housing/tables/HU-EST2004-05.csv

U.S. Department of Commerce. (2010). *Census Bureau online.* Retrieved July 27, 2010 from http://www.census.gov/population/www/projections/reports.html

U.S. Department of Health, Education and Welfare. (2010). *What are programs of all-inclusive care for the elderly (PACE)?* Retrieved July 27, 2010, from http://www.medicare.gov/Publications/Pubs/pdf/11341.pdf

U.S. Department of Housing and Urban Development. (2006). *Section 202 grants.* Retrieved July 27, 2010, from http://www.hud.gov/offices/hsg/mfh/progdesc/eld202.cfm

Review Questions

1. What are the characteristics of a senior for:

    •   At-home assisted living

    •   Assisted-living communities

    •   Full-care living centers

    •   Respite care

2. Describe the type of services offered at each of the following:

    •   At-home assisted living

    •   Assisted-living communities

    •   Full-care living centers

    •   Respite care

3. What is the PACE program and why is it important to seniors?

4. Describe the expected assisted-living potential market and explain what factors contribute to this market.

5. What job characteristics at assisted-living centers are similar to:

- Private clubs

- Hotels

- Restaurants

- Resorts

Education Careers in Hospitality

Linda J. Shea, University of Massachusetts, Amherst

 **LEARNING OBJECTIVES**

- To recognize the growing need for educators in hospitality and tourism.
- To gain an understanding of educators' qualifications, responsibilities, and characteristics.
- To understand the differences in types of schools offering educational opportunities in hospitality and tourism.
- To become familiar with compensation ranges and lifestyle characteristics for faculty.
- To be able to recognize some professional associations for hospitality and tourism educators.

CHAPTER OUTLINE

There's only one career more exciting, challenging and rewarding than working in the hospitality and tourism industry, and that is *teaching* in hospitality and tourism educational programs. With the growth in the industry and in educational programs to support them, the opportunities for careers in hospitality and tourism education abound. Whether the job is in a culinary school in Switzerland, a research university in the United States, or anywhere in between, the possibilities for a fulfilling career as an educator are limitless.

In this chapter, the need for hospitality and tourism educators will be presented. The types of educational institutions, the responsibilities of educators, as well as the skills, experience, academic preparation, and compensation will be reviewed. Finally, professional associations for hospitality and tourism educators will be provided.

Growth in the Industry

The demand for hospitality and tourism educators is derived directly from demand for people working in the hospitality and tourism industry, all of whom have to be educated and trained in some fashion. Tourism is the largest industry in the world and the third-largest industry in the United States. The segments of lodging accommodation and food service comprise almost 8 percent of all employment nationally (U.S. Department of Labor, 2010). According to the Bureau of Labor Statistics (BLS) of the U.S. Department of Labor, the hospitality industry is expected to increase 17 percent in wage and salary employment between 2004 and 2014 (U.S. Department of Labor, 2010). For example, wage and salary jobs in food services and drinking places are estimated to expand 16 percent between 2004 and 2014, whereas wage and salary employment in all industries combined is expected to have a 14 percent growth (U.S. Department of Labor, 2010).

More specifically, according to the National Restaurant Association (NRA, 2010), $580.1 billion sales are forecasted with an estimated 12.7 million employees for the restaurant industry, representing 9 percent of the U.S. workforce. In addition, employment in the restaurant industry is expected to increase by another 1.3 million jobs by 2020, with employment reaching 14 million by 2020 (NRA, 2010).

The U.S. travel and tourism (T&T) industry is also expected to contribute 3.4 percent to gross domestic product in 2010, generating $510.9 billion. The T&T industry is expected to increase to $916.5 billion by 2020 (World Travel & Tourism Council [WTTC], 2010). In terms of employment in the T&T industry, it is expected to expand to 9.9 percent of the total employment in 2010 to 10.7 percent of the total employment by 2020. All this projected growth in various sectors of the industry points to a substantive need to prepare individuals for careers in hospitality and tourism. It is no surprise that formal programs in schools, colleges, and universities around the world are experiencing growth to meet the needs of the industry.

Growth in H&T Education

Although career-oriented vocational and culinary schools have been a part of the educational system in the United States and abroad since the early 1900s, growth in the late 1900s and twenty-first century has been in the four-year baccalaureate-granting institutions offering degrees in hospitality and tourism management. In the early 1970s, there were only about 40 such hospitality management programs. According to the *Guide to College Programs in Hospitality, Tourism, & Culinary Arts* (2006), there were more than 170 undergraduate programs, and this number has grown to more than 250 in recent years.

Among the United States schools in hospitality and tourism education, two-year institutions ranked the first in total number, followed by four-year institutions and culinary programs, as illustrated in Figure 33.1.

FIGURE 33.1 Types of Schools in U.S. Hospitality and Tourism Education

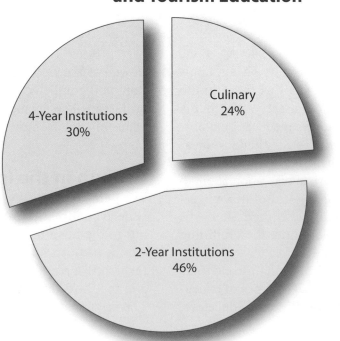

As shown in Table 33.1, the numbers of schools in each category are identified based on the *Guide to College Programs in Hospitality, Tourism, & Culinary Arts and College-source Online* database. Although all schools may not be represented, it is apparent that there are close to 800 schools of various types in the hospitality and tourism arena.

Hospitality and Tourism Educators' Qualifications and Responsibilities

Educators of all subjects require different sets of skills, experience, and academic preparation, and hospitality and tourism educators are no exception. Differences in the duties, the number of courses taught, the type of academic research, and the salaries are related to the type of institutions in which they work. In this section, a review of these key factors in secondary or vocational, culinary, two-year, and four-year colleges are presented.

Careers in Secondary and Vocational Schools

Students taking hospitality courses at the high school or vocational level are preparing for entry-level positions in food service and lodging operations. Educators' primary responsibility is to teach daily and follow a secondary school, with hours extending from morning to midafternoon on a 9-month schedule. Careers in secondary and vocational schools typically require a bachelor's degree and a teaching certificate. Those teaching are expected to demonstrate their own skills as they train the students.

Culinary Schools

As implied in the name, culinary schools focus on teaching culinary-related skills. They are engaged in activities that prepare students for careers in

Culinary schools focus on developing skills and training for entry-level positions. © 2011 by Diego Cervo. Used under license of Shutterstock, Inc.

restaurants, banquets and catering, and institutional food service in settings such as hospitals, schools, and corporate facilities. Courses on beverage management, food purchasing, preparation, presentation, and service, as well as food safety, are taught. Instructors are usually required to have a substantial number of years of experience in the field, and many have baccalaureate degrees or hold certificates from culinary schools themselves. Culinary schools focus on developing skills and training for entry-level positions in food and beverage operations, with an emphasis on back-of-house functions. Many of the international (non-U.S.-based) hospitality programs are in the culinary school category.

Two-Year Schools and Colleges

Students in two-year programs are typically in community colleges, where they earn an associate degree. The curriculum is broader than a vocational or culinary program and includes some general education courses. The focus is on entry-level positions

| TABLE | 33.1 Schools with Hospitality Programs |

TYPES OF SCHOOLS	NUMBER OF SCHOOLS
Culinary	177
Two-year institutions (associate degree)	330
Four-year institutions (bachelor degree)	214
International opportunities	54

in food service or lodging operations, clubs, or catering companies. On completion of the program, some students transfer to baccalaureate degree-granting four-year institutions to earn a bachelor of science in hospitality and tourism management. Faculty teaching in two-year associate degree programs are often required to hold a master's-level degree and to have a few years' experience in at least one sector of the industry. They will teach three to four courses per semester or manage several laboratory classes. Other duties may include sponsoring a student club, student advising, and serving on college committees.

Four-Year Colleges and Universities

The job of faculty in four-year colleges and universities is to prepare students for management positions in the industry. Students earn a bachelor's degree and assume positions in hotels, restaurants, resorts, or clubs. Faculty members teaching in these institutions are usually required to have a PhD from an accredited hospitality or business program. Some faculty members hold other terminal degrees, such as an EdD (doctorate of education) or JD (jurist doctorate). The duties are typically threefold and reflect a mission that includes teaching, research, and service components. Research universities often offer graduate degrees, a master of science and or PhD. Faculty in these positions are expected to advance the discipline of hospitality and tourism management through scholarly research published in academic journals. Teaching loads in these universities are likely two courses or fewer per semester, with research publication requirements and service duties. Service duties demonstrating good citizenship include such contributions as serving on committees at the departmental, school/college, or university level; graduate student advising; and student club sponsorship.

International Opportunities

Although the majority of hospitality and tourism institutions outside the United States are culinary or two-year certificate or associate degree programs, there are some four-year and graduate programs offered as well. European schools tend to be two-year, and Asian and Australian schools tend to be four-year. It is quite common for international programs to link with U.S. programs to offer exchange, internship, and summer abroad opportunities. Faculty and students alike enjoy and benefit from these collaborations.

Characteristics of Educators

Regardless of the type of school setting, there are several skills all hospitality and tourism educators should hold. They should be good communicators, both in writing and speaking. They should be educated in, and have some degree of experience in, the content areas in which they teach. They have a responsibility to keep abreast of the discipline and any changes occurring. They should have respect and admiration for students who want to learn from them. Finally, they should have a strong love of learning themselves and an ability to think creatively.

Compensation

There is a wide range of salaries for hospitality and tourism educators. An instructor-level educator may earn $55,000 base salary per nine-month contract, whereas a distinguished professor earning additional compensation may earn up to $245,000 or more. Differences in salary levels are related to professional rank (instructor, assistant professor, associate professor, full professor, and distinguished or chaired professor. Furthermore, many faculty members earn additional compensation by taking on administrative duties, by teaching additional courses (for instance, summer or online courses), or from consulting work. Differences can also be accounted for between two-year and four-year institutions, public versus private, U.S. versus international, and gender. Average salary figures for faculty in different ranks in private and public institutions are presented in Table 33.2 (Shea & Roberts, 2009).

Faculty rank was the strongest indicator of salary category, despite institutional differences. Overall, salaries are higher at four-year institutions than at two-year, at U.S.-based institutions over non-U.S.-based, and at public over private institutions.

In general, base salaries at private four-year institutions were about $7,500 lower than at public institutions. Total compensation earned from all sources was also lower at private schools, with about an $8,000 difference overall.

About 50 percent of two-year and four-year college faculty participate or are interested in pursuing administrative positions. Some hold positions such as graduate program director, chief advisor, internship coordinator, associate chair, department head, or dean. Each of these positions may add year-round obligations as well as additional compensation. The

TABLE 33.2 Faculty Salaries at Public and Private U.S. Four-Year Institutions

	PRIVATE				PUBLIC			
	N	BASE	ADD'L	TOTAL*	N	BASE	ADD'L	TOTAL
Instructor/lecturer	14	55,143	5,420	61,554	14	67,219	6,167	71,911
Assistant professor	22	61,967	11,579	80,427	80	65,796	13,226	75,284
Associate professor	21	74,822	22,578	106,028	93	84,234	12,970	108,185
Full professor	21	100,729	21,321	120,565	47	119,893	21,493	148,501
Weighted average =	78	74,639	16,052	94,733	234	84,095	14,649	102,984
Distinguished professor	7	143,929	38,429	245,571	8	129,938	19,583	178,750
Overall average =	85	80,345	17,895	107,155	242	85,611	14,165	105,489

*Includes external work

difference in total earnings, which includes outside income, was markedly greater for distinguished professors at private institutions: $245,571 versus $178,750. Full professors at public institutions earn, on average, $20,000 annually from work performed outside their home institutions.

Regarding gender in the Shea and Roberts study (2009), there is about an $8,000 to $18,000 pay differential, depending on rank. The largest difference was seen at the full professor rank: the difference in favor of the men was distinctive: $107,385 for women and $125,200 for men.

It's More than Money

In addition to monetary compensation, careers in hospitality education offer many other benefits. Full-time positions often offer standard kinds of health insurance and retirement benefits, and most positions allow an attractive lifestyle. Unless administrative duties are involved, faculty often work 9 or 10 months of the year with frequent one-week-to one-month-long holiday and break sequences. Working with young people in a campus environment is intellectually stimulating, interesting, and frequently entertaining. Compared to the fast-paced, long, nontraditional hours (late nights, early mornings, weekends, and holidays) and often stressful working conditions of those with careers in hospitality and tourism operations, educators enjoy an equally meaningful, slightly more relaxed, but dynamic lifestyle. Similar to careers in the industry, educators have opportunities for travel for the purposes

of collaborating in teaching and research with colleagues around the world, attending academic conferences, and sponsoring student programs overseas or in other nontraditional venues.

Professional Associations for Educators

Additional information can be found through some of the professional associations for educators in the hospitality and tourism field. Some of these are listed next.

- American Society of Travel Agents
- American Hotel & Lodging Association
- Educational Institute of the American Hotel & Lodging Association
- International Council on Hotel, Restaurant, and Institutional Education (ICHRIE)
- International Society of Travel and Tourism Educators (ISTTE)
- International Hospitality Information Technology Association
- Hospitality Financial and Technical Professionals
- Hospitality Sales and Marketing Association International
- Meeting Professional International
- National Restaurant Association Educational Foundation
- National Restaurant Association
- Professional Convention Management Association

- Travel and Tourism Research Association (TTRA)
- Travel Industry Association of America
- Tourism Cares

Membership in professional associations keeps faculty members in touch with industry professionals and other academics. Each association sponsors annual conferences where ideas are exchanged and innovations in teaching, program development, and research are discussed. Workshops, panels, and symposiums and research presentations offer opportunities for educators to hone their skills in these areas. These ideas are then brought back to the classroom to benefit the students they serve.

Summary

The benefits, lifestyle, and sheer joy of a career in hospitality and tourism education make it an attractive option for many interested in the industry. Although four to six additional years of education beyond the bachelor's degree is required for four-year and graduate-degree-granting colleges and universities, the benefits are worth the extra effort. The education industry offers a plethora of opportunities to which potential educators can match their various combinations of background experience, education, and interests. Having the appropriate academic degrees, a connection to the hospitality industry, effective communication skills, and a creative imagination all contribute to a successful career as an educator.

RESOURCES

References

National Restaurant Association (NRA). (2010). *2010 restaurant industry: Pocket factbook.* Retrieved from http://www.restaurant. org/pdfs/research/2010Forecast_PFB.pdf

Riegel, C., & Dallas, M. (2006). *Hospitality and tourism: Careers in the worlds' largest industry. Guide to college programs in hospitality, tourism, & culinary arts* (9th ed.) [CD-ROM]. Richmond, VA: International CHRIE.

Shea, L. J., & Roberts, C. (2008). Compensation analysis: The 2008 I-CHRIE salary study. *Journal of Hospitality and Tourism Education, 20*(4).

U.S. Department of Labor. (2010). *High growth industry profile: Hospitality.* Retrieved from http://www.doleta.gov/Brg/Indprof/Hospitality_profile.cfm

World Travel & Tourism Council (WTTC). (2010). *Travel & tourism economic impact: United States.* Retrieved from http://www.wttc.org/bin/pdf/original_pdf_file/unitedstates.pdf

Review Questions

1. Describe the growth trend of hospitality and tourism education.

2. Why is hospitality and tourism education important to society? Why is it important to the economy?

3. List the three types educational institutions that provide some form of hospitality and tourism education.

4. Describe two primary characteristics of each type of educational institution listed above.

5. What education-degree and/or work experience is required of faculty teaching hospitality and tourism education at a two-year school? Four-year school?

6. List 3–5 variables that affect compensation of hospitality and tourism educators.

7. Describe several ways many hospitality and tourism educators use to supplement his/her salary.

Management Consulting

Joe Hutchinson, University of Central Florida

 LEARNING OBJECTIVES

- To learn about different types of consulting firms.
- To understand what it means to be a management consultant.
- To know skills, requirements, and personality traits.
- To understand ethics.
- To learn how to develop a career path.

CHAPTER OUTLINE

KEY TERMS

Consultant
Consulting careers
Consulting firms
Consulting qualifications
Consulting skills
Hospitality consultant
Management consultant

A person with years of experience, a talent for identifying problems, and the ability to find creative solutions may want to become a consultant. The consulting industry is a rapidly growing segment in the service sector of the U.S. economy. Consultants offer a wide range of professional services to clients in many different fields.

A consultant may be any individual who has a specific area of expertise and is compensated for providing advice or other services to a client. Sometimes people are hired as consultants after firms downsize and then hire them back as independent contractors. This allows the firm the advantage of retaining the expertise without the former budgetary constraints or expenses. Other times, a firm may be looking for an objective viewpoint to convince the board of directors or upper-level management that their plans and strategies are sound and feasible.

A hospitality management consultant would be a consultant who serves only hospitality industry clients and provides services in one or more functional areas. Hospitality organizations may hire an external consultant because specialized expertise may be unavailable within their organizations to complete the specific tasks within the necessary time frame. For example, consultants may be hired to design a food service facility or to conduct a hotel feasibility study. Even when an organization has adequate internal expertise to complete the necessary tasks, an outside consultant may be hired because of the sensitive nature of the issues involved, the objectivity provided by an outsider, and/or the reputation and credibility of the consultant or the firm that he or she represents.

This chapter provides an overview of the management consulting profession. Topics discussed include the types of management consulting firms, the nature of the work, the consultant's lifestyle, consulting skill requirements and personality traits, ethics and professional development, and the consulting career.

Types of Management Consulting Firms

Management consulting firms may be classified according to a number of characteristics, such as their size, level of specialization, industries served, geographical location, or types of clients/industries that they serve. Consultants who provide services to clients in hospitality organizations are often found in the following types of firms.

General Management Firms

These firms provide general management consulting services to international clients in many different industries. Consultants in these firms may be referred to as generalists who provide a broad range of services to their clients and tailor their services to the specific needs of each client. In some cases, they can assess an organization's structure and recommend restructuring and position cuts and/or additions. Other times, they can examine management practices or organizational efficiencies. With today's prevalence of corporate mergers, consultants provide an objective approach to blending companies together with services that may include strategic planning, psychological testing for compatibility, skill assessments, or recommendations for department restructuring. The better-known international firms that provide general management consulting services to a diverse base of clients include McKinsey and Company, Boston Consulting Group, and Booz Allen Hamilton.

Management Consulting Divisions of Certified Public Accounting (CPA) Firms

Large international CPA firms may have a consulting presence in the hospitality industry. These firms are staffed with consulting professionals who have backgrounds, experiences, and education in the hospitality industry. These firms often perform project feasibility studies or recommend improvements in areas such as strategic planning, operating efficiencies, product/service quality, or customer service. PricewaterhouseCoopers is an example of a larger international accounting/consulting firm that includes a consulting division specializing in the hospitality industry. Hospitality consultants in these larger firms often focus on the lodging industry, particularly with respect to hotel development.

Functionally Specialized Firms

A number of consulting firms may serve clients in the hospitality industry and many other industries by providing their expertise in a specific functional area. Specialists in these firms focus on their narrow area of expertise. For example, a firm that specializes in management information systems may develop the system requirements for a large hotel. Another consultant may be the advertising agency that creates the media campaign for the company.

Industry-Specific Firms

Some firms serve only the management of organizations in the hospitality industry. These firms often provide specialized consulting services to their clients by focusing on a specific industry segment (i.e., food-service industry), an industry subsegment (i.e., full-service restaurants), and/or a specific functional area in certain industry organizations (i.e., facilities/ equipment layout and design in food service operations). PKF Consulting is a national consulting firm that specializes in the lodging industry. Some of you may have seen their reports on salaries for different positions in different segments of the hotel industry across the nation. They also track and report various lodging statistics for various regions of the United States. On the other hand, Cini-Little International serves clients in a wide variety of food service operations. A large number of small firms and sole practitioners also specialize in the layout and design of kitchen facilities. In fact, most consultants specialize in hospitality industry consulting do work for either small firms (2 to 10 employees) or operate as sole practitioners (one-person firms).

Internal Consultants

External consultants serve clients of different hospitality firms, whereas internal consultants serve only one hospitality organization. These consultants may be on the payroll of the organization or they may serve on a contract basis exclusively with that one organization. These individuals are often referred to as "troubleshooters" or "field consultants" and perform many of the functions that external consultants perform. Most large restaurant and lodging chains have in-house personnel who provide operational support and assistance to both company-owned and franchised units of those organizations. For example, chain hotels or restaurants often have in-house consultants or troubleshooters who conduct on-site visits to specific units or properties in the chain to identify problems and develop solutions for implementation. Others might locate sites for new development and evaluate their feasibility for success.

The Nature of the Work

Although the work of a consultant varies significantly among individuals and firms, there are three major steps in the consulting cycle that are common to most consultants: marketing, the consulting engagement, and administration.

Marketing

The marketing of consulting services is usually designed to build the reputation of an individual or a firm as a leading expert in a specific area. Every consulting firm, irrespective of size, must generate and sustain enough work to stay in business. Marketing in consulting involves the direct or indirect solicitation of new clients and/or efforts to generate additional business from existing or previous clients. Forms of indirect marketing include active membership in trade associations, serving on industry boards and panels, writing books and articles, making conference presentations, or conducting workshops and seminars. More direct forms of marketing would include advertising, direct mail, and meetings with potential clients.

The Consulting Engagement

Each new consulting project is typically referred to as a consulting engagement. Most engagements begin with an initial client meeting to discuss the scope and nature of the client's needs. The consultant may have responded to a phone call or a request for proposal (RFP). An RFP is a document, frequently used by government organizations, that outlines the nature of the work requested and other project details.

The final report to the client usually includes an oral presentation of findings and recommendations. © 2011 by wavebreak-media. Used under license of Shutterstock, Inc.

Following an initial client meeting or the receipt of an RFP, the consultant often prepares a formal proposal. This proposal will clarify the details of the engagement by outlining the project background and objectives, the approach and work plan that will be used to complete the engagement, the final deliverables that will be provided to the client (i.e., oral presentations and written reports), and other project details (i.e., project fees, billing procedures, timing, and qualifications of consultants). After completing all the work steps outlined in the proposal, the consultant usually presents a final report to the client, in addition to an oral presentation discussing the findings and recommendations outlined in the report.

Administration

Consultants must perform other duties in addition to soliciting clients, writing proposals, meeting with clients, and completing consulting engagements. A number of administrative tasks must be completed in every consulting firm. In large firms, there usually will be a project manager who directs the work of the consultants on the project, maintains an ongoing dialogue with the client, and ensures that payments for services are received in a timely manner. These consultants may also be responsible for establishing a project budget and ensuring that each consulting engagement is completed within the allocated amount of time and dollars. Larger firms have support staff to perform necessary administrative and clerical tasks within the firm (report production, telephone calls, graphics, copy services, payroll, benefits, professional development, taxes, etc.). In small firms or sole proprietorships, consultants typically will be responsible for completing all relevant administrative tasks required to operate the business.

The Consultant's Lifestyle

There is no common lifestyle shared by all individuals in the consulting profession. The lifestyle of a consultant may differ significantly from one firm to another. Factors that may influence a consultant's lifestyle include the size of the firm, the type of services provided, the geographical area covered, and the industries served. For example, sole practitioners may shape their own working conditions to match their desired lifestyle by limiting travel, selecting only certain clients to serve, determining their own work hours, setting their own fees, working out of their own home, or working part time. Conversely,

consultants in large firms usually have little input into the services they provide, the hours they work, the type of clients they serve, the fees they charge, or the geographical locations where they work.

The consulting profession may be vry rewarding for certain individuals. Consultants have the opportunity to help and influence others and may derive a great deal of satisfaction from making a positive contribution to both clients and society. There is also the potential of high earnings, status, and respect. Many consultants thrive on the constant new challenges they are faced with and the opportunities to learn so much in a short period of time.

Despite the many rewards of consulting, there are lifestyle trade-offs involved. Although these job benefits are enjoyed by some consultants, the actual working conditions are usually much different from what they appear to outsiders. Most consultants are required to meet difficult project deadlines by working long hours under intense pressure to complete their tasks. The consultant must become absorbed in these projects and may be required to spend days, weeks, or months of sustained focus on a project until problems are diagnosed and appropriate solutions are generated. This lifestyle can be physically and mentally fatiguing.

Travel demands and uncertain living conditions also present a challenge for most consultants. Significant amounts of a consultant's time may be spent in travel. This often requires an individual to spend weeks at a time away from home. Although a sole practitioner may have greater control over travel demands, most successful independent consultants will be required to travel frequently over a wide geographic area.

Consulting Skill Requirements

The skill requirements of a consultant will vary according to the nature of services provided, the industries served, or size of the firm. However, a number of skills are required for all consultants. These skills are discussed next.

Technical Skills

All consultants must have a certain level of expertise in a particular industry, function, or technique. However, it takes more than just experience, education, and skills to be a successful consultant. All consultants must have the unique ability to translate their knowledge base into applications that provide value to their clients.

Communication Skills

The ability to communicate both orally and in writing is one of the most critical skills needed to be a successful consultant. This communication may take the form of telephone conversations, meetings, interviews, presentations, or written proposals and reports. Consultants must have the ability to convey information clearly and professionally through every step of a consulting engagement.

Interpersonal Skills

The relationship between the client and the consultant is critical to the successful completion of all consulting engagements. The consultant must have strong interpersonal skills that create a mutual sense of trust and openness with clients. This requires that the consultant remain sensitive to the client's needs and feelings.

Administrative Skills

In addition to performing the tasks of a consulting engagement, a consultant may be required to maintain regular communication with clients, review the work quality of other consultants, keep projects within budgeted hours and costs, and manage the client billing and collection process. As a sole practitioner, these responsibilities are magnified because one individual is responsible for completing all project tasks and managing the business.

Marketing and Selling Skills

A consultant's ability to market and sell a firm's consulting services is essential to the promotion to upper-level positions in a large firm. To build and sustain a viable consulting business, a firm must maintain a strong relationship with existing and previous clients, while continually adding new clients.

Personality Traits

Although a consultant may meet the skill requirements to complete all necessary tasks effectively, certain personality traits are necessary to pursue a career in the consulting profession. The following personality traits are usually required for all consultants, irrespective of the work setting.

Ambition and Self-Motivation

A consultant must have a high desire for personal success and must be internally driven, as there is often little outside motivation or direction. This requires an individual to have the initiative to start and complete tasks in an effective and efficient manner with little oversight and guidance.

Ability to Work with Others

A consultant is required to work with other consultants, clients, and employees of a client's organization on an ongoing basis. Thus, the individual must be able to get along with others and enjoy participating in a team-oriented process. A consultant is also a marketer who must both create and sell the product to the client. Like any good salesperson, they must be able to adapt and modify proposals to address specific client concerns and to know when the sales job is finished.

Self-Fulfillment

Despite the many benefits that a consultant may provide to clients, their contributions often are unrecognized. Consultants usually receive few tangible forms of personal recognition (i.e., certificates and awards) for their accomplishments. This requires the individual to have a strong sense of self-fulfillment.

Mobility, Flexibility, and Tolerance for Ambiguity

Because most successful consultants serve clients dispersed across wide geographic regions, the traveling demands can be rigorous. Further, the nature of projects and the work settings may change on a regular basis, with roles and client problems not well defined. An individual who does not have the mobility to travel extensively, the flexibility to shift directions on short notice, or the tolerance to work in ambiguous situations may have difficulty coping with the challenges of consulting.

High Energy and the Ability to Work under Pressure

The numerous demands and challenges of the consulting profession provide a great deal of excitement but also require high and sustained levels of energy. Most consultants must be able to work long hours on a regular basis. Projects often must be completed under significant pressure to meet multiple deadlines and to satisfy prior commitments made to clients. Although individuals may enjoy the challenges of consulting, it is difficult to maintain such a demanding pace over a sustained period of time.

Self-Confidence

Consultants must be confident in themselves, and they must be able to instill in their clients a strong sense of confidence in them. This often requires an ability to deal with rejection and failure due to lost proposals, mistakes, or a client's unwillingness to accept their recommendations. A consultant must overcome these barriers and continue to move on confidently to each new engagement with a fresh start. A consultant also must have enough self-confidence to think outside the box and be creative in recommending the best possible solutions to a problem or issue, even when those recommendations are not popular.

Ethics, Certification, and Professional Development

Unlike many other professions, there are no government regulations, certification requirements, or codes of ethics that universally apply to all consultants. However, most major professional consulting associations and large consulting organizations have a code of ethics that outlines the consultant's responsibilities to the client and to the public.

Consultants are often faced with a number of ethical dilemmas that are not regulated by law and are not that obvious. Some ethical issues common to the consulting profession include confidentiality, conflict of interest, objectivity, and professional involvement. Specific examples of the type of ethical dilemmas consultants are often faced with include

- The client seeks assistance for services outside the consultant's scope of competence.
- The consultant has an existing relationship or other interests with the client that would influence his or her objectivity in completing the work.
- The client requests the consultant to manipulate the results to favor the client's position.
- The client requests that the consultant omit, conceal, or revise certain information.
- The client requests that the consultant obtain proprietary information from a former client.

Professional development opportunities are available to enhance and refine an individual's technical expertise and consulting skills. Because technical skills can become obsolete quickly, successful consultants stay current by attending workshops, seminars, lectures, and professional meetings. These skills are further updated by reading current books, periodicals, and newspapers. To improve their consulting skills, consultants may attend professional association consulting skills workshops. Large consulting firms usually conduct their own in-house training to further enhance the consulting skills of their professionals.

Summary

The consulting industry is anticipated to continue to outpace the growth of the U.S. economy by a wide margin. This provides a bright outlook for those individuals who desire to pursue a career in management consulting. Consulting can be a rewarding profession for individuals at all ages and career stages, such as recent MBA graduates, individuals in midcareer, retirees, or part-time consultants searching for other outlets to use their skills. The appeal of a career in consulting has continued to grow, as an increasing number of individuals enters the field to utilize their knowledge, skills, and experience.

Individuals who are considering a career in management consulting should take a personal inventory of their interests, skills, and personality traits. Although a person may desire a career in consulting initially, a more thorough examination of the skill requirements, lifestyle, and personality traits of successful consultants may reveal a lack of compatibility with a person's actual needs and desires. However, an individual's talents, interests, and personal situation may change a number of times during his or her career. As these changes occur, each individual should reevaluate his or her fit with a consulting career.

Review Questions

1. Define "consultant."

2. Describe the profile of a "management consultant."

3. Describe the profile of a "hospitality consultant."

4. When is it most likely for a hospitality business to hire a consultant? List three situations.

5. How are management consultant firms classified?

6. Define "generalist."

7. In which hospitality segment is one most likely to find a CPA consultant?

8. Describe the role of an internal consultant.

9. For whom does an internal consultant most likely work?

10. What are the three major steps in the consulting cycle?

11. What is the goal of the marketing phase?

12. What are several forms of direct marketing?

13. What are several forms of indirect marketing?

14. What is an RFP?

15. What are some of the administrative duties of a consultant?

16. Who performs the administrative duties in a large consulting business? In a sole practitioner's business?

17. What are five of the factors that influence a consultant's lifestyle?

18. How does the lifestyle/work style vary between the sole practitioner and the consultant who works for a large firm?

19. What are the rewards associated with a consulting career?

20. What are the drawbacks associated with a consulting career?

21. List the skills required for working as a consultant. What is the progression of skills from the newly hired consultant stage to that of being more experienced?

22. What types of communication skills do consultants need?

23. Why are communication skills particularly important?

24. How do interpersonal skills influence the building of trust with the client?

25. What personality traits are important for success as a consultant?

26. Why is "tolerance for ambiguity" important to a consultant's success?

27. What are some ethical dilemmas common to consultants?

28. What are the projections for careers as consultants?

29. How do consultants stay current in their area of expertise?

30. How many years of work experience does one need before embarking on a career as a consultant?

Acoustical Engineers—Professionals who offer advice and planning for acoustic or sound issues and suggest materials to solve noise problems or enhance sound; usually are employed by the architects

Ad targeting—Through audience-targeting ad technology, consumers form travel-related site content (markets) and it categorizes each individual into groups based on his/her online behavior; market segmentation is based on behavior, allowing companies to reach travelers who are most likely to book reservations

ADR (Average Daily Rate)—This is computed by dividing room revenue by the number of rooms occupied

Advantages of Multi-Unit Business Forms—The advantages include, Market Reach, Economies of Scale, Streamlined Operations, Enhanced Marketing Power, Value-Added Service Options, Access to Financing and Professional Management.

Aesthetics—The beauty of an establishment; can play a primary role in touching the emotions of people and can influence whether they come back or not

Airlines Reporting Corporation—A nonprofit organization representing U.S. airlines that facilitate funds transfer between suppliers and agents, and ensures that travel agencies have experienced management through licensing

Alternating Current (AC)—The form of electricity supplied by local electric utility companies to businesses unless there is an on-site power production plant

Ambience or Servicescape—The landscape within which service is experienced has been used to describe the physical aspects of the setting that contribute to the guests' overall physical "feel" of the experience

American Culinary Federation, Inc. (ACF)—The premier professional chefs' organization in North America, with more than 230 chapters nationwide and 20,000 members. ACF offers culinarians of all ages, skill levels, and specialties the opportunity to further their career, as well as enhance their life

Americans with Disabilities Act of 1990—Federal legislation that forbids discrimination against people with disabilities; expanded the list of included disabilities from earlier legislation

Amperes—Measures the rate of electrical flow through a device or appliance

Amusement Parks—Commercially operated enterprise that offers rides, games, and other forms of entertainment

Angel Investor—An investor who provides lower levels capital to entrepreneurial projects in the early stages. Many times a former entrepreneur who has harvested their business

Animation—Energy, liveliness, vigor, spirit, vivacity, exuberance, cheerfulness

Answer—The responding document filed by a Defendant which responds to the allegations in the Plaintiff's complaint.

AP (As Purchased)—Before a menu item is prepared and any waste has been removed

Appraisers—A professional who is trained to value land and buildings, and is hired to render estimates of value

Apprenticeship—Apprenticeship is an on-the-job training program combined with technical classroom instruction. The American Culinary Federation Foundation (ACFF) operates both 2- and 3-year apprenticeship programs. Currently, there are nearly 2,000 apprentices learning in approximately 80 American Culinary Federation Foundation (ACFF) sponsored culinary apprenticeship programs in the United States

Architects—Professionals that prepare and review plans for the overall facility construction; qualified architects will have an AIA (American Institute of Architects) appellation

Assisted Living Communities—Communities dedicated to seniors, providing support, maintenance, and living assistance in a community environment. These communities often offer a multitude of residency choices including houses, condominiums, and apartments

Association—Membership organizations which are organized around a common interest and the group schedules meetings to explore and discuss their common interest

At-Home Assisted Living—A service that provides support for a multitude of needs such as: light housekeeping, meal preparation and planning, bathing and grooming assistance, medication management, errands and shopping services, to seniors at their private homes

Attractions—Places we visit and the things we do while we are traveling or visiting

Base Fees—These are the basic management fees that contract management companies receive for operating a foodservice or lodging property. These fees are typically a percentage of gross revenues

Bed and Breakfast—Lodging facilities with 2–12 rooms, which are either current or former private residences converted by the owner to accommodate guests

Berth—A bed on a ship

Board Plan—This is a type of meal plan offered on college and university campuses. The board plan allows students to pre-purchase a certain number of meals in the dining halls

Boutique Hotel—Small uniquely designed hotels with 100 rooms; contemporary, designed-led hotels, which offer unique levels of personalized service and high-tech facilities; niche emerged from society's growing interest in history, art, culture and design

Bow—The front of the ship

Brand—In a brand management form a mega-corporation owns multiple chain operations under the same parent umbrella structure. A mega-corporation that owns multiple chains under the same umbrella would prefer to refer to treat each of the chains as a separate brand to emphasize the different images projected by the chains

Branding—This term refers to the foodservice products offered in on-site foodservice locations. There are national brands like Quiznos or Pizza Hut, as well as regional brands, which are specific to a region of the country. On-site foodservice operators also have their own brands

Brand Heritage—An emerging topic within the marketing discipline, that suggests that the consumer appeal of products and services offered by older companies may be enhanced by the historical characters of their brands

Bridge—The navigational and control center of the ship

Broker—A professional who serves as an intermediary in a real estate sales transaction

Bunker—A hole or depression on a golf course that is often filled with sand (sand trap) or some other material of similar consistency; provide challenges to the golfer

By-Laws—Governing rules for an organization

BYO—An acronym used to communicate "**B**ring **y**our **o**wn" alcoholic beverage to a public establishment because it is not licensed to sell alcohol

Cabin—A room on a ship; also called a stateroom

Capital Projects—Projects that require major cash outlay when either replacing or acquiring new equipment

Career Fair—An event where many recruiters come together on-campus or at a local convention center to meet and interview potential employees for employment opportunities

Casual Dining Restaurant—A foodservice establishment that offers food and beverages at moderate prices and offer a level of service below that of an upscale property

Catalyst—An event that brings on a change without being affected itself

Cause of Action—The legal theory under which the injured party believes that someone else should be held responsible for their injuries

Cellaring—The process of storing a wine which will age to a better, more drinkable and mellow wine.

Chain—A company with multiple locations

Chain Operations—Chain-operated hotels, restaurants, and other similar businesses are owned by the same company and offer similar goods and services, but are found in different geographic locations

Chef—A chef is leader in charge of a kitchen and term comes from the French for "chief" or "director."

Today we use this term to describe the chief cook in the kitchen

City Clubs—Establishments that are in urban areas and cater to the businessman or woman, provides dining services and occasionally athletics

Civil Rights Act of 1964—Federal legislation that prohibits discrimination on the basis of race, sex, religion, color, and national origin; it has become the cornerstone piece of legislation protecting workers and their rights

Classic full-service hotel—Hotel properties that provide refined standards of accommodation and service; may be classified midscale, upscale or luxury according to the services and amenities offered, the pricing structure, and location; amenities cater to both the business traveler and the vacation or leisure traveler

CLIA—Cruise Line International Association

Client—This is the specific individual within the host organization that is responsible for monitoring the foodservice operator's performance

Club—A group of persons organized for social, literary, athletic, political, recreational, or other purposes

CMAA—Club Managers Association of America formed in 1920

Code of Hammurabi—Laws established around 1750 BC by Hammurabi, the ruler of Babylonia; regulations for inn-keepers and tavern-keepers on issues related to pricing and licensing are included among others

Color—In design, color can be used to communicate a strong message to the guests, and those messages can be controlled by proper use in layout and design

Commercial Foodservice—A foodservice operation where the primary function of the establishment is the sale of food for profit

Common Law—A system where the courts can apply the "generally accepted rules and principles enunciated by courts in earlier similar cases."

Complaint—The first pleading that lays out of the Plaintiff's cause(s) of action.

Commercial Kitchen Designers—Professionals that provide planning and drawings for commercial kitchens as well as equipment specifications

Conceptual Skills—The ability to see the company or department as a whole and understand how the different parts work together

Conferences—Gatherings that are large business or educational meetings and do not have a trade show; can last from one day to several; held at one venue

Consolidators—Businesses that purchase large blocks of airline seats or cruise berths at a substantial discount and resell them to travel agents or the public at lower than normal fare

Consultant—An individual who has a specific area of expertise and is compensated for providing advice or other services to a client

Consulting Careers—Individuals who work as consultants for many of their working years; the consulting industry is anticipated to continue to outpace the growth of the U.S. economy by a wide margin

Consulting Firms—Business organizations that provide consulting services; may be classified according to a number of characteristics, such as their size, level of specialization, industries served, geographical location, or types of clients they serve

Consulting Qualifications—A person needs years of experience within a specific industry segment and a talent for identifying problems and finding creative solutions to be successful in a consulting career

Consulting Skills—The specific skill set needed by a consultant will vary according to the nature of services provided, the industries served, and the size of the firm; most consultants will need to possess technical skills, communication skills, interpersonal skills, administrative skills, as well as marketing and selling skills

Consumer behavior—The study of how consumers (individuals and groups) behave; used often to increase the effectiveness of marketing to specific target populations

Contract Maintenance—Contractual arrangements with other companies to provide specialized repair service; generally the equipment needing repair is beyond the skill level of the facility staff

Contract Services Management—The term used to describe the segment of the hospitality industry dedicated to operating foodservice locations and lodging properties that are owned by another individual or corporation. Owners contract with organizations in this segment to manage their properties

Contractors—Professionals that are licensed by the state; typically oversee the entire building project; may be hired by bid or recommendation

Control—Comparing the performance of employees in a workforce against the objectives and goals that have been set by the company

Conventions—A special type of meeting held in a specific location often comprised of meetings and presentations as well as a trade show or exhibition

Convention and Visitors Bureau (CVB)—Local area tourism and marketing organizations that specialize in bringing conventions, meetings, conferences and visitations to a city, county or region

Conversational Currency—"Bragging rights" to the latest resort/vacation experience

Core Competencies—Those skills which are necessary for success..

Corkage—A fee charged to bring your own beverage selection if it is not available at the establishment. This is ostensibly used to cover the cost of the beverage service or the profit which would be gained from a sale and/or the ownership of the license.

Cost Control—The management concept of controlling costs through effective management practices

Costs and Reimbursement—The cost of various services provided by living centers and what costs are reimbursed through insurance or other compensation programs

Country Clubs—Hospitality establishments that provide elaborate social events, offer dining, pool, tennis, and golf

Culinology®—An approach to food that blends the culinary arts and food technology. One type of culinologists® are research chefs developing recipes and products for food manufacturers, restaurants, food suppliers, or on-site operators

Cultural Tourism—Travel directed toward experiencing the arts, the heritage, the special character of people and place

Curb Appeal—The attractiveness of the physical operations; the facility's visual appeal

Deck Plan—Diagram that shows the locations and public spaces on a cruise ship

Defamation—An untrue statement about another that is published or communicated to a third party who understood it which resulted in damages

Defendant—The person against whom a lawsuit has been filed

Destination Marketing Organization (DMO)—A company that promotes the long-term development and marketing of a tourist destination by focusing on convention sales and tourism amenities in order to increase the amount of visitors to that specific destination

Disadvantages of Multi-Unit Business Forms—Some of the key disadvantages include Operational Constraints, Financial Strains, and Legal Forces.

Discounting—The method of reducing an item from the regular price

Discovery—The process of taking depositions and requesting documents to learn about the other party's case.

Distribution Services—The vast network of peripheral companies that help hospitality enterprises get their products and services from creation to consumption

Dram Shop Laws—Makes a business which sells alcoholic drinks or a host who serves liquor to a drinker who is obviously intoxicated or close to it, strictly liable to anyone injured by the drunken patron or guest

Duty of Care—"A legal obligation requiring a particular standard of conduct."

E-Commerce—A form of web retailing which features the buying and selling of goods and services on the Internet; characterized by a global reach and twenty-four hour availability

E-Hospitality—An innovative service known as "total solutions" where distributing, servicing, and supporting hospitality products to all size organizations in the industry in order to offer more amenities and support services to potential guests

Economic Growth—The increase over time in the capacity of an economy to produce goods and services and (ideally) to improve the wellbeing of its citizens

Economic Impact—The change in the economy brought about by a specific event or industry segment; examines the economic prosperity of a specific geographic area, such as a town or city; may influence the building up or infrastructure of an area, example the conference and convention industry's economic impact on a city

Effectiveness—Accomplishing the intended outcome; how well a result is produced

Efficiency—The amount of work required to accomplish a task; minimum ratio of time and effort; how resources are productively used

Electrical Engineers—Professionals that are usually employed by the architects and design all of the electrical systems

Electronic Travel Agencies—Providing extensive information and online ticketing via the Internet

Employment Brand—The image of the business as viewed through the eyes of prospective employees. It can also be defined as the image of the applicant as viewed through the eyes of the business

Empowering—Where a contemporary leader has created the organizational work environment in which staff members are trained in necessary skills, enabling them to handle most customer service encounters; management must support the decisions made by the staff members

Energy Management—The management and control of heat, air conditioning, water usage, electric usage, and gas usage

Engineering Systems—The physical plant operating systems, comprised of the water and wastewater systems, refrigeration systems, heating, ventilation and air-conditioning systems, electrical systems, and safety and security systems; knowledge of these various systems help the manager adequately explain what needs to be accomplished by the facilities management team

Entrepreneur—A term often used to define risk taking behavior that results in the creation of new opportunities for individuals and organizations

Environmentally Friendly—Integrating strategies into the design that reduce consumption of raw materials as well as favorably influence the establishments practices

EP (Edible Portion)—After a menu item has been prepared and all waste has been discarded

Equity Clubs—Those facilities owned by their membership, are nonprofit; oldest form of clubs

Ethics—A set of principles that managers apply when interacting with people and their organizations; fair and equal treatment, truth, lack of bias, consistency, and respect of others

Etiquette—Socially understood rules of conduct.

Evaluation—Employee evaluations take place after an employee has been selected, trained, and been on the job for a period of time; provides official feedback; used as backup documentation necessary if an employee is terminated based on performance

Event(s)—A type of meeting or a function within a meeting; see APEX glossary

Featherie—A golf ball made in the 17th century consisting of a hand sewn leather pouch and stuffed with goose or chicken feathers; the pouch would be boiled and as it cooled the hide would shrink and the feathers expanded to result in a compact ball

Festivals—Gatherings that highlight local heritage; often men and women with specific skills or trades (artists, musicians, or craftsmen) help preserve many cultures through celebration, demonstration, and education

Flag of Convenience—When a ship is registered in a foreign country for purposes of reducing operating costs and avoiding government regulations

Flow—An important factor in making a decision about how a hospitality facility should be planned and maintained; different layouts can influence guest perception positively or negatively and affect whether or not they return for future business

Food Cost—The cost to produce a food item for sale; this includes actual cost of the food, labor costs, and energy costs

Foreign Independent Tour (FIT)—A travel package which normally includes airfare, lodging, and some recreational activities, but is not necessarily just in foreign countries. The traveler is independent when it comes to travel and must get from destination to destination on their own by driving a rental car or catching trains and busses

Forms of Ownership—Senior living centers can be owned by private groups, religious orders, corporations, and trusts (REITs)

Franchise—A form of business organization in which a firm that has a successful product or service (the franchisor) enters into a contractual relationship with other businesses (franchisees), operate under the franchisor's trade name, and use the franchisors methods and expertise in exchange for a fee

Franchising—A widespread method of growing restaurant brands, where an independent entrepreneur pays for the right to use the brand, recipes and operating system of a leading restaurant company

Full Care Centers/Nursing Homes—Residency centers for seniors who need the most care. These facilities offer the full array of support including medical, pharmacy, and personal services

Full Membership—Entitles a member to full use of the club, all amenities during any hour of operation

Function—An important factor in layout and design that addresses how a facility will be operated and maintained; can also affect guest perception of the facility and whether or not they come back

Furniture, Fixtures, and Equipment—A major portion of hospitality capital expenditures

Galley—A kitchen on a cruise ship

Game Show—Involves members of the public or celebrities, sometimes as part of a team, competing for points or prizes

Gaming/Gambling—Casino style activities offered on a cruise ship or at a resort

Globalization—The concept that companies are conducting business transactions with both consumers and suppliers who are located around the world. Historically businesses were limited to a smaller local marketplace but the Internet and expedited shipping services have created a worldwide marketplace for conducting business

Golf Club Head—The lower end of the golf club which strikes the ball

Golf Club Shaft—The upper part of the golf club which is a long, tapered tube, usually made of graphite or carbon steel, that connects the club head to the golfer's hands

Golf Management Companies—Companies that have the expertise and resources needed to operate and manage golf courses

Global Destination Systems—Powerful database systems, such as Apollo, Sabre, and Amadeus, that list and offer ticketing for millions of air, hotel, and rental car services and provide worldwide attraction information

Grand Tour—A kind of education for wealthy noblemen. It was a period of European travel which could last from a few months to 8 years

Green Hospitality—Where hospitality industry operators have implemented 'green' initiatives in response to demands from the government, environmental groups, and the general public; common goals are twofold (1) enhancing broader appeal to improve business, while (2) having an increasingly positive impact on the environment

Gross Profit—Sales revenue minus sales cost

Gross Registered Tonnage—A measurement of a ship's enclosed space

Growth and Demand for Living Centers—Senior Living Centers have an extremely high potential for growth with the number of senior citizens expected to be 36,818,000 by 2010 and 81,999,000 by 2050

Guestroom maintenance—An activity applied to guestrooms of a lodging establishment, a form of problem prevention conducted to ensure guest comfort

Health Inspectors—Professionals that are employed by the state and interpret state codes; they inspect existing facilities and must review and approve plans for new or remodeled food preparation areas, service areas, and restrooms

Heating, Ventilation, and Air Conditioning (HVAC)—This system is an infrastructure of pipes, ducts, pumps, thermostats, valves, and pressure sensors that should provide suitable temperature and humidity levels for guests, staff and management

Heritage Tourism—The practice of people traveling outside of their home community to visit historic sites, to participate in local festivals, to enjoy local arts and crafts, sightseeing, and recreation

Hospital Consultant—An individual or business organization that serves only hospitality industry clients and provides specialized consulting services by focusing on a specific industry segment or sub-segment and/or one or more functional areas

Hospitality Managers—Professionals that may represent the owner of the facilities; within layout and design he/she will coordinate the design team and keep them on track with the concept and budget; often is the final decision maker

Hospitia—Guest places or lodging venues for travelers along an extensive network of roads throughout the Mediterranean region; built by Romans during the classical period of the Roman Empire

Host—This is the organization that hires the foodservice operator to manage their foodservice locations

Hotel Ratings System—The system or process by which hotels are evaluated, usually by independent auditors

Human Resource Management—The process of how organizations treat their people in order to accomplish the goals and objectives of the firm; the department within the organization that handles the paperwork regarding selection, termination, legal mandates, benefits, training, and compensation

Hybrid Restaurant—A restaurant unit that combines two different styles of establishments to make a new concept; provides more options for the consumer within one location

Incentive Fees—These are additional fees given by owners to contract management companies to encourage them to manage the lodging or foodservice property in a way that increases the property's overall profit

Incentive Travel—A vacation package offered to employees as a bonus to motivate them to achieve a certain goal

Incentive Travel Houses—These agencies develop customized programs for corporations who offer incentives to induce high employee productivity by providing deluxe travel rewards

Independent—A single unit operation without any franchise or chain affiliation

Independent Business Owner—Similar to the entrepreneur with the distinction that they prefer operating a single business operation on a smaller scale than a entrepreneur

Independent Operation—Operations that have one or up to a few units that have distinct characteristics from other units; differences often occur in how the operations look and feel

Industrial Attractions—Consist of operating concerns, manufacturing, and agricultural, whose processes and products are of interest to visitors

Industry Association—An association or organization that represents the needs of members of a certain profession

In-house training—That training which is provided by the company, usually by the management team as a normal part of the training process of a new employee.

Intangibility—Not perceived by touch, cannot be visualized. Service would be an example of an intangible in the hospitality industry

Interior Designers—Professionals that design interior spaces involving materials, finishes, colors, space planning, and layout; can be employed by the architects or have their own firm

Interior Plantscapers—Professionals that advise the proper selection and positioning of plants as well as their maintenance; generally are hired by recommendation

International Special Events Society (ISES)—A professional organization that seeks to promote, educate and advance the industry of special events and its network of professionals as well as related industries

Internship—A paid or unpaid temporary employment experience designed to acquaint the student to business operations by providing them an opportunity to shadow managers in various positions within a foodservice or lodging facility

Interpersonal Skills—The ability to understand people and work well with them on an individual basis and in groups

Interview—A formal meeting between two or more individuals

Interviewee—Person being interviewed

Interviewer—Person conducting the interview

Interviewing—A formal meeting between a company's representative and a job candidate where one questions or evaluates another person who is applying for work within that company; goal is to ensure fairness to the applicant and yet evaluate him/her sufficiently to achieve the best match for the job

Inventory Reconciliation—A physical count of inventory which is matched to the sales figures in order to determine discrepancies which can point to problems with the control systems.

Job Analysis—An HR tool that focuses on what work needs to be accomplished within a specific job

Job Descriptions—A written document that identifies the tasks, responsibilities, and duties under which jobs are performed

Job Design—The task of determining how the job should be performed; examines how the job is organized and how it can be planned to provide both productivity to the organization and the most job satisfaction to the employee

Job Enlargement—The process of broadening the job by adding tasks

Job Enrichment—The process of adding responsibilities to the job

Job Rotation—Allowing an employee to work different jobs within the same operation; requires cross-training

Job Simplification—The process of determining the smallest components of the job and assessing how they fit into the whole job

Job Specifications—A list of the knowledge, skills, and abilities necessary to perform a specific job successfully

Labor Cost—The cost of labor in running your operation; this includes wages and benefit costs

Labor Intensive—The business or industry that employs a large number of employees to provide customers with a product or service

Labor-Intensive Business—Many of the services provided by the industry require high levels of personal service and attention to detail. This is a key element of the hospitality industry

Leadership—The influencing of others to channel their activities toward reaching the goals of the business

Liability Insurance—Most businesses carry liability insurance in case of accident. If you have auto insurance, this is a type of liability insurance coverage. Some businesses are self-insured which means that they have to absorb the costs of legal judgments or settlements.

Life Cycle Costing—The process of judging the selecting and analysis of capital projects; including the consideration of all aspects of the initial costs, operating costs, fixed costs, and tax implication

Lifespan—An attraction classification according to their lifespan or time-related criteria based upon their duration

Limited-Service—Lodging facilities that provide a limited number of services to the guests

Liqueur—A distilled beverage with a higher sugar content

Long-Term Stay—Lodging facilities where all guestrooms include a kitchenette and provide clean, comfortable, inexpensive rooms that meet the basic needs of the guests

Luxury Hotel—Properties with an emphasis on service often providing extraordinary experiences that exceed customer expectations and create life long memories; a small hotel segment yet these hotels enjoy high profile status within brands and customers

Man-Made Attractions—Owe their very existence to the intervention of humans

Management—The process of getting tasks accomplished through people.

Management Consultant—An individual or business organization that are considered generalists; they provide a broad range of services to their clients and tailor their services to the specific needs of each client

Management Contract—A contractual arrangement between a property owner (who is often an independent investor) and a hotel company to operate the facilities to the specifications of that hotel company's brand name

Meetings—A gathering that brings people together for a common purpose such as conducting business, engaging in social ritual, educating people, and fundraising

Meeting Professionals International (MPI)—The leading international organization of professional meeting planners

Member—Regardless of type of club, each is made up of members, who have applied for and been accepted into membership

Member Benefits—Products, services, or perks available to an individual as part of an organizational membership

Merit Pay—The management approach that connects employee performance to pay raises; it identifies employees, who are performing at, or above, expected levels and provides them with increased wages

Military Clubs—Cater to enlisted men and women and the noncommissioned officer; provides a social outlet, often has golf

Mini-Bar—In room units (usually refrigerators) which contain snacks and beverages for the guest's convenience at a charge. These are found in full service hotels.

Mission Statement—A statement of purpose that defines an organization. A mission statement is usually one to two sentences long and outlines the values and identity of the organization

Moment of Truth—Actual person-to-person interactions between the customer and the person delivering the service experience

Moral Development Theory—Lawrence Kohlberg's conception of the three components for morality and leadership: preconventional; conventional; and postconventional

Multi-Unit Business forms—Broadly, four types of multi-unit or chain operationa exist in hospitality: simple form, mixed form, management-franchise form, and brand management form.

Multi Unit/Chain Operation—Often started as a single unit operation where the business grew and the entrepreneur opened additional sites; has a corporate headquarters that can help by providing advice and support to an individual unit's management staff

Municipal Golf Course—Golf courses that are owned by the government (city or state); operated similarly to daily fee courses

Museum—Typically a nonprofit, permanent institution in the service of society and of its development and open to the public, that acquires, conserves, researches, communicates, and exhibits for purposes of study, and education enjoyment, the tangible and intangible evidence of people and their environment

Myth—A false belief

Natural Attractions—Those that occur in nature without human intervention

NCA—National Club Association

Negligence—The cause of action that arises when a duty owed to someone on the property is breached, resulting in injury or damages to the individual

Networking—The process of connecting with people of like interests who may be of help to you and you a help to them

Noncommercial/Institutional Foodservice—Food service operations where the service of food is not the primary function of the operation where food is being served

Nonprofit Organization—An economic institution that operates like a business but does not seek financial gain

Occupancy Percentage—The ratio relating the number of rooms sold to the number of rooms available

Official Rules of Golf—A specific set of rules developed by the USGA that govern the game of golf; provides the universally accepted rules of the game of golf

On-Site Foodservice—Noncommercial food service usually thought of as institutional that serves the dining needs in areas such as health care, schools and universities, corporate and manufacturing operations, military, children and adult communities, and correctional facilities

On-Site Foodservice Management—This is the term used to describe the contract foodservice segment of the hospitality industry

On the Floor—An expression to indicate the sales floor or where food and beverages are sold. Usually refers to the area where guests can sit at the tables.

Operator—The individual or organization that manages the day-to-day operations of the lodging property or foodservice location

Operator Loan and Equity Contributions—This is a way for contract management companies to contribute to reducing the debt incurred by the owners. It is also a method of gaining some ownership (equity) in the property. Operators may offer loans to the owners the help offset start-up costs or cover initial cash flow losses. Operators may also offer funding or equity in the property. These equity contributions are typically 5 to 15% of the total equity investment

Operator System Reimbursable Expenses—These are the funds paid to the operator by the owner for property management systems, marketing programs, management information systems, foodservice management systems, etc

Organization's Culture—A system of shared meaning held by members that distinguishes the organization from other organizations

Organizing—The efforts involved with determining what activities are to be done and how employees are grouped together to accomplish specific tasks

Origin—Classifies if the attraction is natural or man-made

Outside Sales Agents—Individual who is affiliated with the travel agency, acting as an independent contractor, not employee, who sells travel products and shares commissions with their affiliated agency

Owner—The individuals or corporations that legally own the lodging property or foodservice location

Peripheral Careers—The employment opportunities that help hospitality enterprises get their products and services from creation to consumption

Perishability—A product with a determined shelf life. Food would be an example of a perishable product in the hospitality industry

PGA Professional—A professional who has successfully completed specific education and experience criteria as defined by the Professional Golf Association (PGA) including passing a PGA Playing Ability test

Plaintiff—The alleged aggrieved person who commences the lawsuit

Planned Play Environments—These provide recreation and entertainment sporting facilities, such as ski and golf resorts; commercial attractions which include theme and amusement

Planning—The establishment of goals and objectives and deciding how to accomplish these goals

PMS—The computerized systems used by hotels to manage its rooms revenue, room rates, reservations and room assignments, guest histories, and accounting information, as well as other guest service and management information functions

Portfolios—A collection of holdings, consisting of different hotel brands, assembled by the major hotel companies

Portion Control—The designation of specific portion size as a means of controlling costs

POS (Point of Sale)—A network of electronic cash registers and pre-check terminals that interface with a remote central processing unit

POS Terminal—A location at which goods and services are purchased. Often referred to as a cash register, this type is connected to a computer system which manages the revenue.

Preferred Providers—Agencies sign contracts with specific suppliers to try and sell their services first and in return receive a large sales commission

Preventive maintenance (PM)—Includes the routine duties of the facility maintenance personnel who possess advanced skills, such as conducting inspections, minor repairs or adjustments

Price Points—The set pricing for categories of the beverages which, when compared to the costs the establishment, determine the cost percentages, hence the profit margins for those categories.

Profitability—What is left over from a sales transaction after all of the costs are deducted is the profit. Profitability is the mweasure of how a business performs financially.

Progressive Discipline Policy—An employment policy where an employee's performance is scrutinized, warnings are given, and an opportunity for retraining is provided before termination might take place; it allows employees to receive increasingly more stringent discipline for infractions

Property—A specific hotel site or individual location

Property Operation and Maintenance (POM)—The line item of the income statement where the actions of the facility manager are reported

Proprietary Clubs—Those owned by a corporation, company, business, or individual; they are for profit businesses

Purchasing—The job of procuring general and specialized equipment, materials, and business services for use by an establishment

Purser—The person on a ship responsible for the handling of money on board

Quick Service Restaurant (QSR)—Considered to be informal dining establishments that specialize in delivering food quickly

Real Estate Representative—A person who works for the hospitality firm that specializes in real estate transactions, including site location and analysis

Recreational Amenities—Amenities such as golf, tennis, scuba diving, spa, fishing, and hiking activities that are provided to the guest at a resort

Receptive Operator—A company may meet and greet groups at airports, make arrangements for lodging, and shuttle them to the lodging at one particular destination and offer foreign language interpreters

Recruiting—The process communicating job opportunities to larger populations of people in an attempt to acquire qualified job candidates

Refrigerant—A fluid with a low boiling point that starts as a liquid, absorbs heat, and becomes a gas, and then is placed under pressure to become a liquid again

Relocation—The act of moving from one place to another for employment advancement

Request for Proposals (RFPs)—A document used to solicit bids from service providers and used to determine price and availability of goods and services; can be used to outline the planner's needs for the meeting/convention, including dates, meeting and exhibit space, lodging, food and beverages, telecommunications, audio- visual requirements, transportation, and any other necessities

Resort Cruise Ships—Floating resorts that offer a wide range of recreation, entertainment, and programming activities for guests

Resort Hotel—Range in size from few to thousands of rooms and as self-contained environments appeal to business and leisure guests seeking relaxation, lodging, recreation activities, and meeting facilities on site

Resort Spa—Located on resort property, offering many spa treatments that are often available to both resort and outside guests

Respite Care—Short term care designed to fill the needs of an individual who may need assistance in recovery from surgery, injury, or other ailment and only needs temporary assistance during recovery and rehabilitation. Respite care generally lasts from one week to a few months

Restaurant—An establishment where meals are served to customers

Restaurant Ratings System—The system or process by which restaurants are evaluated, usually by independent auditors

Resume—A brief account of one's educational, professional, or work experiences and quantifications submitted for consideration of employment

Return on Investment—Measure of profits achieved calculating the ratio of net income to total assets (simplest version)

Revenue Per Guest Usage—Total resort revenue (includes all supporting recreation amenity activity) divided by the total number of guest visits

Routine maintenance—Includes the general everyday duties of the facility staff, which requires relatively minimal skills or training, such as emptying trash cans or picking up litter Royal and Ancient Golf Club of St. Andrew's—One of the oldest and most esteemed golf courses in the world; located in St. Andrews, Scotland; many championship tournaments are played there and it is considered to be the 'home of golf'

Sales Commission—A percentage of the sales price paid by the supplier to the agent upon the purchase of a travel product or service

Seasonality—The time frame of the year when a property is at its peak business demand, often includes several months, a property may have more than one peak season

Secondary Attraction—Of lesser importance to the traveler and might be considered simply a stop along the way to get to the primary attraction

Segment—Different price and quality levels that progress upward from the economy segment to the luxury segment.

Segmentation—Allows companies to reach travelers who are most likely to book reservations based on their past behavior

Selection—The act of choosing the best job candidate to hire for a position to achieve the best fit for the organization

Self-Operators—These are organizations who manage their own foodservice locations, even though foodservice is not their area of expertise

Service—A type of product that is intangible, goods that are inseparable from the provider, variable in quality, and perishable. The reason why private clubs exist; members receive high-end, personalized service at their club

Service Experience—Sum total of the experience that the customer has with the service provider on a given occasion

Service Product—Entire bundle of tangibles and intangibles in a transaction which has a significant service component

Shared technological services—A method of sharing many technological services in order to improve the functionality of operations such as standards of delivery, quality, and performance for hospitality technology

Shopping—Searching for or buying goods or services

Shot—A measure of alcohol to be used in a recipe. Standards of measure may differ from establishment to establishment, but 1 oz., 1¼ oz, or 2 oz. are often used. In order to control costs and ensure consistency a shot glass or jigger can be used or a measured pourer.

Silk Road—Encompassed of a variety of ancient routes between Europe and points in Asia; used by merchants and traders to transport goods

Single Unit Operation—The independent operator; can be used when referring to managing one unit; that unit can be part of any industry in the economic sector of the world

Social Media—Internet applications that help consumers share opinions, insights, experiences, and perspectives

Social Membership—Entitles a member to limited use of a country club, typically dining, pool, and tennis, but not golf; reduced initiation fee and dues structure

Social Networking—Interacting with people who can impact your career options or advancement

Social Responsibility—Alcohol so alters one's perception of reality that it is not responsible to allow an intoxicated person to be put into a position where they could harm themselves or someone else. The sale or service of alcohol creates a social responsibility to both the guest and society at large to act in a manner to protect everyone from harm.

Sommelier—A wine expert employed by a beverage serving establishment to help the guests select the best wine for their meal.

Space Ratio—An approximation of how much space is on a cruise ship; divide the GRT by the number of passengers

Spirits—Common distilled beverages (spirits) are vodka, gin, whisky, tequila, etc.

Sponsor—A person, group or corporation that provides funds for an event or activity

Stabilizer—Winglike projections on a cruise ship that is used to reduce and eliminate roll (side-to-side movement)

Staffing—Supplying the human requirements necessary to service guests

Status of Attraction—The importance or interest to the traveler

Statute of Limitations—The minimum timeframe during which a plaintiff must file their lawsuit in order to proceed with the litigation

Student Organizations—These are groups of students that come together in their free time to organize activities to support their common vocational interests

Style—A particular, distinctive mode or form of construction or execution in work

Supplier—A person, group or corporation that provides something that is required, needed or desired

Support Services—Services provided in addition to basic living, such as transportation, housekeeping, laundry, pharmacy, and more

Support Staff—Professionals who work in hospitality and tourism but not in an operations management position

Sustainability—The capacity to maintain, support, or endure; an ecological term that describes how biological systems remain productive through diversity over an extended period of time

Sustainable competitive advantage—Unique attributes or characteristics of a business that attracts customers; goods or services a consumer is willing to pay for; if consistently delivered it will facilitate the customer becoming loyal and returning for repeat business

Sustainable Design—Integrating strategies into the design for reducing consumption; involving design practices that are environmentally friendly

Team Building—Views employees as members of work groups, rather than as individuals

Technical Skills—The skills involving knowledge of and the ability to perform a particular job or task

Tender—A boat that ferries passenger from the ship to the port when the cruise ship is too big to dock at the pier

Term—This is the length of the contract between the operator and owner

The Training Cycle—A systematic process used by human resources departments to determine what training knowledge or skills is needed for an individual to successfully perform their job; used to assess the needs of both newly hired individuals and tenured employees

Theme Parks—Offer escape; as a result of modern technology they replicate both real as well as "unreal" places that may or may not exist beyond the gates

Ticketing Fee—An additional charge above the base cost of the ticket that is charged by a TMC to cover their ticketing costs

Top Down Approach—Is a method of attempting to sell the most expensive item first and then offering a less expensive item next if there is continued sales resistance

Topography—Can be broadly subdivided into three areas of interest: landforms, wildlife, and ecology

Torts—A large classification of different types of civil wrongs that result in injury or damages to either people or property

Tour Escort—A person who travels with a group and acts as guide and business manager, using the skills of a teacher, entertainer, accountant, doctor, and psychologist

Tour Operators—Organize market and operate packages of travel services with a variety of themes, ranging from adventure to sightseeing, for groups or individuals

Trade Show—A large gathering of suppliers who display, demonstrate, or exhibit their new or existing products in a common marketplace

Travel Agent—Individuals within a travel management company that match and ticket the travel desires of leisure and business travelers with most appropriate suppliers of tourist services

Travel Management Company—A contemporary term for travel agencies that provide consulting, ticketing, and management of travel products for leisure and business traveler

Turnover—The situation created when an employee leaves (voluntarily or involuntarily) and must be replaced

Units—A term used in the hotel industry that is more commonly referred to as a hotel room

Universal Design—The term used to convey the idea that products (furnishings, hardware, etc.) and architectural changes could be made to make life easier for all people whether or not they have a disability

Upscale Restaurant—A foodservice establishment that offers the best in food, beverages, and level of service

Up-Selling—A selling technique used to convince customers to purchase one of your more expensive items first

USGA Handicap—A scoring procedure used in the game of golf; it allows for golfers with different skill levels to compete equally

Vacation-Ownership Firm—A business focused on selling long-term vacation packages to guests; these "slices of time" may be hotel rooms or condominium units located at a specific property, or they may be sold as "points" which are used for future vacations

Vacation Ownership/Timeshare Resorts/Condo Hotels—In the most basic form it is the right to accommodations and use of recreational facilities at a vacation development for a specified time period for a defined number of years or into perpetuity, as defined in the purchase agreement or redeemable through purchased vacation club points

Venue—The facility where an event is hosted

Virtual Meeting—A business discussion that is carried out through an Internet broadcast, e-mail or similar mode

Vision—Leadership quality for creating the future. An essential quality for leadership; a successful vision is leader initiated, shared, and supported by followers

Volume Purchasing—Purchasing in bulk volume in order to save money as most suppliers will offer a discount for volume purchasing

Yacht Club—Establishments near or on the water, activities center around sailing and boating, dining also available

Yield Management—A combination of occupancy percentage and the average daily rate